Missionaries and Muckrakers

MISSIONARIES
AND
MUCKRAKERS

THE
FIRST HUNDRED YEARS
OF
KNOX COLLEGE

HERMANN R. MUELDER

UNIVERSITY OF ILLINOIS PRESS

Urbana and Chicago

This book is printed on acid-free paper.

Unless otherwise indicated, all illustrations
are courtesy of Knox College.

Library of Congress Cataloging in Publication Data

Muelder, Hermann R., 1905-
Missionaries and muckrakers.

Bibliography: p.
Includes index.
1. Knox College (Galesburg, Ill.)—History.   I. Title.
LD2813.M83   1984   378.773'49   83-9320
ISBN 0-252-01106-6

TO
Richard, Marcia, and Owen

CONTENTS

FOREWORD

Admiration for my alma mater has prompted this study of its history to the completion of its hundredth year. By that time, my own involvement in the affairs of Knox College made my recollections an important and sometimes an essential source of information. My opinions about people, my perception of events, and my convictions about academic policies would surely bias statements about the history of the college during the last fifty years. Any account by me of Knox during that half century had better be written as a memoir, subject to critical use by another historian who could write about that period with a greater degree of detachment. Therefore, this history of Knox concludes with the commencement of 1937. Writing of a memoir has begun.

Several people have contributed a great deal to the writing of this history. Lynn Harlan has often located materials in the College Archives. Rose Hane has transformed messy pages into a handsome typescript. Douglas Wilson carefully read all of the manuscript, correcting many errors of composition, untangling snarls of exposition, and suggesting very significant improvements in the emphasis placed upon parts of the historical narrative. N. C. Dvoracek provided assistance with the illustrations. The grateful author acknowledges their assistance, while accepting full responsibility for this history as it is herewith presented.

CHAPTER I

THE YEARS WITH A MISSION

The colony that founded Knox College and that settled Galesburg came from upstate New York, from an area so frequently scorched by fires of religious enthusiasm that it was sometimes called the Burned-over District. The flames became most intense during the so-called Great Revival that started in the late 1820s along the Erie Canal and Mohawk River Valley.[1]

The leader of this colony was the Reverend George Washington Gale. The two leading evangelists of the Great Revival had both been prepared for the ministry under the personal tutelage of the Reverend Gale while they were living in his home in Adams, New York. Indeed, one of these men, Charles Grandison Finney, had experienced a crucial religious conversion from Gale's preaching. Finney became a very popular preacher and was most responsible for the intensity of the Great Revival, for its broad scope, and for the depth of its social significance. Gale may rightly be regarded as the mentor of the Great Revival. From a desire to provide an education to converts of the revival who felt called to the ministry, Gale became the founder in 1827 at Whitesboro, New York, of the Oneida Manual Labor Institute.[2]

The idea of combining manual labor with academic work was popular between 1825 and 1840, and Oneida Manual Labor Institute became a widely admired model of how this educational scheme might work. It suited well the spirit of religious benevolence and rising democracy of this Jacksonian era. It was a system that promised to equalize opportunity for rich and poor without the evil of charity and without weakening the important sense of self-dependence in young men. Health and bodily vigor were to be preserved and developed, and future ministers were to be toughened to endure the hardships of the frontier. Moral character, diligence, and self-reliance were to be stimulated. That mutual regard and sympathy between different strata of society essential to a democratic state were to be fostered by the discipline of manual labor for all students. And finally there was the argument that helped to bind the manual labor leaders to the antislavery movement, namely, that this educational innovation helped to make manual labor respectable.[3] Carried away by the success of his school during the early years at Whitesboro, Gale wrote to Finney that it was an "impulse to a system of education that is to introduce the millennium."[4]

To understand the extraordinary impact that converts from the Great Revival, in general, and students from Oneida Institute, in particular, had on the humanitarian causes of the second third of the century, one must appreciate that in the Burned-over District, even before the evangelism of Finney, the area had been seeded with a number of religious and social eccentricities, though none that grew to the stature of Mormonism and Millerism and the anti-Masonic movement in that section later.[5] A feature distinguishing the Great Revival from other waves of religious emotionalism in American history was its greater lasting power. It resulted in a kind of practical Christianity. Finney taught that conversion meant a change in the individual from self-interest to unselfish benevolence. As part of his evangelistic technique, he learned that to make men anxious about their souls it was quite as effective to discourse at length about particular evils in society as to arouse them to extravagant descriptions of the parlous state of the sinful individual. About the time that Finney transferred his evangelistic headquarters to New York City after 1830, that city became the administrative center of a benevolent system based on the interlocking of the personnel of a number of national societies. Leadership for the activities of these societies and coherence in their activities were provided by Congregationalists and New School Presbyterians whose interdenominational agencies were the core of the system.

During the early 1830s this benevolent system reached rapidly westward to the Mississippi Valley, particularly through the means of men who had been associated with Oneida Manual Labor Institute. Most important in this westward movement of moral reform was one of the Oneida Institute students who had lived for a time in the home of Gale. This was Theodore Dwight Weld, who was sent west as the agent for the Society for Promoting Manual Labor in Literary Institutions. Following his recommendation, philanthropists in New York gave their support to a new manual labor theological seminary at Cincinnati. For this school, Lane Seminary, Weld recruited students. A particularly large number migrated under his leadership from Oneida Institute to Lane, where he became, though himself a student, the leading influence.[6] When the trustees of Lane tried to suppress the antislavery activities of the "Oneidas," they withdrew. These "Lane Rebels," rather famous in their time, formed their own temporary school, and then many of them went to Oberlin, transforming it into one of the truly avant-garde colleges of that time. It was at Oberlin that Weld recruited many students for the "Seventy," a band named after the New Testament apostles, to serve as agents for the American Anti-Slavery Society that was organized in 1833.[7]

During the next decade several of these Lane Rebels frequently were associated in their reforming agitation with the colony that founded Knox College and Galesburg. For by 1834 the faculty, some alumni, and former patrons of Oneida Manual Labor Institute were becoming interested in the establishment farther west of a new manual labor college. Associated with Gale in the promotion of this venture was the Reverend Hiram Huntington Kellogg, a fervent follower of Finney, who had founded at Clinton, in Oneida County, a Young Ladies Domestic Seminary. His pioneering of manual labor in a woman's school would have direct influence on the style of education labor established at Mount Holyoke, but in the early 1830s more excitement was engendered by Kellogg's admission of "coloured ladies" with "social and literary privileges" equal to those of the white students.[8] He was supported on this issue by the influential antislavery philanthropist Gerrit Smith, with whom Kellogg had attended college, as he had with the Reverend Albert Barnes, the leading spokesman for the New School Presbyterians, whose theological opinions, support of continuing cooperation with Congregationalists, and attacks on slavery were, during the mid-1830s, bringing him to trial in the General Assembly of the Presbyterians. Kellogg clearly belonged to the clique of New York reformers.[9]

There was a speculative side to Gale's project during this time of rather feverish interest in western lands. The cheap price of Illinois prairie land was no doubt part of the attraction for the Galesburg pioneers. Certain members of the committee who came west to select and buy land for the colony also came prepared to buy land on their own account. One of them was Sylvanus Ferris, who wished to secure for each of his six sons and one daughter an entire section of land. Special problems existed for farmers of New York and New England in the 1830s. Many of those who had been growing grain were suffering from increased competition from western farmers. The Erie Canal, opened in 1825, was bringing grain to the eastern seaboard by the hundreds of thousands of bushels; in New York the loss from poorer prices for grain was aggravated by the taxes to pay for and maintain the canal. There was a kind of agricultural depression in that region which heightened interest in the more productive western lands.[10]

Quite often the project of an academy or college was one of the means used by speculators to stimulate sales of the lands in which they were interested. The sincerity of many such enterprises was questionable, and astounding numbers of educational institutions were projected, even chartered, but never materialized.[11] In the case of the Galesburg colony, however, educational institutions were the true and primary objectives of the enterprise. Cheap land was to be the means by which a colony committed to social reforms was to establish a college, a female seminary, an academy, and a theological seminary. In the "Circular and Plan," which Gale published in 1834, these were the essential features:[12]

1. $40,000 were to be secured from subscribers, who were to elect a board of trustees with a committee to purchase western lands.
2. A township was to be secured at the government price of $1.25 an acre. Three contiguous sections were to be set apart for the purposes of the college and the village. Much of it was to be sold back to the subscribers at an average of $5.00, thus making a profit of $3.75 on each acre for the colony and its institutions. Proceeds from the remaining lands (not

4

set apart and sold to subscribers as farms or village lots) were to be used to build up endowment funds for educational buildings, scholarships, teachers' salaries, and similar expenditures.

3. Every subscriber who purchased at least eighty acres of land, or who took village lots in payment of his subscription, was to receive title to free instruction of one youth in the college, preparatory school, or female seminary for twenty-five years, which title could be sold, used, or rented at his pleasure.

Gale's plan to finance the educational institutions by anticipated rise in the price of land (the "unearned increment") was fulfilled, though considerably modified in the details of its application. Only about $21,000 in subscriptions were actually secured and not all of that advanced. A loan of $10,000 had to be negotiated, largely on the security of Ferris, who had accumulated wealth from the dairy industry that flourished in New York as grain growing became less profitable. It was not possible to buy a whole township; only twenty, not thirty-six, sections of land were purchased. Furthermore, the full advantage of rise in land values was delayed by the Panic of 1837 and by the following hard times until the boom years of the 1850s, when the railroad came to the village.

By November 1835 a son of Ferris was on the colony site, cutting timber for the buildings that had to be erected, plowing the first of the land at the site where it was expected that a seminary was to be constructed, and setting a fire to the prairie grass that blazed north with a frightening fury to the edge of the grove at "Henderson" where "Hoosiers" had their cabins in the timber. Here in the groves at "Log City" the first "Yankees" of the colony arrived on June 2, 1836, to establish a temporary settlement.[13]

Even while other parties of migrants arrived and as the plowing and the planting began, the streets were surveyed, the town lots were platted, the first buildings were being raised, and the land was allotted for a cemetery, the colonists did not wait to renew the religious, educational, and moral purposes by which they had lived in their eastern homes. Already on January 7, 1836, while still in New York, they had elected a Board of Trustees for their

"Prairie College," and about a year later they sent one of their members to the state legislature of Illinois to procure a charter for the Knox Manual Labor College. On February 15, 1837, the day that incorporation of the college was granted in Vandalia, the colony met for the formal organization of a church. Organization for other good purposes was not neglected. The deeds that were granted to those who bought lots in the village stipulated that no intoxicating beverages should ever be sold on the premises. On June 25, 1837, there was an antislavery prayer meeting and, on the following Sunday, which was Independence Day, after appropriate remarks by the Reverend Gale, $100 was pledged to the cause of abolition, and an antislavery society was organized that was auxiliary to the American Anti-Slavery Society that had been formed in Philadelphia.[14] The presiding officer of the convention that organized this national society in Philadelphia in December 1833 had been the head of Oneida Manual Labor Institute; at the conclusion of the meeting he urged: "Let us fasten ourselves to the throne of God with hooks of steel."[15]

The arrival of Gale's colony in Knox County, Illinois, was reflected immediately at the post office in the county seat by a swelling of subscriptions to the *Observer,* an antislavery paper published in Alton, Illinois, by Elijah P. Lovejoy; when the first press of that paper was destroyed by a mob, the Galesburg subscribers met to express their disapprobation and sent Lovejoy $50 to help him reestablish his publication. When Lovejoy circulated a call for a convention to organize an Illinois Anti-Slavery Society, forty signatures came from the newly settled community of Galesburg, the second largest number of the state. Ten days after this state society was formed (despite the interference of a hostile crowd) in October 1837, Lovejoy, while defending the fourth press for his paper against another Alton mob, was shot and killed. When the *Observer* then published another issue in Cincinnati, a letter from Galesburg expressed concern for its continuing publication.[16]

Another paper that circulated in the colony during its first year was a weekly called the *Advocate of Moral Reform and Family Guardian.* This was the organ of a national society, with headquarters in New York, called the Female Moral Reform Society, which was devoted to the rescue of "fallen women." On November 23, 1837, women in the colony organized an auxiliary to this national organization.[17]

Meanwhile, in a cabin at the grove, schooling could also continue while houses were being built out on the prairie village site. On hand to do some of the teaching was Nehemiah Losey, formerly of the Oneida Institute faculty and now a trustee of the projected Knox College—also the first postmaster, and the surveyor, and soon to be professor of mathematics. During the autumn of 1838 a building for the Knox Academy was completed. In addition to its use for teaching it also was, for several years, the meeting place of the colony church. It was located at the northeast corner of Main and Prairie streets, only a half block from the village square. Four years later the Ladies Seminary was built at the eastern boundary of the village where Tompkins Street ends at Seminary Street. It was a three-story wooden building that cost $5,000. Its cupola was covered with burnished tin and as it reflected the sun a flash might be seen for miles over the prairie.[18] Temporarily it was used for male students of the college.

In 1841 the Reverend Kellogg, who had been acting as agent for the trustees in the East, arrived to assume his duties as president. With him was his sister-in-law, Miss Julia Chandler, who was to be "Preceptress of the Female Department." During the academic year of 1841–42 the enrollment in the Academy, which had started with a total of forty students in 1838, had reached 147, nearly half of whom were women. In addition, there was now the first freshman college class of ten men. In addition to the Reverend Kellogg and Miss Chandler, other faculty were the Reverend Gale, Professor Losey, and Professor Innes Grant, a Scotsman who had been a teacher at Oneida Institute. Grant had come west with another colony from the Burned-over District that had settled the town of Lisbon in Kendall County. But by 1842 he joined the Knox College faculty to teach the "Ancient Languages" that were then so important a part of the curriculum.

That curriculum was so uniform for all students and so common to colleges that it could be printed on one page of the first catalogue, which was published in the summer of 1842. The courses were strong on classical languages and literature, mathematics, and philosophy or religion. There was some science but no modern literature, no modern languages, and no modern history.

A study of the geographical origins of students coming to the Knox Academy, College, and Female Seminary during the first two decades shows that localities where there were other colonies from the Burned-over District were most likely to send students to Knox. These places included Lisbon; Lyndon in Whiteside County; and Geneseo. The last of these, in Henry County, just to the north, had close relations with Galesburg during the pioneer years. The Geneseo and Galesburg colonies paralleled each other almost exactly in their religious and educational attributes. The Lane Rebels associated with Knox were naturally interested in their former classmates at Geneseo, where four Lane Rebels became residents. Another "Yankee" colony, though not from the Burned-over District, that sent students frequently to Knox was the Hampshire Colony that settled in Princeton, Illinois.[19]

Ministers and laymen from these and similar colonies saw each other regularly in the presbyteries, synods, associations, and missionary societies of New School Presbyterians and Congregationalists in Illinois. Men from the Burned-over District also often had reunions at the antislavery conventions during the late 1830s and early 1840s. Here were made the covenants, perhaps unspoken, for help on the underground railroad or a vote for the Liberty party. Amongst these "Yankee" communities Knox College and Galesburg assumed a kind of primacy in religious affairs, education, and reform agitation, comparable to that of Oberlin in Ohio.

On a day in March 1843 Knox College suffered a severe setback. Students who were living in an attic room of the new Seminary building carelessly emptied hot ashes from their stove into a wooden box.[20] The building burned to the ground. On a more modest scale, but of brick, the colonists in 1844 and 1845 erected two buildings on the grounds just south of the village that had been originally set apart for the manual labor college and its farm. They were named "East College" and "West College" but soon were more commonly called the East and West "Bricks." Each of these structures consisted of a two-and-one-half story building facing the village to the north that had attached to it a row of one-story rooms trailing to the south. The one-story rooms, each heated with its own stove, opened directly out to the campus and served as dormitories. The taller front buildings were for classrooms. Their attics would soon become halls for literary societies.

By this time the College finances were in straitened condition. President Kellogg, in April 1843, summarized the situation as follows: "We are not only in debt but we are limited in our resources, having only $25,000 permanently invested at 7% of interest, and as much in unsold land besides our large college farm of 720 acres."[21] The original scheme to finance the College had been based on overly optimistic expectations of a rise in land values. There were also several private projects that presumed early prosperity for that segment of the frontier. Two of these special enterprises, large-scale cheese manufacture and wool production, were realistic enough, though optimistic of a market, but in the realm of fancy were the plans to process sugar from cornstalks and to plant mulberry trees for silkworms. When the depression that followed on the Panic of 1837 frustrated such expectations, the College leaders looked for funds to the East, to the reform-minded philanthropists who had underwritten the antislavery movement, who had favored Oneida Institute, who had rescued the Lane Rebels, and who had taken Oberlin under their wings.

The disastrous burning of the new seminary building in March 1843 hastened a plan, contemplated since 1841, that President Kellogg should go to Britain to raise money among wealthy men who were friendly to the antislavery cause. It was not far-fetched to presume a connection between the abolitionism of the Mississippi Valley and that on the Thames, for in both places the main force of the antislavery impulse came from evangelical religious circles, and the development of the abolition movement in the United States had been directly affected by people and events originating in Great Britain. In fact, a favorite theme for discussion at antislavery meetings in Illinois, at which Gale was frequently a speaker, was the emancipation of slaves in the British West Indies. When, at last, they were also freed in the United States, the Emancipation Day that was celebrated for years after the Civil War by the blacks of Galesburg was the anniversary of August 1, 1833, when Parliament abolished slavery in the British colonies.[22] That act had crowned the long life-work of William Wilberforce, who was a member of the evangelical party in the English church. His name would be carried by Wilberforce Churchill, son of a Galesburg colonist and a student in the Knox Academy, to his death in the campaign to capture Vicksburg.[23]

Oberlin agents who had gone to the World Anti-Slavery Convention at London in 1840 had been very successful in raising money for their institution,[24] and Kellogg planned to go in the same capacity. The executive committee of the Illinois Anti-Slavery Society appointed him the Illinois delegate to the world convention of 1843, and at its annual anniversary appointed a committee to raise funds to help defray his traveling expenses.[25] Kellogg wrote to James Birney, Liberty party candidate in the presidential election of 1840, for an endorsement, for Birney had attended the world convention in London in 1840.[26] Kellogg's traveling companion was the Reverend Jonathan Blanchard of Cincinnati, one of the two American vice-presidents of the convention. Within three years he would succeed Kellogg as the president of Knox College.

At this world convention Kellogg's assignment was to deliver one of the longer formal addresses, his subject being: "United States—Prejudice Against Color." In this discourse he cited at some length the absence of a color line at Knox College. Kellogg also prepared a circular appeal "To Christian Philanthropists in Great Britain and Ireland" in which he said of Knox: "It is not exclusive in its privileges. This is true with respect to persons of different complexions. Colored youth will be welcomed and treated with equal kindness and attention with others."[27]

Kellogg was abroad for about a year. His activities there much enlarged the reputation of Knox as an antislavery school through the thirty-eight letters that Kellogg provided to the *Western Citizen,* the antislavery paper that was published in Illinois. From April 1843 to June 1844, these Kellogg letters were usually given the leading place on the front page and did much, certainly, to advertise Knox College. But though he toured widely in Britain and visited and spoke in many places, Kellogg did not raise much money. He collected only $900 and some gifts of books, which, in view of the embarrassed circumstances of the College, was seriously inadequate. Kellogg offered to relinquish his claim for salary and expenses during the year he was abroad. Though the trustees' minutes vaguely record Kellogg's report about "the influence of certain causes" that kept Knox from obtaining "remedial aid to the full extent that was desired," the implication was clear that Kellogg had failed as a money-raiser.[28] While Kellogg was in England, Gale was in the East during the winter of 1843–44 trying to secure funds. After traveling expenses were deducted his labors netted the College only about $180.

The man who would succeed Kellogg as president of Knox College first appeared in Galesburg in April 1845. The members of the colony congregation came to hear him preach on a Sunday morning in the Academy building. Considerable excitement attended his arrival, for he was a famous abolitionist preacher, and many of those present knew that the colony leaders wanted this man to become president of the College. They would remember the sight of the visitor at this time because he now opened a very lively chapter in their lives. They remembered the pleasure of their surprise as he removed his hat, proceeded to the preacher's desk, and stood before them, a young man of medium height but erect and with "but little of the student's stoop of the shoulders," his raven-black hair just beginning to recede from a high, full forehead that beetled over dark, flashing eyes—"truly a lion looking man."[29] He would earn enemies at this place in time, but to his death, decades later, he would keep the most fervent of followers. In May 1845 Kellogg resigned, suggesting Blanchard as his successor. The next month the Board of Trustees resolved unanimously to ask Blanchard to become president; he accepted and the following February took up his duties in Galesburg. It was he who presided in June 1846 at the first Knox College commencement, in which nine seniors were graduated. And there were those who felt it was pretentious for him to wear academic regalia in the yet unfinished building of the colony church where the services were held.

Blanchard's appearance in Galesburg seemed "providential" or "unexpected" to some, but it was not unplanned. The choice of Blanchard had Gale's approval because it was expected that Blanchard would be able to find support for the college in the East, particularly in the more radical antislavery churches with Congregational and New School Presbyterian connections. For he was well known as a former agent of the American Anti-Slavery Society; he had become a friend of Thaddeus Stevens and of Salmon P. Chase; he had become identified with the Liberty party; he was pastor of the Cincinnati church that had supported the Lane Rebels, and, soon after accepting the presidency of Knox, he had engaged in a great public debate with one of the foremost leaders of the Old School Presbyterians on whether slaveholding was a sin. The record of this debate was published and went through many editions. Such in fact was the notoriety of it that Mrs. Blanchard, on her way to Galesburg with their children, was afraid as she got off the boat at Cape Girardeau, Missouri, to rest over the Sabbath, lest proslavery people identify them through the names on their baggage as the family of the man who had taken the unpopular side in the recently published contest.[30]

It was the task of the new president to find support for Knox College in spite of, or because of, its reputation as an abolitionist center. For Knox men had been leaders in the affairs of the Illinois Anti-Slavery Society and in the starting of the Liberty party. Mrs. Kellogg was president of the convention that organized an Illinois Female Anti-Slavery Society in Peoria in May 1844. Along the border of Illinois with Missouri, Galesburg was acquiring a reputation as "the little nigger stealing town . . . a nest of nigger thieves."[31] In 1842 and 1843 Gale himself and another trustee of Knox were under the indictment of the grand jury for helping runaways from slavery.[32]

It was the widely reported case of the border fugitives that brought Knox to the attention of the man who gave the college its first substantial help from outside. This was John P. Williston of Northampton, Massachusetts, whom Gale had contacted in 1843, and who, after a visit to Galesburg in the summer of 1844, determined that Knox, like Oberlin, deserved his special charity because it advocated practical Christianity. Blanchard's high reputation among antislavery men confirmed Williston's confidence in Knox College. They became very good friends. To the end of Blanchard's tenure at Knox in 1858 he was a regular donor, his gifts aggregating about $8,000, exclusive of the $2,000 or more he expended for needy students.[33]

In 1843 the most common channel for contributions in the East, by New School Presbyterians and Congregationalists, became the Society for the Promotion of Collegiate and Theological Education at the West. Gale discovered that it was difficult to raise money for Knox in the wake of the agents of this society. The leaders in founding this "Western College Society" had been men associated with Illinois College in Jacksonville, Illinois. When Knox, in 1844, approached this organization for aid, it was rejected on the ground that the interests of education in the state would not justify aiding more than one college. The Western Society indicated that it might help Knox if it were only a preparatory school. The leaders at Knox rejected these terms as degrading. It was their belief that the real reason the society rebuffed Knox was its militancy for the antislavery cause. About the time that Blanchard took up his duties as president, Gale wrote to him: "In regard to the College Society, I am not (and that is the feeling of the trustees) desirous of a connection with them; at least we would take no special pains for a connection of that kind. The friends of Anti-Slavery and Reform generally will the sooner confide in us, if we stand by ourselves."[34]

Blanchard did, however, undertake to put pressure on the Western College Society. He went to a convention of "Western Congregationalists" held in 1846 at Michigan City, Indiana. This was a gathering of Congregationalists who were increasingly self-conscious about preserving their own church polity and uneasy because the mutual benevolent agencies they shared with Presbyterians were being used to promote the Presbyterians' ecclesiastical methods. It was the first exclusively Congregational convention to be held in the Old Northwest. Blanchard's name headed the roster of a dozen men from Illinois. It also augured well for Knox at the convention that the man chosen to preside was the Reverend John J. Miter, a former student of Gale's at Oneida Institute, one of the Lane Rebels, and a minister who for three years was associated with the Galesburg colony as home missionary in west central Illinois.[35]

Blanchard addressed this convention on the "claims of Knox College," and the convention responded with a resolution expressing its confidence in Knox and commending it "to the benevolent regards of the Society for Collegiate and Theological Education at the West." No other college got such an endorsement. Blanchard was thus well girded when he appeared two months later before the Western College Society. He made it clear that if Knox was again rejected he would take this special endorsement of the western Congregationalists directly to the eastern Congregationalists. The society voted a donation of $2,000 to Knox College. Until 1856, when the prosperity of Knox made appropriations from the

Western Society unnecessary, it continued to give Knox some funds. But these were always less than the amounts given to Illinois College, Wabash, Marietta, and Western Reserve. Blanchard believed the discrimination was due to the antislavery stand of Knox. Over the ten-year period from 1846 to 1856 the College received a total of $5,864 in yearly subsidies ranging from $450 to $750.[36]

This money helped to carry the College to the boom times of the 1850s, when the building of a railroad transformed the village into a thriving industrial and market center and the value of College lands increased. Because the twenty-five-year scholarships issued to the original settlers deprived the College of most of the tuition income, Blanchard continuously sought smaller gifts in many places so that the College might conserve its real estate assets. In 1853 the College received a gift of eighteen quarter-sections of land, with an estimated value of $30,000, from Charles Phelps of Cincinnati. In a letter to Blanchard, Phelps stated that he wished to assist the youth "who must at no distant day, take part in the great and never ceasing struggle between right and wrong, between Freedom and Slavery, Liberty and Tryanny."[37]

Significantly, Phelps stipulated that his gift should endow professorships "for the equal benefit of males and females." The crusade to abolish slavery had become involved with agitation for the rights of women. For example, when Mrs. Blanchard in 1847 became associated with a Peoria feminist in circulating a petition against the "black code" of Illinois, this project was criticized as inappropriate activity for women, and this controversy led to the question of whether with all the other current reform movements, such as antislavery and temperance, there might not be some reform of women's rights.[38] It is not surprising that among the students at Knox before the Civil War were two men who with their wives would be leaders after the war for emancipation of women from male bondage.[39] And what was "equal" in education also became a vital issue.

Gale's plan for a colony stressed the education of women because they would be much more important in the "conversion of the world" than had formerly been assumed, though his prospectus perceived of them only as ministers' wives, public school teachers, and mothers.[40] Women were admitted on the same basis as men to the Knox Academy and attended the same classes with men. A more advanced program for women was delayed by the burning of the Female Seminary building in March 1843. When a larger two-story Academy building was erected in 1847–48 on the village square, across from the colony church, the upper floor was given to the "female branch." In 1848 the catalogue announced a "systematic course of female education," which by 1850 was organized under the title: "Female Collegiate Department." This program extended over three years and was quite as demanding as that which men pursued to earn the less prestigious bachelor of science degree. It was also assumed that women might choose, for an extra fee, to take some of the "Ornamental Branches," which included music, art, and French. The course of studies for women did not, however, lead to a bachelor's degree, nor in fact did females usually attend the same classes as men, exceptions being allowed only for "experimental lectures" and courses in modern languages.

Yet it is significant that when prosperity permitted the College to erect a new main building for the College men in 1856–57, a building was also constructed for the Female Seminary. The Seminary building cost $30,000. A "large edifice" for that time, this five-story structure accommodated sleeping, dining, and studying facilities for eighty to ninety women and provided them a chapel, recitation rooms, and studios for music and art. Later they would be given a sunny room on the south side for their literary society meetings.

The oldest of the College literary societies was the Adelphi, which was organized in 1846. It replaced a society, existing since 1843, which was disbanded because it was secret. Opposition to secret societies was one of the principles of the benevolent and reforming movement to which the founders of Knox belonged. The Galesburg colony came from that part of the Burned-over District where the anti-Masonic sentiment developed into the first American third party. The Galesburg colony church would not even let the Sons of Temperance use its auditorium because they were a secret fraternity.[41] The General Association of the Congregationalists of Illinois in 1846 condemned such "works of darkness" as "opposed to the Church of Christ and a Republican State," as "peculiarly liable to corruption," and "interfering with

... the freedom of elections, both in Church and State."[42] Blanchard, to the end of his long life, was a staunch supporter of this anti-secret-society principle.

In 1849 men of the College organized a second literary society, called the Gnothautii. The contribution of the two men's literary societies to the education of Knox students was great. They maintained libraries that were an important supplement to the rather meager collection of the College itself. At their weekly meetings the students learned parliamentary law, debated, declaimed, and practiced their carefully composed orations. To sustain their activities they sponsored each year a series of lectures by well-known speakers or concerts by professional artists to raise money from the community. Though the theater was morally suspect, they did stage "colloquys" on contemporary problems that were dramatic in form.[43] And during the 1850s both the Adelphi and the Gnothautii published the first student magazines at Knox. The women's society, formed in 1861, was called the LMI, which was briefly a secret for "Ladies Moral Improvement."[44] Though important as an extension of their intellectual experience, the affairs of this society were more limited than those of the men. It is significant that their forensic events did not include oratory, for that activity brought the most prestigious of all campus honors and was to provide the first well-organized intercollegiate competition.[45] In 1864 a literary society was organized for the Academy.

Twenty years after the arrival of the Galesburg colony the town and the College truly were thriving. Enrollments at all three departments of Knox had grown to 446 students during the year 1856–57. There were fifty-one men in the College, and sixty-six women in the Seminary, the largest number that would ever enroll in the Female Collegiate Department. In the Academy there were 329 pupils and a year later this would reach 366, the greatest number ever to attend that department. Under construction at a total cost of $100,000 were two buildings that 120 years later would still be used by the College—the buildings now known as Whiting Hall and Old Main. And the College, whose founders had difficulty raising $21,000 in 1835, now had property estimated to be worth $400,000.

Mostly this wealth came from real estate values that were increased as the railroads that later comprised the C.B.&Q. entered the town in 1854–55. This had been accomplished by trustees of the College and elders of the colony churches, who somehow raised the $300,000 that was required by the New England capitalists whose money had come from the China clipper trade. The right of way for the railroad touched precisely at the southeast corner of the village, and here the College donated land for the depot, yard, and shops from what had been the College farm of 1,200 acres. The remaining College land, which could now command higher prices, was laid out in city lots, comprising the first addition to the original village.[46]

In October 1858 the thriving town, which could now be reached by rail from four directions, became for the first time a center of national attention when the fifth of the Lincoln-Douglas debates was held on a platform built against the shelter of the new building on the Knox College campus.[47] There was no doubt where Knox stood in this preliminary to the presidential campaign of 1860. Soon after Lincoln was nominated, the faculty and trustees gave him formal endorsement, in time for commencement, by voting him the degree of Doctor of Laws, the first degree conferred upon Abraham Lincoln and the first doctorate ever granted by Knox.[48] This was indeed a partial fulfillment of the long mission of the College against the evil of slavery.

Yet this kind of militancy was now rending the community in a bitter dispute for control of the College. This quarrel, which did great injury to Knox, was a local example of the dissolving of the Plan of Union for Presbyterians and Congregationalists. Though the most discernible breach was along this denominational fault, the disruption got much of its energy from the slavery controversy. From the time of its formation, the Knox Presbytery, to which the Galesburg church belonged, had urged its supreme tribunal, the General Assembly, to excommunicate all slaveholders. In 1843 that presbytery seemed about at the breaking point and raised the question "whether it is not the duty of this presbytery to renounce all connection with the General Assembly of the Presbyterian Church, until they shall lift up their voice in solemn rebuke against the sin of slavery."[49] A decade later, however, it was apparent that Gale and other Presbyterians in Galesburg had become more cautious on this issue. But not so Blanchard. When he became president at Knox, he was already committed to the principle that those who favored slavery were sinners and must be denied communion and membership. He became a national leader in the movement for the "disfellowship" of all those connected in any way with slavery. He bore considerable responsibility for the strain which this put on the Plan of Union. He was the leading figure from the West in the reviving sense of a Congregational identity and in the calling of the first national Congregational convention in 1852.[50]

In Galesburg the tensions led to the withdrawal from the original colony church of Gale and others to form a strictly Presbyterian Church in May 1851. In personnel these schismatics coincided with a party that had developed in the Board of Trustees and that had already contended with Blanchard in 1849, when Gale's followers tried to elect certain members to the board. This precipitated litigation over the legality of the board's membership. Among the supporters of the Gale or the Presbyterian party was a prominent lawyer from Quincy, Orville H. Browning, a conservative Whig who would for a time embrace the Republican party, but who would oppose the Emancipation Proclamation and later serve President Andrew Johnson as secretary of the interior and as attorney general. On the other hand, Blanchard sought legal advice from Senator Chase whom he had known in Cincinnnati. Chase had already, like Blanchard, joined the third-party movement against slavery, and eventually he would be one of the Radical Republicans. The differences between the two men reflect the fact that the trustees supporting Blanchard were those more militant in civil as well as ecclesiastical politics.[51]

A compromise gave both sides equal votes on the board, but in June 1856 a new member of the board, proposed by Browning, tilted the balance in favor of the Gale faction. At the next annual meeting, commencement of 1857, Blanchard was forced out as president. The clamor that followed among both town and gown showed that the board's action was most unpopular. One of the men's literary societies at the College voted that Gale's picture should be taken down from the wall of the society hall and "placed out of sight." The other society concurred in voting to support the seniors, all but one of whom were refusing to appear in the graduation exercises. So many of the undergraduates declared that they did not intend to return to Knox the next fall that it seemed doubtful whether the students' organizations would have the membership to carry on, and therefore they made preparations to wind up their affairs, such as the publication of their literary magazines, and selected special trustees to act as custodians of their society effects. Having done this they adjourned *sine die*.

By special action of the executive committee of the board, Blanchard was retained for a year while a new president was sought. That year and the two following were filled with controversy, reported in the press and in the polemical literature of religious bodies, about the "rights" of Congregationalists in Knox College. The rancor was enhanced by the rhetoric of Dr. Edward Beecher, who in 1855 had come to Galesburg to be pastor of a Congregational Church that was built immediately north of the College grounds, adjacent to the Female Seminary. The Reverend Beecher was a theologian of national repute and belonged to the most famous minister's family of the nineteenth century; the author of *Uncle Tom's Cabin* was his sister; Henry Ward Beecher, the great pulpit orator, was his brother.[52]

When the new president, the Reverend Harvey Curtis of Chicago, a Presbyterian, was inaugurated in 1858, it was clear that Knox College would no longer have the sense of mission for social reform with which it had begun. Blanchard had called for a "martyr-age of Colleges and Seminaries" whose "Faculties ought to . . . infuse into the youth a zeal for reformation." The new president in 1858 declared that "the college is not the place . . . in which to inculcate distinctive opinions on doubtful or contested points, either in religion or morals. . . . Teachers in public institutions may form their own opinions on every question of religion, or reform or politics; and may utter or publish those opinions at their discretion, in fitting ways and on appropriate occasions. But they should not compromise the character of the college by becoming propagandists of any individual or partisan peculiarities, nor should the college chapel or lecture or recitation rooms be misappropriated to the inculcation of any such peculiarities."[53]

At the Knox commencement of 1860, when Knox College awarded Lincoln its highest honor, the first Knox senior to speak his graduation oration predicted a "probable dissolution of the Union."[54] The following Thanksgiving Day, when South Carolina was already taking the lead toward just such a dissolution, the

Reverend Beecher told his congregation that he hoped that the Union of the states might continue unimpaired but warned "it may be the design of the Almighty to separate the slave from the free states, that he may deal with slavery itself, and hurl against it His bolts of wrath."[55] During that autumn and winter the Adelphi frequently debated the meaning of the political troubles that threatened the nation, and about the time that Fort Sumter was attacked they were scheduled to debate the question: "Resolved that the system of government planned and adopted by our fore-fathers has been a political failure."[56] But such irresolution was gone after Fort Sumter fell and President Lincoln called for 75,000 volunteers. In late May the Adelphi debated whether or not it was "right for the citizens of Northern States to make persons who sympathize with secession raise the American flag, take the oath of allegiance or leave."[57]

The temper of this proposition likely reflected the feelings that attended the excitement at the railroad depot in Galesburg in May 1861, when a large crowd gathered to witness the departure of the "Galesburg Fencibles," who were going to join other companies of volunteers for the Seventeenth Regiment of Illinois that was to rendezvous at Peoria. There were at least ten former Knox students in this regiment, particularly in Company E, where Knox men were the captain, two lieutenants, and two sergeants. They would become part of the American Iliad, following General Ulysses S. Grant in the great thrust of the western armies down the Mississippi Valley; the capture of Fort Donelson (where one of the Knox men was killed); the battle near Shiloh Church (where this regiment had 130 men killed and wounded); the slow advance on Corinth; the long investment of Vicksburg.[58]

More than a third of the graduates of Knox College since its founding served in the armies of Union volunteers. More than 170 of the men who had since 1838 attended the Academy or College were soldiers in that war, serving in many different units from several states. At least half a hundred became commissioned officers, three of them brigadier generals, and seven of them colonels.[59] At least eight Knox alumni were commissioned as officers for "colored troops," such as the Corps d'Afrique organized in Louisiana. One of these was a son of Professor Losey, who had surveyed the village of Galesburg; two were grandsons of Ferris (one was named George Washington Gale Ferris). It was his namesake, "the Founder," who on a Fourth of July in 1838 had made a speech that had spoken of the need to trumpet the "principles of liberty" until the "walls and ramparts of slavery like those of Jericho fall to the ground."[60]

Also of particular symbolic significance for Knox College were two companies of the "Brains" or "Teachers" Regiment, the Thirty-third Regiment of Illinois Infantry Volunteers. It was the men of this regiment and those of the Seventeenth from Illinois who were the first from that state to have a "baptism of fire," and it was in this battle in eastern Missouri that Knox County soldiers "burnt powder" during "their first fight." In Company E of the Thirty-third about half the men were from Knox County. Company H came largely from Knox and from neighboring Warren County.[61]

There were eight Knox alumni in Company E, including a lieutenant, and a first sergeant, George Gregory Foster, who had been at Knox since 1857 and who would have graduated in June 1862. But at Big River Bridge in Missouri, which he was guarding, he was killed on October 15, 1861, the first soldier of the Thirty-third to die in battle and the first Knox alumnus to die in this war. The telegraph carried such news more quickly than in earlier wars, and the day after Sergeant Foster was killed, his brothers in the Adelphi ordered that the society hall be draped in black and that members wear crepe arm bands in mourning for thirty days. This early in the war there could hardly be a sense of how common the early death of young men would become. Yet for at least two decades the Adelphi remembered Foster. When spring came in 1862, the brothers had his remains removed to a lot in the town cemetery and procured subscriptions for a tombstone. After the war, they cared for the grave marker and at Memorial Days marched to the burial site and decorated it with flowers.[62]

In Company H the captain was James A. McKenzie, who had graduated from Knox in 1859; two lieutenants were also Knox alumni. And one of the corporals was John Mart Bruner, who interrupted his studies at Knox to serve as a volunteer. According to Captain McKenzie, Corporal Bruner was involved in an incident that "would have been enjoyed by Wendell Phillips and William Lloyd Garrison." (While McKenzie was a student, the

Gnothautii brought Phillips to Galesburg on their lecture series.) The significance of the event was heightened by the fact that during the early part of the war it was Lincoln's political strategy not to alienate the border states, such as Missouri, by interfering with slavery. Thus, General John Frémont, the Republican candidate for president in 1856, was removed by Lincoln from his command from the Department of the West because he issued an emancipation of the slaves in Missouri. Yet some time in late September 1861 or early October 1861 Lieutenant Julian Bryant from Princeton, Illinois, and Corporal Bruner led an attack by forty men on a plantation that was a rendezvous for Confederate soldiers. They captured the owner, several of his sons, some Confederate recruits, and a supply of arms. The arms were given to about twenty blacks from the plantation who marched the prisoners back to the Union camp. The colonel rebuked Captain McKenzie for undertaking to do what the president would not yet do, "liberate and arm the slaves." And the blacks were sent back to their owner. Captain McKenzie, however, remained proud of this effort, and after the war believed that this was the first time in the war that "slaves were liberated and armed."[63]

Some of the Knox men who enlisted in the army during the last half of the war would have received some military training at the College. The Knox Board of Trustees, at their annual meeting of June 1862, appointed a committee to look into the establishing of a military course. In August one of the trustees, Dr. James Bunce, who had been the physician of the Galesburg colony, was sent to Springfield to procure "suitable drill officers" and to ascertain whether "suitable arms" might be obtained for the Knox military department. He was told about a German officer, Major Julius Standau. Accordingly, Major Standau was hired as a "Professor of Military Tactics" as well as instructor of German and French; it also turned out that he could tune the pianos in the Female Seminary.[64]

At 4:30 P.M., September 15, Standau met the students to arrange for military drill. Two weeks later a faculty committee, including the major, consulted with the students about uniforms and reported the following stipulation about what the Knox men should wear: "That the uniform for military drill would consist of a flannel shirt and a cheap pair of overalls with a suitable cap, the whole not to cost over $2.00 or $3.00, and that to secure uniformity of dress, students be recommended to wear black, the pantaloons to be plain, the vest to be ornamented with brass or gilt buttons, the coat to be single breasted, straight in front, but with a turned down collar, the cap to be of cloth and may be ornamented with brass buttons."[65]

So that all members of the senior and junior class might in turn be officers, the faculty voted that Standau appoint the officers in rotation. The major also used a scheme that transformed twenty-four cadets into an "entire regiment": "Two men would take a long rope which stretched at full length would then constitute a 'platoon' or 'company.' They would under this arrangement have grand reviews and maneuvers of all kinds."[66] Most of these campus soldiers used old flintlock muskets as the rifle needed for close order drill. Some of these old weapons probably came from Henry County, for in November the treasurer of the College was sent to that county "for the purpose of getting the Arms in the hands of the Swedes there." Later in the year a bugler was employed in order that the students might learn "Signals."

The drill and military training were compulsory, but the requirement encountered some resistance from the first. At their second meeting of the year the Adelphi scheduled a debate on the question: "Resolved that the uniting of a thorough course of military science with a college course is impolitic." One student was excused already in September from military drill by vote of the faculty when he presented a request from his father and indicated that if not excused he would withdraw from the College. Two others were excused during the winter. Another was disciplined for "irregularities during the military drill."[67] By September 1863 the program was discontinued. Then, too, many of the men at Knox by now had already done some military service. They might serve for a short period and return to school. During the summer of 1863, for example, thirteen Knox men served in the Seventy-first Regiment of Illinois for "Three Months" service. They relieved veterans from guard duty at various camps and strategic points so that the veterans might be sent "to the front." Again in the summer of 1864 thirteen Knox soldiers were "one hundred day men" doing duty at forts, arsenals, and similar places.[68]

One of the important lasting consequences of the war was to

make the Republican party the "respectable" party for decades to come in communities such as Galesburg and on campuses such as Knox. Democrats would be stereotyped for rebellion, as well as for Romanism and rum. In 1863, when local branches of a "Union League" were organized in the North to support the Republican party, the Knox Board of Trustees voted that a "Union League" on the campus might use a room in the East College Building.[69] In September 1864, while the presidential contest occurred between Lincoln and the popular General George McClellan, the Knox faculty responded to a student's petition by suspending classes on the day of a Republican convention in the town. The partisan feeling is reflected in a letter that a student wrote to his girl friend:

> Tonight there are great demonstrations down town over the glorious (and ain't they glorious) returns from Indiana, Ohio and Pennsylvania, anvils booming, or rather bonging, and bells ringing. The Copperheads Mass Meeting held here last week was a grand fizzle, as every thing Copperhead is, not worth a Copper cent. One man was put in the calaboose for shouting for Jeff Davis, another collared, and the torch light procession in the evening was so largely made up of Unionists that their shouts for Lincoln drowned out the faint peeps for Little Mac.[70]

As a student in the Female Seminary wrote to her mother on the occasion of the fall of Richmond in April 1865, "The scholars are all pretty patriotic. Last Monday evening there was great rejoicing in town on receiving news that Richmond was taken. All the College boys assembled in front of the college, having gathered flags, horns, drums, etc. They marched all over town and at last in front of the Sem. The girls were all out on the front steps singing 'The Star Spangled Banner.' The boys halted and joined in the chorus. We all sung patriotic songs and gave three cheers for the Union."[71]

Only eleven days later the news came of Lincoln's death; the executive committee of the board ordered that the College "be draped in mourning." Wrote trustee Reverend Samuel Guild Wright in his journal: "We felt God's hand was in it preparing the way for the perfect eradication of slavery, and visiting justice upon the leading rebels. We never hated Slavery so much as now."[72]

At least four Knox alumni remained with the Union armies that had occupied the South, became carpetbaggers, and achieved important civil offices in the Reconstruction governments.[73] Two were members of the congressional delegation from Mississippi that were readmitted to the national legislature in February 1870. One of these was the black senator, Hiram Rhodes Revels, who took the seat last occupied by Jefferson Davis. Revels had attended the Knox Academy in 1856–57. During the war he had helped to recruit black regiments in Maryland and Missouri and had been an army chaplain. He served for a short time as provost marshal at Vicksburg. After a short term in the Senate he became president of the recently established Alcorn University, a school for blacks.[74]

It was as educational missionaries in the South that Knox students would have their most significant role during the Reconstruction. More than a score of Knox men and women were teachers at schools for the freedmen in the South during the last third of the nineteenth century.[75] Most of them were sponsored by the American Missionary Association (AMA), a society founded before the war upon the most radical antislavery principles. Even before the war, a Knox man had been one of the missionaries of this society that was driven out of Kentucky while attempting to establish an antislavery school at Berea. President Blanchard, Dr. Beecher, and the Reverend Flavel Bascom (pastor of the original colony church) were among the leaders at Knox who were officers of this society. Next to Oberlin, where the primary impulse came, Knox was the most active center for the AMA in the Old Northwest. In fact, though the offices for the association were far away in New York, the annual meeting of the society was held in Galesburg in 1866.[76]

During the Reconstruction of the 1870s, when the AMA worked hand in hand with the Freedmen's Bureau in establishing education for the illiterate freedman, a dozen Knox men and women taught at colleges, normal institutes, and schools for freedmen in Charlotte, North Carolina; in New Orleans; in Memphis; in Marshall, Texas; in the state of Mississippi at Cotton Gin Porte, Woodville, and Columbus; in the state of Alabama at Montgomery, Selma, Talledega, and Mobile.

Recent graduates from Knox were particularly active in Mobile, at Emerson Institute. Edward P. Lord (1871) was the superintendent from January 1873 to July 1876; he was succeeded by another Knox man, Albert Barnes Irwin (1871) when Lord became principal of the college for "colored people" at Talledega. During

Lord's superintendency at the Emerson Institute, five Knox graduates were on the faculty.[77]

The colleges that the AMA founded in the South were described by the distinguished black historian, W. E. B. Du Bois, as the "finest thing in American history, one of the few things untainted by sordid greed and cheap vulgarity." They were "not alms, but a friend; not cash, but character."[78] Lord reported occasionally that he had won admiration or respect from certain whites in Mobile, but he and other AMA missionaries, when sharing their experiences, agreed that most southern whites were indifferent at best and often hostile to the education of blacks. Even seventy-five years after the military occupation of the South had ceased, the head of the history department at the University of Alabama pointed out that there had been "pedagogical carpetbaggers" as well as political and ecclesiastical carpetbaggers. The religious and educational missions, he declared, were "essentially a continuation of hostilities against the conquered people."[79]

It was such resentment that probably led to the burning of Emerson Institute during the night of April 16, 1876. The teachers were convinced from the manner of the starting of the fire that it was the act of incendiaries who were resentful of the influence of Emerson Institute. Back in Galesburg, the leading newspaper urged the clergymen of the city to raise money so that Emerson Institute might be rebuilt.[80] And it was, for the work of continuing was started at once by Albert B. Irwin (1871) who, with his sister Sara Irwin (1869), remained there for the next year. From 1883 to 1885, the principal at Emerson was again a man from Knox, Milton Churchill (1877), the son of the principal of the Knox Academy. With him at this Mobile school was his wife of the class of 1878 and two other Knox women of 1884.[81]

In 1878 the Reverend Joseph E. Roy, a Knox alumnus who had been the western agent of the AMA before the war, became the field superintendent of the activities of that society in the South, overseeing what was done to foster universities and colleges such as Talledega, Straight (now Dillard), Atlanta, Fisk, Hampton, Tillotson, and Tougaloo—altogether some twenty-nine schools in all parts of the region. He and his family made their home in Atlanta and lived for seven years "in the midst of people who but lately had been slaves," encountering the "scorn and obstracism from their former masters."[82] In 1870 Knox College had made him an honorary Doctor of Divinity, and in 1887 he was elected to the Board of Trustees. In November of the fortieth year after his graduation (1848) he stood on the platform of the old colony church where his commencement ceremonies had been held and lectured on "Slave Songs." Negro spirituals were sung by the choir to accompany the lecture.[83]

Hundreds of independent colleges, seminaries, and academies were founded in the United States during the half century between the War of 1812 and the conclusion of the Civil War. Most of them failed. Knox College, like some others, provides for the historian a good case study of religious institutions that appeared on the frontier of the upper Mississippi Valley during the second quarter of the nineteenth century. Better than most it affords an example of thoughtful exploitation of the rise of value of land very cheaply bought from the federal government and also an instance of successful speculation in railroad construction. Most distinctive, however, was the role of the College in the crusade against slavery, an issue which by mid-century could no longer be repressed, whether in ecclesiastical or civil politics. The founders of Knox College in 1836 had already committed themselves against slavery, but they could hardly have foreseen that thirty years later Knox alumni would be serving the cause in West Africa, in the Reconstruction government of Mississippi, and in schools newly established to educate the freedmen of the South.

NOTES

1. Cross, *Burned-over District.*
2. Gale, "Autobiography."
3. Muelder, *Fighters for Freedom,* 29–30.
4. George Washington Gale to Charles Grandison Finney, Jan. 29, 1830, Finney Papers.
5. Cross, *Burned-over District,* 8–12.
6. Thomas, *Theodore Weld,* 34–43.
7. Fletcher, *History of Oberlin College,* 1:169–85, 242.
8. Harriet Tenney to Mary Ingall, Feb. 27, 1840, MS, Knox College Library; British and Foreign Anti-Slavery Society, *Proceedings of the General Anti-Slavery Convention, 1843,* 265.
9. Muelder, *Fighters for Freedom,* 80–83.

10. Calkins, *They Broke the Prairie*, chs. 2, 3.
11. Muelder, *Fighters for Freedom*, ch. 7.
12. Webster, *Seventy-five Significant Years*, 9–12.
13. Calkins, *They Broke the Prairie*, ch. 3.
14. Muelder, *Fighters for Freedom*, 117–18.
15. *Ibid.*, 33.
16. *Ibid.*, 118.
17. "The Diary of Jerusha Loomis Farnham," in Calkins, ed., *Log City Days*, 54.
18. Webster, *Seventy-five Significant Years*, 60–61.
19. Muelder, *Fighters for Freedom*, 89–101.
20. Henry E. Hitchcock to John H. Finley, Feb. 1, 1898, Hitchcock Family Papers. Hitchcock inaccurately recalled the fire as occurring in Feb. 1843. A letter in the Knox College Archives established the time as the morning of Mar. 15, 1843 (Hannah Chambers to Cordelia Willard, Mar. 15, 1843, MS, Knox College Library).
21. Kellogg to James G. Birney, Apr. 13, 1843, in Birney, *Letters*, ed. Dumond, 2:729.
22. Galesburg *Republican*, Aug. 6, 1870, 1; Galesburg *Republican Register*, Aug. 8, 1874, 3; Aug. 4, 1877, 5. The editor of the *Republican Register* noted the connection with the West Indies emancipation on Aug. 5, 1876, 1.
23. Bentley, *History of the 77th Illinois Volunteer Infantry;* "Biographical Scrapbook," 1:17–18, Galesburg Public Library.
24. Fletcher, *History of Oberlin*, 1:457–69.
25. *Western Citizen* (Chicago), Mar. 30, 1843.
26. Kellogg to Birney, Apr. 3, 1843, in Birney, *Letters*, ed. Dumond, 2:729.
27. Muelder, *Fighters for Freedom*, 153–55.
28. Knox College, Trustees' Minutes, July 13, 1844.
29. Muelder, *Fighters for Freedom*, ch. 13.
30. Blanchard and Rice, *Debate on Slavery;* Fisher, *Blessed Memory.*
31. Galesburg *Free Democrat*, Sept. 16, 1857.
32. Muelder, *Fighters for Freedom*, ch. 12.
33. *Ibid.*, 249–51.
34. Gale to Blanchard, Oct. 17, 1845, in *Report on Knox College. Presented to the General Association of Illinois, May 24, 1861* (Quincy, Ill.), 39–40.
35. Muelder, *Fighters for Freedom*, 73–75, and *passim.*
36. *Ibid.*, 253–58.
37. *Ibid.*, 259.
38. *Western Citizen*, Aug. 3, 24, 1847; Nov. 28, 1848; Feb. 27, 1849.
39. See references to Charles Burlingame Waite and his wife, Catherine Van Valkenburg Waite; also to James R. Bradwell and his wife, Myra Colby Bradwell; also to Edward Beecher in Stanton and Gage, eds., *History of Woman Suffrage.*
40. Webster, *Seventy-five Significant Years*, 10.

41. Knoxville *Journal*, Sept. 17, 1850; Nov. 7, 1854; Galesburg *Free Democrat*, June 22, 1854.

42. Reprinted in the *Minutes of the General Association of May, 1862* as Appendix J, 27–28 (Congregational General Association of Illinois, 1862).

43. Muelder, *Fighters for Freedom*, 336–37.

44. Amelia Carey to Parents (Rufus Carey, Princeton, Ill.), Nov. 1866, MS, Knox College Library.

45. See ch. 3 herein.

46. Calkins, *They Broke the Prairie*, 7.

47. *Ibid.*, ch. 9.

48. Knox College, Faculty Minutes, June 29, 1860; Trustees Minutes, July 3, 1860.

49. Presbytery of Knox, Records, 1839–44, 133–34, MS, Knox College Library.

50. Muelder, *Fighters for Freedom*, 277–301.

51. *Ibid.*, 379–82.

52. Calkins, *They Broke the Prairie*, ch. 6.

53. Curtis, *Inaugural Address*, 12–13

54. Galesburg *Free Democrat*, July 6, 1860.

55. *Ibid.*, Nov. 30, 1860.

56. Adelphi Society, Program Meeting Minutes, Apr. 17, 1861.

57. *Ibid.*, May 15, 1861.

58. Oquakwa (Ill.) *Spectator*, May 16, 1861.

59. During the Civil War centennial Craig Lovitt compiled from alumni files and other records a list of Knox men who served in the Union armies. I supplemented this record by research in county histories, regimental histories, and other sources. A card file of this list is deposited with the Knox College Archives.

60. Peoria *Register and Northwestern Gazetteer*, July 14, 1838.

61. Elliott, *History of the Thirty-third Veteran Volunteer Infantry*, 8ff.

62. Adelphi Society, Business Meeting Minutes, Oct. 16.1861; Apr. 8, May 14, 1862; May 16, 27, 30, 1869; Galesburg *Republican Register*, May 26, 1883, 9; June 2, 1883, 1.

63. Elliott, *History of the Thirty-third Veteran Volunteer Infantry*, 11–26.

64. Knox College, Trustees Minutes, June 25, 1861. Executive Committee of the Board of Trustees, Aug. 25, Sept. 9, 1862; June 10, 1863.

65. Knox College, Faculty Minutes, Sept. 19, 1862.

66. Thomas Willard in the Knox College *Alumnus*, 10 (Mar.-Apr. 1927), 133.

67. Knox College, Faculty Minutes, Mar. 16, 1863; see also minutes for Sept. 26, 1862; Jan. 9, May 1, June 8, 1863.

68. *Report of the Adjutant General of the State of Illinois*, 4:449–69, 524; 7:3.

69. Knox College, Executive Committee Minutes, Sept. 17, 1863.

70. Thomas Willard to Mary L. D. Wolcott, Oct. 12, 1864, Willard Papers.

71. Augusta Leland to her mother, Apr. 6, 1865, Alumni file for Augusta Leland Case, MS, Knox College Library.

72. Wright, Journal.

73. George P. *Carr* attended Knox intermittently between 1853 and 1863. He became a captain in the Arkansas Cavalry and remained in the South to become a judge in Louisiana (Galesburg *Free Press*, Nov. 24, 1869, 3; Galesburg *Republican*, Jan. 6, 1872, 4). William C. *Craig*, class of 1864, became a second lieutenant in the 137th Illinois Volunteers Regiment and remained in the South as U.S. district attorney in Memphis, Tenn. (Knox Alumni Association Minutes, MS, Knox College Library). Brigadier General George C. *McKee* attended the Knox Academy seven years, from 1845 to 1853, and then attended the Liberal Institute (later called Lombard College) in Galesburg in 1854–55. He helped to frame the new constitution of Mississippi, under which he was elected to the Congress, where he represented Mississippi until Mar. 3, 1875 (*A Biographical Congressional Directory with an Outline History of the National Congress, 1774–1911* [Washington, 1913]; Galesburg *Republican Register*, Dec. 27, 1873). See also Garner, *Reconstruction in Mississippi*, 186–87, 246.

74. Muelder, *Fighters for Freedom*, 332; Galesburg *Republican*, Apr. 9, 1870, 1; Dec. 3, 1870, 4; Dec. 10, 1870, 4.

75. This list, given by last year of attendance at Knox, is compiled primarily from the archives of the AMA and from the missionary lists published in the *American Missionary*. Other sources were the alumni files for the several classes to which the missionaries belonged. Notes also came from College publications and local newspapers. In the archives of Knox College is an unpublished monograph on Knox College during the Civil War and Reconstruction by the author. This manuscript details the sources of information for the following list: Joseph E. Roy, class of 1848, and his wife, Emily Stearns Hatch, who served with him in the South, was a student at Knox from 1844–49; Sarah A. Allan, Female Seminary, 1857–58; Frances Candee, Female Seminary, 1863–64; James A. Adams, 1867; Robert Hall, 1869; Sarah Jane Irwin, 1869; Barnabas Root, 1870; Albert Barnes, 1871; Abby Smith Colton, 1871; Lulu Dunn, 1871; Marrietta Jenney, 1871; Edward P. Lord, 1871; Emma Willard, 1871; Milton Churchill, 1877, served with his wife, Ida Post, 1878; Charles Wychoff Dunn, 1881, served with his wife, Ann Wildman Somers, 1882; Nettie Lay, 1884; Gertrude Wyckoff, 1884; Mary Hyde, 1885; Mary Wyckoff, 1885; Mary P. Roberts, 1886.

76. *American Missionary* (New York), Dec. 1866, 265–68. For the origins of the AMA see Dunning, *Congregationalists in America*, 351–52.

77. See the reports on Emerson Institute in the *American Missionary* beginning in the number for Mar. 1868, 61. The issue for June 1869 (p. 61) presented a picture of Emerson Institute. There are many letters and reports from Edward P. Lord regarding Emerson Institute in the AMA Archives, which are administered by the Amistad Research Center at Dillard University, New Orleans. See the letters from Lord, Dec. 17, 1872, to Dec. 20, 1878. See also

reports in the Galesburg *Republican Register,* Aug. 3, 1873, 1, 6; May 6, 1876, 4; Nov. 25, 1876, 1.

78. Quoted, proudly, by David Sandstrom, *Notes to Friends,* 34 (June 1977), of the occasional reports, reflections, and quotations regarding the USA mission of the United Church of Christ Board for Homeland Missions, New York City.

79. Moore, *History of Alabama,* 487; see also 514–19.

80. *American Missionary,* June 1876, 126; Abby Holton to the Reverend M. E. Streiby, Apr. 18, 1876, AMA Archives; Galesburg *Republican Register,* May 6, 1876, 4.

81. Galesburg *Republican Register,* Sept. 1, 1883, 1; Nov. 19, 1883, 2; Dec. 15, 1883, 1. Knox College *Coup D'Etat,* Jan. 1884, 62; Sept. 1884, 14; Nov. 1884, 45; Mar. 1885, 108; Apr. 1885, 125; May 1885, 133; Oct. 1885, 29; Nov. 1885, 41.

82. Barton, *Joseph Edwin Roy,* 36.

83. Galesburg *Republican Register,* Dec. 1, 1888, 6.

CHAPTER II

YEARS OF UNCERTAINTY

During the lifetime of the founders of Galesburg, profound changes in American civilization altered in significant ways the cultural environment and even the physical setting in which Knox College conducted its affairs. A stronger national government used its public land to subsidize the development of state universities that rapidly hastened the secularization of American education. During the same middle third of the century, millions of immigrants from Europe settled not only in the older communities of the East but also on the frontier of the West, to which they were carried on the relatively new railroad system that was subsidized by very favorable policies of the federal government. All of these changes to some degree affected the history of Knox, which in any event would be involved in the national controversies, nonpolitical in character, over coeducation of men and women, secret societies, and preserving a classical emphasis in the curriculum.

Hard times had come on Knox during the war years. In 1866, when the old timers commemorated the thirtieth anniversary of the arrival of the first families, Professor George Churchill made a statistical summary showing that since 1858 all departments of the College had suffered serious declines in enrollment. He queried why Knox had not kept up with the growth and prosperity of the community.[1] Obviously the disruptions from the Civil War would partly account for the decline, following as it did the general depression of the late 1850s. But there were particular local developments that had also affected the ailing College.

Churchill's own dedication and integrity could partly explain the decreased enrollment in the Academy, which in 1862–63 fell to 94, the lowest since the first catalogue was printed in 1842, and drastically down from its highest in 1857–58, when it had reached 366. Though principal of a private school that once had enrolled students as young as the age of ten, he took the lead in overcoming indifference to good public schools. To stimulate opinion favorable to improved and free graded public schools he brought to Galesburg, partly at his own expense, experts who could speak on this subject. One of these was the distinguished Horace Mann. Churchill had been warned by some partisans of Knox that he was injuring Knox and was "jeopardizing his own position by his activity in promoting public schools."[2]

All departments at Knox were also hurt by what the trustees' minutes recorded as "the unforeseen and radical derangement of the monetary affairs of the country." On the commodity index, the numbers rose from 61.3 in 1861 to 132 in 1865. During this inflation expenses increased much more than the value of the land holdings upon which the College primarily depended for income. The total "means" of the College, mostly land contracts, notes, and real estate, were in June 1860 $373,045; by June 1865 these "means" had declined to $333,157 in badly depreciated dollars. To cover its deficits much of the income-bearing property was sold, and, by the end of the decade this practice seriously threatened the future of the College.[3]

The trustees had during the war insisted on a reduction in the size of the faculty and the teaching duties of each remaining faculty member had been accordingly enlarged while his salary was reduced. When early in the summer of 1861 they were asked to effect certain economies, the faculty responded with a resolution that called the attention of the board to the harmful sectarian controversy among the trustees and urged that the trustees effect a broader denominational appeal by the College.

The spiritual homogeneity that had prevailed when the founders had worshiped in the first small Academy building had changed to the rather considerable sectarian diversity of a railroad center. By the end of the 1860s all of the important American Protestant varieties had been planted at churches within walking distance of the College grounds. There could hardly be an excuse for a student not to obey the requirement that he attend a church on Sunday, for the choices ranged in polity and dogma from Episcopalian to

Universalist. Furthermore, there developed, no doubt after the successful example of Knox College, a concentration of six denominational schools within fifteen miles of the public square in Galesburg. At the seat of Warren County the "Reformed" Presbyterians had established Monmouth College. At the seat of Knox County in Knoxville, there was the Episcopalian St. Mary's School for girls. Also within the county, at Abingdon, the Methodists and the "Christians" had each a college. And in Galesburg, in addition to Knox, there was Lombard University. Occasionally, Galesburg called itself "The College City."

The most important competition came from Lombard, which was located about a mile east of the Knox College grounds. The beliefs of the Universalists separated them far indeed from other sectarians, most of whom refused to accept Universalists as truly Christians and charged that they undermined the very foundations of morality. Universalist creed cut straight through the thickets of Calvinism by assuring the salvation of all souls, rejecting the doctrine of vicarious atonement, and introducing a unitarian concept of God. Since they stressed tolerance of diverse convictions and freedom of individual interpretation, it is not surprising that the Academy they first chartered for Galesburg should have been named Illinois Liberal Institute. Freedom from sectarian restraints were set forth as reasons for its foundation. By 1855 it had become Lombard University.[4] The danger that Galesburg might become the center of Universalism in the West was one of the factors that attracted the distinguished Edward Beecher to Galesburg about that time, for the nation must be saved from this extreme deviation from orthodoxy just as it must be defended against the expansion of Roman Catholicism.[5]

Prominent in the leadership that founded this Universalist college were families that had been in the colony that settled Galesburg and thus endowed Knox College. There can be no doubt that Lombard University attracted students who otherwise might have enrolled in Knox College. By 1860 there were nearly 300 students at Lombard. Certainly some of them were there only because it was Universalist, but of the 120 who came from Galesburg a significant number must have attended Lombard only because it was another and more liberal alternative.

The "younger neighboring institutions" at Knoxville, Abingdon, and Monmouth had a better opportunity to develop because Knox College wasted its initial advantage over them in the bitter quarrel between Congregationalists and Presbyterians, which had reached its climax in 1857 with the ousting of Jonathan Blanchard. This was the judgment of the Reverend Flavel Bascom, pastor of the original colony church during much of the 1850s and the trustee who tried to maintain a balance between the George Gale and the Blanchard parties on the board. He made this observation: "Had the Faculty and Trustees of Knox College obeyed the injunction of Joseph to his brethren, 'See that ye fall not out by the way,' it is probable that it would have attained to an overshadowing preeminence, by drawing to itself that patronage which has now ministered to the growth of younger neighboring institutions."[6] A student editor who had attended Knox from 1864 to 1870 noted an indifference of people in Galesburg toward the College and attributed this attitude to the denominational strife of previous years.[7] It is revealing that sectarianism was a recurring subject for debate during the 1860s in the meetings of the Adelphi.[8]

The "battle of the books" between the Congregationalists and Presbyterians concluded with a *Report on Knox College* that was presented to the General Association of Congregationalists of Illinois, which met in Galesburg in May 1861. The Congregationalists denied any desire to control Knox College, but they expressed the hope that it would not become Presbyterian. If so, they declared that the College would lose patronage in the surrounding area, where Congregationalists greatly outnumbered New School Presbyterians, a claim confirmed by the census of 1860. Furthermore, the Congregationalists wanted to sustain the interdenominational principle that once had been honored. They expressed concern that if Presbyterians took over the College they "would impose upon a liberal institution the yoke of sectarian littleness," which would "demoralize and desecrate it." They stated that the "spirit of aggressive denominationalism, alike in Congregationalists and Presbyterianism, is utterly unlovely."[9]

Sectarian competition in the community was compounded by the arrival in the community of substantial numbers of ethnic minorities. Galesburg was no longer a Yankee village. A concentration of Swedish immigrants in the area had followed upon the attention given to the communal religious settlement of Swedes at Bishop Hill in the next county north. A significant number of Irish Catholics found jobs in the growing railroad town. And during the war the number of blacks multiplied many fold as fugitives from slavery in Missouri (the so-called contrabands) sought out Galesburg, where it was known they would be tolerated, for the laws of the state until 1865 were still hostile to the immigration of blacks.[10]

Unlike the several Protestant sects, the Catholics did not build their church within the bounds of the original village, but rather, as if beyond the pale, they located it well outside, along the railroad right of way. It is evident from recurring discussions in the literary societies during the 1860s and 1870s that Knox students were truly heirs of the prejudices and anxieties of Roundheads and Covenanters, concerned about the growth of Catholic churches and schools and fearful of their effect on the American political system.[11]

Toward the Swedish immigrants the feeling from the first was quite positive. Blanchard had used his influence to get missionary subsidies from 1850 to 1857 for the two pioneer Swedish clergymen who founded a "mother church" at Andover, Illinois, and who made Galesburg for a time the center from which other Lutheran churches were organized, a Swedish synod established, a denominational press started, and the Augustana College colony sent out.[12]

First an "African" Methodist and then a "Second" Baptist Church were established for the increasing population of blacks, being located then, as they would be for the next century and longer, immediately east of the College grounds, on Tompkins and South streets, respectively. On occasions the churches associated with the College had joint services with these "colored" people, and sometimes students from the College helped out with church school and choir activities in these neighboring congregations.[13] Such associations, while not very frequent, were a great deal more than would exist a century later. In fact, the separate churches confirmed the pattern of residential location for blacks that was already taking its present shape. Mary Allen West, a graduate of the Knox Female Seminary and sometimes a teacher in the Academy, volunteered as a teacher of both black children and adults when they became a considerable community of recent migrants. But as this effort became part of the regular public school program, it developed into a segregated system, the controversy over which extended well into the 1870s.[14]

In dealing with these crises the College had the bad fortune to have the office of the president vacated or interrupted frequently during the fifteen years following the inauguration of the Reverend Harvey Curtis (the Presbyterian choice) in 1858. During his fourth year he was ill so much that the trustees offered to put him on half-pay. He died after a long sickness in September of 1862. His successor, another Presbyterian, William S. Curtis, did not assume his duties until the summer of 1863. Then in March 1868, a student strike and the threatened resignation of the faculty of the Female Seminary forced him to resign. By June the Reverend John P. Gulliver had been elected to the office, but four years later he resigned when the trustees no longer would allow the increased costs of his ambitious plans for the College. And then it was almost three years before the next president was on hand to provide executive leadership.

Fortunately, able and dedicated faculty members carried on despite disappointment and uncertainty. Of the original faculty, Professor Innes Grant continued to teach the ancient languages until 1869; Professor Nehemiah Losey stopped teaching mathematics and astronomy during the war but remained on the Board of Trustees, serving as secretary or treasurer until his death in 1875. In the Female Seminary Henry Eaton Hitchcock, a member of the first class graduated from the College and a son-in-law of George Gale, remained on the faculty until 1872. But most valuable of all to the future of Knox were the men who carried through to the end of the century, earning from the admiring alumni and respectful citizens the sobriquet: "The Great Triumvirate." When the Civil War began, these three men were still in their thirties. The senior of the trio was Albert Hurd, whose specialty was natural science, but who, when the College was very poor, could and did teach Latin as an extra assignment. President Blanchard had discovered him at his own alma mater, Middlebury College, and appointed him to the Knox faculty in 1851. The other members of the Triumvirate were Milton Comstock and George Churchill, both graduates of the Knox class of 1851 and very close friends, indeed, brothers-in-law. Comstock first taught at Knox in 1851; Churchill became principal of the Academy in 1855.

The faculty in June 1859 voted to establish a "scientific course" that made it much easier to earn a degree, of sorts, from Knox College, and this action was approved by the trustees. This new course omitted from the studies that led to a bachelor's degree all the Latin and Greek courses. In this way the student could earn the degree of bachelor of science in three years. Because the admissions requirements were fewer, it was also easier for the student entering the scientific course to be enrolled in the College. The only language expected of a bachelor of science was a year of German, and, in this sense, some students must have regarded this degree as easier to attain. It did not mean that the student had studied any more science than those who became bachelors of art.

The degree of bachelor of science was not highly regarded. Though a good many students enrolled for the "scientific course," during the ten years 1859 to 1869, only half a dozen actually became bachelors of science. When at the commencement of 1867 a candidate for this degree was the valedictorian, the local *Free Press* noted that he "was only a scientific." On the program was printed, without the foreknowledge of faculty or graduating class, a motto that some regarded as a joke on this student whose name, White, was last on the class list: *Diabolus ultimum rapiat,* "The Devil take the hinder most."[15] Even the College authorities acknowledged that the degree was inferior. In an advertisement provided by the College for a Galesburg city directory in 1870, the arts degree was praised without stint but the science degree was presented with an apology: "While no one is advised to take this course in preference to the regular course, yet every facility is given to those who enter upon it, to do thorough and scholarly work, so far as they go. While the Faculty of Instruction would awaken no such delusive expectations as are often encouraged in connection with such a course, they feel, all the more, the necessity of making it as advantageous as possible to those whom either choice or necessity induces to enter upon it."[16]

Obviously the science degree was an act of expediency. The same may have been true of the effort by the trustees to make Knox an agricultural and industrial college by procuring the money due to Illinois from the land grant of $480,000 under the

Morrill Act of 1862. In the Midwest this act of Congress would be responsible for starting several "land grant" universities that became in the twentieth century huge academic municipalities. But in 1862 it was not wrong to assume that the Morrill Act funds might be allocated to private colleges; indeed, this was done for Yale, Brown, Dartmouth, Rutgers, Transylvania, Purdue, and Cornell. Knox trustee Senator Orville H. Browning was one of the two Illinois senators who voted for this bill.

In Illinois the foremost protagonist of land grants for industrial universities had himself once been a professor in one of the numerous Illinois church colleges. This was Jonathan Baldwin Turner of Jacksonville. The beginning of his thinking about an agricultural school can be documented from a letter he wrote to President Blanchard of Knox College in 1848, the year after Turner gave up his professorship at Illinois College, partly because of the antislavery issue. Turner suggested that he become a professor of agriculture at Knox and that the College farm, which originally had been reserved for the manual labor program, become an agricultural experimental farm. Blanchard replied that though he "pined for a professorship of the 'blessed green earth,' " he could not see how Knox Manual Labor College could acquire the funds for establishing a professor of agriculture.[17] Fifteen years later Turner no longer believed that an agricultural educational program should be combined with some classical school and wanted all the funds from the land grant under the Morrill Act to be used to establish one agricultural and industrial institution independent of any existing denominational college.

In his annual message following the passage of the Morrill Act the governor, Richard Yates, on January 5, 1863, reminded the Illinois legislature that they must act to accept the land grant within two years. Four days later a bill to accept the grant was introduced into the Illinois senate by Albert C. Mason, Democrat from Galesburg, who lived close by the Knox campus, near the corner of West and Tompkins streets.[18] Mason was chosen to be chairman of the joint committee to consider the best way to use the land grant money. Events moved with impressive speed. On January 26 the executive committee of the Board of Trustees of Knox College voted that two trustees should "be employed at the expense of the College to proceed to Springfield to aid in the preparation and passing of an act by the Legislature to give to the College the benefit of the Act of Congress for the endowment of Agricultural Colleges." The two trustees that went to Springfield were W. Selden Gale, who had succeeded to his father's seat on the board, and Thomas Gold Frost, a lawyer.[19] During the last days of January and the first weeks of February, bills were introduced for both Knox and Shurtleff colleges, which would have made each an agricultural and mechanics college eligible for the land grant money. In the committee of which Mason was chairman these aspirations were combined into one bill to establish two agricultural colleges, one in Galesburg and one at Alton by using the facilities already in existence at Knox and Shurtleff and naming as trustees men connected with these two institutions. In the Senate the bill progressed rapidly and by February 13 had been engrossed, read for the third time, and was ready for action in the lower house. But the next day the two colleges from Alton and Galesburg lost the advantage of their quick start for the land grant money when the legislature took a recess until June 2, 1863. The delay gave Turner and the editor of the *Prairie Farmer* time to agitate for an independent agricultural school and to call a convention to meet in June in Springfield. The secretary of the State Agricultural Society got the committee of the lower house to hold up action on the Knox-Shurtleff bill until after this convention had met.[20]

At this convention the case for Knox was presented by A. S. Bergen of Knox County and that of Shurtleff by a Mr. Underwood from St. Clair County, but the delegates rejected this proposal and voted for postponement of action on the pending bill until there was more time to study the matter. Such postponement did in fact occur when the Republican governor took the unprecedented step of proroguing the General Assembly for fear that its Democratic majority would take certain steps that would be inimical to the war effort. During the ensuing months a wide scramble for the benefits of the land grant was made by lobbyists from a number of places. A kind of last ditch stand for the existing colleges was led in 1866 by President Blanchard, now at Wheaton College, but failed. Turner's plan for a single agricultural and industrial school won out, but to his chagrin it was located between Champaign and Urbana where, on the open prairie, speculators were promot-

ing an "Urbana and Champaign Institute."[21] The editor of a
Galesburg newspaper declared that to locate it at Champaign
would be a "slur" on the faculties of Knox and Lombard in Galesburg.[22] Turner, who wanted it located in Jacksonville, used a
stronger Latinate word suggesting "dung."[23]

A future president of Knox College had a major role in the
beginnings of the Industrial University of Illinois, which opened
its doors to students on Monday, March 2, 1868. This was Newton Bateman, who during most of the preceding decade had been
the superintendent of instruction for the State of Illinois. The governor appointed him to the committee that was to work with the
"Regent" on courses of study of the new university; and he would
be a member of the board for several years to come. At the inauguration of the new university he gave a long opening address that
made that of the regent himself anticlimactic. He stated that it was
essential that the education that it provided "must be equal in ALL
ESSENTIAL POINTS, in extent, in comprehensiveness, in thoroughness, and in inspiration and power, with that afforded by the old
colleges and universities of the country." As for schools such as
Knox, to which he would within six years be elected president, he
spoke as follows "Let church colleges keep right on their appointed course, neither abandoning the whole field to public systems of education, nor yet courting the favor and patronage of the
state. Their work . . . demands freedom from outside control; it is
utterly incompatible with the embarrassing restrictions of legislative supervision."[24]

The "freedom from outside control" of which Superintendent
Bateman spoke had been enhanced at Knox in 1866 by a compromise between Presbyterians and Congregationalists that assured
that neither sect would control the College. An accommodation
between the two parties was made easier following the death of
Gale in 1861. Feelings about him had been so bitter that the
customary resolutions of respect were not adopted by the board,
and a proposal among the Adelphi to hang his picture back on the
walls of the Adelphi Hall was voted down by its members.[25] At
the commencement meeting of 1862 the Board of Trustees
adopted conciliatory resolutions presented by the Reverend Samuel Guild Wright, a pioneer Congregational missionary in central
Illinois, who had always striven to restore amity in the board.

Unanimously the board declared that Presbyterians and Congregationalists should "henceforth" avoid "all denominational contests and rivalry so far as Knox College is concerned," and that the College should "not be employed as an instrument for the promotion of denominational views."[26]

Jockeying for advantage between the two parties, however, still occurred. There was nothing in the election of the new president, the Reverend William Curtis, at the next annual meeting to reassure the Congregationalists, except that this Presbyterian delivered an inaugural address that was purely academic in tone and avoided relating the College to politics either civil or ecclesiastical.

What was to be an important turning point occurred in 1865 when Charles B. Lawrence was elected to the board, for it was he who worked out an agreement among the trustees that at last restored mutual trust. Lawrence was a highly regarded judge of the circuit court, who in 1864 became a justice of the Supreme Court of Illinois, and soon thereafter the chief justice. His own religious convictions were Unitarian,[27] but his family belonged to the local Episcopal church, where Lawrence served as vestryman. He had earned the respect of the strong antislavery Republicans of the town by carrying on a widely publicized controversy with the bishop of the diocese in defense of the local rector, the Reverend John W. Cracraft, whose militant antislavery, pro-Lincoln, pro-Union sermons had offended some of the Episcopalian parishioners.[28]

At the June 1866 meeting Judge Lawrence submitted resolutions that not only agreed in spirit with those presented by the Reverend Wright in 1862 but also stipulated what should be done to effect them. The board agreed that the College should "not in fact nor in appearance" be under the exclusive control of either Presbyterians nor Congregationalists. To prevent such "exclusive control" both denominations "should as nearly as possible be equally represented" on the board, but neither party should have a majority. Enough members of other sects should be board members so as "to prevent the control of the College from falling exclusively into the hands of either denomination through the accident of death, resignation or nonattendance."[29]

The board adopted Lawrence's resolutions and then appointed

him chairman of a committee that was charged to carry out the spirit of his own motion. The recommendations of this committee were accepted by the board, and this apparently was the signal for two old-time members of the board to vacate their places, one being a former Gale partisan, James Bull, the other being a former Blanchard supporter, Matthew Chambers. The latter was one of the original charter members of the Knox College corporation and was now eighty years old. He had previously tried to arrange for his own resignation but held to his place on the board when it refused to let him name the Congregationalist that would succeed him.[30] The timing of these two resignations certainly appears to have been part of a prearranged compromise, as does the smooth progression by which each of four vacancies on the board were now filled, each unanimously.

Chambers's place on the board was in truth filled by a Congregationalist and by none less than Dr. Beecher, who had been such a stormy protagonist of Blanchard. His election was a genuine sign of reconciliation. Another place went to Dr. George Duffield, pastor of the New School Presbyterian church that had been founded by followers of Gale when in 1851 they left the original colony church with the "express purpose of having a strictly Presbyterian Church." The two remaining vacancies were filled in accordance with the intent of Lawrence's plan that, while the Congregationalists and Presbyterians were equally represented, enough members of other sects should be on the board to assure that no denomination had a controlling majority. One of these two was a Baptist, Deacon Clement Leach, a cattle dealer who resided immediately southeast of the College grounds, and whose son was a Knox student. The other was the Episcopalian rector, the Reverend Cracraft, who at that time was still defying the order of his bishop not to officiate in the local church.[31]

Though there would sometimes be signs of Congregational-Presbyterian rivalry, the compromise of 1866 eliminated the factionalism that had brought so much harm to the College since the 1850s. The arrangement was confirmed when the board unanimously elected a Congregationalist, the Reverend Gulliver, as president in 1868. During the hard times of the mid-1870s there was discussion of the financial advantage that might come from

43

giving control of the College to either the Congregationalists or the Presbyterians. Indeed, the Presbyterian Synod of Central Illinois offered generous assistance toward an endowment if Knox College were connected with it. But even the Honorable Orville Browning, once again active in the affairs of the trustees after serving in the cabinet of President Andrew Johnson, belived this could not not be accomplished. And he had once been a strong Presbyterian partisan.[32] It was obviously a proud boast, when a student editor at Knox in 1870 wrote that Knox was "the most unsectarian college in the state."[33]

Becoming nonsectarian did not signify being irreligious—far from it. The trustees resolved still to maintain "scriptural morality," "pure religion," and "evangelical Christianity." And so they did, for many years to come. Not until a century later, after World War II, would Knox become a thoroughly secular institution with no reference in its catalogue to the fact that it was "Christian," with no chapel, no baccalaureate service on the Sabbath before graduation, and no clergyman on the Board of Trustees. Yet already in the late 1850s one can read from the minutes of the faculty intimations of more worldliness, of some playfulness, and suggestions even of some pranks. There was a hint in the spring of 1857 of what some day would come when, on the motion of one of the sons of Dr. Beecher, the Adelphi challenged the Gnothautii to three games of football. This would have been an unprecedented extension of their literary and forensic competition, and the proposed athletic contests were reconsidered a week later and given up. On Christmas Eve of 1851 students had unsuccessfully tried to keep classes from meeting the next morning by removing the bell, stealing the keys to the recitation rooms, and locking the doors after having fastened back the window catches with plugs. A two-day Christmas holiday was specifically refused in 1856, and it was not until 1859 that such a recess was permitted and then, so it was explained, only to accommodate the three-day sessions of a state teachers' convention. Finally, the catalogue printed in the summer of 1860 did schedule a Christmas recess for the year 1860–61. Times were changing.[34]

In 1860, apparently as a kind of editorial afterthought, the "College Laws" were inserted into the catalogue.

Years of Uncertainty

The following provision of the laws are inserted for the information of persons receiving students into their families.

The College Laws forbid:

Leaving town in term time;

Absence from public worship on the Sabbath;

Absence from room in study hours, or being abroad at unseason-
able hours at night;

Avowing or propagating infidel principles;

Breaking the Sabbath by noise, excursions, &c.;

Using profance or obscene language, or being guilty of lewd
conduct;

Playing at cards, billiards, or any unlawful game;

Using intoxicating drinks, or carousing or sharing in any conviv-
ial meetings or entertainments, either in or out of College;

Visiting any place where intoxicating drinks are sold;

Allowing disorder in one's room, or making disturbance in or
about the College, especially at night.

The time had obviously come when it was deemed best to fore-
warn students of what was exptected of them. The year 1859–60
had been difficult for the faculty, filled with disciplinary problems
of the kind that would often recur in the decades to come. Students had an ugly town-and-gown confrontation with the volunteer fire department, which had been aroused in the middle of
the night to put out the fire started by students in "Room Number Seventeen," the College privy. While investigating this incident, the faculty discovered that card playing had become
"common practice" and that some students even indulged in
"refreshments with ale and milk-punch made of whiskey." The
faculty then as later were baffled by the "false code of honor
among students which requires them to conceal the doings of
their fellows even when encouraged by proper authorities."
Later in the year, when the faculty disciplined four students for
their part in a drinking party at which there was a noisy
"Serenade," use of "profane language," and an "irreverent cari-
cature of religious things," thirteen other students in effect tested
the authority of the faculty by coming forward to protest the
punishment only of those who had been discovered and by
stating that they themselves had to a greater or lesser extent broken

45

the same rules. The year was, it seems, one of greater troubles over student behavior than those later in the 1860s, but it was evident that by now the faculty were enforcing "laws" that some of the students no longer respected.[35]

The discovery of most lasting significance during 1859–60 was that some of the revelry on the campus was associated with a secret society, what later would be called a fraternity. Its existence surprised and seemed to confuse the faculty. It adopted a rule that "no Society shall be formed or exist in this college without the express sanction of the Faculty after a full exhibition of all rules, regulations and objects of such society."[36] Nevertheless, apparently unknown to the faculty, there was in existence another secret society. Suddenly, in the spring of 1861, it made itself publicly known. The event was reported in the *Adelphi Quarterly* as an event "out of the ordinary course," which "startled out of their propriety" both Knox students and the "good people of Galesburg." The secret society was the "Eleventh Chapter of Beta, Theta, Pi."[37]

Lists of the Betas that were published in later years show that between 1855, when the chapter was first established, and 1865, thirty-two college students belonged to this secret society. So long as Blanchard was president, by their own admission, they had not dared come out into the open, but by the mid-1860s the faculty were at least willing to tolerate them. In October 1862 a Knox junior wrote to a Beta brother in Ohio: "It is no easy thing to be a Greek at Knox. . . . Every measure which we wish to carry has to be fought through against a large opposition with the most untiring perseverence."[38] In 1863 a Beta reported to the secretary of the Ohio University chapter that the Knox chapter was "getting along very well. . . . Although of course we have to encounter much opposition from the barbarians, still, as the Faculty do not persecute us, we are able to hold our own, and much to the discomfort of the aforesaid gentlemen are considered as *the* boys of the college."[39]

The tolerance for the Betas and of other men's fraternities during this decade would eventually have significant effects on the future history of Knox. The very best midwestern colleges such as Oberlin, Grinnell, and Carleton, which like Knox shared Congregational antecedents, were successful, unlike Knox, in preventing the development of the fraternal system on their several campuses.

What happened at Knox reflected a softening of the disapproval to secret societies that once had been unqualified on the part of the Congregationalists in Illinois. Shortly before he became a trustee of Knox, the Reverend Beecher prepared a long and learned report on secret societies that was adopted by the General Association of the State of Illinois. This report deplored but did not absolutely condemn secret societies; it concluded that some organizations, such as "associations for purely literary or reformatory purposes—are not to be sweepingly condemned by reason of a thin veil of secrecy covering their precise methods of procedure." Yet Beecher's report still deplored such "secrecy" as "unwise and undesirable, inasmuch as it holds out needless temptations to deeds of darkness."[40]

Secret societies with their mysterious emblems, officious titles, initiatory rituals, and impressive names had great fascination for Americans during the nineteenth century; many social purposes or causes were served by such organizations. The female literary society at Knox was open to all of the women, yet they tried to keep the meaning of LMI a secret, though one of the seminary girls did tell her parents that it signified: "Ladies Moral Improvement."[41] For a short time in the mid-1860s the Adelphi was connected with a national organization that wanted it to become a secret society.[42] It was therefore meaningful that the Adelphi, Gnothautii, and LMI remained open organizations, and it was important that they retained their dominant place in the social life of Knox, while the secret fraternities all declined during the 1870s and would not reappear until the next decade.

That these literary societies admitted members without discrimination was exemplified in the case of Barnabas Root, who was probably the first black man to receive a college degree in Illinois. Root came from the colonies on the West African coast where British reformers and naval authorities and American philanthropists resettled black men who either had been rescued from the slave trade, had mutinied or otherwise won their freedom, been manumitted, or had been transported back to Africa by the American Colonization Society. The American Missionary Society, in which faculty members, trustees, and alumni of Knox were deeply involved and to which the local Congregational churches contributed very generously, established a mission for the coastal area where Liberia and Sierra Leone are now located. This region would soon be called a "Grave Yard of Whiteman" because of tropical diseases, and eventually the AMA abandoned missionary efforts there because of the numerous casualties from sickness.[43] In 1855 Mary McIntosh graduated from the Knox Female Seminary; she was sent, with special assistance of the ladies of the local Congregational churches,[44] to become a teacher at this mission. Among her pupils was a seven-year-old youth, Fahma Yahny, who was renamed Barnabas Root. His maternal grandfather had been an American slave who was returned to Africa by the American Colonization Society; a granduncle was a tribal chief. In 1860 the mission was joined by the Reverend Charles Finney Winship, who had graduated from Knox in 1853; later that year the two Knox alumni were married. Within three years, because of chronic sickness, the Reverend Winship and his wife had to return to his home in Princeton, Illinois. In order that he might continue his studies of the native language, Winship brought with him to this country their student and protégé, Barnabas Root.[45]

In September 1864 Root was enrolled in the Knox Academy[46] and six years later was graduated from the College with the arts degree, having excelled in the study of Greek, Latin, and German and in general having earned the high regard of the faculty for his academic competence. He also had the full benefit of that part of his literary training that came by participation in a literary society. As a freshman he was elected to the Gnothautii and was regularly scheduled for debates, essays, and orations in its weekly meetings, held offices of importance in the society, shared in its business affairs, and was accorded honors for its public events.[47]

Root lived at first in the home of Daniel W. Burton, the layman who superintended the AMA mission in West Africa and who resided in Galesburg during the mid-1860s while his wife recovered from malaria. Then for a time Root lived in a private home located in that part of Galesburg near the campus, where already at that time there was a concentration of black residents.[48] His last years at Knox were lived in a room in one of the Bricks on the campus. For Congregationalists, how this educated black man was treated in hotels and restaurants became a kind of test of racial prejudice in the North. A letter that, at the prompting of Mrs. Winship, he wrote to an officer of the AMA gave meaningful insight into the experience of American blacks with prejudice.

Galesburg, Ill.
Sep 23rd 1868

Mr. Whipple

Dear Sir:

. . . In regard to the influence and effect of the prevailing feeling [of] prejudice of which you desire an expression of my thought; . . . I have felt it very keenly since I have been here and more so during the past year being perhaps more exposed to it than hitherto. . . . I have asked God to show me my duty in this matter and to keep me a humble Christian out from that blighting degrading feeling of self abasement which I see in almost every one of my race in this country, the legitimate effects of this feeling.

I think my feeling on this subject since my conversation with Mrs. W. has considerably changed. That this feeling of prejudice is almost universal in this country is a very plain fact; that it ought to be and must in some way be destroyed is equally plain but that it cannot be done altogether by the efforts of kind Christian friends also patent.

The more I think of it the more I see that the most effectual instrument for its destruction lies in the hands of its present victims, and that instead of fleeing or trying to flee from it we ought to meet it manfully.

In taking a sober view of my own personal experiences I think that compared with a great many I had little of it.

One great cause of this feeling I think with many is unacquaintance with us or rather not being accustomed to come in daily and familiar contact with the blacks on the part of the whites. I have found that among my fellow students who entertained much of this feeling when I first came here lost at least much of it. I think not for what I have done but as the natural result of better acquaintance. I think in this way much can be done to help do away with it.

I desired much last Spring to go to Oberlin feeling that there I would meet less of it than here but since the course of study is about as good here as there and matters not really quite so bad as I saw them last year I think it will be best at present to go on here. . . . I feel after much sober thought on the subject it will hardly look right for me to leave Galesburg merely on account of the feeling of prejudice. . . .

Yours Sincerely
Barnabas Root[49]

Obviously Galesburg was not altogether a pleasant place for a black student to live. Though the classes and membership in the literary societies at Knox were open to blacks, this was not true of the fraternities that appeared during the 1860s. Their social patterns reflected those of the larger community. During the last quarter of the nineteenth century there was usually one black student at Knox, but hardly ever more. Only after a bitter controversy in the local public schools were separate buildings for blacks discontinued. Significantly, it took special action by the Galesburg School Board to admit the first black student, a woman, to the high school.[50] No black student completed the course of studies in the high school until 1881.[51]

It was often noted during these years that while black men might be emancipated and enfranchised, white women were not. It was not until the year that Root was graduated that the trustees of Knox voted to admit women to the same course of studies as the men. Perhaps the most troublesome crisis at Knox during the postwar years developed over this question. Women pursued a program of studies quite as demanding as that available to the men when the "scientific course" was authorized during the first year of the war, but women completing the Female Seminary curriculum did not receive a degree. In the mid-1860s the women of LMI would still debate whether "the mind of women is not inferior to that of men" and raise the question whether "accomplishments were more essential to young ladies" than a thorough education.[52] But by that time there were strong advocates for giving women academic as well as civil equality with men. In 1867 Samantha Chloe Whipple read a poem at an LMI meeting that dealt with the fact that women from the Female Seminary building, "across the way" from the Main College Building, were told: "Females are not admitted here." Years later Whipple, now Samantha Shoup, who wrote for the *Youth's Companion* and the *Atlantic Monthly*, would recall that this poem was written "in the last year of President Curtis's reign, when co-education was tabooed."

ODE TO COLLEGE CUPOLA

Hail thou that dar'st the raging storm,
And o'er those ancient walls sublime

Does proudly rear thine awful form,
Too dingy to be dimmed by time!
When Cyllenius' wings
From the far heaven his dazzling flight,
Aside in mid-career he springs
Lest he should be transfixed quite
On the sky-piercing summit's height.
Apollo strikes his lyre in thy praise
And seated on the college roof doth gaze
Upon thy form with breathless admiration,
But if the shielded Pallas come,
Or if the Muse should thither roam,
Drawn by some Junior's piteous invocation,
Austerely gazing on the mighty dome,
Thou dost with stately majesty proclaim,
"Across the way, my dear,
Females are not admitted here!"
Beneath thine overshadowing pride,
With voice of destiny resounding wide,
The college bell, stern arbiter of fate,
Doth evermore abide.
When bursting on the air in tones of doom,
It shatters golden dreams with summons dread,
The manly youths aroused from visions blest,
List to its call, make haste!
Make haste! make haste!
Or, shuddering, hear the doom,
You're late! you're late! you're late!
The maidens also hear thy high behest,
And then "*plangoribus aedes femincis ululat.*"
But thou, great cupola, alone dost rest,
Serenely as a mighty stove-pipe hat,
Doth sit upon a Senior's rounding head.[53]

The Latin line, translated "the house resounded with female wailing," was quoted from Book II of the *Aeneid* that describes the invasion of Priam's palace by the Greeks.[54]

Evidently there had been, previous to the administration of the Reverend Curtis, who became president in 1863, a drift in the direction of coeducation, meaning the teaching of men from the College and of women from the Seminary in the same classes. President Curtis undertook to correct this tendency and to separate men and women entirely, even in the Preparatory Department, where classes had been mixed from the beginning. In so doing he was acting contrary to educational customs that were becoming quite common in the Midwest, as for example in Lombard University. He made his preference for the eastern practice of strong but separate education for females clear in his address to the graduating class of the Female Seminary in June 1867. He recognized the need to give women a "higher and more comprehensive education"; but he believed that woman's place was in the home and that she would be "out of place in the pulpit or the legislative halls"; he stated that the constant mingling of the sexes was undesirable and that "separate education was more beneficial to women than competition in classes with the other sex."[55]

At the beginning of that same academic year the new principal of the Female Seminary was Lydia Howard, who later as the first president of Wellesley College would be the first woman in the world to be the head of a college. She had been graduated from Mount Holyoke and had served on its faculty. In June 1867 President Curtis proposed and the trustees approved a plan by which Howard would help establish another "Mount Holyoke" in Galesburg. Accordingly, the new catalogue published that summer came out in two entirely separate books, and the one for the Female Seminary used language that for years had appeared in the catalogue of Mount Holyoke. The course of studies for females was extended to four years; their faculty was enlarged; and so as to separate the two sexes entirely, "as though there was no male department," the Academy classes for women were also to be held in the Female Seminary building.[56]

Howard was well liked by the students, well regarded by the faculty, and respected by the trustees. But Curtis became quite unpopular. His policy for separating classes that formerly had been mixed was disliked by faculty; students were irked by the stricter social isolation of women from men.[57] In the larger community he offended townspeople with his eastern ways, in contrast to the "wide-awake, progressive elements of Western life."[58] Tensions also developed between the president and Howard, who was overworked with administrative, counseling, and teaching duties. The women teachers of the Seminary had been asked to put up with lower salaries until the new program had proved itself. It was reported that the president, in a quarrel with the principal over copy for the next year's catalogue, had seized the manuscript from the lady's hand. On Friday, March 20, 1867, Howard and two other women of the Seminary faculty tendered their resignations to the executive committee of the board "in consequence of personal difficulty between the Principal and President Curtis."[59]

On the morning of the next day, a Saturday, all of the town was aroused to the knowledge that something excited the Knox students. The bell in the main College building was ringing and kept ringing. Occasionally shots were heard. Those that went to discover what the noise was about could see that College and Academy students had mounted the roof of the main College Building, cut the bell rope from below, and that some of them carried the old muskets that had been used by the student cadets during the war.[60] The students of the Seminary met to resolve that President Curtis had "by his opprobrious conduct insulted our beloved Preceptress and disgraced the entire Institution." Fifty-seven of the women signed a petition that called for his "*immediate* resignation" and declared that if he did not resign they would feel constrained to leave the institution." The signers included all but two students in the upper three classes of the Seminary and nearly half of the girls in the junior (i.e., freshman) class and in the Preparatory Department of the Seminary. This same day a meeting of the men of the College and of the Academy "unanimously adopted" resolutions pledging their "support and hearty concurrence in the petition of the young ladies of the Seminary requesting the President to immediately resign."[61]

On Monday morning all but six students stayed away from chapel and from the classes that should have followed. They resolved, again, not to attend any recitation until the president resigned, and sat around on the grass, talking, laughing, and singing. On Tuesday they did the same until the middle of the afternoon, when they were informed by the chairman of the executive committee of the board, His Honor Chief Justice Lawrence of the Supreme Court of Illinois, that Curtis had resigned. As one of the students recalled, there was still time to go to the three o'clock class. "Every student present jumped up and, grabbing his hat and books, ran for the recitation room yelling, 'Hurrah for Knox College!' or words to that effect."[62]

Almost immediately there were signs of a relaxing of the severe separation that had been imposed upon men and women. The mood is suggested by a debate question that the Adelphi scheduled the following spring: "Resolved that it would be advantageous to keep geese at the Seminary since geese saved the city of Rome."[63] Following what one trustee called the "fall" of President Curtis,[64] a new president, the Reverend Gulliver, was found. Though Dr. Gulliver indicated in his inaugural that he favored the separate education of men and women, he also stated that he had no objection to a union of recitations when that was suitable. And at the end of his second year as president, the trustees finally took the big step of granting women the privilege of taking the regular College courses with the men and of earning the same degrees they did.

From 1870 to 1891 a woman had four educational options at Knox: the College curricula leading to the bachelor of arts or the bachelor of science degree; a four-year Seminary course that included music and art and did not lead to a degree; the College course combined with the Seminary course, in which case, it was assumed, in 1870, that she would need six years of study. For some years most women preferred to seek a Seminary certificate rather than a College diploma. A distinctive course of studies for women was not abandoned until 1891, and even then for another decade the College continued to award a lesser "literary" degree, the bachelor of literature. Academy parity for women had come slowly, as Professor Hurd reminisced in 1906: "the advocates of co-education in Knox College have been obliged to carry on a long and sometimes a hotly contested warfare in order to secure conditions which now prevail. Although from the beginning claiming to be a co-educational college, it has taken us sixty years to reach the time when men and women were in reality on equal terms in college life, college studies and college honors."[65]

During President Gulliver's years important changes began to occur in the immediate environs of the Female Seminary and the College. With the completion of two buildings in 1857, it had been determined that the two block area between Seminary and College should be developed as a College park. Certain structures that had encroached on this space were removed. The trustees attempted unsuccessfully to have Tompkins Street in front of the

Seminary closed, but they did succeed in getting the city council in 1859 to close the segment of Broad Street that had run between Tompkins and South, thus unifying the park. During the war the College grounds were graded and trees were planted, and the park shared in this landscaping, particularly in the planting of some evergreens.[66]

By 1869, however, the Galesburg elders, including trustees of Knox College, were looking upon College Park as a possible site for a county courthouse. They had been attempting for at least a dozen years to move the seat of the county from Knoxville to Galesburg. The political leader for Galesburg in this bitter contest (which included three county-wide elections and charges of voter fraud that were disputed to the Supreme Court of Illinois) was William Selden Gale, eldest son of the founder and his successor on the Board of Trustees of Knox College. In order to make the relocating of the county seat more attractive to the voters, the city of Galesburg promised to pay for a new jail and offered as a site for a new courthouse the grounds of the College Park.[67] Apparently a deal between the city and the College became public knowledge in March 1869, for the Adelphi debated the proposition "that the Knox County Courthouse should not be situated between the present College and Seminary buildings." And a week later the faculty adopted a resolution against giving up the grounds for a courthouse, declaring that to do so would "ultimately necessitate the removal of the College."[68]

Nevertheless, the trustees closed the deal with the city. Though the price of $21,000 may have been fair market value, the land was potentially worth a great deal more to the College and the sale must be regarded as a bargain for the city, in effect, a College contribution to the county courthouse cabal. Accordingly, when the Supreme Court of Illinois finally determined that the county seat would be in Galesburg, the county received from Knox College a warranty deed for block number thirteen in the original plot of Galesburg, "being the east half of the ground known as the 'College Park.'" The record also showed that this "deed is upon the express condition that the ground shall be used for a courthouse and for no other purpose." The remaining block, the western half of College Park, now became city park.[69]

Fortunately for the College and the city these grounds during the mid-1870s began to receive the dedicated attention of Lombard Professor John Van Ness Standish, who lived across Cedar Street from the College grounds. Under his direction (as an original member in 1876 of the city park board) many of the more ordinary trees, such as soft maples, that had grown too densely in the park, were cut down, and along the diagonal walks that crisscrossed the park "more handsome" trees, such as catalpas and magnolias, were planted. The vicinity of the College became a very "delightful and desirable" place for family residences. Along Cedar Street "elegant" houses were built, with well-kept lawns and flowering gardens. Along South Cherry Street the fine chestnut trees were full of blooms at mid-summer, and across the street immediately east of the campus the new county jail, completed in 1874, presented on its College side an Italianate facade that belied the prison behind it.[70]

By comparison the Knox campus, with its shaggy great old cottonwood trees that had seeded themselves readily where the prairie was broken, came to appear shabby. At the March meetings of the Galesburg Horticultural Society in 1880, which were held in residences across from Cedar Street, Professor Comstock was apparently embarrassed by criticism of the appearance of the College grounds and resigned as secretary of the organization.[71]

Professor Comstock's action reflected the frugality practiced at Knox during the late 1870s, after the College had overextended its resources earlier in the decade during the presidency of Gulliver, when an effort was made quickly to achieve a reputation "as high as in the Northeastern colleges," to become "the Yale of the interior." These are the words of the Reverend Wright, who had much to do with the choice of Gulliver as the fifth president of Knox. Gulliver was a Congregationalist clergyman of the "New England Church" of Chicago, who had been elected to the board in 1867, but who had not yet attended a meeting when in March 1868 the Reverend Curtis suddenly was forced to resign. When the Congregationalists met the following May in Jacksonville for their annual state convention, the Reverend Wright got the other trustees of Knox who were present together (six in all) to discuss means by which Gulliver, who was moderator of the convention, might be made interested in the presidency of Knox. When Gulliver came to the board meeting in June 1868, he captivated the

Presbyterians as well as others such as Chief Justice Lawrence and they elected him unanimously. To Wright it "seemed too good to be true" that the Presbyterians should thus have confirmed the denominational compromise of 1866 and thus have "restored the captivity of Knox College."[72] Gulliver was known to be a brilliant writer and speaker and was evidently a person of fine bearing and engaging manner. In its enthusiasm the board, on the motion of Judge Lawrence, offered Gulliver a salary more than twice that received by the last incumbent. In addition to the fixed amount of $4,000 he should also receive "fifty per cent of the increase upon tuition fees of the last year," and furthermore 10 percent of the amount that he as agent for raising funds contributed to the College.[73]

It is a measure of the able new faculty members that were brought to Knox under Gulliver's leadership that five of them would later be listed in *Who's Who in America.* Their Ivy League credentials were impressive: four from Amherst, two (Gulliver himself and a son) from Yale, and one (a brother-in-law) from Williams. These new appointments were particularly strong in the area of classical languages and literature. Toward the end of his first year as president, Gulliver negotiated the retirement of the lone remaining member of the original Knox faculty, Innes Grant, professor of ancient languages. Two men, one for Latin, the other for Greek, replaced him and other new teachers of Greek and Latin were brought for the Academy. Exceptional also were the qualifications of the new principal of the Female Seminary, Susan Hayes Ward. She and her sister Hetta Hayes Ward, who was appointed at the same time (1869) to the faculty of the Academy, came from a distinguished Yankee family that had provided Congregational ministers for several generations. Their father had taught them languages at an early age, Susan beginning with Hebrew at the age of six. She had then been educated at Wheaton Seminary and had studied art in Europe. Shortly before coming to Knox she had published a novel, *Sabrina Hackett,* and in 1872 she published a volume of religious poetry under the title of *Christus ad Portam.*

One of Gulliver's most popular faculty choices was that of John W. Burgess as "Professor of Logic, Rhetoric, English Literature and Political Science." It was not the least of Professor Burgess's credentials that he was a "Captain," that he had an excellent Civil War record, and that though a native of Tennessee he had fled north when Union troops invaded his state and joined the Army of Ohio in 1862.[74] Graduated from Amherst in 1867, he accepted the Knox teaching position even though he had just been admitted to the bar. Later, after he had established at Columbia University the first school of political science, he would regard his teaching at Knox as an unfortunate interruption of his legal career, a "grave mistake." Yet his own reminiscences suggest that at the time he found Galesburg, if not entirely a satisfactory academic location, at least a congenial place to live. With the Amherst graduates and the other colleagues gathered at Knox by Gulliver, he perceived that these new arrivals "practically ruled the institution. . . . The 'hayseed' methods of the West were supplanted by the new modes and manners of the East, and a new era in education and in society was inaugurated in Knox College and in the town."[75]

Dr. Gulliver may very well have been the first president of Knox to be more interested in the scholarly attributes than in the piety of faculty members. Such is the judgment of a scholar who has made a comparative study of the intellectual history of Knox and Wheaton colleges, where Jonathan Blanchard for many years was able to preserve the principles that once had prevailed at Knox.[76] In the case of Mary Ives Seymour, however, Gulliver's latitudinarian policy was apparently tested beyond tolerance. Madame Seymour (as many, particularly students, called her) was appointed in 1870 to teach music, French, and light gymnastics in the Seminary. About the time that she arrived in Galesburg she published her biography of Louis Moreau Gottschalk, the distinguished American pianist and composer who had been her teacher. In this book she revealed in considerable detail a very familiar friendship with her mentor, and, though the leading local paper gave the book a good review, others regarded it as "indiscreet" and "very Frenchy."[77] She became popular, "fairly lionized," for she was a good musician who was generous with her talent, and she had a "magnificent presence and a courtly manner,"[78] and what in that Victorian era would not have been called sex appeal. Undergraduates were fascinated. Toward the end of her first term she staged an exhibition of "musical gymnastics" according to the methods of Dr. Dio Lewis of Boston. Groups both of men and of women performed, for she expressed "no sympathy for those very proper persons who think it indelicate for girls to run or jump." The exhibition was a very successful event for Galesburg society.[79]

Then, suddenly, near the middle of her second year at Knox, the executive committee of the board, in a special meeting in the home of President Gulliver, acted to remove her "immediately" from the Seminary. Seymour later stated that she had resigned from Knox because she could no longer endure the "abominable Presbyterianism,"[80] but it is clear from the record that she was dismissed. Though no public explanation was given, a tradition developed early that (in the words of one who was a youth at the time) "the prairie town" was "too unsophisticated for her accomplishments, and the trustees were unable to adjust themselves to so vivid a personality," and that she "brought to the town a flavor of cosmopolitanism . . . and must have seemed to those staid burgers a creature from another world."[81] Significantly, Eugene Field, who as a student belonged to one of her classes and to two of the musical organizations that she directed, wanted to write a pamphlet in her defense.[82] He, too, was a free spirit who departed from what he found the rigid limits of campus and community.

Many recognized that during his four years Gulliver raised the educational standards at Knox and widened its reputation for greatly improved scholarship. Some would look back at his brief tenure as a "Golden Age."[83] But not everyone appreciated what he was trying to do. When Gulliver pleaded that the scholars he brought to the faculty should have their work arranged so as to have time for study and research, one old trustee objected that "he had always reckoned it was the *pupils* who come there to study. And as to teacher *he* wanted teachers who had learned their lessons before they began to teach them."[84] Gulliver was called an "old fogey" because he wanted to extend the study of classics. He had what one could call a public relations problem, for there were four competing local newspapers ready to publicize any dispute, however minor, that collected in the local teapot, such as the faculty refusal to graduate a senior with important local political connections, or Gulliver's alleged part in the removal of the silver-haired Reverend Beecher, who some believed could no longer save the souls of the young people, or the president's identification with Liberal Republicans.[85]

In truth Gulliver was among Lilliputians. It was easy to make fun of his Yankee speech, just as it was obvious that he was filling his western faculty with eastern teachers. There was criticism of his "lavish" expenditures for the College and of his "showy" lifestyle. From his handsome home at the corner of Cherry and North streets, then a fashionable part of town, he might drive to the campus with his fine "two horse trotting team." On one occasion his eldest son, in jockey garb, drove this team to the first prize at the county fair; on another occasion a younger son, driving at breakneck speed, had an accident in which his passenger, Professor Churchill, was pitched out and incurred painful injuries. Such horsemanship still offended many townspeople, though one of the local editors did argue that it was right in a farming community for the College president to have good horses just as it was good for him to have a herd of fine cattle. The stubborn truth was that as late as September 1868 the executive committee of the board had spelled out expectations of faculty conduct that stipulated that they "refrain from all drinking and billiard saloon, and race courses."[86] Among the faculty it is certain that at least Professor Churchill came to dislike the president. He had been irked over the forced retirement of the elderly Professor Grant, and he had "supreme contempt" for Gulliver's "kid-gloved, orange-eating, horse driving, high-falutin', Gale imitating, West-decrying, New England applauding, big I and little you policy."[87]

Gulliver's high aspirations for Knox collapsed when the board insisted on an immediate and severe cutback in expenditures. In his letter of resignation, dated "Commencement Day" 1872, the president made the point plainly that with a "little more of sympathy and aid" he might have succeeded in the "development of a first rate college." But he also agreed that, having failed to raise more endowment, the College, with a steadily recurring annual deficit, was "gradually destroying the foundation from which it rests," that foundation having been its land.[88]

Outwardly, in some respects, the College seemed to be doing well. During Gulliver's last two years enrollments at the College were the highest they had ever been; Seminary enrollments were higher than they had been since before the war. Unfortunately, for Knox such increased enrollments might not signify larger revenues, for the College still had to carry a burden of a debt in the form of scholarships granted by the founders, and, though this obligation was approaching cancellation, the College would have to wait for a few more years before tuition income truly reflected enrollments. These scholarships, which had originally amounted to 2,150 years of tuition, in 1871 still remained at 288 years.[89]

To some degree Gulliver and the College were victims of the severe agricultural depression and of the financial instability that plagued the country after the war and reached its climax in the Panic of 1873. Between 1866 and 1870 the wholesale price index of farm products fell from 140 to 112; by 1876 it would be down to 89. By 1871 "everybody" in Galesburg was complaining of "depression," after "recent years of short crops and general business stagnation."[90] At the College there was a "sudden falling off of its land sales from an average of $21,000 a year to an average, since the present president came into office, of less than $300 a year." The need to raise "cash capital, independent of its land" was obvious.[91] In early May 1871 the faculty voted their "unanimous conviction" that unless $100,000 was added to the productive funds of the College it probably would be necessary to abandon the "College department." The board in June agreed to raise $200,000 but, having fallen far short of that amount a year later, insisted on a policy of acute retrenchment. Gulliver then resigned, and so did several faculty members. Indeed, by September 1872 of the nineteen faculty appointments made by Gulliver during four years no teacher remained except for Mary West, who was hardly new to the Knox scene, having served previously on the Academy faculty. Of the faculty serving Knox the year before Gulliver came, only three would be serving the year after he left, the triumvirate of Hurd, Comstock, and Churchill.

The resignation of Gulliver distressed many students. According to a local report when the class of 1876 was graduated it "numbered only five," whereas at its admission to college it consisted of thirty-one and this "disorganization was . . . wrought when Dr. Gulliver retired from the Presidency of Knox."[92] That Amherst became the alma mater of two members of 1873, two from 1874, and two from 1875 undoubtedly reflected continuing attraction

61

of those brilliant young Amherst men that for a time had served at Knox. An interregnum of nearly three years ensued, for the finding of a new president was bungled by the trustees when an election occurred; a public announcement was made, and the choice was rejected by the Presbyterian minister who had been elected.[93] Leadership was divided among three men: Justice Lawrence for the board, Professor Hurd as chairman of the faculty, and a new faculty member, the Reverend Dr. Alexander F. Kemp, who performed so many of the public or ceremonial functions of a college president that some people in the community thought he was the acting president.[94]

"But we shall live somehow," wrote Professor Churchill in a pessimistic summary of the situation in March 1872.[95]

NOTES

1. Perkins, *Statistical Paper*, 66.

2. W. L. Steele, "Early History of the Galesburg Public Schools," in Perry, ed., *History of Knox County*, 1:552.

3. William E. Simonds, "Knox College," in *ibid.*, 1:562–77. Selby et al., eds., *Illinois and Knox County*, 684–89 (article on Knox College). One of the editors of this work, W. Selden Gale, was a trustee of Knox, beginning in 1861. See also Knox College, Journal, a ledger (MS, Knox College Library) containing a "Recapitulation" for each of the years 1859–60 to 1864–65 of salaries, receipts, expenditures, and means of the College.

4. Charles W. Chapman and Co., *Portrait and Biographical Album of Knox County*, 1019. The catalogues of Lombard University, later renamed Lombard College, are preserved in the Archives of Knox College (1854–1930).

5. Meredith, *Politics of the Universe*, 201, 120–25.

6. Bascom, "Autobiography," 202. Muelder, *Fighters for Freedom*, 380–81.

7. Knox College *Pantheon*, 1 (1869–70), 46–47.

8. Adelphi, Program Meeting Minutes, May 16, 1866; Jan. 23, Sept. 25, 1867; Oct. 20, 1869.

9. *Minutes of the General Association of the Congregational Churches and Ministers, 18th Annual Meeting, Galesburg, Illinois, May 23–26, 1861* (Quincy, 1861), 74. General Association of Congregational Churches, *Report on Knox College, May 24, 1861*. The phrase "battle of the books" is from Calkins's account of this sectarian quarrel in *They Broke the Prairie*, 184–90.

10. Lewis C. Carter, "The Negro Race," in Perry, ed., *History of Knox County*, 1:761–66. Cole, *Era of the Civil War*, 333–36. *American Missionary*, June 1863, 133–34; Apr. 1865, 84.

11. During the year that Edward Beecher came to Galesburg he published *Papal Conspiracy*.

12. Muelder, *Fighters for Freedom*, 346–48.

13. Faculty Minutes, Oct. 13, Dec. 1, 1865; Jan. 19, 1866; Galesburg *Free Democrat*, July 3, 1860; Galesburg *Republican Register*, Dec. 21, 1871.

14. Steele, *Galesburg Public Schools*, 41–46. Galesburg *Republican*, Sept. 17, 1870, 1; Jan. 28, 1871, 3–4; Oct. 17, 1871, 1; Oct. 28, 1871, 6; Nov. 18, 1871, 3–4; Jan. 13, 1872, 1; Galesburg *Republican Register*, Feb. 28, 1874, 1; Mar. 28, 1874, 1; Mar. 13, 1875, 5.

15. Galesburg *Free Press*, July 4, 1867, 2.

16. *Holland's Galesburg City Directory, 1870–71*, 14–15.

17. Powell, *Movement for Industrial Education*, 1:12–13, 357–62.

18. *Ibid.*, 178–80.

19. Executive Committee Minutes, Jan. 26, Apr. 6, 1863.

20. Powell, *Movement for Industrial Education*, 183.

21. *Ibid.*, 193–222.

22. Galesburg *Weekly Register*, Jan. 17, 1867, 2.

23. J. B. Turner, "Report of Committee on Location of Industrial University," Mar. 4, 1867, published in Jacksonville *Journal*, Mar. 16, 18, 1867, and reprinted as Document Number 19, in the appendix to Powell, *Movement for Industrial Education*, 492–505. This quotation is on 503.

24. Rammelkamp, *Illinois College*, 239.

25. Adelphi, Business Meeting Minutes, Oct. 23, Nov. 6, 1861.

26. These resolutions were inscribed in the minutes of the board when the resolutions were reaffirmed on June 24, 1868. This was the session at which Dr. John P. Gulliver, a Congregationalist, was elected president. Original holograph on p. 235 of the minutes.

27. Galesburg *Republican Register*, Apr. 14, 1883, 1.

28. Brown, "Question of Conflict and Consensus," chs. 3, 4, 5, 25–50. The Galesburg *Republican* reprinted on Oct. 8, 1870, 6, from a Cincinnati source a review of a book by the Reverend J. W. Cracraft, *Old Paths*. The review makes it clear that he is a controversial figure in the Episcopalian denomination, having been an antislavery activist.

29. Trustees Minutes, June 26, 1868.

30. *Ibid.*, June 25–26, 1862.

31. Brown, "Question of Conflict and Consensus."

32. Browning, *Diary of Orville H. Browning*, 2:390.

33. Knox College *Pantheon*, 1 (1869–70), 46–47.

34. Muelder, *Fighters for Freedom*, 334–35.

35. Faculty Minutes, for 1859–60, *passim*.

36. *Ibid.*, Nov. 30, 1859.

37. Knox College, *Adelphi Quarterly*, 1 (July 1861), 158.

38. O. H. Pitcher to E. H. Guthrie, Oct. 7, 1862, MS, Knox College Li-

brary. See also Samuel Caldwell to David Moore, Feb. 23, 1856, Knox College Library.

39. Pitcher to the Secretary of the Ohio Chapter, Feb. 21, 1863, MS, Knox College Library.

40. *Minutes of the General Association of Congregational Churches and Ministers of Illinois 23rd Annual Meeting—Ottawa, Illinois— May 23–29, 1866* (Ollown, 1866), 23.

41. Amelia Carey to Parents (Rufus Carey, Princeton, Ill.), Nov. 1866, MS, Knox College Library.

42. Adelphi, Minutes of Business Meetings, May 28, 1862, to Nov. 16, 1864, *passim.*

43. The account that follows of the missionaries in West Africa and of the career of Barnabas Root at Knox is based largely on the letters from the persons named in this narrative to the officers of the AMA. Because the correspondence was very extensive between 1855 and 1876, when the AMA despaired over the location of this mission, footnotes to the text have been used only at points of singular significance. Another important source has been the *American Missionary;* see, for example, "Mendi Mission. Its History, Condition and Wants," *American Missionary,* Mar. 1862, 49.

44. Holmes, *Knox Missionaries,* 24.

45. *American Missionary,* Aug. 1865, 181.

46. D. W. Burton to the Reverend George Whipple, Sept. 2, 1864, AMA Archives.

47. Gnothautii Society, Program Meeting Minutes, Dec. 21, 1868, to May 1870, *passim;* and the Gnothautii Society, Business Meeting Minutes, for the same period, *passim.*

48. In *Dewey's County Directory,* for 1868 the "colored" residents of Galesburg were identified.

49. AMA Archives.

50. Galesburg *Republican Register,* Jan. 18, 1873, 1.

51. *Ibid.,* June 11, 1881, 6.

52. L.M.I. Minutes, Dec. 3, 1863; Oct. 12, 1866.

53. *Coup D'Etat,* 13 (May 1894), 153.

54. As noted by Stephen Fineberg, assistant professor of classics at Knox College.

55. Galesburg *Weekly Register,* June 25, 1867, 3; and Galesburg *Free Press,* July 4, 1867, printed the full text of this speech.

56. Galesburg *Weekly Register,* July 27, 1867, 125; Trustees Minutes, June 27, 1867. *Annual Catalogue of the Female Collegiate Department, 1867–68. Dewey's County Directory,* 1868, 36, stressed that "the trustees have recently adopted substantially the four year's course of Mt. Holyoke."

57. Amelia Carey to her parents, Oct. 19, Nov. 6, 1866; Adelphi, Program Minutes, Jan. 30, 1867; Feb. 12, 1868; Trustees Minutes, June 29, 1866.

58. Galesburg *Weekly Register,* July 25, 1867, 2; Dec. 5, 1867, 2. Galesburg *Free Press,* July 4, 1867, 6.

59. Executive Committee of the Board to the Trustees, at the annual meeting of June 1868.

60. I have seen three accounts of this students' strike. One is by James Julius Parks and is filed with the materials of the class of 1872, with which Parks was graduated (MS, Knox College Library). Another reference to this event was found in Scrap Book Number Two, p. 39, of the Galesburg Public Library before the library building was destroyed by fire in 1958. A note made by me ascribed the information to George A. Lawrence and reads as follows: "The insurrection of the students to demand the withdrawal of Dr. Curtis as president was the occasion of great excitement. The old arms from the war period, stored in the college, were taken and the students paraded the streets under arms to such affect that a resignation was forthcoming." I have not been able to find the document itself in the new library building. A third account of the strike, agreeing substantially with the recollections of Parks, occurred in a contemporary publication at Monmouth College. *College Courier*, 1 (Apr. 1, 1868), 5.

61. Though the minutes of this Executive Committee of the board for these dates cannot be found, the petitions addressed to the committee by the students at this time are preserved in the College Archives.

62. Parks, account of students' strike; Faculty Minutes, Mar. 23, 24, 25, 1868.

63. Adelphi, Program Minutes, May 6, 1869.

64. Wright, Journal, June 29, 1868.

65. Albert Hurd, "Reminiscences," *Knox Student*, 11 (Feb. 18, 1904), 305–8.

66. Perry, ed., *History of Knox County*, Vol. 1: 410–11; George Churchill, "Galesburg History," Galesburg *Republican Register*, July 29, 1876, 3; Executive Committee Minutes, Oct. 2, 1865.

67. Calkins, *They Broke the Prairie*, ch. 10.

68. Faculty Minutes, Mar. 23, 1869.

69. Minutes of the Board of Supervisors for Jan. 30, 1873, quoted in full in Perry, ed., *History of Knox County*, 1:142–43.

70. Knox *Alumnus*, 2 (Feb. 1919), 87–91; Galesburg *Republican Register*, May 17, 1879, 1; July 10, 1880, 1; Aug. 13, 1881, 6; Apr. 29, 1882, 1; May 6, 1882, 2; May 20, 1882, 2.

71. Galesburg *Republican Register*, Mar. 20, 1880, 2; Mar. 27, 1880, 5. A note in the author's file (which is too inadequately documented to quote) states that Comstock defended Knox as cultivating minds rather than lawns and parks.

72. Wright, Journal, July 10, 1867; June 3, 29, 1868; July 27, 1870; June 26, 1871.

73. Trustees Minutes, June 26, 1868.

74. Galesburg *Free Press*, Dec. 16, 1869, 2.

75. Burgess, *Reminiscences*, 77.

76. Askew, "Liberal Arts College Encounters Intellectual Change," 64–70.

77. Seymour, *Life and Letters of Gottschalk*. Gottschalk had died in Dec.

1869 while on tour in Brazil. See the unfavorable review from the Peoria *Democrat* quoted in the Galesburg *Republican Register,* Aug. 16, 1879, 8. Local mention of the book occurred in the Galesburg *Republican,* Nov. 26, 1870, 4; Dec. 3, 1870, 3.

78. Galesburg *Republican Register,* Aug. 16, 1879, 8.

79. Galesburg *Republican,* Dec. 17, 1870, 6.

80. A letter from Mrs. Seymour to the *Isrealite* quoted in the Galesburg *Republican Register,* July 17, 1873, 1.

81. Calkins, *They Broke the Prairie,* 377.

82. Eugene Field to Fannie Bagby, June 5, 1872, MS, Knox College Library. *Mischmasch,* the Knox yearbook for 1870–71, lists members of student organizations directed by Madame Seymour.

83. Calkins, "Past and Present of Knox College," *American University Magazine,* 226–33, in Calkins Papers. Trustees Minutes, July 18, 1872.

84. Arthur W. Little, "College Days," *Gale, 1894,* 56–60.

85. Muelder's monograph entitled "Gulliver among the Lilliputians" deals in detail with the difficulties Gulliver encountered in Galesburg.

86. *Ibid.*

87. George Churchill to "Will and Mary," Mar. 7, 1873, MS, Knox College Library.

88. Trustees Minutes, June 27, 1872.

89. Galesburg *Republican,* Feb. 28, 1871, 4; June 10, 1871, 4.

90. *Ibid.,* June 24, 1871, 4.

91. *Ibid.,* Feb. 18, 1871; June 10, 1871, 4.

92. Galesburg *Republican Register,* June 24, 1876, 4.

93. *Ibid.,* June 26, 1873, 4; July 17, 1873, 1; Aug. 23, 1873, 1.

94. *Ibid.,* June 26, 1873, 4; July 3, 1873, 1; Sept. 26, 1875, 1; Oct. 17, 1874, 5; Nov. 14, 1874, 3; Mar. 20, 1875, 5.

95. Churchill to "Will and Mary," Mar. 7, 1873.

CHAPTER III

STUDENT INITIATIVES

During the last third of the nineteenth century the quality of life in the Knox community was considerably transformed by activities initiated by the students themselves. The intellectual as well as the social character of the College was changed in ways not anticipated by the founders, and sometimes not approved by those who succeeded the founders in formal authority.

After the Civil War the academic routine for the men at the College changed little until the closing years of the century. The curriculum, except that Latin and a fourth year were added to the "Scientific Course" in 1873, remained essentially the same. The "triumvirate"—Albert Hurd, Milton Comstock, and George Churchill—remained the leaders of the faculty, though they were joined by two alumni right out of College, Thomas Willard in 1866 and Henry Read in 1875, who as teachers of Greek and Latin became permanent members of the teaching staff. Otherwise the new men who taught at Knox remained for only brief terms. The longest tenure of outsiders was that of three women: Sarah M. McCall, who taught thirty years in the Preparatory Department; Maria Whiting, who was principal of the Female Seminary for fifteen years; and Melvina Bennett, who as a teacher of elocution and coach of the College orators for nine years had a great role in the most exciting extracurricular events on the campus. There was no significant change in the teaching facilities of the College until an astronomical observatory was built in 1888. The method of teaching remained almost entirely the hearing of recitations from assignments in textbooks. In 1886–87, when John Huston Finley was a senior and served as the college librarian, the library was open in the morning from 11:00 to 12:15 and in the afternoon from 1:30 to 2:30. The Adelphi library was open to all students for "a short time" each morning after chapel; the Gnothautii library for five minutes at noon each day.[1]

There was little yielding on the matter of religion. In the 1890s Sabbath was still observed and daily chapel attendance was required. The Society for Religious Inquiry (later renamed YMCA) remained an important campus organization, through which close interest was maintained in the number of students who became ministers or missionaries, and by which were tallied the numbers who were "professors of religion" and the number who had been "converted." There were frequently recurring periods when even weekdays were preempted for intensive religious sessions conducted by a visiting evangelist, who was assisted by members of the faculty as well as by the local Protestant preachers; however, the Universalists connected with Lombard College, who had other ideas about salvation, did not participate. On one occasion during the mid-1870s, they were accused of believing that the visiting revivalist was "a first class hypocrite and fraud."[2]

Student Rebellion: Eugene Field

A legend developed that Eugene Field had been canned by the Knox faculty "following a wild night during which he and a friend marched through the town carrying banners which bore coarsely worded inscriptions attesting the power of God to do certain ungentlemenly deeds. The whole parade was a burlesque of a popular evangelist who was 'reforming' the city at the time, but the college authorities' sense of humor was not unbounded."[3] A variant recollection of this same episode or the memory of a similar one was that Field set out to provide a "counterirritant" to a "spell-binding revivalist" whose services were causing a "great to-do" among townspeople and students. "He secured yards of loud, patterned calicos and had made outlandish robes and hoods. Gathering together a number of his fellows in a secluded place he dressed them in the gowns and caps. Then with great solemnity they proceeded to chant a litany written by Field and said to have been rather profane."[4]

These and other pranks devised by Field were a kind of preliminary practice of the humor he provided years later for his important column, "Sharps and Flats," in the Chicago *Daily News*. They are significant not merely because he attained among certain Knox alumni "the title of being the greatest of all the 'play boys' who ever attended Knox College"[5]; nor only because he remained, even when he became the leading literary figure in Chicago, an inveterate practical joker and a humorist so subtle that readers, even friends, often could not be certain when he was serious. There was a relationship between such campus acts of humor and his later journalistic role as a critic, as a satirist of Chicago manners, and of the materialism and pretentiousness of its culture. There was a continuity between the amusing tricks he staged at Knox and his later role as a columnist, who in his "Sharps and Flats" directed his "satirical barbs" at the "get up and—git" culture of the rising "Porkopolis," where (in Field's words) "the creme de la creme of our elite lift up their hands, and groan, when they discover that it takes as long to play a classic symphony as it takes to slaughter a carload of Missouri razor-backs, or an invoice of prairie racers from Kansas."[6]

At the age of twenty-one, which would be on a day in September 1871, Field would inherit some $50,000. As he awaited his majority and independence, impatient with Professor John W. Burgess, who was his guardian, for keeping him in college, he had an allowance of $800 a year, a most generous provision for an undergraduate. Yet, though he was better dressed than most and had what were called "Eastern notions," he was popular with students. They delighted in going to his room, where one student later recalled Field taught him to play his first game of cards. At the Union Hotel he "lived amid surroundings that quite dazzled his fellow students," and where he kept a "very considerable library" that was a "wonder to them." Here, too, he began the school year of 1870–71 with a pair of guinea pigs that were duly noted in a local paper.[7]

President John P. Gulliver's son, who was a student at Knox, was at least twice involved with Field in escapades that prompted faculty censure. One of these occurred during Field's first year, one night early in April, after the freshmen had finished the two terms that they were required to study the Latin histories of Livy, an author whom most of the students detested. Field and John

Gulliver arranged to bury Livy in a "highly sacrilegious" burlesque of an ancient funeral. A procession bore a life-size effigy of
Livy to a great pile of boxes and barrels that had been collected in
what was then still the College park, between the College and the
Seminary. A devil clad in red tights, with horns and tail, kept
dashing out of the dark, trying to snatch the corpse away. When
the celebrants gathered at the pyre, kerosene was thrown on the
fuel; it was ignited in a flash, and the flames made the spring sky
glow and shadows flicker against the budding park trees. Field
read the dirge that he had composed for the occasion; the first
stanza was:

> Oh! Titus Livy, art thou dead?
> Oh! Auctor misere.
> And hast thou now to Hades fled?
> Nos Deploramus te.

Soon firemen and police were on hand to end the obsequies. When
the faculty censured the mourners the next day, students felt they
came off the better because it had been young Gulliver who had
played the devil.[8]

Obviously Field found the expected academic performances
tedious. At the end of his first year he participated with others in
his class in the declamation contest that was one of the usual
features of commencement week, which in those days was an
important civic occasion. This was a very hot June night, in the
old colony church, but the declaimers fortunately were down front
in the amen-corner, which was located by a large open window.
Field, who was first on the program, strode up on the stage, with
an American beauty in the buttonhole of his tailcoat, the only
student so dressed up. In a deep sonorous voice he rendered "Spar-
tacus to the Gladiators" with such a dramatic power that at its
close he had to rise twice from his pew to acknowledge the continuing rounds of applause. But all the other pieces followed, and
then a half hour wait for evaluation of the scores, and then a judge
delivered a critique of each speaker's performance. At this point
Field nudged his roommate, Frank Sargent Hoffman, whispered,
"Come on," and the two of them jumped up on the cushion of
their pew, plunged through the open window, disappeared out-

side; inside there was no little hub-hub and distraction to the speaker.[9]

For these graduation ceremonies, Field was quite likely the author of the humorously irreverent account of the baccalaureate services that was published in the Galesburg *Republican* and that was in style and substance so utterly unlike the prosaic reports of such events that ordinarily filled the columns of the local newspapers. He reported in detail how, after the choir had finished its first number, a bass note on the organ kept sounding and how Professor Charles Fuhrman (a Bavarian music teacher in the city) "struck a full chord, which only made it worse, for the 'blowist' supposed the piece was not finished and he sent in another blast which gave a beautiful prominence to that one note. Professor F. became excited and struck wildly here and there, first at one stop and then another. The result was a most delectable conglomeration of inharmonious tones, bars from a treble flute to a thundering bass." Faithfully also the reporter told of the two deacons who prompted "irreligious smiles" when they mistakenly arose for the second hymn. "None others rose and when these bashful ones saw their mistake down they went in a manner which provoked much merriment." The text of the sermon was from Matthew 10:16: "Behold I send you forth as sheep among wolves," so said the reporter. As for the preacher's homily to the seniors, this was the author's summary: "President Gulliver is a very profound and metaphysical writer. . . . We do not think that the students to whom he talked will ever gain much from it . . . still the most illiterate could not fail to be impressed with the soundness of the arguments and beauty of the language."[10]

By the summer of 1870 Field was writing regularly for the Galesburg *Free Press*. Though the files of this newspaper have been lost, one amusing sample of his journalistic apprenticeship was well remembered by George Lawrence, a fellow student and close friend. In this story Field was reporting the performance of a cantata about the biblical Esther by the Galesburg Philharmonic Club whose members were mostly members of the Knox faculty. According to Field, when they performed at Abingdon, about ten miles away on the C.B.&.Q., they created quite a sensation in their oriental costumes. "Special mention was made of the shapely

71

shanks of some of the faculty ladies and how the inhabitants fled to the woods, but were reassembled and reassured." Field's review concluded: "Emboldened by their success at Abingdon and Kewanee, where the show was also given, it was understood that they were planning shortly to produce a cantata to be called Adam and Eve, also in original costume."[11]

Field obviously cut a wide swath in a short time at Knox College. How much learning he gleaned for himself seems doubtful. He was only a perfunctory student; faculty minutes would use the word "nominally." The circumstance that he would later with his brother share in a widely admired translation of Horace does not mean that his was the Latin scholarship that went into the work. As a student he did demonstrate often his talent for fluent speech and for ready versification. But only for occasions and on topics that suited him, for Adelphi Society members discovered that they too could not rely on his performance. From the beginning of his membership the minutes often recorded that his literary assignments were, when due, "postponed" or that he was "fined" for failing to deliver the speech for which he was scheduled.[12]

Yet he was well liked. The Adelphi made him its membership chairman. Though not handsome, he was attractive, lank of figure, lean of face (perhaps even "raw-boned" and "rather gawky"), but fascinating. He wore his hair long. He was known to smoke a corncob pipe. He was reputed to spend much time at the Female Seminary. Professor Burgess noted that it did not help his standing with the men on the College faculty that the women of the Seminary faculty found him likeable.

It is significant that the Knox senior who formally welcomed Field at his induction into Adelphi in the fall of 1869 was William Mackintire Salter, who the following June ruffled trustees with his commencement oration, "Is Orthodoxy in Theology Necessary for the Christian?" a question that he would answer with a long career of intellectual heterodoxy and social dissent.[13] Field was also ready to challenge orthodoxy. As chairman of a program committee of the Adelphi, on February 8, 1871, he reported a question to be debated on Washington's birthday, which was an important day for general campus festivities. The question, which the society accepted, was "Resolved that Thomas Paine's theory of noninspiration of the bible [sic] is probable." For the first time since he had joined Adelphi he was scheduled for a debate, and on the affirmative team. But when the day came for the debate this question was "thrown aside . . . on motion," and a topic that was utterly noncontroversial was substituted. Possibly this incident added to his uneasiness at Knox, which in a few weeks would lead to his departing for the University of Missouri, where he joined his brother.[14]

In fairness to the faculty of Knox College, it should be noted that he stayed only a few weeks at the University of Missouri and that even before he came to Knox he had been asked to leave Williams College by its president, Mark Hopkins, who explained to Field's guardian, Professor Burgess, that his ward was a "general nuisance." Which is what he became to the faculty at Knox.[15]

Within a dozen years after he dropped out of Knox, students treasured his reputation as a poet. During 1881–82, the year that S. S. McClure and John S. Phillips edited the Knox *Student,* two of the monthly issues proudly included poems by Field. East from the campus across the railroad tracks a former Knox student impressed on her grade school pupils, who included Carl Sandburg, that a living poet, to be compared with the greatest from the past, had attended Knox College.[16] The third number of *McClure's Magazine,* in 1893, presented Field as one of America's leading literary figures, and, in this interview by Hamlin Garland, Field referred to the fact that he had that same year received an honorary master's degree from Knox College.

But sometimes there seemed to be a kind of chilled restraint about the attitude toward Field. On the only occasion when Field, as a famous man, is reported to have returned to Galesburg, the student magazine merely noted that he provided a "delightful entertainment."[17] The delight in his rather sentimental verse was apparently not matched by an appreciation for his role as a critic of the glittering culture, of the pretentious new wealth, and of the rapacious society that was evolving in that "Porkopolis"—the city of Chicago—and that was admired in Galesburg. There were those in Galesburg who believed that he had, while a student, acquired a "strong prejudice" against Galesburg, and that this was evident in the way he made fun in his *Daily News* column of Galesburg's leading politician, the well-padded and rather pompous Clark E. Carr, who had become a Knox trustee in 1881. The Galesburg

Republican Register in 1885 attributed Field's dislike of Carr to jealous competition, when Field was a student and Carr was still a bachelor in his mid-thirties, for the attentions of "a very beautiful and attractive young woman."[18]

In August 1870, while Field was a student at Knox, Carr became the owner of the *Republican*. In the special Christmas number of this paper for that year there was much written about "Eushene Fweeled." It was obviously intended to be funny, but it was so extreme and repetitive as hardly to be amusing. These are samples of Carr's humor:

> There is an adolescent hybrid inflicting himself upon Knox College, Knox Female Seminary, and the poor old played-out gin and cabbage sheet, who, when asked his name, opens an aperture of the dimensions of the Mammoth Cave, revealing the principal ingredients of several days diet, and pronouncing something which sounds like
>
> E-U-S-H-E-N-E F-W-E-E-L-D. . . .
>
> He is not without accomplishements, being not only remarkable for his literary genius, but a musician. He sang a piece in public a short time ago, taking the character of an infant ox, which would have rendered to the perfect satisfaction of the assembly, but for the painful anxiety experienced when he lifted up one of his feet and the dizziness when he opened his mouth. There was "rest for the weary" people when he got through, who had been holding on to the benches with all their might and main and the opinion was unanimously expressed that as a braying donkey Eushene Fweeld was a decided success. He is always a chief fugle man at public entertainments because he applauds everything, and on account of the size of his hands, he is able to make himself heard. He is regarded at the seminary as a convenience, at the newspaper office as an oracle, by the young men of the city as a blatherskite, and at the college as a dunce and blockhead.[19]

It would indeed appear that Carr disliked Field and that Field already as a student was irritating several important people.

The kind of jokes that Field played are better appreciated if compared with the more ordinary tricks played by students during the years that Gulliver and Newton Bateman were president (1868–92): stealing the clapper from the College bell, scattering cayenne pepper on the chapel floor and thus cutting short one of the speakers, burning a mathematics teacher in effigy, stealing the handsled of the "colored" washer-woman from where she left it at the south gate of the College grounds while she picked up the College boys' washing. One autumn morning in 1871 a professor found in his lecture room "a pair of nice porkers." In 1889 Edgar Lee Masters versified about borrowing the janitor's rooster. The leading prankster at the College in his day repeated the old stunt of putting the janitor's cow in the chapel.

The barnyard quality of so many of these escapades fit the College environment, for the habits of frontier farmers persisted within the city limits. The range law that allowed livestock to rove (while fences were built not to confine but exclude the animals) had been established while Galesburg was still a frontier settlement. By 1872 public sentiment supported an ordinance that required livestock be confined, but the law was not enforced against milch cows, for there was considerable feeling in many parts of the town that those who needed the animals for food should be allowed to let them forage freely, particularly during the months from May to November. So the cattle continued to foul the pathways, to break the boards of sidewalks, to jump over or through fences, and to spoil parks, lawns, flower beds, and vegetable gardens. In the mid-1880s the cows that ran at large were still a political issue.[20] The fences around the Seminary and the College were not merely ornamental but also strong enough to exclude such vagrant creatures. The protected spaces were entered through gates consisting of "smooth poles set at angles which would admit men and women but not cows and horses which roamed at will just outside the fence." As late as the semicentennial year at Knox College (1887) the grounds were enclosed by a "cattle proof" board fence.[21]

The Literary Societies

To appreciate the lifestyle of that era it is helpful to know that "Old Main" had no indoor plumbing until it was restored and rebuilt in 1936 and that it had no central heating until 1890, when by construction of the new Alumni Hall the *"Main"* Building became *"Old."* A vivid impression of campus housekeeping is provided by the minutes of business meetings of the two men's literary societies. They were responsible for maintaining and furnishing their meeting halls, which were in the attics and later on the second floor of the East Bricks, where the Gnothautii were located, and of the West Bricks, where the Adelphi held forth. These societies looked to the College trustees or to the faculty for services such as lengthening the chimney when poor draught caused smoke to fill their rooms from the woodburning stove; or papering and whitewashing the stairway and entry leading to their halls; and when the spring thaw came they would ask that a walk be built from the main College building to the East and the West Bricks. But ordinarily they cared for their society rooms themselves.

Each of the College societies chose a janitor, sometimes given the more impressive title of *factotum,* which was the Latin for "do everything." This job was awarded to the member of the society who offered the lowest bid for his services. The *factotum* might be instructed to buy a new lock for the door or to have the windows repaired. As janitor he did the more repetitive chores of having the window curtains and walls washed, of removing the accumulated clutter, of blacking the stove, of procuring fuel for the stove, of supplying oil for the lamps, and of replacing or cleaning lamp chimneys. Each autumn the stove and stove pipes were brought up and installed; each spring they were removed; for this he would need help from other members of the society.[22]

The more interesting business of buying new furnishings for the hall was assigned to special committees—new muslin curtains, a new carpet, a new marble-top table for the presiding officer and two wooden ones for the secretary and the "critic." Obviously each society was proud of its hall furnishings, which by special vote might be lent to the "Preparatory" society. The Adelphi had a particularly fine "chandelier," which was lent out for a Seminary "sociable." The Gnothautii were very proud of the busts that adorned their meeting place—Daniel Webster, Henry Clay, Stephen Douglas, and Abraham Lincoln. For special outlays of this kind the members assessed themselves, courted alumni, and staged lectures and concerts off campus in the old colony church or in the Opera House, which was also located on the town square.

It was under these simple circumstances and in this humble setting that Knox students greatly enriched the academic life of the Midwest by starting a system of interstate competition among orators from the colleges and universities. These contests not only provided during the 1870s and 1880s the most celebrated student activities on the Knox and other campuses; they also created a pattern that affected the growth of intercollegiate athletics and other extramural events. This important contribution by Knox men occurred when, otherwise, the College was at a very low point, being without a president for nearly three years and experiencing confusion about the interim leadership.

Interstate Oratorical Contests

That the intellectual training and the forensic experience encouraged by the interstate competition had genuine educational relevance to the times is evident from the careers of those who were winners at the annual interstate contests. Of those who won first place during the twenty-five meetings from 1874 to 1899, seven champions would later earn essays in the *Dictionary of American Biography*. Of six others who were to be listed in *Who's Who*, certainly two more, at least, will also be included in the *DAB*. Of those winning second place in the contests during the same quarter century, six more were to be listed in *Who's Who*. All but a few of these winners became lawyers, clergymen, college professors, or college presidents, vocations of the spoken word. The impact of their careers upon American political and social life is exemplified in the lives of Robert M. La Follette (University of Wisconsin) and Albert J. Beveridge (DePauw College), both of whom were important leaders in the Progressive movement; in the work of Howard H. Russel (Oberlin), who was a founder and the first superintendent of the Anti-Saloon League; in the career of John H. Finley (Knox) who became editor of the New York *Times;* in the achievement of James A. Blaisdell (Beloit), who instituted the plan of the Claremont group of colleges in California and became its first president.

The importance of what Knox students had started in 1874 was widely acknowledged, and the manner in which this had been done was proudly retold on the Knox campus during the following decades. Though the Adelphians could rightly claim the distinction of having, rather audaciously, inaugurated the interstate contests, the Gnothautii had already shared in a broadening of local

77

forensic activities into intercollegiate competition. A tentative effort at solving the problems of staging such contests occurred in the early months of 1872, when the Adelphi and Gnothautii accepted a challenge from the men's literary societies of neighboring Monmouth College and appointed committees to prepare, jointly, the terms, rules, and procedures for holding competitions in essay writing, debate, declamation, and oratory.[23] A date in May was selected for the event, but apparently it never took place, very likely because it was impossible to agree on all the rules for so comprehensive a contest. The mutual distrust was evident in the long and elaborate rules formulated by the Gnothautii to assure fair competition. Thus section six, of sixteen sections, provided:

> The judges shall be men of good literary and moral character. They shall be men who have no interest in either College. They shall be men who have not now, nor ever have had a relative in either College. They shall not be personally acquainted with any of the contestants. They shall be non-residents of either Galesburg or Monmouth. They shall be men who are not members of either of the churches under which the Colleges are conducted. Any one of the judges can be objected to by either of the four societies. A duplicate of each of the letters sent to the committee must be furnished to each society.[24]

Such a regulation suggests paranoia about one's opponents, but at the time that degree of distrust seemed quite reasonable under the conditions of fierce competition then flourishing. This was well exemplified in an episode bitterly recalled by George W. Prince, who attended Knox from 1872 to 1878. Even the public honor that he later earned as a congressman from the Galesburg district did not efface the humiliation and the resentment over losing, he thought unfairly, in the oratorical contest during his senior year. As a freshman, as a sophomore, and as a junior he failed to win even a second prize and thus missed the honors at the banquet given to the contestants by the prize winners, to which each contender took "his very favorite girl." His lady companion for the senior contest was Sadie Bateman, daughter of the president. Again he failed to win a prize, but, worse than that, the judges this time reported the relative standings and Prince ranked eighth, at the bottom of the list. "I was extremely mortified and felt keenly the position I had been placed in." After the banquet he walked the lady home from the church on the square, but at the corner by the old village cemetery "I dramatically stopped . . . and in her presence made a vow that I would work my fingernails off until I had beaten in life in a successful way every contestant who took part that night, with the exception of one who really deserved the award and won it."[25] The deserving winner, according to Prince, was his classmate, Edgar A. Bancroft, who one day would be the U.S. ambassador to Japan.

During Prince's first year at Knox, students staged what a historian asserts was the "first intercollegiate oratorical contest in America."[26] That year, 1872–73, it was the Gnothautii's turn to conduct the annual lecture series for town and gown. Already in September the lecture committee of the society proposed that one of the four events be an "intercollegiate contest between the four colleges: Knox, Monmouth, Abingdon and Lombard." With the approval of the society, the committee was able to announce by November 2 that on the following February 11, there would be an "entertainment" consisting of two orators from each of the four colleges contending for a second prize of $25 and a first prize of $50. The winners would be chosen by a "committee of award" consisting of "twelve competent men," to which the president of each college would appoint three men. Except that the judges would not be announced earlier than a week before the intercollegiate meeting, there were no other specifications for choosing the judges, but there were rather detailed rules stated for the manner in which the "committee of award" would select the prize orators.[27]

The contest did take place in Galesburg as scheduled, with Knox represented by a senior, Samuel D. Dunlap, president of the Gnothautii, and by Frank I. Moulton, a junior who during the next year would be president of Adelphi. Unfortunately there exists no record of the outcome of this contest. A Galesburg paper did, however, take special notice of the fact that one Abingdon College orator was a woman. At Knox the competition in oratory belonged to the men's societies and the women of LMI were not involved except as observers. The lady from Abingdon did not, apparently, win a prize, as this laudatory but patronizing comment indicated: "We have heard so many complimentary remarks concerning the literary effort of Miss Ada Byram, of Abingdon, in the later Inter-College contest, that we feel constrained to note the fact in the columns of our paper. Her subject was one entitled 'Wife, Man's Best Treasure,' and the pleasing and highly cultivated manner in which she handled her theme, had converted a large number of our unbelieving bachelors to a truism which heretofore they have been perversely disinclined to admit."[28]

Any profits made from this "Grand Inter-College Prize Contest," which was held in the Galesburg Opera House, could be put to good use by the Gnothautii to pay for the improvements that they made in their meeting hall. The Gnothautii, which once had used only the attic of East Bricks, were now allowed to combine the second and third floors. Partitions were torn away, creating a much larger meeting place, thirty feet by forty feet (nearly the entire area of the building) and with a higher ceiling. By the commencement of 1873 the society was able to dedicate this "commodius hall," with its walls "frescoed in the highest state of the art," with its new furniture and with its "appropriate pictures and busts of prominent statesmen." Gnothautii boasted that its new hall was as "convenient and commodius" as any to "be found east or west."[29]

Improving and adorning their halls was one of the ways in which Adelphi and Gnothautii tried to outshine each other. This extended to securing "the services of the most desirable ladies to assist them in the decoration of their halls" and "furnishing music" at their anniversaries, exhibitions, and annual reunions. At the commencement of 1874 there was a "Society Riot," when on the Monday morning before the events began the Gnothautii discovered that "a lot of evergreens" used to decorate the hall had been carried away. Suspecting their "rivals," a "possee" of Gnothautii armed themselves with baseball bats and broomsticks, secured a search warrant from a police magistrate, and followed the constable into Adelphi Hall, where they found the evergreens. Some Adelphians tried to prevent the recovery of the greenery by burning it with kerosene. Fortunately, Professor Comstock appeared and broke up the fight.[30]

At the reunion of June 1873, an alumnus of Adelphi, Judge Arthur A. Smith, was given the "toast":

"Will Adelphi ever grow beyond her garret?"

for the new Gnothautii Hall had alerted the Adelphi to the need to improve its meeting hall. Just as school was about to close the society appointed a committee to take charge of building a "new hall," and, when school reopened, while the work was completed on the old hall, the Adelphi held its meetings, until the end of October, in classrooms or in the Adelphi library or in the chapel in the main College building. It cost about $1,000 to reconstruct and to refurbish the hall. Much of this was done on credit, and as late as December 1873 the "Frescoers" had still not been paid for their work.[31]

The Adelphi needed money. Fortunately, it was their turn to conduct the annual lecture series in the community in 1873–74. Indeed, at the very first meeting of Adelphi in September 1873, immediately after Moulton had been elected president of the society, the lecture committee was asked to report. There was discussion of a "prize contest" with other colleges and a special committee was appointed to "negotiate" for that purpose. This special committee consisted of Moulton as chairman, Lawrence, and Read, three men who over many years would have important roles in the affairs of Knox College. One evening when they were meeting in the room in the northwest corner of the East Bricks that Read shared with his brother Charles, Lawrence suggested that the contest be enlarged from the rather localized meeting of the preceding February, at which no college representative had to travel more than fifteen miles. Henry Read later recalled that Lawrence said: "Let us invite the best colleges of the state each to send an orator to a contest here, and we will jam that old opera house and fill our treasury." At this point, Read's brother, who had been kibitzing, broke in to say: "Why don't you do a big thing while you are about it? Have your state contest here; let other states have their contests; then match up the champions." According to Read, the men looked at each other only a brief time before Moulton stretched out his hand across the table, saying: "Boys, shake, we shall do it."[32]

By November 15 it was announced that one of the four events of the "Knox College Adelphi course of winter entertainments" would be a "grand Inter-State College contest . . . which is expected to be of an extraordinary character." Since there were as yet no state organizations to choose the state champions, Adelphi directly invited two colleges or universities each from Iowa, Wisconsin, and Illinois. Regional pride or prejudice was plainly apparent in the preamble in which Adelphi proposed an oratorical competition "feeling that it would be for the mutual benefit of Western Colleges to engage in a friendly rivalry and preferring the culture of the rostrum to that of the oar." Knox kept itself out of the contest because of the obvious advantage of speaking to a home audience. The Adelphi offered prizes of $100 and $75 and agreed to pay the expenses of participants. The governors of the three states were each invited to appoint one member of "an awarding committee of three" to judge the winners.[33]

The proposal was forcefully and cleverly promoted. Moulton took advantage of the fact that he was the Galesburg reporter for both the Chicago *Tribune* and the Chicago *Times*. "We arranged to have the Governor of Illinois announce his appointment of the judge, and I immediately wired the information to the Chicago papers. We waited about a week, got the Iowa governor to make his appointment, and again bombarded the Chicago papers. A week or two later, the Wisconsin governor announced his appointment, and again we wired the Chicago papers."[34] Local papers in the three states, especially in the college towns, played up the affair prominently, and students at other campuses also involved the metropolitan dailies: "In one college a student fell in with a *Times* reporter and a column article on the approaching contest appeared in the *Times*. At another place a *Tribune* reporter was interviewed, and in the same manner the *Inner Ocean* was written to."[35]

Already by November 27 it was announced that six institutions had accepted the Adelphi proposal. They were: Illinois State Industrial University (now the University of Illinois); Chicago University; Iowa State University (Iowa City); Iowa College (now Grinnell); Wisconsin State University (Madison); Beloit College.

The contest proved to be an immense success.[36] It was held on a Friday evening, February 28, 1872, in the Galesburg Opera House, which at that time was being used during the daytime as a makeshift courtroom, for the county had not yet built the courthouse required by the recent removal of the county seat from Knoxville to Galesburg. There was some difficulty and delay in transforming a "court of justice to an entertainment hall." A large crowd was kept standing outdoors for upward of an hour, and when about 7:30 the doors were opened people poured in "like an avalanche, and rushed for seats regardless of ushers, which was the source of considerable annoyance to those who came afterwards" and "found their 'reserved' seats already occupied." The auditorium was literally "packed . . . to an uncomfortable condition," and "hudreds were turned away for lack of room."

Moulton presided over the event, which went on until after 11:00. In addition to the six orations there was music before, between, and after the speeches: three soprano solos, two of them operatic arias, and at least three pieces by the "Grand Orchestra" consisting of four pianos, two organs, and ten "other orchestral instruments," all played, gratuitously, by local musicians. Though "good order" was maintained, there was some annoying restlessness apparent at this entertainment; a newsman complained: "It is surprising that persons having neither literary nor musical taste will attend such entertainments, and by talking, giggling, and other unseemly conduct during the performance, seriously mar the enjoyment of those who are so unfortunate as to sit near them. We also chronicle the fact that the usual number of peanut crunchers were present, in the galleries, who thought it smart to pelt the people under them with the shucks."[37]

After the last orator had finished, the judges deliberated while the soprano sang "Five O'clock in the Morning." Moulton announced their decision and awarded first prize to the orator from Chicago University and second prize to the speaker from Beloit. Afterward the contestants and delegates from the colleges participating were guests at a "free banquet" by the Adelphi Society, a "fitting close" to what was the first of the Inter-State Oratorical contests.[38]

Action to assure continuation of interstate contests had already been taken. The Knox men had invited other colleges and universities to send three delegates each to a convention, at which a committee appointed jointly by Adelphi and Gnothautii would be ready to present a plan that would "include all the states of the Northwest." The delegates met in a parlor of the Union Hotel, where a University of Chicago student presided while Moulton served as secretary. They discussed the formation of associations in each of the states. For future interstate contests they adopted a constitution for the "Inter-State Collegiate Association," elected officers for the new organization, and agreed on a meeting place for the next year. By 1888 this association embraced ten states and included over fifty colleges.[39]

An "Illinois Collegiate Association" was organized at Bloomington early in April 1874 by representatives from Chicago University, Northwestern University, Illinois Industrial University, Wesleyan University, Knox College, Monmouth College, and Shurtleff College. Its stated purpose was to hold prize contests in oratory, and it adopted rules and procedures for such contests. Moulton of Knox was elected permanent president of the Illinois Collegiate Association. Anticipating the "first annual contest" to be held at Bloomington the next autumn, Knox by June 1874 had chosen Lawrence to be its contestant.[40]

In 1880 Knox College entertained the state contest. The event would later be often recalled because of a contender from Illinois College who would later make some of the most famous speeches in American history. His name was William Jennings Bryan. On this occasion he got only second place, though he made a favorable impression on local critics. At the reception before the contest, given at the Seminary by the LMI, he gave a toast to "The Girls." At the banquet the Knox woman who made arrangements insisted that he be her dinner partner.[41] Fifteen years later the Honorable W. J. Bryan (along with a senator, a governor, and a distinguished university professor) would again be in Galesburg to serve as a judge at the Inter-State Oratorical Contest.

When the first *Gale* (a yearbook) was published in 1888, a student writer boasted that no other institution could match the record of Knox in oratory. The facts support this claim. At fifteen statewide contests since 1874, Knox had won prizes seven times: in 1876, 1877, 1881, 1883, 1884, 1885, and 1886; four of these prizes were for first place. By the end of the century Knox, representing the state of Illinois seven times at the Inter-State Oratorical Contest, had carried off the first prize six times. Once it had to settle for the second prize when Victor Bender in 1885 lost the first place to Albert J. Beveridge, who later would become a distinguished Progressive senator from Indiana.

The first Knox man to win the first prize at an Inter-State Contest was Edgar A. Bancroft, who was a senior prep at Knox when Moulton, Read, and Lawrence initiated the regional competition.

Bancroft was president of Adelphi for two years (1876–78), an unmatched distinction in the history of that society. In October 1876 he was elected president of the Illinois Inter-Collegiate Convention. He won the college declamation prize as a freshman and again as a sophomore. These declamation contests were a preliminary preparation for the "art of Demosthenes and Cicero," for in a declamation contestants used "the words of others," "concentrating on delivery." As juniors and seniors they "spoke their own productions and were graded on thought and wording as well as delivery."[42] In the spring of 1877 Bancroft was chosen College orator; the following autumn he won the state championship at Monmouth; and in May of his senior year, at St. Louis, he won first prize in the Inter-State Contest. Among his judges was, from Indiana, the son of a president of the United States, who was only a decade from being elected to that office himself. Also, from Ohio, was the Honorable Alphonse Taft, recently a member of President Ulysses Grant's cabinet and himself the father of a future president.

Great intensity and amazing excitement were generated by the interstate contests. The frenzy can only be compared to that of a football championship, decades later. A good example was the Inter-State Oratorical Contest of May 1887, when Finley represented the state of Illinois, the third time in four years that a Knox man had that honor and responsibility. The competition occurred in Bloomington, Illinois, where on the day before the contest about twenty-five Knox men joined the delegations "from nearly every western state and all the colleges of Illinois," attired in "plug hat and broadcloth." To save Finley from the stress of attention from the crowd in the hotel, he was sent off to bed and a Knox man (Harry McCorkle) was "passed off" as the Knox orator.[43]

There were orators from nine states: Ohio, Indiana, Illinois, Wisconsin, Minnesota, Iowa, Nebraska, Kansas, and Colorado. Finley was the sixth to speak. His subject was "John Brown." He began quietly:

> Far up the wooded slopes of one of the Adirondacks there is a lone grave. It is marked by no tall monument, and but for its remoteness and seclusion there in the wildness of those enchanted hills, it might pass unnoticed.

Finley concluded with a peroration that ascended with Brown's famous and familiar words when he was sentenced to death in a Virginia courtroom and reached its climax in Finley's own rousing rhetoric:

> Byron dying amid the marshes of Missolonghi, LaFayette bleeding at Brandywine, and shall I say Washington at Valley Forge, showed not such disinterested bravery, such generous devotion. Traitor? Then were the brave who fell at Lexington traitors. They taught us this, "that we may resist with arms a law which violates the principles of natural justice." Emmet did it in Ireland; Wallace, in Scotland; Garibaldi, in Italy, and we honor them; John Brown did it in America, the land of the free, and we hanged him.
>
> Is this his fitting and final reward? The soaring shaft that stands by Potomac's stream answers, No. The monuments, which a grateful people have erected to the memory of those who died for the slave, say, No. The gratitude of millions freed from bondage says, No. And the day will come when even the mountains of Virginia will echo back the answer, No.[44]

After the last speaker had finished, there was a long delay while the scores of judges were gathered and tallied. There were six judges, three on "thought and composition," three on "delivery." One of them was the great Episcopalian preacher from Boston, the Reverend Philips Brooks; one was a senator from Connecticut; another the governor of Ohio; another the editor of a widely circulated Methodist magazine, published in Chicago; there was a layman from Iowa and another from Missouri.[45]

Meanwhile, back in Galesburg about 100 Knox College students went to the telegraph office at the C.B.&.Q. depot to wait for the news of the outcome of the contest in Bloomington: "As late as half past twelve o'clock no word had reached the anxious throng. At that time the depot master turned the students out of the depot. The boys gathered just outside. A policeman was invoked to send them away. The students began to sing, 'Here's to Good Old Knox,' and other inspiring tunes. Jeffery and others killed time in arguing with the officer."

A pistol shot rang out. It was the signal agreed upon that a telegram had come and that the news was "Illinois first." Immediately the crowd at the depot dispersed, to rouse the town. Students entered half a dozen churches to ring their bells. The bell at the Main College building was cracked by the frenzied ringers. Other students scoured Main Street and the public square for boards and boxes to make a huge pile before the Female Seminary, while the girls "swarmed" out of the building to join the jubilee. Soon the great bonfire cast a ruddy glow over the celebrating crowd. After a time the students in body marched to the home of President Bateman and announced the victory to him. After an apology for his night clothes ("unbecoming attire"), he made a "few appropriate remarks." Friday morning was mostly gone when the students withdrew and retired.

When Finley arrived back in Galesburg on Saturday evening, the celebration was renewed. A large number of students awaited him at the depot. The rail shop whistle blew—"a long time." The College cadets were there to head the procession in which the champion was driven in a barouche down Seminary and Main streets, President Bateman and the city mayor riding with him. The "equipage" was escorted by students and headed for the Female Seminary, "where the young ladies gave a fitting and enthusiastic greeting."

The next day was Sunday, which was still the Sabbath; Monday was needed for preparations; and then on Tuesday evening came the formal reception and the victory banquet. Finley "took his stand" in the "front parlor" of the Female Seminary and received congratulations. Then the celebrants gathered in the chapel of the new wing of the Seminary for the ceremony devised by the Knox "Preps." They presented to Finley, in a "beautiful plush box," "a fragment of the old College bell . . . which had been broken out of the bell at the late oratorical jubilee." The fragment, measuring about four cubic inches, had been polished on one side and upon it was engraved:

K. C. BELL, BROKEN FOR JOHN H. FINLEY, MAY 5, 1887.

After singing "John Brown's Body" the gathering dispersed, but promenaded about the rooms and halls until about 11 o'clock.

Then came the banquet at the "depot hotel," which was attended by 120 guests. The menu was "elaborate and promptly and neatly served." There followed a program of toasts, responses, and other victory speeches. It had been a long "jubilee."[46]

Understandably, some Galesburg citizens, kept awake by the

students' "jollification," grumbled about the noisy disturbances. But many proudly shared the students' pleasure. Earnest Elmo Calkins, who grew up in Galesburg and attended Knox between 1885 and 1891, recalled years later the "saturnalia" that occurred in 1884 when Charles Wyckoff brought home the first prize from Iowa City. On this occasion the city's lawyers had a "lark" while the students and faculty of Knox had an uncalendared holiday. Trouble with the police had developed while students waited for news of outcome of this interstate contest: "An officious policeman arrested a dozen ringleaders. The faculty recognized the futility of holding classes, and the students attended court in a body. As one man the Knox County bar tendered its services to the defense; and the city attorney, himself a graduate of the College, spent the unhappiest day of his life. A triumphant acquittal turned malefactors and confederates loose to continue the celebration, stepped up by the presence of its central figure who had by now returned."[47] The editor of the student magazine explained trouble with the policeman on this occasion by describing him as "intoxicated" and accused the local police officials of wanting "to get even with the students for voting the temperance ticket at the recent elections."[48]

Another Galesburg youth who retained vivid memories of these events was Carl Sandburg. He was seventeen years old when the Inter-State Contest of 1895 was held in Galesburg. The Illinois representative was Otto Hauerbach (later Harbach), who had been attracted to Knox by the fame of Finley's achievements, which had been proudly broadcast by Knox students and alumni as far west as Salt Lake City, whence Hauerbach had come. When Hauerbach won the first prize, pandemonium once more broke loose. Sandburg recalls the incident in the autobiography of his youth.

> One June night in the year of 1895 the town of Galesburg was, as people said, "turned upside down." Church bells and the Knox College bell rang all night. You could hear gunshots. Cannon cracked and boomed. Fireworks sprayed the sky and firecrackers snapped. Railroad-engine whistles tooted. City and farm boys rampaged around bonfires on the campus and in the streets. Glee clubs sang and wild yells came on the air from before midnight till past

daybreak. You could hear voices getting hoarse from crying "Hurrah for Knox" followed by "Hurrah for Harbach!" . . .

The Knox Silver Cornet Band, the Glee Club, and a wild mob followed the students who hauled Harbach to the campus on their shoulders. With songs, bells, yells, bonfires, they not only made the welkin ring but they swept the deck and threw the broom in the sea in so far as that could be done in a prairie town.[49]

Alumni Hall

In 1889–90 a building was erected that fulfilled the aspirations of both Gnothautii and Adelphi for better meeting halls, the aspirations that in 1873 and 1874 prompted them to initiate intercollegiate oratorical competition and to start the interstate oratorical association. Since both societies had improved their quarters in the mid-1870s the space had become too cramped, for the College enrollment had increased; there were thirty-eight men in 1875–76 (the lowest since the last year of the Civil War); five years later it had doubled; ten years later it had tripled. The East and West Bricks were deteriorating. In 1882 a wall of West Bricks "began to give way and threatened to 'bring down' " the Adelphi. In 1885 the roof of East Bricks took fire from a faulty flue and badly damaged the Gnothautii Hall. The following year both these societies were harmed by the burning of the Opera House, where the Adelphians and Gnothautii staged many of their lectures and concerts; they had to hire a smaller auditorium and their profits were considerably diminished. The situation clearly indicated that the College needed its own auditorium.[50]

Both of the men's societies could well envy the women of LMI, for when an east wing was added to the Female Seminary in 1885 they had the entire third floor as their own "beautiful new hall." Furthermore, they raised the money for this hall themselves, so that it was entirely their own property. The men's societies were also garnering gifts from their alumni so that each of them might have a new hall, which they assumed would be a single and separate building. However, at the urging of the faculty and the Board of Trustees a special committee negotiated an agreement with the Adelphi and the Gnothautii for a "Union" building, as it was at first called. The plan that was adopted provided that a large College chapel, or auditorium, would join two single society structures into a tripartite but combined building. This would be called "Alumni Hall"; its western wing would be identified by Latin letters carved in stone over the north portal and by Greek letters over the south entry as the hall of the Adelphi; in the same manner the east wing was identified as the hall of the Gnothautii.[51]

The late 1880s and early 1890s were boom times for the College enrollment, which for the first time exceeded that of the Academy. President Bateman had been for years frugal and financially cautious; now between 1885 and 1892 much building occurred; for the Seminary, an east wing in 1885 and a west wing in 1892; for the teaching of science, an observatory in 1888; and in 1890–91 the most ambitious of all, the structure that would be three in one, Alumni Hall, Adelphi Hall, Gnothautii Hall. By April 1890 the plans were essentially complete. The architect, E. E. Myers of Detroit, was well known for his design of several state capitol buildings; locally his work was already apparent in the recently completed county courthouse that the ladies of the Seminary passed on their way to the College.

It was intended that each of the societies would contribute $7,000 to the total expense, which was estimated at between $35,000 and $40,000. The society wings were to be two-story buildings, the second floor of which would for each society have a spacious meeting hall, with a stage and dressing rooms, a reading room, a library, and a cloak room. The first floor of each wing would have a large parlor that students might use "between recitations for study or such other purposes as may be desirable." The remaining areas of the first floor, it was assumed, would be rented to the College to use for recitations, for the College library, and possibly for a museum. The basement was planned for furnace and for fuel storage, for this was to be the first building on the campus designed totally with central heating. Other basement areas might be used for bathrooms, "water closets," and lockers. The central chapel, or auditorium, would accommodate 450 persons on the ground floor and nearly that many in the balcony.[52]

The site selected for this structure required the demolition during the summer of 1890 of the West Bricks. It was one of the choicest locations in the city. North, across South Street, was the two-block park area on which, to the right, a county courthouse had been newly erected. Immediately to the front this park was still receiving the special nurture of Professor John Van Ness Standish of Lombard College, who with his wife was particularly active in the local horticultural society and who was the most active member of the park commission. This area of the park, which would one day carry his name, was thoughtfully planted with a diversity of trees and shrubs, native and exotic. To the west across Cedar Street was the residence of Professor and Mrs. Standish. Their gardens, where the flowering of plants followed the advancing seasons, were greatly admired. The ginko tree that still grows before the Knox Library is a reminder of this enterprise in landscaping.

The College now undertook to improve the appearance of its own grounds. In the spring of 1889, the landscape architect, A. N. Carpenter, laid out the campus "in the most approved modern style, as regards grades and walks and providing for adequate drainage." In 1891 brick sidewalks replaced the wooden walks.[53]

At the dedication in October 1891 there were three ceremonies, just as there had the year before been the laying of three cornerstones. The three petroglyphs spoke for themselves. The cornerstone was near the center of the north front of the building:

OCTOBER 8TH   LAID BY BENJ' HARRISON
PRESIDENT OF THE UNITED STATES

As eyes looked up from this inscription they saw another in the stone beneath the crown of a great Romanesque arch; it gave the name:

ALUMNI BUILDING

President Harrison had been previously committed to come to Galesburg to participate in a reunion of the brigade he commanded during the Civil War. The laying of this cornerstone became only one event in a great gathering of war veterans from all over the Midwest. For this occasion town and gown staged a civic celebration that opened with a grand parade in which Knox cadets as well as the ladies of the Seminary passed in review before the U.S. president. On the campus President Harrison must have stood near what was to be the entrance to a large auditorium that might seat as many as 1,000 persons. It was intended for the almost daily religious assemblies or special events of the College and also for the more secular programs that were shared with town. When finished this chapel extended the full width of the building from the street side to the large semicircular alcove, where it was hoped an organ would someday be installed behind the stage.

To the west from this central arch, at the northwest corner of this complex, was another cornerstone that read: "ADELPHI FOUNDED 1846." In the stone above the doorway that entered this part of the building was carved "ADELPHI HALL."

In a corresponding location at the northeast corner, on the street side of this structure, was a cornerstone that read: "GNOTHAUTII FOUNDED 1849," and here again the name was repeated in the stone above the entrance, being inscribed: "GNOTHAUTII HALL."

A certain kind of academic life at Knox had reached its zenith.

Athletics

Though athletics had become very important by 1890, they were still subsidiary to forensic competition. Earnest Elmo Calkins, who had grown up in Galesburg and attended Knox between 1885 and 1891, referred to these "pre-football days" when "public speaking was a stepping stone to campus prestige" and oratory "almost the only road to fame." In fact, during his youth there was confusion at Knox about the rules with which the game of football should be played. Most athletic contests of any kind were intramural and those played away from home usually were incidental to the intercollegiate oratorical competition for which Knox students had initiated the permanent organization.

Alumni from antebellum years all recalled that the work done to earn a way through school provided ample physical activity and that there were really no organized sports. Erastus Wilcox, who was graduated in 1851 with Comstock and Churchill and served on the faculty with them from 1855 to 1863, stated positively, "In the bright lexicon of our youth there was no such word as athletics." He did remember that there had been long-jumping contests and that "we had a few common old fashioned games of ball," played, if Comstock is correct, with a ball that was soft and not hard.[54]

The word *athleta* did appear twice in an article in the April

1857 issue of the *Oak Leaf,* a monthly magazine published by the Gnothautii. The title of the article was "A Gymnasium." Well versed in the classics, a Knox student would know that *athleta* were those who competed for a prize in the public games of ancient Greece and Rome. The Knox author of the *Oak Leaf* essay had a very low opinion of these "useless and senseless games" of the "heathen Greeks." Especially he despised the Spartan concern with "symmetrical beauty" of the body and a "commanding appearance." He associated the "glory of the *athleta*" in wrestling, boxing, jumping, running, and the "Pancratium" with less attractive features of Greek culture, such as slavery, the degradation of women, and the exposure of infants that were uncomely or deformed. In short, the Knox writer denied that in America gynmasia were needed "to educate the body in mere play." America already had a great gymnasium:

> A Gymnasium that God has given us. . . . It extends as far as our dominion extends. What fields for the development of the muscular system! What forests of pine, oak, hemlock, cedar, and walnut, are to be removed from their proud positions. . . . What quarries of gold, silver, iron, copper, and lead, to be raised from their dark beds! How science may be enriched by gems from every hillside, valley, tree, and flower! What mechanic arts to be sustained! What agricultural interests to be advanced! What unnumbered square miles of land to be brought under cultivation! What lines of railroad to be extended athwart our continent, bearing intelligence, and manifold blessings to the millions who shall gather on our western borders. . . .
>
> Then let the educated man, Cincinnatus-like, betimes resort to useful bodily labor. Let him mingle with the unlettered and lead them along in the paths of knowledge. He will thus develop his own manly proportions, and unfold the mental powers of the poor despised laborer. And before many decades have passed, we will be a nation of men. Yes, men! Not senseless giants, or spindle-shanked philosophers. In stature, how like angels, in apprehension, *How like God.*[55]

This essay was a response to proposals for building a gymnasium on the Knox campus. Already in 1859 a Knox student wrote to a friend that "next summer they are going to build a gymnasium for the students," and the men's literary societies both debated the desirability of constructing a gymnasium during the early 1860s.

Some of the Adelphi argued that the College needed a cistern more.[56]

A gymnasium at that time was intended, of course, for gymnastics, not for basketball as it would be half a century later. It was in the Female Seminary that gymnastics were first officially recognized. Interest in such activity was evident in a debate by the LMI in 1863 on the proposition, "Resolved that the Olympic and other games had a favorable effect upon the ancient Greeks."[57] During the first year that Ada Lydia Howard was principal of the Seminary (1866–1867), Professor Henry Eaton Hitchcock, who taught mathematics and natural philosophy in the Seminary, also directed exercises for the women. A young woman wrote to her parents about what they did in the "exercise room": "Perhaps you would like to know what we do at recess. We go up to the exercise room and Professor Hitchcock gave us gymnastic exercises until today we had a game with the corn bags. It is real fun. There are two divisions and Professor counts three and then the one at the head commences and hands the bags around. The division that gets through the first five times gets the game. It is a very exciting game." Considerable research into Knox history suggests this is the first explicit account of an athletic event at Knox.[58]

The first specific faculty appointment for physical education was made for the Seminary during the second year that Howard was principal. This was the year that the trustees, led by President William S. Curtis, undertook to make the Seminary totally separate from the College and to provide a more comprehensive education for women, conducive "to physical health as well as to mental and moral development." By far the most novel feature in this new Seminary program was the education offered by a new faculty member, Mrs. A. A. Douty, in "Musical Gymnastics." Under a bold type heading, the Seminary catalogue (for this year an entirely separate publication) had this paragraph:

GYMNASTICS

Dr. Dio Lewis' system of Musical Gymnastics has been recently introduced and promises to be of essential service in physical culture. These, interspersed with Calisthenics, give grace of manner, and afford amusement and healthful exercise, in which each young lady will be expected to engage.

Obviously this "physical exercise" was something more than the casual "exercises" offered by Professor Hitchcock the previous year. Dr. Dio Lewis's system of calisthenics had attracted much attention since he introduced it in the normal school he founded in Boston in 1861.

For the men of the College the earliest evidence of gymnastics is found in the first College yearbook that was published for the year 1869–70. At that time there were gymnastic "captains" for each of the four College classes. "Captain" was a title that would recur frequently during the next dozen years for the leaders or instructors in gymnastics for men.[59] Apparently there was some expectation that the men would participate regularly in gymnastics, for there is a recollection by the roommate of Eugene Field that he acted the fool in his gymnastic class to make the exercises seem ridiculous. When his guardian rebuked him, Field, who lived in the next room, got up in the middle of the night and went through the gymnastics with great commotion.

While Field was a student, the colorful, cosmopolitan, and sometimes controversial Mrs. Mary Ives Seymour (often addressed by students as "Madame") gave faculty supervision to this art— or sport. Her duties during a brief teaching tenure included instruction in French, music, and "light gymnastics." The *Mischmasch,* the student yearbook for 1870–71, described her as "Instructor" of the "Cynsarges" whose motto was: "He is a cripple who cultivates his mind alone, suffering his body to languish through inactivity and sloth."[60] The membership of the group consisted of twenty-eight "gymnastes" (women) and twenty-three "gymnasts" (men). Already at the end of her first term as instructor, Seymour presented in the Seminary gymnasium on the top floor an exhibition that was an important social event in the city. Unfortunately, the detailed newspaper account of this occasion tells us nothing about the gymnastics themselves, but it does report in full the speech with which Madame Seymour opened her program. It began with an account of the high place that Greeks accorded to gymnastic education: "Gymnastics . . . from the earliest ages of Grecian . . . have ever been associated with all that is highest and most beautiful in art. . . . Women as well as men were instructed in physical culture, and amid the 'classic groves of the Cynsarges' a portion of ground was set apart for use by women. . . . Many of the gymnasiums were dedicated to Apollo, the god of physicians and the works of Hippocrates and Galen are full of testimony as to the necessity and benefit of physical culture." Madame Seymour carried her discourse on physical culture through Roman, medieval, and modern times until Lewis, her mentor, had restored it to its proper importance in the education of youth.[61]

A gymnasium for the College men was finally built by the students themselves. In September 1876 they organized a "Gymnastic Club," and elected as president a junior, Nicholas Edwards, who belonged to a family that figured prominently at Knox during the 1870s and 1880s. The students proposed to have a gymnasium "ready for tumblers by the first of November," a short time, indicating either the simplicity or flimsiness of the structure, but also manifesting the genuine intensity and speed with which the ground was prepared and the carpentry done. By mid-October the stakes had been driven, the lumber was on the ground, and the construction started. Students helped "to forward the work . . . with spade and shovel, ax and hammer, and saw and plane." President Bateman "illustrated his skill in using a spade."

By the third week of October the frame was up and most of the siding was on. During the first week of November the gymnasium was opened "with great eclat" and an "excellent supper." It stood on the east side of the campus, a little farther south than the main College building; it faced north and was located where a second gymnasium building would be erected in 1908. It was seventy-two feet long, thirty-six feet wide, and in height reached twenty-three feet from foundation to plates. It was dark brown. A large double-door opened at the north entrance, and just within, on either side, were two wardrobe or dressing rooms, nine feet by thirteen. The floor was of double thickness, with tar paper between the layers of wooden flooring. There were fourteen large windows, five on the long sides and two at either end. The walls were wainscoted up to the level of the window sills, seven feet from the floor. The building could be heated by the two stoves in the dressing rooms and by the large stove at the opposite (south) end. The windows could be opened for ventilation. There was a little gallery for spectators above the entrance.[62]

The Gymnasium cost $1,473.19. President Batemen estimated

that student labor had been worth about $200, that students had raised $324, and that the dedication supper organized by Knox women had netted $90. Because the College finances were still tight, President Bateman was unwilling to burden it with this debt for the gymnasium. Therefore he and "one or two others" personally "assumed" the debt on the gymnasium that in March 1878 still amounted to about $1,000, including accumulated interest and the "expenses incidental to the management of the gymnasium."[63] Students therefore felt "honor bound" to raise the money to pay off the indebtedness and resorted to such means as bringing to Galesburg well-known lecture programs, including the famous Wendel Phillips. Even that notorious infidel, "Bob" (Robert Green) Ingersoll from Peoria, agreed to deliver one of his spellbinding orations in a gymnasium "benefit."[64] One wonders that the great agnostic should have been invited; no doubt his religious skepticism was more than compensated by his fidelity to the Republican cause, for he was the great oratorical voice of that party, the speaker who had nominated James G. Blaine for the presidency in 1876, awarding him the famous sobriquet of "plumed knight," and who at many other times and places "waved the bloody shirt," recalling his own service in the Union army and reminding his auditors that Confederates had been Democrats.

Gymnastics had a kind of official status not yet accorded to other sports. In June 1879 a program of gymnastics was included in the events of commencement week. That year for the first time there had been on the staff a "Director of the Gymnasium"; he was "Captain" Loren Morrison, himself in the graduating class. The detailed newspaper report of this event indicated some of the ideology as well as the action of the occasion. The little gallery in the gymnasium was filled with the party of the president, "distinguished visitors," trustees, faculty "with their wives, their sisters, and their cousins and their aunts, and a goodly number of alumni and friends." Amongst the returning alumni was Samuel S. McClure's uncle, the Reverend Joseph Gaston; his seat was on one of the rafters, with his feet swinging over the gymnasium floor.

First the men marched "in file in line in platoons" and then performed vigorously but precisely with dumbbells. And then the "class of young ladies" came to the floor. President Bateman called them "this pioneer class in calisthenics." They were:

in their pretty costumes of navy blue and white, and of grey and blue. With what a charming grace they marched in line, in twos, in fours; and with what military precision they wheeled to the right or left and charged with all their chivalry. With an elastic step far handsomer than the languid gait of city belles, they took each one her wand and moved into position. Then it was that the celerity and ease of the former exercises became awkwardness in the light of girlish quickness and grace. They rested their wands upon the floor, and we thought of the lovely Minerva leaning upon her lance; then holding them horizontally with both hands, they raised them above their heads and lowered them again in rapid repetition, and we thought of clothes-frames; but when they seized them in one hand and held them high in the air, we thought it best to be out of reach. . . . It was a beautiful sight, made doubly beautiful by the beneficence of the drill. It gave a healthy glow to many cheeks, and a brighter sparkle to many eyes.

Of course, even this event concluded with a number of speeches. One of the distinguished visitors told the young ladies that "the beads of sweat" on their faces were "worth more" to them "than diamonds hung about your necks." To his surprise, Gaston was called upon to speak extemporaneously for the class of 1877, who, said President Bateman, "started the Gymnasium." From his perch in the rafters Gaston quickly recovered, announced his text, and spoke humorously and aptly about the rich publican, Zacchaeus, who being of little stature climbed a sycamore tree so that he might see Jesus.[65]

By 1882 the gymnasium was equipped with trapezees, parallel bars, rings, a springboard, a rowing machine, and a "health lifting machine." In an exhibition that year the audience particularly marveled over the performance of student and "teacher" Charles Lincoln Johnson, who did a "Giant Swing" upon the parallel bars that ended with "a somersault in the air."[66]

It is not surprising that a building so hastily erected soon needed repairs. In 1881–82 the gymnasium could not be kept warm because of "cracks and knot holes," and classes at times were excused because it was too cold. To improve this condition, workers boarded the building inside so that it became "tight and comfortable"; to pay for this improvement the student who was director of the gymnasium, or "Captain," sought subscriptions around town. During the 1890s the gym work was transferred to the basement of the new Alumni Hall, [67] and the older wooden structure fell prey to the winds until by 1904 only a decrepit frame was still standing. It was then torn down to clear the ground for the new gymnasium that was completed in 1908.

For the women, meanwhile, an improved gymnasium of their own had been included in the wing that was added to the Seminary in 1885. Arrangements were made at that time for the director of the College gymnasium to give the women "instruction in physical development."[68] They had on occasion used the same gymnasium as the men, but there were complaints that organization of the men's activities tended to leave the women out of consideration. Even more significant, however, had been the evolution on the part of male students of sports activities that soon made gymnastics relatively insignificant.

The first sport to be well organized on the Knox campus was baseball, and it remained the most important athletic competition until the late 1880s. There was a baseball diamond on the back campus of the College at least as early as 1867, but it was used during the next two years only for games among Knox students themselves. The first explicit report of a game by Knox men is of the baseball game played between freshmen and juniors for the "Championship of Knox College" on a Saturday afternoon late in October 1869 on the "beautiful grounds in the rear of Knox College." A large crowd was on hand. The freshmen won; the score: 49–37.[69]

Newspapers reported a "Knox Baseball Club" in 1867, but there are indications that this was not composed exclusively of Knox students and that it was more of a city team. Certainly the contests were interurban rather than intercollegiate. To some students the game was still rather new. A Preparatory student who entered Knox in 1869 recalled that it was still played without gloves and that novices had to learn how to catch a swiftly thrown ball with bare hands. One of the best players, a senior, took the thrown ball in front, where it came into his hands "with a resounding slap." The method admired by others was that of Eugene Field, who received the ball "at the side with a graceful yielding of the hands."[70]

The first College yearbook, for 1869–70, lists the members of four baseball clubs. One, the Roscoe Base Ball Club, had a first nine that consisted of members of the senior (1870) and junior (1871) classes. In addition there was a Junior Class Club (overlapping the Roscoe Base Ball Club in membership), a Sophomore Club, and a Freshman Club. Field was a catcher on the Freshman Club's First Nine. The next year he played second base on the "Knox College Base Ball Club."[71]

An intraurban baseball competition for "College City" championship with Lombard University began at least as early as 1870 and continued in 1871, 1872, and 1873, the Lombard Osceolas rather consistently defeating the Knox College club. In 1873 the latter were calling themselves the Modocs, that being the name of an Indian tribe in the Pacific Northwest that during the early 1870s was fighting the U.S. Army. For the game with Lombard played in the fall of 1872, the pitchers were both faculty members, a practice that was accepted, at least until the early 1880s, for intercollegiate competition.[72]

There was genuine amateur spontaneity about a game played with Chicago University, possibly the first collegiate athletic competition with a team from beyond Galesburg. It occurred in June 1872, when the seniors of the Chicago college stopped in Galesburg on their way back from a two-week geology trip along the Mississippi River in the areas of Gladstone and Quincy. They visited the Knox campus and "a friendly game of ball was played with a picked nine of Knox on Saturday morning." Unfortunately, one of the Chicago players "was severely injured, being hit by a very hot ball"; he was still "suffering considerable from the blow" when he boarded the early afternoon train to return home with his team and classmates.[73] The first game with Monmouth College was played on the Knox campus in the year 1872–73, according to the recollection of a contemporary student.[74]

From 1872 to 1880 there was a student in the Knox Academy and in the College who earned a special kind of fame as a baseball player. His name was William S. Harvey and later in life he became a distinguished physician and surgeon. But he always remained proud that at Knox he had been a star pitcher and asserted that he was the first student to throw curves in intercollegiate competition. He learned the art of throwing an "in-shoot" and an "out-curve" during a summer baseball tournament (for "prizes") in Princeton, Illinois, from a professional player who, it was said, became the first curve pitcher in the National League.[75] When the phenomenon was reported to the professor of mathematics and astronomy, Milton L. Comstock, he pronounced such curves impossible, whereupon a demonstration was arranged with the doubting professor behind the catcher. With his long, full beard, Comstock must have looked like an Old Testament prophet come down to umpire! Comstock accepted this proof of curves and later explained them. Even the more conservative professor of natural science, Albert Hurd, who was in the crowd of witnesses, was impressed.[76]

In 1879, with Harvey as pitcher, Knox made its most extended athletic expedition to that date. It sent a team to Jacksonville to play "the first game of ball between Knox and Old Illinois." Contributions to cover expenses were made by both students and faculty, the trip being lengthy, requiring a change of trains, and concluding with a connection by horse-drawn hack from Chapin to Jacksonville. The Knox Club won, 20 to 13, with the assistance of costly errors made by Illinois College in the first four innings. For the latter school this was probably the first intercollegiate ball game played on their campus. The Knox men were cordially treated; they were taken in the evening to visit the two men's literary societies that paralleled the men's organizations at Knox and were entertained overnight in private homes in Jacksonville.[77]

About this time Illinois College, along with Monmouth and the Illinois Industrial University at Champaign, became the most regular baseball competitors of Knox. The contests with the Jacksonville and Champaign schools were held in conjunction with the annual state oratorical competitions, the first of which had occurred in the fall of 1874. This collegiate association provided the framework for the athletic events that were still definitely secondary to the main program of oratorical competition. In October 1880 the state oratorical meeting was scheduled for Galesburg and the baseball nines from both Jacksonville and Champaign announced that they would also be on hand.[78] Knox beat Illinois College in baseball 5 to 1, though the Jacksonville student paper raised questions about the legitimacy of Harvey as the Knox pitcher. Captains of both teams agreed beforehand "that no one should be played on either nine who was not either a student or a teacher in the institution represented by the club." "On this ground an objection was entered against Knox playing Harvey, but he claimed to be taking a special course in chemistry and confirmed his statement by Gas-ing the umpire all through the game."[79] Harvey had been a senior at Knox in 1879–80, and had been graduated in June 1880. The College catalogue for 1880–81 lists a category of "irregular" students, but Harvey is not on this list either. It may also be noted that he continued to play collegiate baseball at the University of Michigan, where he went for medical education.

At this same intercollegiate gathering in October 1880, Illinois Industrial University beat Knox 14 to 8. For some reason, the losers a few days later sent the Champaign team a purse of $15 to help defray expenses. That the Knox men made so "handsome" a gesture suggests that there may have been a profit from the main event, the oratorical contest, for it should not be overlooked that the baseball game had been only an "overture to the oratory."[80]

The Illinois Industrial University was embarrassed because its team had taken to the diamond at Knox in rather "motley garb." By spring, when these same teams played again at Jacksonville, the men from Champaign had new uniforms.[81] The special occasion was again the Interstate Oratorical Contest. Jacksonville was "overflowing" with college students; among them eighty from Monmouth, sixty from Champaign, and from Knox a "car load"—that is a *train car* load. Unfortunately an early May rain washed out most of the baseball games.[82]

At the statewide oratorical contest in October 1881 football as well as baseball games would be part of the intercollegiate competition. The Knox yearbooks of the early 1870s make no mention of football until the academic year of 1872–73. In October 1872 a local newspaper reported: "The Knox College students now amuse themselves playing football" and observed that their style of playing was "a somewhat feeble imitation of the stirring struggle we have read about in the admirable work of 'Tom Brown at Oxford.'" The reporter noted that the players obviously needed practice before they would be able "to kick one another's shins in the most manly and independent manner."[83] According to the *Pantheon* of that year there was on the campus "the Accidental Foot-Ball Club." Its origins were explained thus:

This organization was "put on foot" by certain youths, who preferred broken heads, sore shins and goodly exercise to *ennui,* indigestion, and general "gone-upativeness." It flourisheth, and hath a brave band of devotees, who have as their motto, "Live and let live," but it is to be regretted that this sentiment is hardly carried out, as their victims are almost numberless. With cheeks stained with tears, shed in remembrance of our fallen braves, we can simply sigh in the language of the high-toned but sadly immoral Billings, "Sich is life!" The members "aim" high, hence it is no fault of theirs if the consequences are adverse.[84]

The membership or "faithful few" allegedly included twenty-nine men.

Six years later the *Knox Student* suggested that football "seems to be the favorite game at present in western as well as eastern colleges," but indicated that it was not certain whether a team should have eleven or fifteen men. In fact a game played during the first week of December 1878 had thirteen men on each side, the one team being freshmen and the other being a combination of sophomores and juniors. The size of the team may very well have been determined by the number of healthy men available, for counting those enrolled as "irregular" there were only thirty-two men in the junior and sophomore classes together and thirty-two freshman.[85]

Until 1881 football games at Knox were contests between classes. This is specifically evident in an editorial in the student paper published when S. S. McClure was chief editor, during his senior year. This editorial urged that "we might have a game or two with our Abingdon, Monmouth or Lombard neighbors." But to do this, it was asserted, "we sadly need some definite and different rules of play. . . . We have been playing by these old half-American half local rules long enough." The writer suggested that a committee of students "draw up some rules."[86] Yet, four years later, when the first game was played with Monmouth, "a great deal of time was taken out in discussing the rules. . . . Constantly situations were developing for which no existing rule would fit."[87]

The need for uniformity in rules for which the *Knox Student* editorialized in November 1881 may have been prompted by an intercollegiate contest the preceding month, probably the first game off campus. On October 21, 1881, a Knox team played and defeated the "Normal University" club on the "University campus." This game occurred in connection with the Interstate Oratorial Contest, which was held at Illinois Wesleyan University at Bloomington. The newspaper that reported this football game gave no further details. Was it impromptu? Very likely some of the Knox men who participated in this football game also played in a baseball game with Illinois Wesleyan, for that game occurred so late in the afternoon that it could not be completed; at the end of three innings, with Knox ahead 9 to 4, "darkness stopped the game."[88]

The first detailed account of an intercollegiate football game is about one played in late November 1885 against Monmouth at that campus.[89] In many respects this contest would now hardly be recognized as a football game. The men merely wore old clothes, without benefit of cleated shoes, shin-guards, shoulder pads, or head protectors. As much time was consumed arguing over the rules as was used in playing, for the Knox men themselves had never definitely agreed on the character of the sport, which was during the 1880s a mixture of rugby, soccer, and an eastern game, as Knox men learned about it from men who had attended one of the eastern colleges and who sometimes did some of the coaching. It is certain that the ball was round and not oval, and that a goal was won by advancing the ball between two upright posts. A team that scored three goals won; thus a game with a score of three to nothing might be quickly completed; a game scored three to two might last over parts of two days because it was interrupted by nightfall.[90] Late in the 1880s there was agitation for adopting the rugby rules, but that was changed because the games proved to be very rough. Until about 1891 it is evident that the rules were changed locally from season to season or even "amended or revised to suit exigencies" of the occasion. Certainly before 1891 there was more kicking and running with the ball. Though a man might not be tackled nor tripped, he could be blocked by an opponent who refrained from using his hands or his forearms. He might run with the ball only so long as he kept it in motion—by bouncing it in the hand or by dribbling it on the ground. A player who caught the ball got a free kick or he might punt, that is, propel it by hitting it with his hand. Knox won the game with Monmouth in 1885 because one of its players could hit the ball with his fist to a distance of sixty yards, which was quite as good as a kick. As understood today, there would be some question whether the games played in the 1880s were football.

By the 1880s sports in great variety had developed on the campus. An area was prepared on the back campus for lawn tennis, and space was kept clear for archery, both men and women enjoying these activities.[91] The diversity of physical recreation was displayed during commencement week of 1886 in what was called "The First Field Day." It started with an intramural baseball game that was followed by many of the events that today commonly occur at a track and field meet: the 100-yard dash, the mile run, the two-mile walk, the hammer-throw, the high jump, the long jump, and the hop-skip and jump. But there were other contests among the Knox students that would not today occur at a track meet, such as the jumps with weights, or tumbling, or the 100-yard bicycle race, or the three-legged race, or the sack race, or the wheelbarrow race, or the potato race, the baseball throwing contest, the bayonet drill, and the closing event of the day, the "class pulls," in which teams of twelve men and a captain from each class competed in a tug of war. The sophomores won. Local business men donated prizes for all of the many winners. It was much fun for participants and entertaining for spectators, and to a large extent this "Olympic Day" was impromptu.[92]

Thomas Gold Frost of the class of 1886 had been a very active promoter of athletics during his years at Knox. He took them seriously all his life. Fifty years after his graduation he would write and publish a reminiscence of his years at Knox in which he bitterly criticized the president of Knox, Albert Britt, for not emphasizing athletic winning as much as good Knox men should. Already during his first year as an alumnus, Frost in April 1887 urged that better preparations be made for the "second annual celebration of 'Field Day' at 'Old Knox.' " It should include "hurdles, pole jumping, and putting the shot." It should be better organized. There should be better training in advance of the contests by the athletes. For this purpose Frost recommended the standards suggested by the president of the "Inter-Collegiate Association," whose rules, furthermore, ought to "govern in all contests."[93]

From Frost's reference to an "Inter-Collegiate Association" it was evident that an athletic bureaucracy that one day would govern scholastic institutions was already evolving. As late as October 1893 and October 1894 Knox sent to the Illinois Inter-Collegiate Oratorical contests not only an orator, but also teams for football, baseball, tennis, and track and field events.[94] However, on the Knox campus a special Athletic Association had been formed in the spring of 1881[95] and by the year 1886–87 such a local society had taken over from the original "Contests Association" the management of the local sports, including the scheduling of games and the selection of the teams.[96]

The beginnings of a similar separation at the intercollegiate level of organized athletic competition from oratory was initiated by Knox. The Knox *Coup D'Etat* in October 1889 made the following boast: "With pardonable pride, Knox claims the title of 'Mother of Western Inter-Collegiates.' Here many years ago was born the idea of oratorical contests . . . and here, October 8, 1889, under the auspices of the home association was organized the Illinois Athletic Association." Furthermore, from the profits of the recent Inter-Collegiate Oratorical Contest in Galesburg, the Knox men provided a "beautiful gold and silver cup, which will be presented to the new Illinois Inter-Collegiate Athletic Association . . . as a prize to be carried off annually by the college that excels in athletics."[97]

According to this new plan both the state oratorical society and the new state athletic association met at Bloomington in October 1890, Knox sending tennis, field and track, baseball, and football teams.[98]

A similar joint meeting of both associations occurred at Monmouth in October 1891,[99] but on this occasion this basic statewide structure began to break up. The eight students from the University of Illinois showed only a "boorish interest" in the oratory, and before the next annual October meeting the University of Illinois took the lead to form a separate "Western Inter-Collegiate Field Day."[100] Knox and other schools in the fall of 1891 formed an Illinois Inter-Collegiate Football League.[101] In October 1896 the "Board of Control" for athletics at Knox decided not to send Knox athletes to the annual October meeting for the first time since the formation of the Illinois Inter-Collegiate Athletic Association.[102] When the statewide oratorical meeting was held at Illinois Wesleyan that month, it was decided that hereafter athletics should no longer be associated with the oratorical contests.[103] Certainly by this time a plenitude of athletic contests were being scheduled in other ways and at other times. The Years of Old Siwash had already begun.

NOTES

1. Galesburg *Republican Register,* Sept. 11, 1886, 5; Sept. 18, 1886, 5.
2. *Ibid.,* Jan. 2, 1875.
3. Galesburg *Register Mail,* Dec. 6, 1933, 4.
4. Emmet Smith, "Field at Knox," *Knox Alumnus,* 14 (Apr. 1931), 195.
5. Frost, *Tales from the Siwash Campus,* 132.
6. Conrow, *Field Days,* 153.
7. Burgess, *Reminiscences,* 82; correspondence between Field and Edward P. Chambers during the summer of 1870 in Field Papers; Henry Read as reported in the *Knox Alumnus,* 20 (Jan.-Feb. 1937), 61; J. L. Pearce, *ibid.,* 20 (Mar.-Apr. 1937), 100–101; Smith, *ibid.,* 14 (Apr. 1931), 194; Galesburg *Republican,* Oct. 8, 1870, 1.
8. Pearce, *Knox Alumnus,* 20 (Mar.-Apr. 1937), 100–102; a somewhat variant account by Henry Read makes Field out to be the "Devil." See *ibid.,* 20 (Jan.–Feb. 1937), 61–63. A legend persisted for more than forty years about Field's chewing of tobacco in his Latin class, a habit sternly to be rebuked at any time anywhere. The Latin professor noticed a small roll of what appeared to be tobacco near Field's seat and inquired, grimly, "Quid est hoc?" Field disarmed the questioner with a quick reply. "Hoc est quid." *Knox Student,* Feb. 1, 1916, 4.
9. Hoffman, *Tales,* 20–22.
10. Galesburg *Republican,* Extra, June 21, 1870, 4.
11. Smith, *Knox Alumnus,* 14 (Apr. 1931), 195.
12. Adelphi Society, Program Minutes from Oct. 6, 1869, to Feb. 22, 1871, *passim.*
13. Wilson, "Howell's Unpublished Letters," 5–19.
14. Adelphi Society, Program Minutes, Feb. 8, 22, 1871. There is no mention of Field in these minutes after Feb. 22, 1871.
15. Burgess, *Reminiscences,* 80–83.
16. Sandburg, *Always the Young Strangers,* 117.
17. *Coup D'Etat,* May 1894, 1.
18. Galesburg *Republican Register,* Aug. 15, 1885, 3.
19. Galesburg *Republican,* Dec. 30, 1870, 1, 4.
20. Galesburg *Republican Register,* July 22, 1882, 5.
21. Recollection of Mina Weinberg Allensworth of the class of 1879 (file for the class of 1879, Knox College Library); James J. Needham, "Some Knox

Academic History," *Knox College Fifty Year Club Bulletin*, 36 (June 1953), 4–8.

22. Adelphi and Gnothautii societies, Business Meeting Minutes, *passim*.

23. *Ibid.*, Jan. and Feb. 1872, *passim*.

24. Gnothautii Society, Business Meeting Minutes, Feb. 13, 1872.

25. Prince, "Autobiography."

26. Askew, "Liberal Arts College Encounters Intellectual Change," 72. The "Forensics" file of the Knox Archives contains a program dated Oct. 18, 1877, with the following title: "Fifth Annual Oratorical Contest Between the Colleges of Illinois, in Union Hall, Monmouth, Illinois." This would place the first in this series in the year after the intercollegiate oratorical contest staged by the Gnothautii.

27. Gnothautii Society, Business Meeting Minutes, Sept. 25, 1872; Galesburg *Republican*, Nov. 2, 1872, 4; Dec. 21, 1872, 1; Jan. 25, 1873, 1.

28. Galesburg *Republican Register*, Feb. 22, 1873, 6.

29. *Ibid.*, June 12, 1873, 7; June 26, 1873, 4.

30. *Ibid.*, June 27, 1874, 3.

31. Adelphi Society, Business Meeting Minutes, Oct. 15, 22, Dec. 9, 1873.

32. Henry Read, quoted by Thos. C. Trueblood, who published a history of the Inter-State Oratorical contests in *Werner's Magazine*, Nov. 1897, that was extensively reprinted in the *Knox Student*, May 19, 1898, 1–2. This account conforms closely to an earlier statement that appeared in the *Knox Student*, Nov. 1881, 22. This was signed by "Knox Man," who was probably Read, who in 1881 was a member of the Knox faculty.

33. Galesburg *Republican Register*, Nov. 15, 22, 1873.

34. Frank Moulton to Frederic Bancroft, July 17, 1929, Bancroft Papers.

35. *Knox Student*, Nov. 1881, 22.

36. A good account of the Inter-State Oratorical contests was written by Wade Arnold: "College Hero Old Style" and published as a pamphlet by Knox College in 1948.

37. Galesburg *Republican Register*, Mar. 7, 1874, 3.

38. *Knox Student*, Nov. 1881, 22.

39. Galesburg *Republican Register*, Feb. 14, 1874, 3; Mar. 7, 1874, 3. Knox College *Gale*, 1888, 88; Faculty Minutes, Feb. 19, 1874.

40. Galesburg *Republican Register*, Apr. 11, 1874, 4; June 6, 1874, 4.

41. *Knox Student*, Oct. 1880, 15; Galesburg *Republican Register*, Oct. 16, 1880, 1; *Knox Fifty Year Club Bulletin*, 4 (June 1948), 4.

42. Calkins, *and Hearing Not*, 100–101.

43. Galesburg *Republican Register*, May 14, 1887, 2.

44. The oration was printed in full in *ibid.*, May 14, 1887, 2. It is more readily available in Prather, *Winning Orations*.

45. Galesburg *Republican Register*, May 7, 1887, 5.

46. *Ibid.*, May 7, 1887, 5; May 14, 1887, 6.

47. Calkins, *and Hearing Not*, 101; Frost, *Tales from the Siwash Campus*, ch. 4.

48. *Coup D'Etat*, May 1884, 115.

49. Sandburg, *Always the Young Strangers,* 303.

50. Galesburg *Republican Register,* Sept. 22, 1882, 1; *Coup D'Etat,* Mar. 1885, 99, 105; Knox catalogue for 1887–88, 38.

51. Galesburg *Republican Register,* Feb. 9, 1889, 1; Oct. 17, 1891, 10.

52. *Ibid.,* Apr. 12, 1890, 1; July 26, 1890, 6.

53. *Ibid.,* Christmas ed., 1887, 5; May 17, 1890, 5; Sept. 12, 1891, 1; Oct. 10, 1891, 7; *Knox Alumnus,* 2 (Feb. 1919), 87.

54. *Coup D'Etat,* Sept. 1897, 2.

55. *Oak Leaf,* 1 (Apr. 1857), 215–19.

56. D. H. Waterbury to George P. Davis, Oct. 19, 1859, MS, Knox College Library; Adelphi Society, Program Minutes, Jan. 11, 1861.

57. LMI, Minutes, Feb. 27, 1863.

58. Amelia Carey to her parents, Nov. 7, 1866, MS, Knox College Library.

59. *Pantheon,* 1 (1869–70), 33.

60. *Mischmasch,* 1870–71, 36–37.

61. Galesburg *Republican,* Dec. 17, 1870, 6.

62. Galesburg *Republican Register,* Sept. 30, 1876, 1; Oct. 14, 1876, 1; Nov. 11, 1876, 1, 3; June 28, 1879, 4.

63. *Knox Student,* Mar. 1878, 9.

64. Galesburg *Republican Register,* Dec. 7, 1878, 1.

65. *Ibid.,* June 28, 1879, 4.

66. *Ibid.,* Dec. 17, 1881, 6.

67. *Knox Alumnus,* 3 (Feb. 1920), 87.

68. Catalogue for 1886–87, 50.

69. Galesburg *Free Press,* Oct. 25, 1869, 1. Field is listed on the freshman team roster as the catcher.

70. As reported by Henry Read in the *Knox Alumnus,* 20 (Jan.-Feb. 1937), 61–62.

71. *Pantheon,* for 1869–70, 34–35; *Mischmasch,* for 1870–71, 43.

72. Frost, *Tales from the Siwash Campus,* 115. The pitcher for Lombard in the fall of 1872 was David Starr Jordan, a role which he recalled in his autobiography, *The Days of a Man,* 1:105.

73. Galesburg *Republican,* June 22, 1872, 3.

74. Frost, *Tales from the Siwash Campus,* 114.

75. *Ibid.,* 116–17. William Harvey's brother, Andrew M. Harvey, Knox, 1889, in a letter dated June 10, 1931, to Zens Smith, Galesburg, stated, "I think he was the first college pitcher in the West, if not in the whole country, that pitched the curved ball in college baseball competition." MS, Knox College Library. A biography prepared at the time of his death stated more cautiously that William Harvey "was credited by contemporaries as pitching the first curved ball in a baseball game that was ever seen in Galesburg" (George Harvey to Office of the President of Knox College, Nov. 23, 1950, MS, Knox College Library).

76. Frost, *Tales from the Siwash Campus,* 117–18. There is confusion in the chronology of these events. Harvey begins the narrative in *ibid.* by referring to a trip made in 1877 by the Knox baseball team to Jacksonville in

connection with the state oratorical contest for which Illinois College was the host. But the oratorical contest in 1877 was held not in Jacksonville but in Monmouth (Galesburg *Republican Register*, Oct. 27, 1877, 60). Furthermore, as related above, the first trip made by a Knox baseball team to Jacksonville occurred in 1879.

77. Rammelkamp, *Illinois College*, 283; *Knox Student*, Nov. 1879, 9, 15–16.

78. Galesburg *Republican Register*, Oct. 19, 1880, 1.

79. Rammelkamp, *Illinois College*, 26.

80. Solberg, *University of Illinois*, 313.

81. *Ibid.*

82. Galesburg *Republican Register*, May 7, 1881, 1.

83. Galesburg *Republican*, Oct. 19, 1872, 1.

84. *Pantheon*, 2 (1872–73), 84.

85. *Knox Student*, Dec. 1878, 14; Knox College catalogue for 1878–79, 54–58.

86. *Knox Student*, Nov. 1881, 21.

87. Frost, *Tales from the Siwash Campus*, 70.

88. Galesburg *Republican Register*, Oct. 1881, 6.

89. Frost, *Tales from the Siwash Campus*, 15, and *passim*.

90. *Coup D'Etat*, Nov. 1887, 44; Dec. 1887, 58.

91. Galesburg *Republican Register*, June 24, 1882, 1; Apr. 16, 1887, 5.

92. *Coup D'Etat*, June 1886, 158.

93. *Ibid.*, Apr. 1887, 120–21.

94. *Ibid.*, Oct. 1893, 28–32; Oct. 1894, 26–27, 31–33.

95. Galesburg *Republican Register*, Apr. 30, 1881, 6.

96. *Pantheon*, III (1888), 58.

97. *Coup D'Etat*, Dec. 1889, 50.

98. *Ibid.*, Oct. 1890, 31–34.

99. Galesburg *Republican Register*, Oct. 10, 1891, 12; Oct. 17, 1891, 6.

100. Solberg, *University of Illinois*, 381.

101. *Coup D'Etat*, Nov. 1891, 88; Dec. 1891, 52; *Knox Student*, Dec. 12, 1894, 1; Jan. 23, 1896, 1.

102. *Knox Student*, Oct. 1, 1896, 2.

103. *Ibid.*, Oct. 8, 1896, 6.

Old Main, 1857. When this building was restored in time for the Centenary in 1937, the multiple chimneys had long since come down and the battlements of the corner towers were no longer in evidence.

There are no good pictures extant of the East Bricks (1844), briefly called East College, and of West Bricks (1845), styled Williston Hall. Earnest Elmo Calkins made these models for the Centenary celebration, showing the location of the Bricks to Old Main.

𝕷𝕴𝕭𝕰𝕽𝕿𝖄 𝕷𝕴𝕹𝕰.
NEW ARRANGEMENT---NIGHT AND DAY.

The improved and splendid Locomotives, Clarkson and Lundy, with their trains fitted up in the best style of accommodation for passengers, will run their regular trips during the present season, between the borders of the Patriarchal Dominion and Libertyville, Upper Canada. Gentlemen and Ladies, who may wish to improve their health or circumstances, by a northern tour, are respectfully invited to give us their patronage.

SEATS FREE, *irrespective of color*.

Necessary Clothing furnished gratuitously to such as have *"fallen among thieves."*

" Hide the outcasts—let the oppressed go free."—*Bible.*

☞For seats apply at any of the trap doors, or to the conductor of the train.

J. CROSS, *Proprietor.*

N. B. For the special benefit of Pro-Slavery Police Officers, an extra heavy wagon for Texas, will be furnished, whenever it may be necessary, in which they will be forwarded as dead freight, to the " Valley of Rascals," always at the risk of the owners.

☞Extra Overcoats provided for such of them as are afflicted with protracted *chilly-phobia.*

George Washington Gale and the "proprietor" of the Underground Railroad had been under indictment for harboring runaway slaves when this cartoon was published by the organ of the Illinois Anti-Slavery Society.

Fellow travelers as delegates in 1843 to London, England, for the World Anti-Slavery Convention: first and second presidents of Knox College, *left,* Hiram H. Kellogg (1841-45) and *right,* Jonathan Blanchard (1845-58).

Beginning with the commencement of 1846, large gatherings for the College were convened in the colony church building, called First Church (top) until it was replaced by the great red sandstone structure, the Central Congregational Church (bottom), erected on the same site at the town square in 1898.

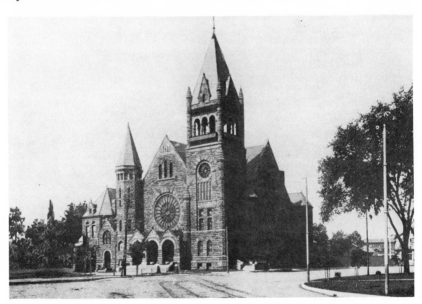

When this picture first appeared in the catalogue for 1863-64, the building was entitled Knox Female College. The next year it was named Knox Female Seminary. Differences over its status became critical between President William Stanton Curtis (1863-68) and Principal Ada Lydia Howard (1866-69), later the first president of Wellesley College.

Dr. John Van Ness Standish, a member of the Lombard College faculty, was a generous donor to Knox College. Among his gifts was his mansion, located where the Library was later built. He managed the improvement of the grounds adjacent to the campus, including the area named Standish Park.

Professor Milton L. Comstock, Knox's professor of mathematics and the physical sciences, at first believed that the curve ball did not exist. (He was later convinced!)

Alumni Hall. The Gnothautii's quarters were on the left, the Adelphi's on the right.

The Old Gym is Gone

(Air, "Old Grimes is Dead.")

GEORGE FITCH, '97.

The gym is gone, that good old gym,
We ne'er shall see it more.
'Twas made of plain unfinished boards
All battened up before.

A thousand years have passed away
Since first that gym was new.
Its sides were open as the day:
The wind blew gaily through.

What memories of the golden past
Its echoing walls awoke.
Its ancient roof was failing fast;
Its stove inclined to smoke.

Something it had for each to learn;
Some help it gave to all.
Its lockers weren't worth a durn;
Its mats were much too small.

Its sons went out to glorious deeds
And on to victory raced.
By carvings and facetious weeds
Its sides were much defaced.

The men of Knox its banner bore,
Nor knew the word "retreat."
Huge splinters graced its ancient floor
And hurt the freshmen feet.

What wealth of muscle and of brawn
It never failed to give !
Its window lights were mostly gone;
Its roof leaked like a sieve.

Right nobly through each college year
It did its duty o'er.
It had no stain on its career;
No handle on its door.

Full well we loved the good old shed
In spite of its decay.
Its outer paint had once been red;
'Twas fallen all away.

Upon its place some day shall loom
A structure grand and great.
Its gallery was short of room;
Its clubs were under weight.

Then let us weep o'er its demise,
Each loyal college man;
And honor it, although 'twas built
Upon a hay-barn plan.

Details of the construction of the old gymnasium were revealed when George Fitch, creator of Old Siwash, mourned its demolition.

A new gymnasium was erected in 1908, complete with battlements.

CHAPTER IV

YEARS OF RECOVERY

It was a "new departure"[1] for Knox College that Newton Bateman was not by profession a clergyman. A graduate from Illinois
College in Jacksonville, he had started and then given up theological studies at Lane Seminary to become a teacher and administra-
tor of schools. By the time he became president of Knox he was
the most widely known professional educator in the State of Illinois. Within fifteen years after his graduation from Illinois College
he had taught mathematics in a private school in St. Louis, been a
public school principal in Jacksonville, twice served as a county
commissioner, edited the *Illinois Teacher,* had become a leader in
the state teachers' organization, and supported the founding of the
Normal School, which was the first of the state-controlled institutions of higher education. In 1858, as a Republican, he was
elected to the relatively new state office of superintendent of public
instruction, which he held until 1875, except for the years 1863–
65. During these two years out of office he served as assistant
provost-marshal general.[2]

During his many years as state superintendent of public instruction he traveled widely throughout the state, observing the condition of its public schools and speaking to many teachers'
conferences and educational gatherings. After he became president
of Knox he remained in great demand for such occasions. In 1860
he began to publish a series of masterly biennial reports on the
Illinois school system, which were widely read beyond Illinois for
their information and comment on the content, method, and administration of public schools and their relations to political and
social conditions.[3] As superintendent of public instruction he sup-

ported the establishment of the state university at Champaign,[4] helped to plan its first educational program, and spoke at the inauguration ceremonies.

He was not able to assume fully his duties at Knox until March 1875, by which time the College had lacked unified leadership for almost three years and was in a feeble condition.[5] In his inaugural address Bateman reaffirmed the importance of the classical studies and what had been for many years the standard college curriculum. The most eloquent passages were those in which he pleaded for thrift, even austerity, in the conduct of College affairs. For Bateman it was a matter of plain honesty that the College should pay its bills as it went along. But Bateman's advocacy of fiscal responsibility went beyond rejection of imprudent frills or impressive but unneeded buildings. He wanted the life of the College to remain simple and unpretentious so that the most impoverished student would not be embarrassed by the tyranny of social customs that he could not afford:

College expenses may become practically prohibitive to this class of young men, without any formal action of the authorities, or any change in the fees and term bills. Extravagant social customs may be allowed to grow up among the students; class and society usages may impose their unwritten but imperative burdens upon the members; costly peculiarities of dress and other personal habits and accessories may assume the form of social laws, not to be evaded or infringed; other elegant and expensive usages and practices may gradually creep in, and become the settled order of college life. True, all these things are wholly outside of college requirements, and, in a sense, matters of class or individual option. But we all know how mandatory and even despotic social customs may become, especially in college communities, in some respects the most unique and peculiar in the world. So intensely true is this, that in some institutions it would scarcely require greater temerity, or involve more serious personal consequences, for a student to defy a written college law, than one of those unwritten but most exacting class or college customs. If these tendencies to lavish expenditures of money are not earnestly discountenanced, instead of being not seldom tacitly encouraged; and especially if there be that in the tone and spirit, the air and bearing, of the college regime itself, which affords a color of approval—then, not if such costly usages were enjoined by the college ordinances, would the sons of the indigent be more effectually excluded from those institutions. . . . While colleges are for all, without distinction, and all are equally welcome; and while the priceless boon of a true culture is intrinsically the same to rich and poor, there is a sense in which a liberal education is the especial hope and refuge of the indigent.[6]

This deeply felt preference for a plain style of living was rooted in Bateman's youth on the Illinois frontier. While studying to prepare himself for college, he lived in the hollow of a great old elm eleven feet in diameter that was warmed by the fire burning outside his study "door."[7] In Galesburg he lived in simple dignity in a house on West North Street just beyond the limits of the original village—in the home that had formerly belonged to Chief Justice Charles Lawrence—in a setting of tall trees and shrubs that Bateman called his "farm." Certainly the manner of his life contrasted sharply with the smart style of his predecessor, Dr. John P. Gulliver, who had a taste for fast horses. The "venerable Doctor" had horses of another kind: "Ned was as sedate in harness as was his master who held the reins . . . never fast except when fast to a post. One day, overtaking Mr. George Davis, the treasurer of the College, and noted for his dry Scotch-Irish wit, the president invited him to ride. 'Thank you,' was Mr. Davis' reply, 'but I'm in a bit of a hurry this morning.' "[8]

President Bateman had the advantage of his wide familiarity with the state Republicans, with the men who for many years dominated the major political party in Illinois. His personal knowledge of Abraham Lincoln, whom he had gotten to know well in the Illinois state house, was the theme of a reminiscent and memorial address that was often in demand. During the first February of his presidency at Knox he started the custom of honoring Lincoln's birthday. His continuing political activity was evident in his appointment to the Illinois State Board of Health, which regulated the practice of medicine in the state and licensed physicians, from 1877 to 1891. In 1878 President Rutherford B. Hayes appointed him to the national Assay Commission. In 1882 it was even rumored that he might again be candidate for superintendent of public instruction.[9]

One may perceive Bateman's appreciation of men in the public sector of higher education in the election to the Knox Board of Trustees of Dr. Richard Edwards, who was the principal of the

Normal School at Normal, Illinois, from 1862 to 1876. Edwards was elected to the Knox board in 1877 and served as its vice-president from 1881 to 1892. Upon retirement from Normal he became a Congregational minister at Princeton, Illinois, but he frequently addressed gatherings such as teachers' institutes throughout the state. His family was deeply involved in Knox affairs, one son being graduated in 1878, another in 1883; a third was on the faculty from 1879 to 1881 teaching logic, rhetoric, and English literature.[10] In 1884 the father was hired by Knox to serve as its "general agent," promoting the cause of Knox, raising money, and encouraging students to come to Knox.[11] He was still serving Knox in this capacity when in 1886 the Republican state convention nominated him for Bateman's old job as state superintendent of public instruction, to which Edwards was elected the following fall.[12] It was the proud boast of a very "regular" Knox Republican, Robert Mather of 1882, that this Knox trustee rescued the office from "the gutter of politics in which it had been the football of demagogues" and restored it to the place of honor and respected leadership that it had held when Bateman was the superintendent.[13]

Bateman's wide familiarity with the state's Republicans helped him to procure for Knox a professorship of military science. This required a federal law enlarging the assignment of officers to educational institutions. For this purpose Bateman sought the assistance of Lincoln's eldest son, Robert, who was now secretary of war, and of Senator John A. Logan, with whom Bateman had campaigned, and of Shelby M. Cullom, the recent governor of Illinois who had just become the junior Senator of the state. As a consequence Knox was the only small college to which military details were assigned among those allotted to universities.[14] It was also politically meaningful that the first army office detailed to be professor of military science at Knox was a brother to Mrs. Clark E. Carr, wife of a leading local politician. This new faculty member was First Lieutenant Stephen C. Mills, a recent West Point graduate who had seen some service fighting Indians on the frontier.[15]

The "Knox College Military Department" was officially established by the executive committee of the Board of Trustees on January 23, 1885. It is significant that at first much of the argument for this new College department was the "good, healthy exercise" that it would provide in "straightening out the backs that are bent over the study table." In the College catalogue the description of the military program was listed under the general heading of "Physical Education," and the primary argument given for it was the health of the students.[16] Whether all students agreed with this rationale may be doubted. Already in September 1885 "inquiries" were "being made as to whether military drill is to be allowed to kill out baseball and every other physical sport."[17]

At first becoming one of the "Cadets" was entirely voluntary, but those that "enlisted" were required to attend "military drill." By September 1892, however, "the drill for Sophomores and Freshmen" had become "compulsory, in fact, as well as name." There were indications of some student unhappiness with this situation, and at least one student left the College "because he objected to compulsory drill in the cadet corps."[18]

The Knox Cadets were in great demand for civic events such as Memorial Day, for College celebrations, and for special occasions such as the parade that honored President Benjamin Harrison when he laid the cornerstone for Alumni Hall. The nearest contact they probably had with actual military action was to march to the depot in the spring of 1886 to welcome home the members of Company C of the Illinois National Guard that was based in Galesburg. Company C, which included seven Knox students, had for sixteen days guarded the freight house in East St. Louis of the C.B.&.Q. during a strike. Much was made over this service which they rendered to their state, and the Knox Cadets escorted them back to their place of mustering out. A speech of gratitude was made by "Col." Clark E. Carr.[19]

It should be noted that Bateman added a professor of military science to the Knox faculty at the expense of the government. The frugality that Bateman had promised in his inaugural address was always maintained. Thus in 1877 he reiterated "that debts should not be contracted unless the means for paying are either in hand or in sight." Getting and keeping the College out of debt was a moral obligation to him. Within months after he became active as the president of Knox, trustees of Knox launched a drive to raise $50,000 among the citizenry of Galesburg, with Chauncey Colton subscribing $5,000 and O. T. Johnson pledging $2,500 to the total of $14,000 that was promised at the opening of the campaign at a dinner in the Union Hotel in July 1875. Six months later about $34,000 had been pledged.[20]

In September 1875, when Bateman was beginning his first full year on the campus, he summarized the situation at Knox to a reporter of the Chicago *Tribune*. Knox was "undenominational," and he, Bateman, preferred that it should remain so. Its fiscal assets were as follows: buildings and grounds worth $120,000; productive investment fund of $120,000. Income from this fund plus tuition was about $20,000. The College owned within the city 350 lots and also "outlying acre property" of 4,000 acres with a combined value of $200,000.[21]

The total enrollment of both College and Female Seminary for the year 1875–76 was eighty-five students. During Bateman's last year as president (1891–92) that number had tripled to 254 in the College alone, there being no longer a separate female school. Out of the Seminary, furthermore, there had developed a Conservatory of Music, which in 1891–92 enrolled 243 students. Early in Bateman's administration it was already evident that the College enrollment more nearly reflected tuition income because the twenty-five-year scholarship granted to the original colonists of Galesburg were now being exhausted. Thus in September 1877, when it was noticed that there was an "unprecedented number of first day attendants, in the history of the college," it was also noted that "no fewer than 150 students prepaid their tuition in full for the term, a fact equally unprecedented with the other."[22]

By June 1881 the finances of Knox could be described as "excellent," but enlarged enrollments were stretching its capacity to fulfill academic needs. The opening issue of the student paper the next fall, edited by Samuel McClure, described the Seminary building as "filled" and the dining room as "simply crowded." McClure pointed out a need for more dormitories, a chapel, society halls, and a "fireproof building" for libraries and the museum. "Most of all," stressed McClure, "we need more professors."[23]

But Bateman remained reluctant to add to the number of the College faculty and its size remained pretty much the same until the latter years of his presidency. At the opening of the year 1882–83 there were still only eight College faculty members, including Bateman himself, and half of these were themselves Knox alumni. Among the recent appointments from other institutions was Melvina Bennett, instructor in elocution, who deserved much of the fame Knox earned for its frequent champions in oratory. A series of able men for relatively short periods of time taught rhetoric and literature in combination with subjects such as logic or political economy. Two of them would later achieve great distinction as scholarly writers:[24] Professor Melville Anderson (1881–86) and Jeremiah Jenks (1886–89). Anderson and Jenks both were greatly admired by the Knox students.[25]

Bateman's thrift in personnel matters was well exemplified by the fact that throughout his presidency the College professorship in Latin was never filled because the teaching could be done by Professor Albert Hurd in addition to his classes in chemistry and natural science. The trustees in January 1884 did offer Hurd additional pay for his Latin teaching, but Hurd accepted it only with the stipulation that he could spend the extra money "in bettering the condition of the museum."[26]

Bateman fully appreciated how much the College owed to Hurd and to Milton Comstock and George Churchill, the three men who in effect comprised the nucleus of the College community. In an address before the Chicago alumni in 1884 Bateman paid this tribute:

> You know them well, their devotion, their fidelity, their abounding labors. Upon them rested the responsibility of sustaining Knox College, through all her vicissitudes and trials, and most nobly have they fulfilled their trust. With quiet courage and unshaken faith they kept right on. When others were ready to falter, they did not despond. But for their cheerful fortitude, unselfish devotion, and willing sacrifices, I know not what may have become of Knox College. To it they have given the dew of their youth and the strength of their manhood, and there they are today, in the grand maturity of their powers, teaching as many hours in the day as the common district schoolmaster—one of them still doing double duty with no additional compensation—all patiently waiting for that increase of resources which will permit the needed reduction of hours, and the concentration of their powers upon their respective departments.[27]

One of Bateman's most important achievements was to persuade Maria Whiting in 1879 to become principal of the Knox Female Seminary. For thirteen years she had been well established as instructor and manager of the Institution for the Blind in Janesville, Wisconsin.[28] Quickly she became not only the well-regarded matron-mother of the Seminary girls but also the energetic prompter of improvements in their educational facilities. Early in 1885 she offered to donate $5,000 of her own money and to raise subscriptions for another $5,000, which would pay for most of the cost of a wing to the east of the Seminary, "for use next fall if possible."[29] This was the first substantial addition to the Knox buildings in nearly thirty years, if one excepts the rather shedlike gymnasium the students had built in 1876. The wing was named Whiting Hall in recognition of her "labors and liberality . . . business tact and enterprise and energy."[30] It was the first building at Knox heated by steam,[31] a feature that was soon extended to the older part of the Seminary.[32] The fourth and uppermost floor became the library, reading room, hall, and dressing room for the ladies of the LMI, and for these quarters they raised the money to make it their own property. The ground floor provided for a new dining room and kitchen. On the first floor would be a new chapel and additional music rooms. The building was nearly completed by the winter of 1885–86, and in justification of Whiting's expectations at the opening of school in 1887 "all the Seminary rooms had been engaged, causing many young ladies to find accommodations in town."[33]

Much of the growth of the enrollment during the 1880s occurred by the development in the Seminary of an autonomous and self-supporting Conservatory of Music. Musical activities had always been an important part of the life of the Galesburg colony, but the very first formal training in music at Knox was provided in 1848 as part of a "systematic course of a female course of education" that became the Female Collegiate Department, or, as it was more commonly called, the Female Seminary. Music along with art and French was one of the "Ornamental Branches" that were "extra" to the regular curriculum. Later they would be listed in the female section of the catalogue under the heading of "Accomplishments." Until the mid-1870s music was something taught at Knox by women to women, a solitary exception being Charles Fuhrman, a male Bavarian whom Knox shared with Lombard in 1859 and 1860.[34] Little is known about the women who taught music for relatively short terms in the Seminary; often they were themselves graduates of the Seminary. It is not at all certain that they were better qualified than some of the dozen music teachers who were available as private teachers in the town by 1860; most of them were young single women living at home, though four of them were male heads of families: one from Connecticut, one from Sweden, one from Saxe-Coburg, one from Kentucky.[35] The Kentuckian, L. B. Miller, and Fuhrman had by the late 1860s established an Academy of Music in a hall downtown, where private instruction and regular participation in musical groups were available.[36]

President Gulliver, as part of his general effort to upgrade the quality of the departments at Knox quickly, in 1870 brought to the Seminary "Madame" Mary Ives Seymour. She was a former pupil and protégé of the distinguished American pianist and composer, Louis Moreau Gottschalk. She was respected for her very competent musicianship; she had "a magnificent presence and courtly manner"; she was generous with her performances; and for some time she was greatly admired by Galesburg society, just as she obviously fascinated the young men on the campus. During the first December of her residence in Galesburg she presented not only an exhibition of "musical gymnastics" by both the young men and the young women but also staged a Christmas concert by the "Music Department of Knox College and Seminary." This title is significant, for the program included performances by men as well as by women, by a St. George Society as well as by a St. Cecelia Society. This indication that music had become a coeducational activity at Knox was also evident in the solo appearances by two men, one a son of President Gulliver and the other Eugene Field.[37] Field was one of the six men enrolled with thirty-eight women in the "Class in Music." Men had for the first time been listed in this class in the catalogue for 1869–70, the men being named at the end of the class list as a kind of editorial afterthought recording the enrollment for a course that was still part of the Female Seminary.

Rather suddenly, the executive committee of the Board of Trustees, in February 1871, dismissed Seymour and asked her "to leave the Seminary at once," on the grounds of the "embarrassment and dissatisfaction" that she had brought the College.[38] The best explanation of how she had brought "embarrassment" to the College is that of Earnest Elmo Calkins, who would as a youth have been well acquainted with the young men who were in College while Seymour was on the faculty: " 'Madame' Seymour had beauty and that undefinable charm sometimes coarsely described as sex appeal. She brought to the town a flavor of cosmopolitanism . . . and must have seemed to those staid burgers a creature from another world . . . and the trustees were unable to adjust themselves to so vivid a personality."[39]

For nearly seven years after the dismissal of Seymour, music received sparse attention. Revitalization came with Carl Laux, who was one of those German intellectuals who as fugitives from the aftermath of the Revolution of 1848 greatly enriched the culture of the United States. He had been born in Rhenish Bavaria in 1821 and at the age of eighteen was already teaching music. After his arrival in the United States he became director of music in a ladies' seminary in New Haven, Connecticut. He would later tell Knox students that he had a share in starting a music department at Yale University. In 1859 he came west to Waukegan, Illinois, and after the Civil War resided in Quincy and Canton until he came to Galesburg in 1873. A city directory of 1877 shows that the Laux family lived at the northeast corner of Losey and Pearl streets, and at this address he and his daughter, Emelia, were advertised as "Music Teachers."[40]

In 1874 a daughter, Adele, enrolled at Knox, the first of four children to attend the Academy or Seminary or College, all of whom would participate in Knox musical activities. The oldest son in the family, Adolphe, who worked as a bookkeeper, also served as one of the important musicians in the city. He succeeded his father as the organist of the Universalist Church when the former became the organist of the First Church in January 1878. Thus, these two members of the Laux family became well known to students both from Lombard and Knox. Adolphe organized and directed an orchestra, which the Methodists might procure for a church program, but which others might use for dancing at Laux Hall. He played the organ for choral concerts directed by his father and made his talents available for affairs promoted by the Knox students, even though he was never one of them.[41]

Carl Laux quickly established himself as a leading musician in the city. Within three years of his arrival he had become organist of the church associated with Lombard College, and in January 1876 he was leading rehearsals of Haydn's *Creation* for the choral society of the Galesburg Academy of Music. The next year he directed a presentation by the Galesburg Philharmonic Society of the *Oratorio of Elijah* by Mendelssohn in the Opera House. Fortunately, reviews by Professor Comstock provide the historian good accounts of this musical event. Adolphe Laux was the organist. There was an orchestra of eight musicians. Of the seven soloists, four were from the Knox community.[42]

Soon after he took over direction of the music department in 1878 Professor Laux called a meeting of the students "of all departments" in the College chapel. At this gathering he "stated that music should be *studied* at Knox College"—the italics are those of the editor of the *Knox Student* and presumably reflect the emphasis on *"studied"* made by Laux. He expressed the hope that "the music box" in the chapel would soon "give way to a 'pipe organ' " and declared his intention of establishing "musical societies" at Knox.[43].

Knox shared the services of Laux with St. Mary's School in Knoxville, the founder and head of which was the Reverend Charles Wesley Leffingwell, who had been graduated from Knox in 1862. Laux became music director there about the same time that he joined the Knox faculty. When the girls of St. Mary's gave their annual concert in June 1879, the public was informed of the thoroughness of the education they received from Laux: "All his pupils are instructed in the theory, as well as the practice of music, and are taught the great principles of harmony, and are greatly aided by Prof. Laux's own work, the Outlines of Harmony."[44]

The catalogue for 1878–79 listed, as it had for years, a "Class in Music," but for the first time there was a record of some differentiation in the subject matter being taught. A special note indicated that there was a "Harmony Class" with twenty-six members, and an "Elementary Singing Class" with sixty-five members, and "The Advanced Singing Class and Beethoven Society" with seventy-four members. The Beethoven Society was organized in January 1879, with an initial membership of fifty-two students "for the purpose of promoting the thorough culture of Music in Knox College." The president of this society and two other officers were men in the College; the vice-president and secretary were women in the Seminary. Their society hall was a large room on the main floor of the Seminary building that formerly had been used as a chapel for the Seminary. Here they met each Thursday afternoon.[45]

In late May 1879 the "pupils" of Professor Laux presented a "Recital"; then in June the Beethoven Society staged a concert, the proceeds from which were for the "Great Organ Fund of Knox College." Admission was twenty-five cents. The first part of the concert consisted of ten vocal and piano numbers, all by women except for performances by quartets from the Adelphi and from the EOD, a men's literary society in the Academy. Two of Laux's daughters sang a duet and were part of a vocal trio. An overture for two pianos with eight hands opened the concert; a "grand duo" for two pianos came just before the intermission. Then the Beethoven Society rendered the "Spring" portion from Haydn's *The Seasons*. It was an impressive event. The opening paragraph in the report in the *Register Mail* made this significant comment about Professor Laux's achievement: "It was no little thing for Professor Laux to attempt the formation of a musical department as a distinct addition to Knox College. But this endeavor the Professor made; and now everything betokens its ultimate success."[46]

As promised in the catalogue published in the summer of 1879, the Beethoven Society in the spring of 1880 presented Haydn's *Creation*. Unfortunately, this was Professor Laux's last major production while on the Knox faculty, for at the end of the academic year he resigned, intending to move to Knoxville, where his time would be "entirely devoted to the musical instruction of the pupils of St. Mary's School." His connections with Knox were not, however, altogether cut off. In May 1883 he was the "Musical Director" for a performance in the Galesburg Opera House of Handel's *Messiah* by the Galesburg Philharmonic Society, comprising a chorus of eighty voices. Of the four soloists both men were from Knox, the tenor, Professor Harry C. Brooks, who was then the instructor in music at Knox, and the bass, Edwin Wyckoff, a student at Knox who had sung solos for *The Seasons* and for the *Creation* under Laux's direction. The piano was played by Harriet Adams, who had been a Knox student and who had taught music at Knox in 1881–82. The organ was played by Edward Quincy Adams, who had been graduated from Knox in 1873 and who

was the organist at the First Congregational Church, immediately
north of the Seminary. The orchestra was directed by Charles
Lindolft, who would be on the Knox music faculty from 1883 to
1885. Though it may not be said that this was a premiere performance of this very popular oratorio, it was regarded in the community not only as a musical but also as a civil triumph. Between the
first and second parts of the performance, the special importance
of the occasion was noted by the leading citizen of the city, Clark
E. Carr, who came down from the gallery to speak to the distinguished assemblage. He spoke of the special "debt" that the community owed to those "pioneers in the musical arts," Samuel
Bacon, Fuhrman, and Miller. He particularly noted what the community owed to the musical talents of its "gifted women." And to
express the appreciation of the citizens to Laux for the performance of the *Messiah* on which the chorus had been practicing since
the previous January, Carr presented the director with a gold-
headed cane.[47]

The effort that Laux had made for a more diversified department, with more demanding emphasis on the study of music, languished. Critics complained that vocal music was neglected after
Laux left. The students themselves reorganized the Beethoven Society in January 1882 and actually started to rehearse Sigmund
Romberg's *The Lay of the Bell*, a work that Laux had previously
presented at the Galesburg Opera House on February 28, 1878. A
soloist at that time had been Wyckoff. He was then only eighteen
years old and was just beginning his six years of study at the Knox
Academy and College. It was he who attempted the unsuccessful
revival by students of Romberg's work in 1882. His unusual musical talent was evident in his role as organist and as director of
the choir in the Old First Church while still a college student.
Under Wyckoff's direction this choir, during his junior year, presented a concert including a cantata entitled "The Magic Wall."
Wyckoff was the organist. He was assisted at the piano and in
certain vocal numbers by Professor Brooks, who had joined the
Knox faculty in September 1882.[48]

The coming of Brooks as "Instructor in Instrumental and Vocal
Music" was welcomed by a student magazine as an indication that
the field of music would now be better nurtured. Brooks was a
graduate from Oberlin, where he had had "the benefit of a thor-

ough course in the Oberlin Conservatory of Music." The Oberlin connection with Knox, which was to be very apparent from now on in the history of music at Knox, had more than artistic significance, for Oberlin had sectarian, evangelical, and humanitarian antecedents that were identical with those of Knox. Both colleges were founded about the same time and in their respective states had similar educational roles. Oberlin had been the leading pioneer in coeducation. In 1865 it had started what was to be one of the oldest conservatories of the nation. A Galesburg newswriter in 1882 spoke of it as "well and favorably known." When Brooks's appointment at Knox was announced, this reporter also explained that Knox too would now have a Conservatory: "Mr. Brooks proposes to lay the foundations of the Musical Department so broad that it will some day develop into a Conservatory of Music, an announcement that will please those of our readers fond of music. Such a department is much needed here, music, and especially instruction in vocal music, being as dead as an Egyptian mummy."[49] This idea of "an established music department" or "Conservatory" reflected also the aspirations of Maria Whiting, who since 1879 had been principal of the Female Seminary.[50] Brooks was an "efficient teacher," and "under his conscientious care the music class of the College was larger than ever before," but like so many of his predecessors he did not return the next year.[51]

Nevertheless in the autumn of 1883 a Conservatory was started at Knox, "patterned after that of Oberlin." At the opening of the College in September the "department of music" was staffed by Lepha A. Kelsey and Florence E. Sperry. These teachers had "been selected with the advice and strong recommendation of Professor Rice, Director of the Oberlin Conservatory of Music."[52] Sperry was to be "Instructor in Piano and Harmony"; Kelsey was "Instructor in Piano and Voice." It was Kelsey who took the lead in designing a "systematic course of instruction in music." Late in November 1883 President Bateman presented to the executive committee of the Board "the question of Inaugurating a Musical Conservatory in connection with the College as outlined by a communication from the young ladies having charge of that department of the institution." On December 3, 1883, the trustees concurred in the "establishing of a Conservatory under the direction of our present musical instructors, Misses Kelsey & Sperry." It was stipulated, however, that this should be done "without any extra expense to the College."[53]

A "Circular" dated December 10, 1883, indicated that Kelsey would be "Director"; it advertised that the next term would begin January 3, 1884, and described the course requirements in music theory as well as the lessons in vocal and instrumental music. Much of the instruction would be in classes that were to be limited to two persons in vocal and instrumental lessons. Because of the "marked diversities of different pupils in talent, and in habits of application," no "fixed limits of time" were prescribed for "completing the courses in Piano, Organ, Singing, and Violin," but it was anticipated that three to four years would be required before the student had earned his or her diploma.[54] In addition to the two women, the other members of the Conservatory faculty were an "Instructor in Violin," Charles A. Lindolft, and an "Instructor in Pipe Organ," Edwin Wyckoff.

Lindolft came from a Galesburg family that lived near the center of town. He was much admired as an accomplished musician. There were only two violin students for him at Knox this year, but on May 6, 1884, his friends staged a "benefit for him that he" might "pursue his musical studies." The musicians who helped in this project included a soprano from Galva, a flutist from Kewanee, and Professor Laux, who was now teaching at St. Mary's in Knoxville. Accordingly Lindolft was able to renew his studies in Cincinnati, at the Jacobsohn School of Music, from which he had been graduated in 1880.

Wyckoff, whose musical activities as a student have already been noted, was a member of the senior class during the year that the Conservatory was founded. His brother, Charles, had that fall already brought further laurels to his musically talented family by winning the Illinois Inter-Collegiate Oratorical Contest. He would win the Inter-State championship the next spring. For Edwin Wyckoff, the eldest child, the musical experience at Knox as a student and as a pipe organ teacher would lead to a career as a church and concert organist, as supervisor of music in public schools, and as a composer.[55]

The trustees had cautiously indicated that the Conservatory plan should be given a one-year trial. It was very successful.

Though only two men enrolled for violin lessons, nine women enrolled for "Harmony," thirty-six women enrolled for "Voice Culture," and sixty-one women and one man enrolled for the "Class in Piano." Four new pianos were added, and a "circulating musical library" helped to lessen the "incidental" expenses of the students.

The growing popularity of music at Knox was shown in October 1884, when a Knox band went along with the baseball team to the annual Inter-Collegiate Oratorical Contest, held this time at Lincoln, Illinois. The organization for oratorical competition was still the primary means for arranging athletic competition. An effort was made to add a band contest to the other events. Though this failed as a permanent project, on this occasion there was a contest between the bands of Knox and of the state university at Champaign, the latter winning the prize of $25 because it "had the advantage in number of pieces."[56] This was very likely the first intercollegiate competition of this kind in the state.

During its second year enrollments in piano, vocal, and harmony lessons held up very well, with some slight increase in the number of men listed for these classes; the number of students of the violin increased from two to seven, all but one being men. The size of enrollment in music classes was particularly critical because the Conservatory was expected to make its own way financially. Not until after World War I would the trustees assume "financial responsibility of the music department or Conservatory." The Conservatory made a "small payment" for use of the rooms that it needed, this rent amounting at first to $500 a year. The director of the Conservatory hired all teachers, guaranteeing them a "certain salary, with a share in their earnings over and above their guaranteed salary," he receiving the entire income from the department and paying all the bills in connection therewith. After the Female Seminary ceased to have a separate educational program in 1890 and the building itself came to be called Whiting Hall, the accounts for such matters as buying and selling pianos, repairs, and fees for practice hours were handled by the director instead of the principal of the Seminary.[57]

It was this kind of financial autonomy that led to the relinquishment of the directorship by Kelsey in the fall of 1885. She had appointed William F. Bentley as instructor in piano, organ, and harmony, and he presumed that she had been acting for the College authorities. But when he arrived he discovered that his warm welcome by the "College authorities" did not mean that they would pay his salary. Instead Kelsey was "personally responsible" for that. The enrollment in his classes "was far from promising." This so worried her that Bentley, in October of the first term, proposed to her "that if she would resign" he "would release her from" his contract.[58] As he became the director he would then pay her "the salary she had guaranteed" to him. Thus began the role of leadership by Bentley in the Conservatory and then in the department of music that, with one interruption of two years, would last for half a century, until 1936, when he died in an automobile accident while on a trip with the College choir.

Bentley had been graduated from the Oberlin Conservatory in 1883 and then for two years at the New Lyme Conservatory in Ohio. At Knox he immediately impressed students with his contagious enthusiasm and amazing energy, traits that would still be noted by an undergraduate forty years later. He started a Conservatory orchestra; by the second term he had inaugurated two "singing classes," one, a "class for beginners" with 120 members, the other, an "advanced class" with seventy members, each meeting once a week. He played the "wheezy cabinet organ" at chapel, but he also was organist for the recently rebuilt instrument at the First Church, where he also became director of the choir.[59] Matching the greater interest in music, the Adelphi in April of Bentley's first year brought to the city one of the most ambitious musical offerings it had ever attempted in its lectures and concert series. This was the "Emma Abbot Grand Opera Company," presenting *Mignon*.[60] The audience was one of the largest ever seen in the Galesburg Opera House. The next month the Knox Conservatory of Music brought Mme. Rive-King, advertised as "the greatest lady pianist in the world."[61] And in June Olive Barnes became the "first graduate of the Knox Conservatory of Music."

In 1887 Bentley and Kelsey interrupted their teaching to study for two years in Leipzig, Germany. During the past decades such departures tended to be permanent, disrupting the continuity of the music education at Knox and spoiling gains that had been made toward a strong music program. But this time Bentley returned to resume his teaching and his role of director of the Conservatory. Joining him on the faculty when he returned in the autumn of 1889 were two women from the Oberlin Conservatory, Adele Matthews and Susan Kellogg Clisbee. Matthews was at Knox only one year, teaching piano and voice, but Clisbee remained on the faculty at Knox for more than twenty years teaching violin and viola and later theory. She had studied at the Oberlin Conservatory for three years before coming to Knox and in 1892 and 1894 studied privately in Berlin. Another graduate from Oberlin, John Winter Thompson, joined the faculty in 1890. He had also studied at Leipzig, with Gustav Schreck. At Knox he taught organ and theory and composed and published organ works, motets, anthems, and a *Course in Harmony* (Boston, 1923).[62] He was on the Knox faculty for forty-eight years, all but two of them as a colleague of Bentley.

Toward the end of the school year 1889–90 the first catalogue of the Knox Conservatory of Music was published, a pamphlet of sixteen pages. The number of students enrolled in music that year had reached 217. The numbers continued to increase with relative consistency even when enrollment in the College and the Academy was falling off. In 1903, twenty years after the Conservatory had been started, when the enrollment was 377 students, it was noted that it was "almost the largest musical school outside a great city."[63]

The transformation of a rather faltering music program into a strong Conservatory probably best exemplified how much stronger Knox became under Bateman's leadership. During his latter years he was truly revered in the community for his intelligence, industry, patience, and geniality. Bateman retained his friendship with officials of the state school system and the leaders of the Republican party, his faculty at Knox improved, and most students acquired a very deep affection for Bateman. His weekly chapel talks were carefully composed and read in a resonant voice with recurring periods of moving eloquence that carried to the far corners of an auditorium. Often townspeople came to hear them, and frequently they were fully reported in a local newspaper. Though he had not followed the plan of his youth to become a minister, there was much about his appearance, including his manner of dress, that suggested that he was a clergyman. His head was very large and well shaped and surrounded with hair and beard that as it whitened made him look like what he indeed was, a patriarch. He was sturdily built, and his short stature in no way detracted from his native dignity. There was a saying often repeated that Lincoln had spoken of him as "my little friend, the big schoolmaster."

During his first years he had been very cautious not to burden the shaky financial structure of the College with any extensive capital expenditures. During his later years as president he was able to supervise the construction of four new buildings: the east wing of the Female Seminary in 1885 and a west wing in 1892; an astronomical observatory in 1888; and the Alumni Building in 1889–90 with its halls for the Adelphi and the Gnothautii. Financially the College was now receiving steady though very modest contributions from its alumni: altogether about $23,000 between 1875 and 1890. Moreover, two friends of the College made substantial donations. One of these was the bequest of about $60,000 from Henry Hitchcock, who was a member of the Board of Trustees from 1872 until his death in 1884. He had come to Galesburg to serve as division superintendent of the C.B.&.Q. The Hitchcock bequest was used to endow a professorship of mathematics. In 1892 the College received a gift of real estate in Chicago (worth about $30,000 when it was sold in 1913) from Daniel Kimball Pearsons.[64] It was used to endow a classics professorship in the name of the Reverend Flavel Bascom, who had been influential in procuring this gift for the College. Bascom served on the Knox board from 1845 to 1884 and had been pastor of the original colony church during the 1850s. It is helpful to evaluate such gifts by noting that for the year 1891–92 the annual expenses of the College were about $28,000 and that tuition income was about $11,000.[65]

NOTES

1. Galesburg *Republican Register*, July 4, 1874, 6.
2. Simonds, "Newton Bateman."
3. Samuel Willard, "Memorial of Newton Bateman," *Coup D'Etat*, Feb. 1891, 141–51.
4. Rammelkamp, *Illinois College*, 239.
5. Galesburg *Republican Register*, Jan. 16, 1875, 6; Mar. 27, 1875, 1; Jan. 1, 1876, 1.

6. Knox College, *Inauguration of Newton Bateman.*

7. *Pantheon,* III (1888), 18–21.

8. Simonds, "Newton Bateman," 36.

9. Galesburg *Republican Register,* Feb. 19, 1876, 1; Dec. 8, 1877, 1; June 17, 1882, 3; Simonds, "Newton Bateman," 32.

10. Galesburg *Republican Register,* Oct. 16, 1886, 3; May 22, 1880, 1.

11. Executive Committee Minutes, Sept. 15, 1884, 65, state that his salary was $3,000. He was rehired in Oct. 1885, but at a reduced salary of $2,000. The Reverend J. M. Cracraft, D.D., had served the College as an agent in 1878 at a salary of $1,200 (Executive Committee Minutes, June 29, July 6, 1878).

12. Galesburg *Republican Register,* Christmas ed., 1885, 7; Sept. 11, 1886, 9; *Coup D'Etat,* Dec. 1888, 57.

13. Robert Mather, "Knox in Politics," a speech delivered at the annual dinner of the Knox Alumni Association of Chicago, Apr. 26, 1893, and printed in the *Gale* of 1894, 62–63.

14. Executive Committee Minutes, Dec. 13, 1883; Jan. 7, Mar. 3, 1884. Simonds, "Newton Bateman," 30.

15. *Coup D'Etat,* Dec. 1888, 57; Nov. 1884, 39.

16. Executive Committee Minutes, Jan. 23, 1885; *Coup D'Etat,* Nov. 1884, 39; Knox catalogue for 1889–90, 57.

17. Galesburg *Republican Register,* Sept. 19, 1885, 5.

18. *Coup D'Etat,* Nov. 1884, 39; Sept. 1892, 13; Galesburg *Republican Register,* Oct. 10, 1885, 5; *Knox Student,* summer ed., 1895, 3.

19. Galesburg *Republican Register,* Apr. 24, 1886, 4–5; May 1, 1886, 6; May 8, 1886, 1; May 15, 1886, 2.

20. *Ibid.,* July 28, 2877, 2; July 13, 1880, 2; July 3, 1875, 4; Feb. 19, 1876, 6.

21. *Ibid.,* Sept. 3, 1875, 3.

22. *Ibid.,* Sept. 15, 1877, 5.

23. *Ibid.,* June 25, 1881, 8–9; *Knox Student,* Oct. 1881, 4.

24. Both of these men have been accorded essays in the *DAB.*

25. Both S. S. McClure and Earnest Elmo Calkins speak highly of Anderson's teaching in their autobiographies. See the high praise of Jenks in the *Coup D'Etat,* Jan. 1888, opening editorial.

26. Executive Committee Minutes, Jan. 7, 1884. For a complimentary student description of Hurd's teaching, see *Coup D'Etat,* Nov. 1884, 3.

27. Newton Bateman Papers.

28. Galesburg *Republican Register,* Aug. 30, 1879, 1.

29. Executive Committee Minutes, Feb. 2, Apr. 20, 1885.

30. *Coup D'Etat,* Nov. 1884, 42; Sept. 1885, 3.

31. Catalogue, for 1885–86, 48. "The design has been submitted to Mr. Cochrane, one of the foremost architects of the state, and returned without change" (*Coup D'Etat,* Nov. 1884, 42).

32. Galesburg *Republican Register,* Aug. 13, 1887, 1.

33. *Coup D'Etat,* Nov. 1884, 42; catalogue, for 1888–89, 60; Galesburg *Republican Register,* Sept. 3, 1887, 5.

34. Obituary of Charles Fuhrman, Galesburg *Republican Register,* Nov. 17, 1888. See also *ibid., Mar.* 12, 1883, 6; Knox catalogue, for 1859–60, 13; Lombard University catalogue, for 1858–59.

35. Henry Walker was born in Connecticut; F. Riemann came from Saxe-Coburg; A. Steinbach came from Sweden; L. B. Miller was from Kentucky (returns from the census for 1860). According to a city directory, published in 1861, Walker was "leader" of a Silver Cornet Band, "reorganized" in 1858"; Miller was "president" of the Galesburg Academy of Music organized in 1859; Riemann was the "Director" and "A. Stenbeck" was the "Leader" of the Galesburg Union Orchestra, organized in 1860 (Root, *Root's Galesburg City Directory*).

36. Galesburg *Republican Register,* Mar. 12, 1883, 6; Mar. 31, 1883, 1; Dec. 15, 1883, 1; Dec. 12, 1885, 5; Dec. 19, 1885, 1; *Holland's Galesburg City Directory,* for 1870–71, 28–29.

37. Program for the "Christmas Concert by Music Department of Knox College and Seminary. Friday Eve., Dec. 16, 1870," Archives, Knox College Library.

38. For a fuller account of her career at Knox, see ch. 2 herein.

39. Calkins, *They Broke the Prairie,* 377.

40. Obituary for Carl Laux in Galesburg *Republican Register,* Mar. 10, 1888, 1; *Knox Student,* Dec. 1878, 14; *Beasley's Galesburg City Directory,* 194.

41. Galesburg *Republican Register,* May 12, 1877, 4; Jan. 12, 1878, 1; July 19, 1879, 1; May 8, 1880, 6; Oct. 2, 1880, 6; Oct. 16, 1880, 1; Dec. 25, 1880, 5; Jan. 29, 1881, 6; Feb. 5, 1881, 1.

42. *Ibid.,* Apr. 21, 1877, 5; May 12, 1877, 5.

43. *Knox Student,* Dec. 1878, 14.

44. Galesburg *Republican Register,* June 7, 1879, 2; June 21, 1879, 1.

45. Knox College catalogue, for 1879–80, 14.

46. Galesburg *Republican Register,* June 7, 1879, 6.

47. The program for this performance of *The Messiah* is in the College Archives; the account of the performance is in the Galesburg *Republican Register,* May 12, 1883, 5.

48. *Coup D'Etat,* Oct. 1882, 3; Galesburg *Republican Register,* Jan. 12, 1882, 1; Aug. 26, 1882, 1; Mar. 31, 1883, 6. A letter from Edwin Wyckoff to Edward Caldwell, June 30, 1847, Caldwell Papers.

49. Galesburg *Republican Register,* Aug. 26, 1882, 1.

50. William F. Bentley, "The Knox Conservatory of Music," *Knox Alumnus,* Feb. 1918, 68–69.

51. Galesburg *Republican Register,* Sept. 1, 1883, 1.

52. *Coup D'Etat,* Sept. 1884, 3; Galesburg *Republican Register,* Sept. 1, 1883, 1.

53. Executive Committee Minutes, Nov. 24, Dec. 3, 1883.

54. *Coup D'Etat,* Dec. 1883, 39.

55. Wyckoff to Edward Caldwell, Aug. 30, 1946, June 30, 1947, Caldwell Papers.

56. *Coup D'Etat*, Oct. 1884, 24.

57. Bentley, *History of the 77th Illinois Volunteer Infantry*, 68–69; Executive Committee Minutes, Feb. 7, 1895.

58. Bentley, *History of the 77th Illinois Volunteer Infantry*, 68–69.

59. *Coup D'Etat*, Sept. 1885, 15; Feb. 1886, 89; Dec. 1885, 55; May 1886, 137; *Pantheon*, III (1888), 66.

60. *Coup D'Etat*, Apr. 1886, 122; May 1886, 137.

61. *Ibid.*, May 1886, 138.

62. *Baker's Biographical Dictionary of Musicians*, 1642.

63. Knox College *Bulletin*, 4 (May 1903), 13.

64. Information about the Hitchcock and Pearsons funds was reported in a study of gifts to the College prepared by Edwin Dunn, who was business manager and auditor of the College, 1914 to 1927, MS, Knox College Library.

65. *Coup D'Etat*, Feb. 1892, 93.

CHAPTER V

THE MUCKRAKERS FROM KNOX

President Theodore Roosevelt, speaking informally at the Grid-iron Club in March 1906, denounced those journalists who were constantly writing about the evils of American institutions; he called them "muckrakers."[1] The word muckraker was quickly taken into the jargon of politics and came to be applied generally to those journalists and other writers who exposed the political, economic, and other social evils of the opening decade of the twentieth century and who prompted the reforms of the Progressive Era. The deprecatory sting of the word was soon dulled and came to have an "honorable connotation of social concern and courageous exposition."[2]

Many of President Roosevelt's contemporaries regarded *McClure's Magazine* as the "pioneer and the best of the muckraking publications"[3] and as the originator or prototype or prime example of muckraking; the "era of the muckrake," these people believed, had been "really inaugurated by McClure's."[4] It was the "first and the best" of the cheap magazines, whose popular circulation made them potent molders of public opinion. "Cheap" did not mean "unworthy," but rather "inexpensive." In 1892 Samuel S. McClure (Knox, 1882) had persuaded his classmate Albert Brady (1882) to join with him and John S. Phillips (1882) in establishing this magazine, thus regrouping the staff that published and edited the *Knox Student* during their senior year in the College. Except for a year at Harvard and a year at the University of Leipzig, Phillips had been associated with McClure ever since their graduation, the collaboration having been begun on the *Wheelman* (a magazine about bicycles) before the end of their first

133

summer out of Knox. Phillips became in 1886 the literary editor of the newspaper syndicate that McClure had founded with the assistance of Harriet Hurd (Knox, 1877), whom he had married in 1883.

McClure's Magazine and this newspaper syndicate were by the turn of the century only the most successful ventures in a comprehensive collection of publishing operations that had been started by McClure and his partners.[5] The syndicate had a significant place in the development of American journalism, in the careers of American and British writers, and in the history of American literature. McClure, Harriet Hurd McClure, Phillips, and Brady were only some of the Knox alumni to become involved in the several McClure publishing enterprises. Altogether there would be more than a score: the earliest to enroll at Knox would be Hurd, in 1868; the last would be Albert Britt, who would be graduated from Knox in 1898. It should be noted that in this group there were four kinship sets that could affect the internal relations of the McClure staff: the three McClure brothers who attended Knox, Samuel, John, and Thomas; the brothers Bancroft, Edgar and Frederic; the brothers John and Robert Finley, and Albert Boyden, brother-in-law of John Huston Finley by the latter's marriage to Boyden's sister Martha.

To appreciate the relations that brought Knox alumni together again in New York City, it is helpful to understand how closely knit the student body was at Knox during the last third of the nineteenth century. There was first of all a very strong sense of class membership, e.g., the class of 1882. It manifested itself in rituals (elections of officers, class projects, programs, and parties), in emblems (class colors, mottos, even items of dress such as freshman caps and senior hats), and in class competitions. Several factors fostered this strong feeling of class identification, one being the smallness of the group. Thus Samuel McClure belonged to seven annual grades of his class (over an eight-year period), ranging in size as follows:

1874–75:	Junior Preparatory	: 48 students
1875–76:	Middle Preparatory	: 10 students
1876–77:	Senior Preparatory	: 13 students
1877–78:	Freshman, College	: 21 students

1878–79:   not enrolled
1879–80:   Sophomore, College : 36 students
1880–81:   Junior, College   : 31 students
1881–82:   Senior, College   : 25 students

In those years there was a second meaning of class in the academic sense, namely, those students who were studying a certain subject together. For example, there was McClure's freshman class; it was during the autumn of 1877 also the class in conic sections; during the winter it was the class in algebra; during the spring of 1878 it was again the class in algebra. This congruence of the two meanings of class resulted from the simplicity of the curriculum, which (at the college level) hardly permitted any electives and really allowed only one choice: between the classical and the scientific courses, the latter differing only from the former in that it did not require Greek. So limited and so stable were the course offerings (and thus so nearly uniform the students' educational experiences), that the catalogue for McClure's senior year, 1881–82, could present on only three pages (one for each term) the full schedule of all courses, day and hour, for the entire year.

The Academy was still the largest department, and its primary purpose was to prepare pupils for the Female Seminary and the College, though the Academy was in fact the terminal academic experience for most of the academical students. Not until four years after McClure was graduated were freshmen allowed to enter Knox College by certification from high schools; instead, they were individually examined on the subjects fully advertised in the catalogues of the College.[6] McClure would study at Knox for seven years. This was not typical, but it was not uncommon. Of the twenty-five students graduated from the College in McClure's senior class, nineteen had been at Knox five or more years.

This extended period of students' association fostered a sense of comradeship that often lasted for a lifetime. Samuel McClure was "in college" for five years with men who would later be associated with him in *McClure's Magazine:* Frederic Bancroft, Charles Churchill, and Phillips. Furthermore, the longer period of McClure's status as a student at Knox meant that he overlapped with students who otherwise would not have been in school when he was. McClure's three years as a prep student coincided with college years of his influential advisor and friend of future years, Edgar A. Bancroft, with his future wife, Harriet Hurd, and with his uncle, Joseph Gaston.

Gaston, who was in the same class with Hurd, was an Irish immigrant who was preparing for the ministry. He was one of fourteen children of a small farmer in Ulster, four of whom had by the mid-1860s migrated to northeastern Indiana. In June 1866 a widowed sister, Elizabeth Gaston McClure, left Ireland with her four sons, of whom Samuel, who was nine, was the eldest. They were met, after a journey of nineteen days, at a railroad station in Valparaiso by Gaston, who took them to the farm home of the married sister with whom Joseph and a brother were staying.[7] It was Gaston who persuaded Samuel, eight years later, to come to Knox College, where Gaston was a respected member of the student body, as indicated by his presidency of the Adelphi and by other student honors.

In early September 1874 Samuel McClure arrived in Galesburg with fifteen cents. He found a vacant room in one of the Bricks, and, though it was furnished only with a box, for the first month he studied and slept and ate there, subsisting on bread, soda crackers, and Concord grapes, which, in the autumn before the frost, he could buy cheaply, three pounds for ten cents. By October he found a place to work for his board and room with the mayor of the city, J. C. Stewart. He earned pocket money by sawing wood about town. Except for a suit of clothes sent by his mother to replace the ill-fitting garments with which he arrived on campus, he got no other help from home that year.[8]

Later that same academic year, his brother John also enrolled at Knox, and he entered even lower on the educational ladder as a kind of "sub-prep," enrolling in the English department of the Academy.[9] John and Samuel would be together at Knox from 1874 to 1878 and then again during the year 1880–81. Though John did not complete his studies at Knox, he was frequently on the campus during 1881–82 when Samuel was a senior. Like his brother he became a member of the Zetetici, one of the Academy literary societies, and was elected a president of that society for 1877–78. A declamation by him at the thirteenth anniversary of Zetetici in the spring of 1877 was highly praised, and it was remarked that he seemed "destined to be 'the orator' of the Class of

'82."[10] Unlike his brother, at the conclusion of his preparatory years he was elected into Gnothautii, rather than Adelphi, thus becoming a member of the same society with Phillips and Brady.

A third brother, Thomas, attended the Academy in 1876–77. Thus that year all three brothers were at various levels of progress in the Preparatory Department and Uncle Joseph was a senior in the College. It should have been a good year to remember, and in some respects it was. A speech given by Samuel at the anniversary of Zetetici was favorably reviewed in the local paper,[11] and he also served as one of the presidents of that literary society.

But Samuel McClure remembered this as his most difficult year at Knox, mostly because of his troubled courtship of Harriet Hurd.[12] She was a senior in the College and he was not yet a freshman. The informal understanding that quickly developed between Harriet and Samuel was strenuously opposed by Professor Albert Hurd, whose position at the College made him a formidable opponent indeed. He was the senior member of the faculty and had recently served as its leader during the three years that Knox was without a president. If McClure became a student in the College, he would have to be one of the professor's students, hardly an encouraging prospect.

Life also was difficult in 1876–77 because McClure no longer could tolerate the tedium and the toil of keeping himself in school by working at chores such as cutting wood, tending to furnaces, and cleaning stables. Hence there were times this year when he went to bed hungry and cold. Until mid-December he had no coal for the stove in his room in one of the Bricks, and then he bought a winter's supply with part of the $5 which was given him by Harriet Hurd from money her father gave her as a birthday present.[13] But when Harriet Hurd's commencement occurred, the celebration was spoiled because Professor Hurd successfully insisted that she break the engagement. He announced that she would be going away to school for advanced studies in French. And for more than four years Harriet and Samuel did not see each other.

Samuel McClure had now completed his college preparatory studies and decided to transfer to Oberlin, but his uncle intervened and persuaded him to stay at Knox, where he became a freshman in the autumn of 1877. His brother John boarded and roomed with Professor Thomas Willard, but Samuel lived at one of the Bricks on the very austere budget of eighteen cents a day. He was elected to Adelphi, where he was immediately involved in the forensic activities that were such an important aspect of the students' intellectual experiences. His first assignment that year was to debate on an issue arising from the violent general strike that had during the summer spread from the eastern to the western railroads and that had provoked serious rioting in Chicago and St. Louis; he was appointed to debate the affirmative side of the question: "Resolved that the R.R. officials were more to blame in the late strikes than the strikers."[14] The topics of Adelphi programs were not always so obviously related to current events; yet later in the year he was on the affirmative side of very significant propositions:

> June 5, 1878: Has Congress in the present investigation a right to touch the validity of Hayes's title to the presidency?
>
> June 12, 1878: Should women receive the same wages as men?[15]

During the summer of 1878 McClure discovered a means of earning money for his college expenses that was congenial to him and that he later declared had contributed greatly to his knowledge of common people and to the kind of understanding that was helpful in the management of a popular magazine. He and his brother John set out to sell from door to door and town to town a new gadget invented by "Professor" E. D. Bangs, husband of the principal of the Seminary, where McClure was a kind of *factotum*. It was a coffee pot that had been given the public endorsement of Professors Hurd and Milton Comstock, who jointly stated in the local newspaper that the contrivance made better coffee than that made by the common method.[16] Though the McClure brothers soon discovered that marketing the new coffee pot was not profitable, they did enjoy the itinerant life of peddling and later shifted their efforts to the sale of notions. Thereafter, each summer until he had finished college Samuel McClure went on some kind of peddler's journey in the Midwest; in 1879 with his brother Thomas; in 1881 with his classmate, Brady, the future business manager of *McClure's Magazine*.[17]

In September 1878 Samuel and John McClure did not return to Knox for the opening of school. Instead they both taught public schools near Valparaiso, Indiana. Samuel got very little satisfaction from pedagogy, which he had tried twice before for short periods of time. Restlessly he looked forward to his return to the Knox campus,[18] and in the spring deserted his teaching duties before the school year was out. By mid-May he was back on the campus, having brought with him as a gift to the Adelphi two small paintings of Lincoln and Grant.[19] This visit to Galesburg had been particularly prompted by news that Harriet Hurd was back in the city, but when he called at her home he was turned away by Mrs. Hurd. Since prospects for Harriet and Samuel were so hopeless, they both returned each other's "remembrances" and the understanding between them was broken.

Samuel McClure returned to Knox in September 1879 to begin his sophomore year and to form close relationships with members of the class of 1882. From its members would come Charles Edward Churchill, who one day would be advertising manager for *McClure's Magazine;* the distinguished corporation lawyer Robert Mather, who would some day influence the finances of McClure's publishing ventures; and Frederic Bancroft, the distinguished historian, who would influence the editorial content of *McClure's Magazine.* Most significantly the class of 1882 included John S. Phillips, who was associated with Samuel McClure in all his journalistic ventures for the quarter century that began immediately after the commencement of June 1882. Phillips's first wife, Emma West, was also of this class. A new member of 1882 was Albert Brady, who, next to Phillips, would be McClure's most important associate in the establishment of *McClure's Magazine.* During that sophomore year Brady left his "good boarding house" to become McClure's roommate, and they roomed together during most of their remaining years at Knox.[20]

Samuel McClure chose to seek the degree of bachelor of arts, which was regarded as more demanding and was more prestigious than the bachelor of science degree. Candidates for the arts degree had to master not only substantial knowledge of Latin but also Greek. McClure looked forward to the required courses in these languages and found them delightful. By the end of his freshman year he had become interested in "comparative etymology" and had already compiled a "thick manuscript" of philological notes.[21] During his senior year, when he was no longer short of money, he purchased several volumes on etymology that he found during a holiday visit to Chicago bookstores, and he presented these books to the College library.[22]

Late in his junior year McClure was the leader of a group that organized to study Anglo-Saxon "and also to engage in philological discussion." This special interest in Anglo-Saxon had been stimulated by a visiting scholar from Oxford who came to Galesburg for the lecture series provided that year by the Gnothautii. During the first term of the next year, the newly appointed professor of literature, Melville Anderson, offered instruction in Anglo-Saxon to those interested in this subject.[23] Among the students enrolled in this class was Harriet Hurd, for soon after College opened that year, she had appeared on the campus. Samuel saw her for the first time in almost five years, and their courtship resumed as if nothing had ever gone wrong between them. Professor Melville's Anglo-Saxon class became one of the means by which they saw each other frequently, until March 1883 when Professor Hurd, still adamantly opposed to McClure's attentions to his brilliant daughter, insisted that she leave Galesburg to become a teacher at the Abbot Academy in Andover, Massachusetts.[24]

Anderson profoundly influenced the career of McClure. In the foreword to his autobiography, thirty years after he was graduated from Knox College, McClure stated: "I owe much to Melville B. Anderson (formerly Professor of English Literature at Knox College, now Professor Emeritus of Leland Stanford), who first encouraged me to hope that I might find a place in the world."[25] Anderson as mentor for McClure, the student, became the trusted advisor for McClure, the journalist, immediately after graduation. A brother of Anderson, who was on the faculty of Michigan State College, became a contributor to the newspaper syndicate founded by McClure.[26]

It is not surprising, in view of his duties as a part-time teacher and of other work to earn his own living and to pay for his schooling, that McClure was not, during his sophomore and junior years, as active in campus affairs as other students, such as the Bancroft brothers or Phillips, who lived at home and did not need to work their way through college. McClure did not, for example, become a leading contender for the forensic honors so highly prized at that time. Of course, as a member of Adelphi he attended the weekly meetings of that society and participated in its programs, though it should be noted that for the second half of his sophomore year and again for the latter part of his senior year he was formally excused because of "extra work."[27] It is worth noting that on some of these Adelphi programs McClure was associated with the future speaker of the House of Representatives of the United States, Henry T. Rainey, who was a year behind McClure. In October 1879, for example, McClure and Rainey were on the negative side of the debate: "Resolved that Grant should accept a third presidential nomination."

McClure's extracurricular achievements compared favorably with those of his classmates by the commencement of 1882, though most of these honors had been earned during his senior year. It was not as a performer that McClure excelled, but rather as the promoter, the manager; not as reporter or author, but as editor or publisher. Thus, in the autumn of 1881 he represented Knox in the prestigious oratorical arena, not as an orator but as an officer of the oratorical association. He was elected president of the Knox Contest Association. In that capacity he attended the state oratorical contest at Bloomington and participated in the business session of the Illinois State Oratorical Association. McClure was one of the two delegates chosen to represent that body at the Inter-State convention the following spring.[28]

In the state oratorical contest of 1881 the second place was won by the Knox man, Nels Anderson, an honor that was celebrated wildly on the campus, reaching a climax at a banquet for which McClure was the toastmaster. In his opening remarks McClure "took special pleasure in the fact that this contest had united all the factions of the College into one harmonious body." He referred specifically to a bitter campus rift that had developed over the College magazine: "There are no longer Adelphians, Gnothautians, '*Students,*' '*Coup d'Etats,*' but Knox Collegians."[29]

It was particularly appropriate that McClure should speak in this conciliatory manner, because he and Mather, who was second on the speakers' list, represented in their roles as competing magazine editors, a deep-seated factionalism that had been disturbing the campus since the preceding winter. The *Knox Student,* though only four years old, had become involved in the intense rivalries associated with college forensic competition. And the campus paper had itself never been free of its own political problems.

The *Knox Student* was started in 1878–79, the year that Samuel and John McClure stayed out of college a year to teach school. There had not, except for programs printed by literary societies, been any student publications since three college yearbooks had been issued between 1869 and 1873. In the spring of 1878 a mass meeting of students appointed a committee of three to make arrangements to publish a yearbook. The chairman, Claude F. Clendenin, proposed that instead of an annual they start a monthly college paper. Clendenin's suggestion was accepted by the committee, encouraged by President Newton Bateman, and approved by the faculty.[30] It was the first magazine published by Knox students since the early months of the Civil War.

Discontent with the character of the *Student* became evident in 1880–81, its critics asserting "that something was needed to shake up the paper and give it an enlivened tone." In March 1881 an editorial in the *Student* called for the formation of a "Joint Stock Company" to replace the existing board that had tried to represent the "student body" by way of delegates from the literary societies. In a joint stock company, it was argued, only those really interested in the *Student* would control it. This plan for reorganization was adopted "by a vote of all students" and accordingly the "ownership and management" of the *Student* came "into the hands of a Joint Stock Company of sixteen members." The capital stock was to consist of thirty-two shares, and none but members of Knox College could hold stock and no member could dispose of stock to another without consent of other stockholders. On this basis in the spring of 1881 the new corporation elected officers for the next year. By September, however, the man elected president had withdrawn from school and when a meeting of the Student Joint Stock Company occurred to fill the vacancy, there was difficulty about the corporation rule that two-thirds of the stockholders comprised a quorum to do business.[31]

McClure had become during the preceding year (1880–81) a member of an anti-Mather minority in the Adelphi, a faction that included Frederic Bancroft, Rainey, and Frank Bellows.[32] In the spring of 1881 these Adelphi under Bellows's management formed a coalition with some of the Gnothautii to control the selection of the orator who would represent Knox in the state competition the next fall. Bancroft, to whom the judges had awarded first place in the spring oratorical contest, was the candidate of this coalition. In the election, with members of the two men's literary societies voting, Bancroft was beaten by Nels Anderson, who was the candidate of the Mather party comprising a majority of the Adelphi and certain of the Gnothautii. Partisan feelings had been sharply shown in this campus rivalry for the honor of becoming the College orator. When judges had awarded Bancroft first place and Anderson second place in the formal contest, there had been hisses in the audience. When Anderson defeated Bancroft in the literary societies' election 45 to 22, the Mather-Anderson faction "hurrahed, rang the bell, and made as much noise as possible."[33] And in the autumn, Bellows, Rainey, and Bancroft did not return to Knox, but instead went to Amherst.

These coalitions persisted into the fall when the students divided over the control of the *Student*. Mather and Anderson, along with other Adelphians and their Gnothautii associates of the spring contest, belonged to one of the groups that tried to control the *Student*. McClure belonged to a party headed by Lyndon Evans, a member of Gnothautii. On September 15, a simple majority of shareholders of the Joint Stock Company elected Evans president of the board and proceeded to choose a magazine staff with McClure as editor-in-chief and with Brady as business manager.

The Mather party protested the legality of the election of Evans and of the other business done by the board of the *Student* on September 15th, on the ground that there had not been the necessary two-thirds of the stock represented at the meeting to constitute a quorum. After two more meetings it became apparent that no one would have the needed two-thirds for legal action. A meeting of both parties with Professor Comstock as moderator was convened but failed to effect a compromise.[34]

By a strenuous all-night effort the Mather group got out a prospectus for the chapel session on the morning of the same day that McClure's supporters issued the prospectus for their *Student*. For this coup the Mather paper named itself the *Coup D'Etat*.[35] At a meeting of students, 130 voted to accept the *Coup D'Etat* as the "official organ" of the students. But the *Student* characterized this as the act of an "unofficial body" and pointed out that the vote was less than a majority of those present at the meeting and that "the *Student* party" refused to vote either way. Editor McClure stated that, whatever the statistics, the vote was irrelevant: "The number of students has nothing to do with publishing the paper. One man or ten or a hundred have a perfect right to publish a college paper."[36]

In his reminiscences McClure recalled his editing of the *Student* as a valuable preparation for his lifelong career as a journalist. It gave him experience in selecting or rejecting or in pruning the writing of others, some of whom, in fact, had a better reputation for literary skill than he did. Those who resented his editing of their contributions actually convened a meeting of the *Student* Joint Stock Company, but Brady showed up with enough voting shares to squelch this threat to McClure's editorship.[37]

The literary features of the *Student* reflected the influence of John S. Phillips, who was McClure's chief editorial assistant. McClure regarded Phillips as "easily the best read student in the College . . . with great natural aptitude for letters." In the Phillips's home on East Simmons Street, only two or three blocks from the College grounds, McClure discovered magazines such as the *Century*, in which he read serials such as William Dean Howells's *A Modern Instance*.[38] Phillips's student relationship to McClure was especially significant, because it was to be repeated so exactly in the careers of both men.

A similar renewal of roles occurred in the case of Albert Brady, who, as McClure would reminisce, already showed "the same unusual business ability that he afterward showed as Business Manager of *McClure's Magazine*." He and McClure were roommates during most of the last three years they were at Knox. They had spent the summer before their senior year peddling microscopes in the cities of the upper Mississippi River Valley and around the Great Lakes from Duluth to Cleveland, traveling some 3,000 miles.

Already as editor of a college monthly, McClure showed that fertility for new ideas, the imagination for large plans, and the disposition to act on them promptly that later made him an acknowledged journalistic genius. The December issue of the *Stu-*

dent reported that Knox had "taken practical steps to form" an organization by which the College Press might "be elevated" through "mutual assistance." The *Knox Student* had invited the leading western colleges to form an Associated College Press. The *Student,* on behalf of Knox, offered "to do all the routine work of such an organization, free of charge. . . . The plan we propose is an exceedingly simple one. Each college sends us items of Inter-collegiate interest. We collect these items, and each week send a printed bulletin to all colleges which furnish items." Knox also offered to make the preparations for a convention of college editors at Indianapolis to meet at the time of the Inter-State Oratorical Contest at Indianapolis in May 1882.[39]

It is not clear how much of this enterprise was conducted by anyone other than McClure himself, but by the time of the Christmas recess he was entitled "manager of the Western College Press."[40] Obviously McClure could not speak for the entire College. Indeed, the *Coup D'Etat* opposed his efforts to establish a "Western College Press Association."[41] However, the *Student* for February 1882 reported "many favorable responses" regarding the "advisability of establishing an Inter-Collegiate Bulletin." The colleges responding included Carleton, Ripon, Northwestern University, Illinois Industrial University at Champaign, Wheaton, Monmouth, Abingdon, Earlham, Milton, the University of Michigan, and even Trinity of Connecticut.[42]

When the Inter-State Oratorical Contest occurred early in May 1882, at Indianapolis, editors of the college journals were invited to hold a meeting. McClure was also on hand as a representative from the state of Illinois for the business sessions of the Inter-State Oratorical Association. He had prepared a constitution for the "Western College Press Association," which was adopted by a convention of "about thirty students from several colleges." In addition to facilitating exchange of editorial materials, the association proposed a prize contest for the best article appearing in any college paper. The *Knox Student* was made the "official organ" of this Western College Press Association and Samuel McClure was chosen its president.[43] A meeting of this new intercollegiate organization was scheduled for July 5 at Iowa College at Grinnell. Unfortunately a storm late in June destroyed both of the large buildings at Iowa College and three students were among the twenty people that were killed. The session of the Western College Association was deferred until fall.[44] But autumn found McClure miles away, in Massachusetts.

McClure profited rather well from the contacts he made with other college editors. In May 1882 the *Student* announced the forthcoming publication, at twenty-five cents a copy, of a *History of College Journalism*, to be edited by S. S. McClure, "Pres. Western College Press Association, Knox College." The book was to consist of histories of journalistic activities, which were prepared by each of the colleges and then compiled by McClure. The article on journalism at Knox, for example, was written by Phillips. From this enterprise McClure admittedly "realized a goodly sum of money," for he sold advertising to a number of national companies that usually placed advertising in magazines.[45] Among these was a Boston bicycle manufacturer, for whom McClure would start a publication soon after graduation. In reaching back to Galesburg for Phillips and for brother John McClure to help, he would be calling on his Knox connections as he would do so often in the decades to come.

On commencement day of 1882 the graduation exercises differed from those of previous years in that, responsive to a request of this senior class, not everyone in the class was a commencement speaker. Only the seniors who were graduated *cum honore* were speakers. The selected group of nine included McClure, Phillips, and Mather.

McClure's brief ("exactly five minutes") commencement oration on "The Nature of Enthusiasm" was described as "most unique in its terseness and scholastic rather than popular style."[46] It is relevant to McClure's later role as a muckraker to quote from his own precis of what he spoke:

> The men who start the great new movements in the world are enthusiasts whose eyes are fixed upon the end they wish to bring about—that to them the future becomes present. It was when they believed in what seemed impossible that the Abolitionists did most good, that they created the sentiment which finally did accomplish the impossible. The enthusiast . . . must always be considered impractical, because he ignores those difficulties of execution which make most men conservative; and his impracticality is his strength. It is not the critical, judicial type of mind, but the Garibaldi type of

mind, that generates the great popular ideas by which humanity rights itself.[47]

McClure's approving reference to the abolitionists is significant. "The Imprint of Abolitionism" is the title of the opening chapter of the scholarly monograph by Harold S. Wilson, *McClure's Magazine and the Muckrakers.* In this historical analysis of *McClure's Magazine,* Wilson stresses the influence of Knox College on muckrakers and Progressives; he links the social, economic, and political reforms of the opening years of the twentieth century to the founders of Knox by way of the faculty and students at that institution during McClure's student years:

> When *McClure's Magazine* was founded in 1893, it was staffed to a great extent by graduates of Knox College. . . . The two dozen Knox alumni who edited, sold, and financed *McClure's* carried to the New York publishing world many of the reform traditions of the Great Revival. . . . Thus evangelical Christianity—although greatly modified—with its injunction to transform an evil world, helped to provide the purpose, technique, and content of many of the progressive reforms championed by the muckraking movement in a later era.

Wilson points out that Knox College was guided by men who had been present during the antebellum abolitionist crusade and that these men would "leave their impression on a score of muckrakers who graduated in the decade after Reconstruction."[48]

When McClure was a student at Knox, there were many remainders and reminders of the abolitionist cause. Knox alumni were serving as educational missionaries to the illiterate freedman, and a graduate of 1848 was stationed in Atlanta to superintend the subsidies of a Congregational missionary society to schools such as Fisk, Talledega, Hampton, and many others. Among the Knox carpetbaggers in the South was the black Senator who in 1870 took the seat once occupied by Jefferson Davis.[49] By the mid-1870s the founders of Knox were the "old settlers" who reminisced about their radical leadership for the antislavery cause and their reckless roles on the Underground Railroad.[50] Former presidents Hiram Kellogg and Jonathan Blanchard, who had been leading abolitionists, returned to speak to the younger as well as to the older generations.[51] Their contemporary, President Bateman, did much to shape the cult of Lincoln as the antislavery martyr. Perhaps most amazing was the heroic status accorded to that genuine revolutionary, John Brown. The blacks in Galesburg celebrated the tenth anniversary of the death of this radical abolitionist, and the leading local Republican newspaper editorialized the next day that Brown's attack on Harpers Ferry had been a noble deed.[52] In 1878 the *Republican Register* noted that one might see in the possession of a Galesburg resident: "One of the famous pikes made for old John Brown—whose soul goes marching on—and with which he essayed to arm the negroes of his historical government."[53] A Galesburg youth, Frederic Bancroft, chose both William Lloyd Garrison and Brown for the subject of orations; both were "heroes" to him.[54] And it was with an oration on John Brown that in the spring of 1886 John Finley won the Knox oratorical prize, and then in the fall the Illinois intercollegiate honors, and in the next spring the interstate championship. In the concluding climax of this oration, Finley (who would one day join the McClure journalistic enterprises) dramatically linked the abolitionist Brown with three great leaders of national liberation, Garibaldi of Italy, Wallace of Scotland, and Robert Emmet of Ireland. The Irish patriot, Emmet, like Brown was tried for treason after he had failed in an aborted Irish uprising and was executed.[55]

Linking abolitionism to freedom for the Irish was not merely a rhetorical invention by Finley. The evangelists that half a century earlier had denounced the sin of slavery had also sometimes condemned the oppression of the Irish peasants.[56] And during the years when Samuel McClure, the young Irish immigrant, was a student at Knox, the righting of the wrongs of the Irish was often debated by the Adelphi on campus and discussed at public meetings in the city.[57] For McClure this translation of the abolitionists' ethic to another social evil was clearly demonstrated in an oration that he delivered to the Adelphi on "Irish Landlordism" in March 1881, a speech published in the *Student*. Particularly bitter and passionate was this Protestant immigrant's characterization of the penal laws devised against Irish Catholics during the eighteenth century, which were "so remorsely cruel, so devilish in their Satanic perfection that they were well said to have been conceived by fiends, written in human gore, and registered in hell." As a consequence, he declared, "nine-tenths of the Irish people" were "degraded to the lowest form of slavery."[58]

It would, however, be most untrue to assume that Knox or Galesburg in McClure's time had made a unified conversion from the evangelical humanitarianism of the antebellum years to radical social and economic reforms as they were being agitated in the 1880s. Two notable instances demonstrate that abolitionists of the 1850s might be reactionary on the new social issues of the later generation. One example is that of Professor Hurd, who had been at Knox since 1851. In a chapel talk in May 1886, soon after a bomb had killed seven policemen in the Haymarket Square in Chicago and provoked frantic persecution of radicals, Hurd defended "corporations," denounced strikes, and condemned the eight-hour day. The style of his argument, as abridged for a local paper, is meaningful:

> Means should be provided for restraining persons who interfere with the operations of large corporations which benefit the people. I do not believe in strikes. Because I work for fifty cents a day you have no right to kill me. The laws of God if fully obeyed would make perfect harmony; we old men are always looking back, while you look forward. We used to work much harder than the people do now. I always arose early and worked until late at night. Work never did me much harm. I do not think eight hours are a sufficient number of hours to labor. Two hours less labor will mean that much more money squandered in drinking and rioting.[59]

This same kind of conservatism was expressed by the Knox alumnus who delivered the oration that culminated the celebration of the Knox Semi-Centennial in June 1887. The speaker who was accorded this honor was Stephen V. White, class of 1854. He reminded his audience of the noble role of Knox in the antislavery movement, how it had spoken out when the other colleges in Illinois were still "mute." But White spoke more about the social unrest of the 1880s, about his horror over the Haymarket Riot, and his desire to regulate immigration so as to keep out aliens with subversive ideas. He strongly opposed the Interstate Commerce Act that had been passed earlier that year, providing for some regulation of the railroads. He decried unionization of laborers. He denounced the ideas of the reformer, Henry George.[60]

When White spoke his oration at the Knox celebration, many

of those listening knew that he had made not merely one fortune but "three fortunes," for he had already "failed twice for very large sums" and then "paid off every cent." The most famous of his New York Stock Exchange operations was the Lackawanna Railroad "corner," which he "engineered" in 1884. In 1885 he was one of the dozen "great speculative operators" discussed in *Harper's New Monthly Magazine*, others being such noted capitalists as W. H. Vanderbilt, Cyrus W. Field, Russell Sage, and Jay Gould. This magazine article presented a portrait of White on the page opposite its picture of the notorious Gould.[61] Though some Knox students and alumni may have been offended by White's gambling in the stock market, the public notices of his career show that by most Knox people he was much respected and admired.[62]

That the Knox students were overwhelmingly Republican in sentiment was exemplified during McClure's junior year by their participation in the presidential campaign and their enthusiastic celebration when Garfield was elected. Furthermore, students insisted that if they were of age they should vote. The Democrats "mindful of Knox's politics" had "challengers" at the polls, but election officials allowed those students to vote who called Galesburg their home, were of proper age, and "had voted at no other voting place within the last year."[63] During this same year Knox students also became active in local politics. Partly this was provoked by posters scattered throughout the city to advertise "a traveling house of ill-fame, under the title of the Hibernian blondes." Students were offended by the "boldness and obscenity" of these advertisements, which they regarded as "heralds of sin," and they held a "mass meeting," at which three students were chosen to join faculty members on a committee to visit the mayor to ask him to suppress the show. This the mayor refused to do (after all, he had not seen it), but the "Hibernian blondes" did not come to Galesburg—they had been jailed in Peoria.[64]

Evidently, sinful shows were only one aspect of the students' indignation, for it was reported that at their mass meeting "Knox boys . . . decided that the present city government is a failure; [and] appointed a committee to get up a better one." At a meeting of the Women's Christian Temperance Union a few days later, a Knox student "in a glowing speech advocated the putting of a full temperance ticket in the field at the spring election."[65] Not surprisingly, there was resentment in the community against the notion that the city be managed to suit Knox College and its sister, Lombard College. In 1884, when there was trouble with the police during celebrations over victories in the intercollegiate oratorical contests, a Knox magazine charged that mistreatment from the police reflected "a desire of the city officials to get even with the students for voting the temperance ticket at the recent elections."[66]

On the question of temperance the activism of the students was consistent with a moral-political principle espoused from the beginning by the College and by the colony that had founded it. The links between the Great Revival and the Progressive movement a century later may here be plainly seen, for *McClure's Magazine* "from its earliest days was an advocate of prohibition" and many of the economic and social reforms it encouraged (much of its muckraking) had some connection with the corrupting business in alcohol.[67] This traffic the founding fathers of Knox had tried unsuccessfully to bar locally by writing into the deeds by which Knox College sold land to the first settlers a provision that if intoxicating beverages were made or sold on the land, it would revert to the College.[68]

Political questions with strong moral or religious accents were frequently debated in the weekly meetings of the Adelphi—issues such as Roman Catholicism, the Bible in public schools, polygamy in Utah, and capital punishment. Theological topics were much less popular than they formerly had been. By far the most common subjects for debate derived from contemporary controversies in national politics: presidential acts and executive misconduct, reconstruction of the South, Chinese immigration, the tariff, treatment of the Indians, and currency questions.

It is surprising that in these debates hardly any attention was given to the agrarian unrest and the third-party organization that reflected the farmers' grievances. One of the leaders of the agrarian crusades of the last third of the century was Alson J. Streeter, who had attended Knox during the 1840s and who lived just across the Knox County line in the little town of New Windsor. When McClure was a prep, Streeter was the state senator for Knox and Mercer counties, and during the next twenty years under the changing party descriptions of Greenback, Farmers' Alliance, Union Labor, and Populist he was a perennial candidate for Congress, for governor and finally for president of the United States.[69] Though he was noticed often in the local press, on the Knox campus he received little attention until he ran for president on the Union Labor ticket in 1888.[70] Among McClure's contemporaries at Knox was a student who joined the farmers' movement about this time. This was Horace Mark Gilbert, who attended Knox from 1879 to 1885. In 1891–92, when the Populist movement was nearing its zenith, Gilbert, a farmer from Geneseo, in the next county north, was president of "The Farmers' Alliance of Illinois."[71]

There were other indications that though the Knox College community was strongly Republican, it was open to more progressive opinions than those that dominated the "Regulars" or Main Street wing of the party. For example, President John Gulliver had been one of the Liberal Republicans who in 1872 tried in conjunction with Democrats to prevent the reelection of President Ulysses Grant.[72] At that time Newton Bateman, the superintendent of public instruction in Springfield, was one of a number of leading Republicans who supported Horace Greeley, the Liberal Republican candidate.[73] Bateman had been a Democrat early in his life, one of those who on the slavery issue had joined the Republican ranks and voted for John Charles Frémont in 1856. Though he held state office as a Republican for many years, "he was not, except during the war, an ardent partisan. He was too well aware of the evils of party government to be a hardy partisan."[74]

In a chapel talk in May 1879, President Bateman denounced the evil of railroad monopolies. His complaints were like those of the third parties of that time, his language was quite as strong as that of the antitrust muckrakers two decades later: "All monopolies tend to injustice and oppression. Take from a man, or a company of men all fear of competition, and sooner or later there will be arbitrary and heartless extortion; for the love of gain is insatiable. . . . Monopolies are gigantic evils, a perpetual menace to the people, a prolific source of popular irritation." To Bateman great wealth gained by speculation violated "immutable truths of political economy."[75] He explained to Knox students at the opening chapel in McClure's senior year that the hard times of the 1870s and the "persistent monetary stringency of unparalleled duration and severity" was God "speaking to this nation, as it were, from Sinai . . . telling us . . . that the laws of political economy are *his* laws, as much so as those of electricity or of gravitation."[76] In a talk to the seniors in 1885 he spoke of the "malign shadow of gigantic, heartless, and banded monopolies" that was "upon the land."[77]

Brief biographies of the members of the senior class of 1882 as published in the *Student* show that all but four were unqualified Republicans. McClure listed himself as a Republican.[78] But it is significant that of the four non-conformists, three had been on the *Student* staff with McClure and that none had been with the Mather group of the *Coup D'Etat*. Furthermore, two good friends of McClure on the anti-Mather coalition of his junior year had been Frederic Bancroft and Henry T. Rainey. Already at Knox Bancroft showed the political inclinations that were to make him a Mugwump who would support Grover Cleveland in 1884; all his life he remained a political independent.[79] Rainey early in the next century would appear in Congress as one of the progressive Democrats and as Speaker of the House three decades later would help push through Congress the first enactments of the New Deal.[80]

There is no basis in the record for ascribing to McClure in 1882 the non-conforming opinions of some of his close associates on the Knox campus. Yet it remaines meaningful that he was drawn to them. For McClure had already shown that he was attracted to that which was novel, unconventional, and unusual or untried.

Nor would he hide his light under a basket. By mid-July, after his graduation, the Galesburg *Republican Register* had been informed that "Sam McClure . . . has obtained a lucrative position in the employ of the Pope Manufacturing Company, Boston," well known as the leading manufacturer of bicycles, then a novelty and all the vogue. Two weeks later the newspaper reported that he had already been "promoted."[81] He had started for the East at the end of June 1882, with money accumulated from sales of his *History of Western College Journalism*, leaving his friend Phillips, who had been associated with him in this publication, to take care of their interests. He set out for the town near Utica, New York, where Harriet Hurd was visiting a friend. Here he was curtly sent away by Harriet and their engagement once more broken. Distraught, he bought a ticket for the first train he could get out of Utica; it was to Boston. When he arrived at the terminal, he discovered that someone had stolen his valise. Thus stranded, he sought out the family home of the Knox instructor in elocution, Melvina Bennett, who lived in a Boston suburb, and was welcomed for the weekend. On Monday he sought out Colonel Albert Pope, who had during the previous spring placed an advertisement for his bicycles in McClure's *History of Western College Journalism*. He got a job in a bicycle "rink," and soon was discussing with Pope his plans for a magazine that would enhance popular interest in bicycles.[82]

To show Colonel Pope what he could do, McClure sent to John Phillips in Galesburg for copies of the *Knox Student* for the year past. When Phillips sent the requested copies, he also wrote a letter to his friend: "You are the surest fellow I ever saw. You always alight on your feet. I wish I had one-half your push and business ability. Great Heavens, I wish I was with you. If you think I can make a living . . . I'll come. Couldn't your office boy become your assistant some time? Just say come & I'll do so. . . . Oh I *do* hope I *can* come. I'd give anything."[83] And so it happened. Colonel Pope put McClure in charge of establishing a magazine named the *Wheelman*, and because he would need help Samuel McClure sent for Phillips and John McClure. The little Knox group that were editing and managing the *Wheelman* in Boston were joined by Harriet Hurd, for she had initiated a reconciliation with Samuel, their engagement was renewed, and in June 1883, despite the very evident displeasure of her father, they were married in the Hurd home in Galesburg. During the next few years she would be a brilliant, patient, and essential associate of her husband in new journalistic ventures. For in the fall of 1883 both John McClure and Phillips interrupted their association with Samuel McClure; they enrolled at Harvard, as at one time Samuel McClure also intended to do.[84] For Harriet and Samuel the future of the *Wheelman* became less attractive, and in the spring of 1884 they moved to New York, where they were employed by the Century Book Company.

In October 1884 the McClures started a literary syndicate for newspapers. From their parlor they stuffed almost a thousand circulars to mail to newspapers, proposing that the McClures' literary syndicate sell work by well-known authors to the newspapers. Since several newspapers would print the same short stories or serialized novels, the shared cost to them would be less than it was to a single magazine. Yet it would be possible for the authors to be better paid than they might be by a single periodical. And the operators of the syndicate, that is, the McClures, would make a profit from the enterprise of finding and buying the authors' works and of vending them to metropolitan dailies. Though the idea was not new, as successfully conducted by the McClures this syndicate was to have profound influence not only on American journalism but on American literary history.[85]

Though the McClures had started on a shoestring, within months the syndicate was a working enterprise, and Samuel not only needed help for the chores of the enterprise but also someone with "decent editorial taste." He was disappointed in the kind of help he got from his brothers, and Harriet, with the care of a second child, was hardly able to give him the assistance that he needed. At this juncture, happily, John Phillips became available, to resume a partnership that would last for two decades. He "soon took over the entire office management," leaving McClure "free to move about the country, seeing editors and authors."[86]

Knox students, faculty, and alumni were kept well informed about the broadening scope and prosperity of the Associated Literary Press, the news often prompted by a visit of McClure to Galesburg. To the land-bound or "freshwater" precincts of Knox College, the direct contacts of both McClure and Phillips with European writers was impressive. Less than ten years after their graduation, McClure stood on the College chapel platform and recounted his experiences with famous English authors.[87] In October of that same year—1892—Knox students were given advance intimations of the new magazine that he was about to launch. Two months later, McClure, while passing through Galesburg, gave out the news that Albert Brady was to join the "firm of McClure and Phillips" that would publish this new magazine.[88] Thus the three men of the class of 1882 that had run the *Knox Student* ten years earlier would be together again in New York.

The most important resource of the new magazine was the "great fund . . . of the most successful stories and articles" that had been used by the syndicate and that might be selectively reprinted in the magazine. It was Phillips who put in most of the cash capital with which the magazine was started, and when later in that first year *McClure's Magazine* was desperate for cash, Phillips got his father to mortgage his home in Galesburg to provide another $5,000.[89]

Circulation of *McClure's* averaged during the first nine months nearly 25,000 copies, reached a monthly average of over 47,000 during the next twelve months, and achieved an average of nearly 150,000 the next year. In February 1896, when a circulation of 300,000 had been reached, some dramatic comparisons were made. *McClure's* now had a circulation "equal to both those giants of the magazine field," *Harper's* and *Century*. The former was "over half a century old"; the latter had "just completed twenty-five years of splendid life." Furthermore, "for three months—October, November, and December—we had, month by month, more paid advertising than any other magazine, while our December number had more pages of paid advertising than any other magazine at any time in the history of the world."[90]

The profits from the syndicate and the magazine only made it easier for McClure to dream up new ventures, some of them successfully discouraged by his partners; others briefly tried but failing. He did profitably form an association with Frank Doubleday to conduct a book publishing firm. During the first three months, beginning in October 1897, it was announced, "nearly a quarter of a million volumes had been manufactured and mostly sold." The climax of this kind of expansion occurred in 1899, when for a time the McClure enterprises controlled Harper and Brothers. In June 1899, when McClure went on his annual trip to Europe, he was "head of the strongest publishing house in the country, comprising a syndicate service, five magazines, a lecture bureau, and two book companies."[91]

To provide the editorial and managerial supervision for all these activities Phillips could be shifted from one task to a new one, Brady might spread himself around, Ida Tarbell might be given new duties, and men such as Doubleday or Walter Hines Page brought over from the older publishing houses. But to a remarkable degree McClure drew upon Knox College connections for new staff members. Particularly important appointments were given during the late 1890s to Robert and John Finley and to a brother-in-law of the latter, Albert Boyden.

The Finley brothers were both graduated from Knox in 1887 and then were graduate students at Johns Hopkins until 1890. When the *Review of Reviews* was started in 1890, Robert Finley was a staff member, became an assistant editor, and often was entirely responsible for its form and contents. In 1896 he joined the other Knox men at *McClure's* and became manager of the syndicate. Unfortunately he died the following year. In the chapel of Knox College, where John Finley was now the president, Samuel McClure in December 1897 gave an "inspiring talk" on the life of this Knox alumnus whose career had been cut off in its prime.[92]

In April 1899 President Finley announced that he would leave Knox to join the McClure enterprises. It was anticipated that he would edit a review that would grow out of the recent "combination of the great publishing firms of the east," *Harper's* and *McClure's*, a "union of the young and the old blood of the publishing business."[93] When this combination failed, McClure put Finley in charge of editing *McClure's*. Though Finley left *McClure's* in the fall of 1900 to accept an invitation of Woodrow Wilson to teach at Princeton, he continued for some time "to read copy and to make editorial suggestions." During his brief formal connection with the magazine, moreover, his influence had much to do with making the magazine famous for its muckraking, particularly for its exposure of trusts.[94]

About the time that Finley assumed the presidency of Knox he had married an alumna, Martha Boyden, who like himself and his brother Robert had entered Knox at the fall term following the graduation of Brady, Phillips, and McClure. Mrs. Finley's brother, Albert Augustus Boyden, was at Knox from 1890 to 1895. At the end of his junior year he transferred to Harvard, from which he was graduated in 1898. He came straight from Harvard to the art department of *McClure's*, where he became a sort of "professional god-son" to Phillips. By 1901 he was assigned general responsibilities for editing the magazine and in 1903 became the managing director of *McClure's*. He retained this post until 1906, when he and some others followed Phillips in the founding of the *American Magazine*, of which Albert Boyden was the managing editor from 1906 to 1917.[95]

Boyden was only one in the "flow of students" to *McClure's* during the 1890s—the years of Finley's presidency, when Knox affairs and those of the magazine were often linked together.[96] Another was Albert Britt, who was editor of the Knox *Student* fifteen years after McClure and then three decades later would be president of Knox College. Britt was disappointed with the job he was given at *McClure's* and changed to graduate studies at Columbia University. Three years later he went to work for *Public Opinion,* which was a "transitory holding" of McClure's supervised by Robert McClure. Britt eventually became the editor of *Public Opinion,* which made "some ventures in muckraking." Later, with a former fellow student from Knox, Thomas Harper Blodgett, he bought and edited the *Outing Magazine.*[97]

Late in the 1890s *McClure's Magazine* also came to have close associations with Earnest Elmo Calkins, who was graduated from Knox in 1891. Like McClure, Calkins acknowledged a special indebtedness for his literary education to Melville Anderson and also to Melvina Bennett. At Knox his journalistic apprenticeship included editing during three summers the Knox *Vacationist* (1888, 1889, and 1894), and reporting (for a weekly feature) in a local newspaper the news from the College. For his senior year he was elected by the *Coup D'Etat* stock company to the post of editor-in-chief. As had McClure, Calkins found this editorial responsibility significant. He recalled it as "the most valuable education he obtained from College," all the more satisfying because the deafness that handicapped him in most situations of college life was less of a hindrance in his editorial duties.[98]

In New York Calkins formed an advertising partnership that has been described as the "first modern advertising company." It was *McClure's Magazine* that particularly helped Calkins's firm get a good start, and the magazine became a "client" of the Calkins and Holden firm "in a large way." To Calkins, who was very close to the affairs of *McClure's,* it was at the turn of the century "the most exciting publication in existence."[99]

The close identification of Knox College with *McClure's Magazine* was exemplified at the turn of the century by the College annual that juniors published for the year 1899–1900. The *Gale* opened with an article entitled: "The Story of McClure's." It summarized the phenomenal success of the magazine and noted that the three men "at the head" were all from the class of 1882, and then added "by the recent removal of Dr. Finley from his field of labor as President of Knox, *McClure's* has gained another loyal son of Knox whose added strength will give new impetus to the great work to be done." Portraits of all four men, McClure, Phillips, Brady, and Finley, illustrated the article.

The Knox College Alumni Association in June 1890 had elected McClure vice-president. Early in 1897 he participated in the organization of an eastern or New York alumni society. The meeting was held in the home of Stephen ("Deacon") V. White (Knox 1854), the well-known speculator, who off and on was a very wealthy man; he became a trustee of Knox that year. McClure was chosen vice-president and Phillips was named treasurer of this New York alumni group.[100]

Already during the first year of the publication of *McClure's*, Knox began to receive public attention through this magazine.[101] During the autumn of 1893 McClure arranged for Knox to be visited by the distinguished French journalist, Thérèse Bentzon, who used the *nom de plume* of Madame Blanc. This was her first visit to an American school. She stayed at the home of Professor Hurd. In October 1894 she published in the *Revue des Deux Mondes* an article: "La condition de la femme aux Etats-Unis (la co-education—Galesburg)." This was translated into English by Mary Hurd, McClure's sister-in-law, who had recently become an instructor in French at Knox and in May 1895 was republished in *McClure's* under the title: "A Prairie College: An Eminent Frenchwoman's Study of Co-Education in America." Madame Blanc reported favorably upon the education for women she found at Knox, sketched a flattering description of the home of Professor Hurd and his family, and presented a nearly idyllic impression of the College city. Her essay, which would be quoted by Edward Bok in the *Ladies' Home Journal,* was an impressive endorsement of the College. McClure supplied Knox with copies of the flattering article, which President Finley might use to raise money and to attract students.[102]

McClure himself responded generously and thoughtfully to the financial stringencies that caused the College during the mid-1890s to reduce its budget and to cut back expenditures for faculty salaries. As a speaker during the ceremonies for the Founders Day Celebration on February 15, 1897, he discussed the financial difficulties of the College and suggested "as a plan of retrenchment a

Committee of Safety, consisting of forty or fifty who would pledge $200 apiece per year to make up any deficit." This plan, which would assure $10,000 annually, was adopted by the trustees. Two years later on Founders Day, when President Finley was able to announce that substantial progress had been made toward raising $100,000 for endowment, the pledge of McClure for $10,000 was by far the largest on the list of subscribers.[103]

To attract more students to Knox College, McClure on Founders Day of 1896 announced "another of the many . . . schemes which he started for the advancement of his Alma Mater." He proposed "to establish at Knox an 'Abraham Lincoln School of Science and Practical Arts.' " Galesburg would become the "great center of interest in Lincoln" by embodying "a memorial to his name in the Scientific department of Knox College."[104]

For this new department at Knox the publishers of *McClure's Magazine* undertook to raise an endowment of $250,000 and to establish 100 scholarships that could be gained by enlarging the circulation of the magazine. These scholarships, which could be earned by securing 500 subscribers to *McClure's Magazine,* would pay the board, room rent, and tuition of a young man or woman for a year. Soon advertisements in *McClure's Magazine* identified this special association of the magazine with Knox College. McClure sent notices of this joint venture to 3,500 papers throughout the nation, and Knox itself widely advertised the scheme.[105] There was no tabulation of the number of students thus attracted to Knox, but Don Marquis, who was to be very briefly a student at Knox, recalled that his interest had been "fired" partly by the *McClure's* proposition, though he was never able to sell more than a dozen subscriptions even after trying for six months.[106]

The proposal for an Abraham Lincoln School of Science and Practical Arts and the scheme for *McClure's Magazine* scholarships were synchronized with the appearance in the magazine of a serialized biography of Abraham Lincoln, and this, in turn, was coordinated with the celebration for the first time at Knox of an anniversary of the Lincoln-Douglas debate that had occurred on the campus in October 1858.[107] The author to whom McClure assigned this biographical series on Lincoln was Ida M. Tarbell, who arrived in Galesburg in January 1895 "for the purpose of gathering reminiscences of President Lincoln."[108] Tarbell stayed at the home of President Finley, who assisted her in gathering newspaper materials and in meeting people who could give her their recollections, especially of the fifth Lincoln-Douglas debate at Galesburg, in which she was particularly interested.[109] Her friendship with John Finley antedated her connection with McClure, for, during their summer vacations, while graduate students at Johns Hopkins, John and Robert Finley both came to the famous Chautauqua assembly, where Tarbell helped publish the newspaper of the Chautauqua Society. John Finley helped, too, proofreading articles that Tarbell wrote for this distinctly liberal and reformist periodical.[110] The Tarbell series on Lincoln did indeed prove to be very successful in expanding the *McClure's Magazine* circulation. Her article on the Lincoln-Douglas debates particularly emphasized the debate held in Galesburg against the back-drop of the main building of Knox College. The article appeared in the issue for October 1896, the month when Knox College staged the first of its anniversary commemorations of the Galesburg debate. The article took notice of this fact, as it did of the other connections among Knox College, Lincoln, and *McClure's Magazine*.[111]

Of these several Knox projects associated with the Lincoln theme, only the celebration of the Lincoln-Douglas debate would be of lasting significance. During the decades to come William McKinley, Theodore Roosevelt, William Howard Taft, and William Jennings Bryan would be involved in anniversaries of this debate. In future years many of the great Lincoln biographers and Civil War historians would assist in the commemorations, and not the least of these, Carl Sandburg, would vividly remember that he witnessed the first of these rituals in 1896 and acknowledged the imprint on him of the bronze plaque that quoted from the speeches made at the Knox Old Main building in 1857.[112]

After President Finley left Knox to join the other Knox men that headed McClure's publishing ventures, the interlocking of the affairs of Knox and of *McClure's Magazine* were not as apparent. But McClure continued to be very much involved in Knox activities. He was a regular visitor to the campus and spoke in the chapel during the fall of 1903 and again in 1906. In June 1906 he spoke at the Alumni Reunion. From 1905 to 1908 his son, Robert

Louis Stevenson McClure, was a student at Knox and his daughter Eleanor was a student from 1903 to 1907 and again in 1909–10. During the year 1908–9 she was instructor in French, taking the place on the Knox faculty of her aunt, Mary Hurd, who was on leave in France. It was while his children were at Knox that Samuel S. McClure, in 1907, was awarded an honorary doctorate, along with his classmates Robert Mather and John S. Phillips.[113]

Though McClure was not as affluent then as he had been at the turn of the century, he supported the special endowment fund drive in 1909, pledging $5,000. Regarding the raising of money for colleges, McClure, at the Founders Day banquet for the seventieth anniversary of the founding of the College, had spoken this warning about "the grave danger in such gifts as Rockefeller is making to colleges is that the spirit of gratitude to the giver would tend to blunt the sense in students, faculty and alumni, of opprobrium which should be maintained toward the manner in which such wealth was acquired."[114] This was an appropriate caution from the editor of the most famous muckraking magazine, which had published the long serialized history of the Standard Oil Company by Tarbell, a series that had an enormous impact on public opinion regarding monopolistic corporations. The *Knox Student* had in 1906, for example, taken notice of the action of William Jennings Bryan, who resigned from the board of trustees of Illinois College because of its solicitation of funds from Andrew Carnegie.[115]

When McClure and Phillips both became Doctors of Literature at the Knox commencement of 1907, it was only fifteen months since President Roosevelt, in a widely reported speech to American journalists, denounced the muckrakers. The Knox muckrakers were not so much the writers of the magazine as they were its editors and managers. McClure and Phillips discovered, attracted, and selected authors such as Tarbell and Ray Stannard Baker[116] and prompted them to their exposure of the abuse of economic or political power. William Allen White was the more readily involved and persuaded to contribute to *McClure's* because Harriet Hurd McClure's father had been the teacher and friend of White's mother when, as an adult, she attended the Knox Academy from 1856 to 1861.[117] Frederic Bancroft brought to *McClure's* the memoirs of that veteran reformer, Carl Schurz, as well as contributions relating to the Civil War and to the postbellum South. John Finley brought to the magazine staff a penchant for reform that had been quite evident during his presidency of Knox College. By his earlier connections with the charities board of New York he put the staff of *McClure's* into contact with social reformers of the East; from the Midwest he first introduced the editors to Jane Addams, Albert Beveridge, Robert La Follette, and Frederic Howe. Finley's role as professional economist was crucial. Viola Roseboro of the magazine staff was greatly influenced by the book on *Taxation in American Cities* that Finley had co-authored with Richard Ely. Finley did much to involve *McClure's Magazine* in the question of the monopolistic trusts as exemplified in Tarbell's work on Standard Oil and by studies of the "Trust Problem" written by Professor Jeremiah Jenks. Jenks had been a faculty member at Knox from 1886 to 1889, while Finley was a student.[118]

Finley, along with Phillips and Finley's brother-in-law, Albert Boyden, were involved in bringing on to the staff Lincoln Steffens, who would write the brilliant series of articles on the "Shame of the Cities." Boyden, as well as Phillips, was greatly admired by Steffens.[119] It was Albert Boyden's brother, William Boyden of Chicago, who first gave Steffens the leads for interviews and information that went into the famous articles on the nature of politics in Chicago, St. Paul, Minneapolis, and St. Louis.[120]

Soon after President Roosevelt denounced the muckrakers, the management and writing staff of *McClure's Magazine* suffered a schism. Most of the remarkable group of writers associated with *McClure's* followed Phillips and Boyden in separating from McClure and establishing the *American Magazine*. This secession of leadership and talent from *McClure's Magazine* was widely regarded, sometimes with joy, as resulting from President Roosevelt's speech against the muckrakers. But this conclusion was erroneous, as those on the inside of the magazine's organization knew.[121]

Frustrations had been building for several years over McClure's visionary projects and about his protracted absences in Europe. There were temperamental differences and personal irritations. These tensions came to a head when McClure insisted on the developing of a second magazine that was to be even cheaper, even more popular, and even more profitable and powerful than *McClure's Magazine*. Furthermore, the money made by this second magazine was, in another of McClure's grandiose schemes, to finance other subsidiary projects.

To Phillips and Tarbell, McClure's new projects would gamble with their own capital investment in *McClure's Magazine;* to staff writers such as Baker and Steffens the scheme threatened their careers. Furthermore, it was believed that the financial backers that McClure was seeking would corrupt the independence of *McClure's Magazine*. Indeed, articles in the magazine itself had recently been exposing the manner in which great corporations, by their subsidies, had been achieving control over the press. The sinister capitalists who in particular appeared to be corrupting McClure were two Knox alumni who had been at Knox College when he was a student and who were now fellow members of the Knox College board of trustees: Edgar A. Bancroft (1878) and Robert Mather (1882). Though McClure might regard them merely as old friends or admirers and though Phillips and Boyden as fellow alumni would know that McClure's relations with them had been sustained by their legitimate common concerns about Knox, yet both Bancroft and Mather had corporate connections that made them rightly suspect to the other muckrakers on the staff.[122]

Bancroft regarded himself as a liberal and supportive of new ideas,[123] but there were reasons in 1906 why he should be regarded as a representative of railroad and other monopolistic interests. He had become connected with the Santa Fe Railroad when it developed its right of way through Galesburg, and in 1892 he moved to Chicago to serve that railroad as solicitor in the state of Illinois.[124] During the railway strike that grew out of the difficulties of George Pullman with his employees and tenants in Pullman, Illinois, Bancroft secured the first of the injunctions used against the American Railway Union and was active in the contempt proceedings that sent Eugene Debs to prison.[125] His role in the jailing of Debs was well known to Knox students,[126] and he defended this punitive use of the injunctive powers in a paper that he read to the Illinois Bar Association, which was published at his own expense.[127] Thus, Bancroft's associations were understandably suspect by 1906, by which time he had served other railroads and had otherwise become a "trust lawyer" by serving the International Harvester Company.

Even more involved in the split that occurred in *McClure's Magazine* staff in 1906 was Robert Mather. Though McClure and Mather had been rivals while students, they remained friends.[128] Mather matched McClure's success in journalism by a rapid rise to importance as a corporation lawyer, and at the time *McClure's Magazine* was launched he was an attorney with the Rock Island Railroad, of which he became general counsel.[129] By the mid-1890s both of these members of the class of 1882 were seeing each other regularly, if not at other times, in meetings of the College Board of Trustees. At the time of the crisis at *McClure's* in 1906 Mather became McClure's "advocate and general counsel" for negotiations with Phillips and Tarbell so that McClure might buy their stock in the magazine. To Tarbell and Steffens, Mather and Bancroft appeared to be "unscrupulous knaves" who were trying to "worm" their way into control of *McClure's* to "throttle" it. The muckrakers were particularly suspicious of Mather because he was an officer of the Mercantile Trust Company, which had become notorious because of its connection with scandals in the insurance business.[130] Among the evils exposed at that time had been the use of funds for lobbying, political bribery, and political espionage.[131]

It was Mather who managed the financial details for separating Phillips, Tarbell, Boyden, and their supporters from the McClure enterprises. Though still burdened by a crushing debt, McClure in 1908 resisted pressure by Mather to sell out his stock to the Crowell Publishing Company; and in 1911 he rejected a refinancing plan proposed by Mather because he feared it would cause his magazine to "pass into the hands of Wall Street." Unfortunately, another scheme devised by McClure's own staff by 1912 did cause McClure to lose control of the magazine that he and Phillips had started two decades earlier.[132]

Meanwhile Phillips and Boyden and Tarbell and the others who had separated from McClure in 1906 had made a successful venture of the *American Magazine*. Though Ida Tarbell claimed this magazine "had little genuine muckraking spirit," it "did have a large and fighting interest in fair play."[133] Phillips used the *American* to support La Follette, and he along with Boyden and

165

McClure all joined the Progressive revolt under Theodore Roosevelt. In 1915 the *American* was sold to the Crowell Publishing Company; the old staff that went back to the days of *McClure's Magazine* was now dispersed.[134]

NOTES

1. Pringle, *Theodore Roosevelt.*
2. Louis Filler, "Muckrakers,' *Encyclopedia Brittanica* (1967), 15:973.
3. Sullivan, *Our Times,* 2:479–80.
4. Faulkner, *Quest for Social Justice,* 112. An English author in the *Fortnightly Review* in 1910, while discussing the impulse that the muckrakers gave to reform, wrote about the "McClure type of magazine" (quoted in Baker, *American Chronicle,* 202).
5. Sources for the history of McClure's journalistic ventures are: Lyon, *Success Story;* Wilson, *McClure's Magazine;* and, of course, McClure's own autobiography, recited to Willa Cather and written by her: *My Autobiography.*
6. The catalogue of 1886–87 (26–27) for the first time has this kind of statement: "Students from certain preparatory schools which have been approved by the Faculty will be admitted to suitable classes without a special examination on presentation of their diplomas of graduation or certificates of class standing. . . . In 1887 . . . students from the following schools will be admitted on certificate: Galesburg High School; Princeton High School; Geneseo Collegiate Institute." These were all schools with which Knox had had unusually close relations.
7. McClure, *My Autobiography,* 60–61.
8. *Ibid.,* 62–65.
9. John McClure to Miss Sandford, Oct. 16, 1923, MS, alumni file for class of 1879, Knox College Library.
10. Galesburg *Republican Register,* Apr. 7, 1877, 1.
11. *Ibid.*
12. McClure, *My Autobiography,* 88–89; Lyon, *Success Story,* 16–20.
13. McClure, *My Autobiography.*
14. Adelphi Society, Program Minutes, Sept. 12, 1877.
15. *Ibid.,* June 5, 12, 1878.
16. Galesburg *Republican Register,* June 8, 1878, 5.
17. McClure, *My Autobiography,* 101–31.
18. *Knox Student,* 1 (Feb. 1879), 13.
19. Adelphi Society, Business Meeting Minutes, May 14, 1879.
20. McClure, *My Autobiography,* 126.
21. *Ibid.,* 90–93, 95.
22. *Knox Student,* Jan. 1882, 58, 62.
23. Adelphi Society, Program Minutes, June 1, 1881; Galesburg *Republi-*

can Register, May 21, 1881, 1; May 28, 1881, 6; Sept. 10, 1881, 1; Sept. 17, 1881, 5.

24. McClure, *My Autobiography,* 158; *Knox Student,* Apr. 1882, 106.

25. McClure, *My Autobiography,* v.

26. Wilson, *McClure's Magazine,* 34, 85; Lyon, *Success Story,* 76.

27. Adelphi Society, Program Minutes, Feb. 4, 1880, Feb. 15, 1882.

28. *Knox Student,* Nov. 1881, 23; Galesburg *Republican Register,* Oct. 22, 1881, 6.

29. Galesburg *Republican Register,* Oct. 22, 1881, 1; *Coup D'Etat,* Nov. 1881, 16.

30. Phillips, "Knox College," in McClure, ed., *History of College Journalism,* 26–29; Galesburg *Republican Register,* Oct. 12, 1878, 4.

31. Phillips, "Knox College," in McClure, ed., *History of College Journalism; Knox Student,* May 1881, 7; June 1881, 16; *Coup D'Etat,* 1 (Oct. 1881), 5–8.

32. Adelphi Society, Business Meeting Minutes and Program Minutes for the year 1880–81, *passim.*

33. *Knox Student,* Apr. 1881, 14–15; Galesburg *Republican Register,* Apr. 30, 1881, 5.

34. McClure, *My Autobiography,* 133–34; *Coup D'Etat,* Oct. 1881, 5–8; *Gale,* 1888, 96, article on "Knox Journalism."

35. Earnest Elmo Calkins, an article in the Diamond Jubilee edition of the *Knox Student,* Oct. 30, 1953, 2.

36. *Ibid.,* Nov. 1881, 21–22.

37. McClure, *My Autobiography,* 135–36.

38. *Ibid.,* 134–35, 149.

39. *Knox Student,* Dec. 1881, 33–35, 36–38.

40. Galesburg *Republican Register,* Dec. 24, 1881, 5. The *Coup D'Etat* also gave him that title in the issue of Apr. 1882, 111.

41. *Coup D'Etat,* Jan. 1881, 57.

42. *Knox Student,* Feb. 1882, 75–76.

43. *Ibid.,* Apr. 1882, 106; May 1882, 113–17; Galesburg *Republican Register,* Oct. 22, 1881, 6; Apr. 29, 1882, 1; May 6, 1882, 1.

44. *Ibid.,* June 24, 1882, 4, 7; July 1, 1882, 1. The Western College Press Association was described as "defunct" in an "exchange" from the Franklin College *Collegiate* published in *Coup D'Etat,* May 1883, 125.

45. Phillips, "Knox College," in McClure, ed., *History of College Journalism,* 26–29; McClure, *My Autobiography,* 136–37; *Knox Student,* May 1882, 120; June 1882, 145.

46. Galesburg *Republican Register,* June 24, 1882, 4–5.

47. McClure, *My Autobiography,* 139. The *Coup D'Etat,* commencement supplement, June 1882, 152, published an excerpt from McClure's speech.

48. Wilson, *McClure's Magazine,* 3–5.

49. See ch. 1 herein.

50. Galesburg *Republican Register,* Ap. 11, 1874, 5; Aug. 1, 1874, 4; Mar. 13, 1875, 3; Oct. 4, 1890, 6; June 28, 1891, 2.

51. Edward Beecher returned to give the Baccalaureate address in 1879; the Reverend Horatio Foote gave the opening prayer (*ibid.*, June 28, 1879, 2). Hiram Huntington Kellogg preached at the First Congregational Church, Apr. 1876 (*ibid.*, Apr. 22, 1876, 1). Dr. Blanchard was a rather frequent visitor. A reminiscent letter by him appeared in *ibid.*, June 5, 1875, 1.

52. Galesburg *Republican*, Dec. 3, 1869, 2.

53. Galesburg *Republican Register*, Dec. 7, 1878, 6.

54. Cooke, *Frederic Bancroft*, 7–8; Galesburg *Republican Register*, Oct. 9, 1880, 6.

55. See ch. 3 herein.

56. Blanchard in the 1840s, having returned from a world antislavery convention in London, lectured on the "wrongs of Ireland" (*Coup D'Etat*, Jan. 1891, 78). When Wendell Phillips returned in 1878, under the auspices of Gnothautii, to lecture for the third time in Galesburg, he spoke on Daniel O'Connell, "the first Liberator of the Emerald Island." Galesburg *Republican Register*, Dec. 21, 1878.

57. Adelphi Society, Program Minutes, *passim;* Galesburg *Republican Register*, Feb. 14, 1880, 1; Apr. 10, 1880, 5.

58. *Knox Student*, Mar. 1881, 5–6.

59. Galesburg *Republican Register*, May 15, 1886, 2.

60. *Ibid.*, June 11, 1887, 4; *Coup D'Etat*, Nov. 1886, 44.

61. Wheatly, "New York Stock Exchange," 829–53.

62. *Coup D'Etat*, Mar. 1884, 92; Mar. 1885, 107; Nov. 1885, 44; Mar. 1886, 108; Oct. 1891, 25; Galesburg *Republican Register*, Dec. 25, 1875, 1; May 21, 1887, 3.

63. Galesburg *Republican Register*, Oct. 28, 1880, 6; Nov. 6, 1880, 4, 5.

64. *Ibid.*, Mar. 19, 1881, 3.

65. *Ibid.*, Mar. 19, 1881, 6; Mar. 26, 1881, 3, 5.

66. *Coup D'Etat*, May 1884, 115; Oct. 1884, 26.

67. Wilson, *McClure's Magazine*, 217–22.

68. Calkins, *They Broke the Prairie*, 23.

69. Newcombe, "Alson J. Streeter."

70. *Coup D'Etat*, Sept. 1888, 11; June 1889, 153; Galesburg *Republican Register*, Sept. 28, 1888, 6.

71. Knox catalogue, 1891–92, 120.

72. Galesburg *Republican Register*, June 15, 1872, 2.

73. Carr, *My Day and Generation*, 323–24.

74. Samuel Willard, "Memorial of Newton Bateman," *Coup D'Etat*, Feb. 1898, 150.

75. Bateman Papers. This speech is in a folder labeled "Chapel Talks."

76. *Ibid.*, manuscript entitled "Loyalty."

77. *Ibid.*, manuscript entitled "Redeeming the Time."

78. *Knox Student*, June 1882, 144–45.

79. Cooke, *Frederic Bancroft*, 19, 126–31.

80. Charles O. Paulin, "Henry Thomas Rainey," in the *DAB*, first supplementary volume.

81. Galesburg *Republican Register*, July 15, 1882, 1; July 29, 1882, 1.
82. McClure, *My Autobiography*, 126–44.
83. Lyon, *Success Story*, 37.
84. Galesburg *Republican Register*, July 29, 1882, 1.
85. Wilson, *McClure's Magazine*, 40–41; Lyon, *Success Story*, 50–62.
86. McClure, *My Autobiography*, 180–81.
87. Galesburg *Republican Register*, Jan. 2, 1892, 2.
88. *Coup D'Etat*, Oct. 1892, 54.
89. McClure, *My Autobiography*, 208–9.
90. *McClure's Magazine*, Feb. 1896, 304.
91. Lyon, *Success Story*, 139–69.
92. Finley, "Tribute to the Memory of Robert J. Finley"; Wilson, *McClure's Magazine*, 22; *Coup D'Etat*, Dec. 1897, 108.
93. *Knox Student*, Nov. 7, 1899, 110; Dec. 5, 1899, 161.
94. Wilson, *McClure's Magazine*, 93.
95. Phillips, *Albert A. Boyden;* Lyons, *Success Story*, 192; Wilson, *McClure's Magazine*, 412.
96. See an unpublished manuscript by Muelder on "Knox College and the Muckrakers."
97. Britt, *Turn of the Century*, 12–20; Wilson, *McClure's Magazine*, 24–25.
98. Calkins, *and Hearing Not*, 102–4.
99. *Ibid.*, 190, 248–49.
100. *Coup D'Etat*, June 1890, 139; *Student*, Feb. 4, 1897, 4; Feb. 18, 1897, 4; *Coup D'Etat*, Feb. 1897, 101.
101. *McClure's Magazine*, Aug. 1893, 198.
102. *Coup D'Etat*, Nov. 1893, 50, 52; *Revue des Deux Mondes*, 125 (Oct. 1894), 885–95; Madame Blanc (Th. Bentzon), "A Prairie College," 541–48; Calkins, *They Broke the Prairie*, 431–32; *Knox Student*, Apr. 17, 1895, 5; May 15, 1895, 3.
103. *Knox Student*, Feb. 18, 1897, 1; Feb. 21, 1899, 242; *Coup D'Etat*, Feb. 1897, 98–99. McClure was probably as impulsive in his giving as he was in other matters. In 1895 he agreed to provide the money ($100) if the executive committee would authorize an increase in the salary of his sister-in-law, Mary Hurd, who was an instructor of French (Minutes of the Executive Committee, June 6, 1895). In 1901 he, with ten others, including E. A. Bancroft and Robert Mather, made a special contribution for football at Knox (*Knox Student*, Nov. 8, 1901, 160).
104. *Coup D'Etat*, Mar. 26, 1896, 33; *Knox Student*, Feb. 20, 1896, 2.
105. *Knox Student*, Mar. 12, 1896, 5; Executive Committee Minutes, Mar. 5, 1896. The advertisement of the scholarships was still being published in the *Coup D'Etat* of Apr. 1898 (p. 199).
106. Anthony, *O Rare Don Marquis*, 494.
107. The coming celebration of the Lincoln-Douglas debate was announced in the same issues of the *Knox Student* and the *Coup D'Etat* that announced the Abraham Lincoln School and the scholarships. By Jan. 1896

Clark E. Carr had already extended the invitation to Chauncey DePew to speak at the debate anniversary.

108. *Knox Student*, Jan. 23, 1895, 4.

109. Tarbell, "The Lincoln-Douglas Debate and Old Main," 30–31; Tarbell, *All in the Day's Work*, 171–72.

110. Wilson, *McClure's Magazine*, 67–69.

111. *McClure's Magazine*, Oct. 1896, 401–13.

112. Sandburg, *Always the Young Strangers*, 301–2, 241.

113. *Knox Student*, Oct. 22, 1903, 72; Feb. 15, 1906, 306; June 14, 1906, 610; Nov. 8, 1906, 136; Sept. 17, 1903, 7; *Gale*, of 1910, 28. McClure's nephew, Thomas Harvey McClure, was a student at Knox, 1905–10.

114. *Knox Student*, Feb. 18, 1907, 333; Feb. 21, 1907, 353; Feb. 4, 1901, 310.

115. *Ibid.*, Feb. 15, 1906, 308.

116. Baker, *American Chronicle*, 77–82.

117. White, *Autobiography*, 12–31, 300–301, 381. White credited McClure with being "the pioneer of a reform that was to surge onward in American life and run for forty years as the dominant note in our political, social, and economic thinking" (p. 386).

118. Wilson, *McClure's Magazine*, 13, 22–24, 76, 130–31, 132, 139, 162–63.

119. Albert Boyden to Steffens, Jan. 2, 1904, in Steffens, *The Letters of Lincoln Steffens*, 162.

120. Steffens, *Autobiography*, 1:357–59, 365–68, 453ff.

121. Wilson, *McClure's Magazine*; Lyon, *Success Story*, 186, 257–96; Tarbell, *All in a Day's Work*, 254–59; Baker, *American Chronicle*, 211, 220; White, *Autobiography*, 386.

122. Lyon, *Success Story*, 280–83; Wilson, *McClure's Magazine*, 178; Steffens, *Letters*, 1:173–75.

123. He supported civil service reform and low tariffs and opposed imperialism. After World War I he served as chairman of the commission on race relations for Illinois, following the Chicago riots of 1919 (Cooke, *Frederic Bancroft*, 54–55). He was a "lawyer friend" of Harriet Monroe and one of the original five-year underwriters of *Poetry*. He was present at the famous *Poetry* banquet for W. B. Yeats in 1914. See Monroe, *A Poet's Life*, 234, 244.

124. Galesburg *Republican Register*, Aug. 27, 1887, 1. For earlier involvement in railroad cases see, Perry, ed., *History of Knox County*, 1:58–59.

125. Cooke, *Frederic Bancroft*, 54–55; *Knox Alumnus*, Oct. 24, 1924, 31–32.

126. *Knox Student*, Oct. 3, 1894, 5.

127. Bancroft, *Chicago Strike of 1894*. The *Knox Student* commented that this booklet was an "excellent source of information on what has been the unpopular side of the struggle" (Mar. 13, 1895, 137).

128. Lyon, *Success Story*, 50.

129. Knox College catalogue, 1892, 117; *Coup D'Etat*, Jan. 1898, 137.

130. Lyon, *Success Story*, 282–85, 291–92.

131. Hendricks, "The Story of Life Insurance," *McClure's*, 27 (May-Oct. 1906), 36, 157, 237, 401, 539, 659.

132. Lyon, *Success Story*, 285, 313, 421, 335.

133. Tarbell, *All in a Day's Work*, 281, 300; Wilson, *McClure's Magazine*, 277.

134. Tarbell, *All in a Day's Work*, 495–500.

CHAPTER VI

EDGAR LEE MASTERS: "the position that was given me at Knox College"

After thirty years as an obscure versifier, Edgr Lee Masters "catapulted" into fame as a significant poet.[1] In February 1915, *Poetry* magazine of Chicago declared that the *Spoon River Anthology* had proved to be "the literary sensation of the year."[2] But not all were pleased with this unconventional work. The reviewer in *The Dial*, which for a quarter of a century had been providing literary guidance to Chicago and the Midwest, was most unhappy about this newest of Masters's books and stated that he was perpetrating "trash" in much of the *Spoon River Anthology*. "Spoon River," he assumed, was a village or a "place peculiarly accursed," in the vicinity of Peoria and Knox College.[3]

Knox College had been publicly associated with the author of the *Spoon River Anthology* when the poems first appeared serially in the St. Louis *Mirror* of William Marion Reedy. Masters used the pseudonym "Webster Ford" for these epitaphs, as he had for some earlier writings. Carl Sandburg was one of the very few who knew who "Webster Ford" was. And while Masters's epitaphs were first appearing in the *Mirror*, Sandburg sent Reedy a tribute to "Webster Ford," which read as follows:

> A man wrote two books.
> One held in its covers the outside man,
> whose name was on a Knox College diploma,
> who bought his clothes at Marshall Field's,
> had his name done by a sign painter in gilt
> on an office door in a loop skyscraper,

and never did any damage to the code of morals
set forth by the *Chicago Tribune.*

The other book held a naked man,
the sheer brute under the clothes
as he will be stripped at the Last Day,
the inside man with red heartbeats
that go on ticking off life
against the ribs.[4]

Sandburg and Masters at this time had known each other for
only a few months. Though Masters had lived in Sandburg's
hometown of Galesburg during the year when Masters was at
Knox College, the first meeting of the men was delayed for a
quarter of a century until Masters, a labor lawyer in Chicago, met
Sandburg when Sandburg was reporting a labor case which Masters was arguing at the time. On this occasion, just before Christmas of 1913, during a recess in the courtroom procedures,
Sandburg came to Masters with a copy of Reedy's *Mirror* that
contained a poem by Masters for which Sandburg expressed
admiration.

Masters and Sandburg shared familiarity with Galesburg,
though they went to different colleges there. They also had in
common an awareness that their college experiences were important influences on their literary careers. Though Lee Masters was
enrolled at Knox College only nine months, in his autobiography,
published when he was sixty-six years old, he placed great importance on that solitary college year: "Whatever my luck has been,
and often it has been bad, I have always been conscious of a good
demon, a brother god, who would guide me along according to
the fortunate direction that went forth at the time of my birth. It
may have been the adoration of my grandmother, the attention
that was paid me from the first at school, *the position that was
given me at Knox College,* that gave me the feeling, the illusion
that I was born to something fortunate and distinguished, come
what might."[5] Masters gave an entire chapter in his memoirs,
Across Spoon River, to his time at Knox College, a chapter sprin-
kled with words such as "enthralled," "wonderful," and "magic"
and filled with memories evoking pleasure, excitement, warmth,

companionship, and intensity. It indicates that Masters made much of the opportunities for studying, for reading and conversation, and for forming enriching friendships.[6]

Knox College, when Masters was a student, certainly exemplified what George Santayana in 1911 described as the "genteel tradition." Dr. William Edward Simonds, who arrived to teach English literature the same autumn that Masters enrolled, was the embodiment of gentility. The "genteel tradition," however, by honoring scholarship, by promoting inquiry, by tolerating criticism, and by delighting in intellectual diversions, also encouraged invention and novelty and possibly even rebellion. This proposition was demonstrated by the Knox muckrakers in *McClure's Magazine.* It was also evident in Masters's experience at Knox and by his continuing relation with Simonds. Reading Homer in Greek was quite as broadening an experience to the youth from a rural county seat in western Illinois as was his subsequent removal to Chicago. At Knox a poet was honored, and his verses, while a student and later as alumnus, might be seen in print, even if he departed from the traditional.

Masters came to Knox in September 1889 from Lewiston, the seat of Fulton County, immediately south of Knox County. It was typical of the origins of Knox students at that time that thirty-two of them came from Fulton County. One-third of the students came from the "Military Tract," the area between the Illinois and the Mississippi rivers, from the country of the Spoon River, a name which suddenly became known throughout the nation when Masters's *Anthology* was published in 1915. When Masters was a student, only a tiny fraction of the students came from Cook County.[7]

Masters arrived in Galesburg on the train from Lewiston with his good friend Edwin Parsons Reese. The two of them found a place to room at $2.00 a week and to board at $2.50. At that rate his total expenses for the year would be $191.50. Unlike many students he did not work for his schooling expenses.[8] The house where Masters roomed was as near as it could possibly be to the College. He and Reese shared a "comfortable room" at the home of Mrs. V. P. Clute,[9] the wife of a train dispatcher for the Burlington Railroad. The Clute's residence was on South Cedar Street and stood on land where the College library now stands. South

Cedar then extended through the city without interruption at the campus; indeed, it formed the western boundary of the campus. Only the previous fall had this section of the street been paved with brick.[10] Before the Clute house ran a "small street car drawn by one rangy white horse."[11]

East across Cedar Street from Masters's roominghouse it was only a minute's walk to a cluster of five College buildings, all of them rather small structures except for the main College building (now called Old Main). And even that, though impressive in its style, was modest in its dimensions. South from that main College building was the newest construction, the Observatory, only about a year old when the College semester opened in September 1889. It had been built to house the telescope and other astronomical equipment of Edgar Lucien Larkin, self-taught scientist and a sort of village genius from the nearby town of New Windsor. (Masters would remember him in one of the epitaphs of the *Spoon River Anthology*.) But the College building nearest to Masters's lodgings was the West Bricks, one of the two oldest College buildings (1844). West Bricks (the name suggests its plain appearance) began at the north end as a two-story building, the lower level being used for classes. From this structure a series of adjoining one-story rooms tailed off to the south, each of them with a door to the campus. A few students lived in these little rooms, and in one of them, Number Two, a member of the junior class maintained a taxidermy shop for his livelihood.[12] The upper floor of the two-story section was the hall for the oldest literary society of the College and for the literary society of the Academy, of which Reese and Masters both became members. It was now very much rundown, its upkeep neglected because during the next summer it was to be torn down and replaced by a larger Alumni Hall, which would provide better facilities for the meetings, social events, and libraries of the literary societies.

Masters had finished high school in Lewiston and after that also attended a private academy in the town for a short time. Even so he was still short of meeting the standards set by the entrance examinations at Knox. He was "mortified" to discover that he "could not even enter the freshman class. . . . All my reading in English literature, in philosophy, availed me nothing. I had too little Latin to enter college, and no Greek at all. . . . By this time I

had read a good deal of the Greek classics in translations, I had
read Faust, and I had been through English literature pretty thoroughly, but having nothing but a beginner's knowledge of Latin
and no start at all in Greek, I had to enter the preparatory
school."[13]

He was placed in the Middle Preparatory Class. His disappointment is understandable for a man who was already twenty years
old. But rightly he should have felt no humiliation, for his situation was quite common, even typical, ever since the College had
enrolled its first students. Of the eighteen senior men who were
graduated from Knox the year that Masters was a student, half
had been at Knox five to seven years. Masters decided to "go on
with Latin," "to resume the study of German," and "to begin
Greek." Though he claimed "good marks" in all subjects, his
study of Cicero under a Knox graduate, Henry Ware Read (1875),
did not overcome his dislike of Latin. Most students then as now
would have recoiled from a course of studies comprising three
languages. But Masters settled down to "hard study," and, in
addition, as he recalls it, "I almost read myself blind" in the books
of the College and the public library, the latter collection of
14,000 volumes being a marvelous opportunity for him. He dis-
dained the way Reese as a cadet was wasting his time at military
drill.[14]

Every Tuesday evening in the Adelphi Hall in West Bricks there
was a meeting of EOD, the literary society of which Masters and
Reese became members. The letters rendered in English the initials
of a Greek phrase: "To Be, Not to Seem." EOD competed with
another men's literary society of the Academy called Zetici, which
also met on Tuesday evenings in East Bricks, in the hall of the
Gnothautii. On the same evenings there would also meet a wom-
en's society for the Academy and the Conservatory; these were the
Oneota. They met in the Seminary building in the Hall of LMI
(Ladies Moral Improvement Society). Thus there were three College literary societies that paralleled the three Academy organizations. All three College groups met regularly on Wednesday
evenings. Masters received early recognition on the campus. Near
the end of the fall term EOD elected him to the office of "critic."[15]
At the beginning of the second term the campus magazine, *Coup
D'Etat,* not given to printing much verse, published one of Masters's poems. In his autobiography Masters mentions this event:

"I wrote humorous verses which were published in the College magazine, verses on the new passenger engine of the Burlington Railroad, called the hog-engine. This was about the time that Kipling had sent forth some verses which attempted to show what Homer would do in a description of the engine."[16] The reader who will see this piece of Masters's juvenilia (if the writing of a twenty-year-old student can be called that) for the first time should note that the steam-powered Burlington trains could be seen, heard, smelled from the Knox campus. He may also notice how the homely theme from the immediate environment was embellished with Greek references to Homer and the "immortal gods."[17] That same blend would occur twenty-five years later in the *Spoon River Anthology*.

The College annual, at the end of Masters's year, applied this quotation to him: "A mighty wonder bred among our quiet crew."[18] Even if there was a humorous sting to this flattery, Masters would have liked the notoriety. Earnest Elmo Calkins, an in-and-out student since 1885, who used to drop into Masters's room between classes along with other Galesburg men, recalled Masters's reputation: "I know I considered you the wickedest person I had had the honor of knowing up to that time, though I now do not know why, unless it was because you used tobacco and did not take seriously the God who was so strenuously taught at Knox College."[19] This recollection by the successful author and advertising man was friendly. Less kindly was the remembrance of a classmate, Arthur Ferris, whom Masters remembered as a friend. Ferris, at the time he wrote this reminiscent profile of Masters, was angered by Masters's biography of Lincoln, but the characterizations are nevertheless revealing:

> Those who remember Masters at Knox College will admit that his description of Lincoln could be applied to Masters in almost every particular. He says of Lincoln as follows: "In the middle western small town there usually was a boy genius who wore his hair long, thought he had superior abilities, studied words and debated; one of his principal gifts was satire, mimicry, histrionic antics, deep seated antagonism, coldness, and a sort of logic such as you would expect the village genius to develope."[20]

Masters, Reese, and six other Fulton County students comprised nearly half the membership of an eating society, the KEK

(Knox Epicurean Klub), which met most of the year on South Broad Street.[21] Of all these companions, it was Reese who outlasted everyone in a continuing friendship with Masters. Fifty years later Masters would remember in a memorial poem—"the long ended years, in which we two had watched the life careers of chums."[22]

Among the upperclassmen Masters's most important friend was a Galesburg student, Oscar "Bum" Lanstrum. His local credentials were impeccable; both his father and grandfather had immigrated from Sweden, both had served in the Union army, and the family had achieved considerable standing in the Republican party. But Lanstrum's father was identified with the local Liberals, who were willing to have licensed saloons. The junior Lanstrum shared with students such as Masters and Calkins an aversion for the YMCA type of student on the campus.[23] Lanstrum compiled a most impressive record in students affairs, notably in College publications, including tenure as associate editor of the *Gale* during his junior year and editor-in-chief during his senior year. As such he was responsible for the publishing of five "Sonnets" by Masters in the College annual a year after Masters had left Knox.

In the poetry section of the *Gale,* where Masters's poems were published,[24] also appeared poetry contributed by a young faculty member, Alphonso Gerald Newcomer. Probably the most important academic event for Masters in 1889–90 was the secession[25] early in the year of a group of students from the Greek class of Instructor Read to that of the younger Newcomer. Like Masters, Newcomer had begun his association with Knox that autumn. He came to Galesburg from his hometown of Mount Morris, Illinois, where he had earlier been a student at the Dunkard College and there been introduced to Latin and Greek by Professor Jeremiah Jenks, who in the June before Newcomer came to Knox had concluded his three years as a member of the Knox faculty. Newcomer had been graduated from the University of Michigan in 1887 and in 1888 had received the degree of A.M. from Cornell University. While at Ann Arbor he was on the staff of the college paper. His twenty-fifth birthday occurred during the month he started teaching at Knox. He was only five years older than Masters.[26]

Master found in Newcomer "one of the most interesting men I have ever known, and besides a very good poet."[27] Instructor and student became friends, sharing common intellectual and spiritual concerns. Masters enjoyed the Greek class under Newcomer's tutelage intensely; it was the "happiest of all my studies. Greek fascinated me beyond anything I had ever studied. The very look of the alphabet gave me a thrill; I found the language easier than Latin, because of the articles and demonstrative pronouns." As soon as he could read Greek at all, he took up the New Testament "and for several weeks made critical notes on the evidence of the Gospels for the credibility of the miracles," an interest that was probably encouraged by Newcomer's talks on "skepticism and faith."

By spring the class with Newcomer was reading about the great adventure of the Ten Thousand—the *Anabasis* of Xenophon:

> Professor Newcomer made it a wonderful study. He gave us the background and topography of the recital, so that we read not merely by way of deciphering the text, but with an understanding of the story. I have never had a more delightful experience with a book than with the *Anabasis* in Greek. As the year ended I was reading Homer in Greek; and finally took up Bryant's translation which I absorbed under the trees of the campus.
>
> Ah, yes, reading Homer on the campus! It was June, and June in Illinois can be as beautiful as anywhere. I sat under the trees reading about the King of Men, and about the swift footed Achilles, with a delight that cannot be expressed.[28]

Masters's fascination with Greek language and literature was manifested in the "Sonnets" of the 1891 *Gale*. The poems, as a group, were headed by a quotation from the *Iliad* in the Greek script. They contained allusions not only to an episode in the *Anabasis*, but also to the Nereids, the Elysian Fields, Prometheus, and Jove's minions.[29]

Masters was not able to come back to Knox College in the fall of 1890; Newcomver left Knox in 1891, to join the faculty of the new Stanford University. Masters in Chicago could readily follow the career of his mentor and friend in the columns of *The Dial*, to which Newcomer was a frequent contributor. In an issue of October 1, 1913, Masters read of Newcomer's death. The very next day he wrote to the editor: "He was my teacher of Greek in Knox College, and I could not help but contrast the fresh delight of those studies under his inspiring companionship with the shadow that falls in thinking that his work is done." And with this note Masters sent a poetic tribute, "In Memory of Professor Newcomer," that was published in *The Dial* and reprinted at Knox in the student paper. In this memorial poem Masters used the theme of the *Anabasis,* which signified an advancing or "going up." He recalled:

> I was a boy when you were young,
> When truth was ours and fame to seek;
> You taught me what the Scian sung
> Of fallen Troy in golden Greek.
>
> In Spring's enchanted long ago,
> In days of April cloud and sun,
> We scaled Armenia's peaks of snow
> Along the page of Xenophon.[30]

Masters failed to return to Knox because, as he himself admitted, he was "very awkward about financing myself, with the result that my father captured me, for the law office."[31] Masters gave two explanations for his father's reluctance to send him back to Knox. In his autobiography he ascribed it to his father's desire to have him as a partner and to the elder's skepticism about the son's literary interests, especially in a literary career. Furthermore, Masters's sister should have her turn at college. The second explanation, given some years after the autobiography was published, suggested that the son did not at the time adequately appreciate his father's political reasons. The latter "was a liberal and hated Knox and all that it stood for." Two of Masters's Fulton County classmates, he now recalled, also failed to return to Knox and "hated . . . its black Republicanism, its Calvinism."[32] For himself, however, Masters affirmed that he had not felt "much the narrow dogmatism of Knox," being "so deep in studies that all that impinged on me very little." Indeed, he said: "It almost broke my heart because I wanted to continue my life at Knox."[33]

To his friends at Knox, Masters became an ex-1894, that is, a non-graduate of the senior class of that year. Until that class was graduated Master remained in direct contact with the campus. A newly founded magazine, of which his friend Lanstrum (1891) was business manager, reported Masters's visit to Galesburg in

June 1891 and commented: "He is a talented writer and has penned many accepted articles for leading papers and magazines."[34] When school opened the next September, the student paper in its first issue reported his admission to the bar and his "copartnership" with his father.[35] During that academic year his sister Madeline attended the Knox "School of Art," returning to Lewiston in June 1892 (according to her brother) "with a little knowledge of French, and with two drawings."[36]

During 1892 Masters arrived in Chicago, as the *Gale* for his year had anticipated would happen to students of his generation. At least three other Fulton County men who were associated with Masters at Knox also became Chicago lawyers. As to Masters, the *Coup D'Etat,* by the opening of the year 1893–94, reported: "His success in the legal profession is a joy to many friends here."[37]

In February 1893 Masters visited friends on the Knox campus, where Reese was now associate editor of the College magazine. Masters probably at this time left with Reese a poem that was published in the February number of the *Coup D'Etat,* in the leading position, on page one: "Helen of Troy."[38]

> This is the vase of love
> Whose feet must ever rove
> O'er land and sea
> Whose hopes forever seek
> Bright eyes, the vermilled cheek,
> And ways made free.
>
> Do we not understand
> Why thou didst leave thy land,
> Thy spouse, thy hearth?
> Helen of Troy, Greek art
> hath made my heart thy heart,
> Thy mirth my mirth.
>
> For Paris did appear,
> Curled hair and rosy ear,
> And tapering hands
> He spoke—the blood ran fast;
> He touched and killed the past,
> And clove its bands.

And this, I deem, is why
The restless ages sigh.
  Helen, for thee:
What'er we do or dream,
What'er we say or seem,
  We would be free.

We would forsake old love
And all the pain thereof,
  And all the care.
We would find out new seas
And lands more strange than these,
  And flowers more fair.

We would behold fresh skies,
Where summer never dies,
  And amaranths spring.
Hands where the halcyon hours
Nest over scented bowers
  On folded wing.

Helen of Troy, Greek art
Hath made my heart thy heart,
  Thy love my love;
For poetry, like thee,
Must love and wander free
  As any dove!

This was the first publication of a poem of which Masters was particularly fond, despite the contemptuous attitude of critics toward this reworking of one of the most shopworn subjects in Western verse. He included it in his first privately printed book; he revived it for *Songs and Satires* in 1916, his first book after *Spoon River Anthology* had made him famous; he included it in his *Selected Works* of 1925, a gleaning from eight earlier publications. Obviously this poem belongs fully to the genteel tradition, but it should be noted that "there is a sense in which the identification with Helen of Troy figures forth Masters' own need to leave his home and seek the 'freedom' of the great world, namely Chicago."[39] The concluding affirmation was that "poetry . . . must . . . wander free."

Masters later wrote that this poem had been written under the spell of a very beautiful, interesting, and bewitching young

woman—in the "days of rapt fascination for Gertrude," a visitor
to Chicago with whom he spent his evenings at the Columbian
Exposition. Gertrude was also the subject of the two poems that
appeared during the autumn after the World's Fair, in the September and in the November issues of the *Coup d'Etat*. Reese was
now editor-in-chief. Again that fall Masters was a visitor on the
Knox campus and could well have shared with his close friend
both the verses and an account of his amours. Masters's memoirs
present "Gertrude" as one with "voluptuous sorcery," who
"worked her strange hypnotism over me." This was a theme in
the verses about her, written "in the manner of Swinburne."[40]

Five years later the student paper would again publish one of
his poems: it came from the volume he privately printed in 1898.[41]
This appearance of his verse was some palliation for Masters's
search for broader recognition. Some of that much needed attention would continue to come from the Knox campus, from Dr.
Simonds, who had begun his life-long career at Knox the same
September that Masters became a Middle Prep. Their relationship
during Masters's months on the campus was not close, yet an
important friendship developed from their mutual identification
with the College, an identification that Masters cherished.[42] When
Master published, or rather had printed, in 1898, *A Book of
Verses*, he "sent . . . copies to some friends and potential review-
ers," but the book was "virtually ignored."[43] Thirty-eight years
later, when writing his autobiography, Masters glossed over the
"virtual silence which had greeted his first book," saying merely
that the reviews were "creditable enough." But the only review
that he recalled specifically was that appearing "in a College periodical," written by "Dr. Simonds, the head of the English department at Knox College." Masters remembered that Simonds
"praised the poems, as much as I could wish."[44]

This Simonds's review appeared early in January 1899 in the
Knox Student under the heading: "Another Knox Poet." The
probable and most flattering reference in that title was to another
Knox alumnus, Eugene Field, of whom the Knox community was
very proud. The magnitude of Field's popularity and the strong
sentimentality associated with it, however difficult they may be
now to comprehend, were very real in 1898, and extended far
beyond the Knox campus and the city where Field lived for two

years as a student. During Masters's youth Eugene Field was "a name to conjure with"; he was bracketed with "Emerson, Dickens, Scott and Thackery . . . Byron and Shakespeare" in the little group of high school friends that met in Lewiston to read and discuss literature. In those days Masters sent poems to Eugene Field, hoping they might be published in Field's famous column in the Chicago *Daily News*. And when the adult Masters started his law practice in Chicago, he found that Field "was the most famous literary man of Chicago."[45]

The Simonds review of Masters's verse was not unqualified in its praise, but did repeatedly emphasize that the poet showed promise of good things to come if he would persist in his writing. Some of these very encouraging comments were:

> Mr. Masters has the happy touch of one who has almost achieved his art and works with the confidence of final success. His phrasings are strikingly effective and at the same time more original than the compositions of young writers have to show. . . .
> Mr. Masters takes his calling seriously and we like him the better for it. While the note of melancholy is dwelt upon perhaps overmuch, that fault is one almost inseparable from serious minded youth and will take care of itself with the years; it is far better than the tone of conscious cynicism sometimes affected by our would-be-poets, young or old.
> Some of these poems surprise us with a promise of more than ordinary power to be expressed more perfectly after experience. . . . The scope of his material is noteworthy.[46]

Not until sixteen years later would Masters "receive any substantial recognition as a poet."[47] During this long disappointment Simonds was one of the few who gave some attention to Masters's continuing literary labors. Simonds, in a reminiscence of his relations with the poets of the Chicago Renaissance, recalled that Masters had "visited" his classes when a student at Knox and "always sent me copies of his earlier privately printed volumes."[48] After the *Book of Verses,* Masters next had printed, in 1902, a drama, *Maximillian.* In a short article reviewing four new plays, *The Dial* gave Masters's work the last and least attention—two sentences or seven lines of faint praise.[49] All the more reason for Masters to be "indebted" for the "inspiring letter" that he received from Simonds about this time. Masters responded: "All you say is disinterested and cordial out of a spirit of literary brotherhood. I feel the imperfections of 'Maximillian' as much as you do and along the same lines. But I may try again and avoid some of the errors into which I fell before."[50]

The letterhead for this letter to Simonds announced: "Law Offices Darrow & Masters," for during 1903 Masters became the partner of the now famous but then often notorious Clarence Darrow. Masters was himself earning a reputation of his own for having radical political and social views. Knox College students noted that before the Jefferson Club of Chicago, of which he was the organizer and first president, he "created a sensation" when he fiercely attacked the federal judiciary "as the tool of the corporate interests."[51] Such unorthodox views had been set forth in a book published in 1904, bearing the title the *New Star Chamber and Other Essays*. *The Dial* this time gave Masters's work three sentences, characterizing this book as a "collection of forcibly written essays upon political subjects, containing much sound doctrine upon imperialism and the dangerous present centralizing trend in our government. We regret that the effect of this excellent writing should be marred by the excessive radicalism evoked by other subjects, and by an occasional intemperance of statement."[52]

In December 1903 the Knox weekly magazine announced that Masters had founded a prize to be given to the best essayist at Knox. To Simonds, Masters explained that he wanted "to stimulate Knox students to think and write about the things which in my judgment relate to the higher life and upon which all else depend. The times are not what idealists wish them; and as hitherto the fight must be carried on."[53]

At the end of that academic year Masters wrote to Simonds that he would "add an additional purse . . . so as to have two prizes ready to be won, that is for two years," and that he would continue it so as to give it a fair trial before withdrawing it. For the academic year 1904–5 he agreed with Simonds that the theme for the contest should be "Thomas Jefferson."[54] The winner, announced at commencement in June 1905, was a junior, James Findlay. Because that was one of the conditions of the gift, this winning essay was published in full in a *Knox College Bulletin*. Masters must have been satisfied with the political position of the essayist. The treatment of Jefferson was ordinary in content, but it was combined with an eloquent description of the Democratic party, its principles and achievements. "Jefferson's party was, and is the people's party." The Republican party was presented as a party that had accomplished its original worthy mission and as now drifting with "no set purposes or principles, but the prey of selfish interests."[55]

In 1905–6 the Edgar Lee Masters' Prize Essay Contest was in its fourth year. Masters and Simonds agreed by correspondence on "John Milton" as a theme. Masters wrote on January 18, 1906: "I will send my check for $35.00 in a few days and in the meantime you can announce the prize and the subject of John Milton. I think he is remembered for what he did for the course of liberty, although he is primarily considered as a poet. Perhaps the contestants will get this idea and will develop it."[56]

The winning student writer did indeed have that "idea." She was Clarissa Atwood, of the graduating class. Milton was presented not only as the prose propagandist for divorce and as author of *Areopagitica* on freedom of the press but as a poet whose "soul grasped and held the thought, the image of freedom . . . the universal truth of liberty." The essay concluded with Wordsworth's famous tribute:

> Milton thou shouldst be living at this hour,
> England hath need of thee;
> Oh! raise us up return to us again
> And give us manners, virtue, freedom, power.
> Thy soul was like a star, and dwelt apart
> Thou hadst a voice whose sound was like the sea:
> Pure as the naked heavens, majestic, *free*.[57]

In 1905 Masters published another volume of poems; they expressed in verse his bitter feelings about corruption of the judiciary, the greed of corporate wealth, the new American imperialism, the spoiling of democracy, and the contradictions of Christianity. For this work Masters assumed the *nom de plume* of "Dexter Wallace." The title, *The Blood of the Prophets,* is suggestive of the mood of the poems as well as of their subject matter.[58] Again, this second volume of his poetry received only the scantiest attention from literary periodicals, but it did become the subject of an extended correspondence with Professor Simonds.[59]

Masters complained to Simonds in several of his letters about the shabby treatment of poets in America: "No matter what you do poetry will not sell. The only satisfaction one has is to see the book in print—get the reviews and note the dissemination of his thought."[60] But there was some inner compulsion that kept Masters composing and revising his verses and seeking critical acclaim. Even before the *Blood of the Prophets* had been printed he was planning for his next collection of poems and for this was salvaging some good from the first of his publishing failures. He wrote Simonds on December 30, 1904: "I am trying to put my poems in order for another book . . . cutting out the chaff [from the *Book of Verses*] and adding to the best poems some written since that book was published." When that new collection appeared in 1910 under the title *Songs and Satires,* Masters again despaired: "I am much satisfied to get your kind letter with its cordial appreciation of the book and your friendship for me and what I do. I wish what I did were worthier but I think that American poets are worse circumstanced than a man like [Burns]. Our country is so large, the audience is so hard to reach, . . . and the age and spirit so commercial that to get a vision and to keep it and express it is hard indeed. Even poor [Burns] found a material for working and an assembled audience waiting to hear."[61] When a review did at last appear in *The Dial,* in March 1911, it was only one part of a general essay. The book also received some attention elsewhere, but Masters felt that he was not appreciated. Even the limited praise given him by *The Dial* was for merits that Masters would not accept as praiseworthy. *The Dial* selected two of Masters's roundels as illustrative of his work, reprinted them, and then commented about the "plaintive strain of . . . decorous but deeply-felt verse" that was "very moving" and about "his graceful measures" that had "charm that is genuine and compelling."[62]

"Plaintive," "decorous," "graceful," "charm" are hardly the words to please the poet that would write the *Spoon River Anthology.* Indeed, when that masterpiece appeared about five years later in book form, *The Dial* described it as "the *reductio ad absurdum* of certain of the new methods, such as the abandonment of conventional form and the fearless scrutiny of disagreeable realities." The reviewer then asked how Masters could "perpetrate, and endure to see in type, trash" such as appeared in *Spoon River Anthology,* especially since he "has shown us before this that he knows what verse is."[63]

Simonds was in Boston on leave during the months when Masters gathered his Spoon River epitaphs into a book and allowed the revelation that he was indeed the Webster Ford who had been credited with writing the poems both of *Songs and Sonnets* and of the *Spoon River Anthology.* Then he began to receive the critical approval for which he had so long yearned. Simonds did not participate in this climax to Masters's career. But the professor of English literature and contributor to *The Dial,* now become dean at Knox College, did have a role in the events that brought another of the rebel poets of Illinois to public appreciation. In this instance, Simonds acted not with Masters nor even with the native of Galesburg, Sandburg, but with Vachel Lindsay, who by a matter of months was the first of this trio to achieve special fame. Masters himself noted this primary event as being the publication of "General William Booth Enters Heaven" in *Poetry* in January 1913.[64]

Simonds may possibly first have seen Lindsay's poetry in 1911, when it began to be published in the *American Magazine,* for that publication was edited and managed by two distinguished Knox alumni, John S. Phillips and Albert Boyden. When these men broke away from *McClure's Magazine* in 1906, they took with them other associates of S. S. McClure, including Witter Bynner. It was the latter who promoted the publication of Lindsay's verse in the *American* and thus brought him to the attention of Reedy's *Mirror* in St. Louis and then of *Poetry* in Chicago.[65]

Furthermore, there was at Knox at this time a student whom Simonds described as "one of Vachel's group of Springfield boys to whom the poet had played big brother."[66] He was Franz Rickaby from Springfield, a freshman in 1912–13, who became an active campus promoter of musical and literary activities. In 1916 the College published the *Songs of Knox* that he had edited. He himself was the author of the words for five of these songs. The importance then accorded to College songs was indicated by the fact that words to seven of the songs had been written by members of the faculty, among them being the "Morning Hymn" by former President John Finley and "Sons of Knox" by Simonds. Three teachers in the Knox Conservatory had composed the music for seven of the songs. When the students in February 1915 launched a new literary magazine, Rickaby contributed four sonnets that had originally been "inspired" by Lindsay. They had first been published in a booklet called *A Set of Sonnets* that Rickaby set in type, printed, and bound. Lindsay provided an afterword.[67] Rickaby's promise as a poet and writer of one-act plays would be confirmed during graduate studies at Harvard, which published a book of folk ballads that he collected. But the promise was cut short by his untimely death in 1925.[68]

It was Rickaby who suggested to Simonds that Lindsay be invited, in the fall of 1913, to the Knox campus. Lindsay did indeed appear and perform. It was a "great experience" for those who heard and saw him and for Lindsay an important incident in his career. Simonds recalled the event, years later, most vividly: "So far as I know, this was probably the earliest of V.L.'s visits to colleges. . . . He recited some of his verses at chapel, and in the evening I had a dozen of my more intimate friends, all men, meet him at dinner in a private dining room at the Galesburg Club. We sat there until nearly midnight under the spell of Lindsay's chant-like delivery."[69]

Lindsay wrote afterward to Simonds that he hoped to return, "perhaps," in the spring of 1915.[70] But it would be in Boston, not in Galesburg, that Simonds would again be Lindsay's host, and, by way of Simonds's old friend Bliss Perry, introduce him at Harvard.

The academic year, 1914–15, we were all in Boston—my year's leave of absence. . . . I was in close touch with Harvard, attending lectures and seeing a great deal of my friend, Bliss Perry. That was the year when Vachel Lindsay came east on his first tour; he had engagements at several eastern colleges—and, incidentally, for one public reading at one of the large Back Bay mansions. . . . For this affair I obtained tickets and asked Perry to attend the reading with me. Harvard was not on the list of Lindsay's ports of call, but I had read some of Vachel's verse to Perry, in my feeble way trying to suggest by my rendering the peculiar chant with which the poet intoned the verse of "Gen. Wm. Booth," "Congo," "The Santa Fe Trail," etc. Thus he was duly prepared for the bard-like delivery of the poet from Springfield, Illinois. . . .

Before we left, Perry invited Lindsay to visit one of his courses and read to the students; this he agreed to do.[71]

Among the students for whom Lindsay made a surprise appearance in Perry's class (expecting to hear a lecture on Tennyson) was Carl Carmer. He recalled that "Tennyson was a pale wraith within us as Lindsay's bold accents beat the living daylight out of our polite conceptions of poetry." John Dos Passos, who also first heard Lindsay while a Harvard student, remembered: "We went to kid, but were very much impressed in spite of our selves."[72]

Thus the vagabond poet, with some help from a college dean, became a successful entertainer, who for the rest of his life earned a living reciting his poetry to audiences from coast to coast. And back in Chicago, Masters was offended, and he believed Sandburg was "infuriated," as Lindsay assumed, at least a little, "the role of the man who had arrived."[73]

Dean Simonds was not one of three faculty members from Masters's time at Knox, who were remembered by him in the *Spoon River Anthology*. It was Newcomer, Masters's Greek instructor, who was named in two of the epitaphs. And rightly, for Masters fully appreciated how the passion for Greek literature engendered in Newcomer's class had affected the form and content of the poems in his most famous work.[74] Masters kept with him all his life the beige-colored notebook containing the translation he made at Knox of the first book of the *Iliad*.[75] Every year during the quarter century intervening between Newcomer's class and the publication of the *Anthology* as a book, he read Homer in some translation.[76] Now and then he brushed up on the Greek language itself, reading the New Testament and some of the *Iliad* in the original.[77] A book of his poems published in 1905 exhibited his familiarity with texts in Greek by printing a sentence in the Greek alphabet on the title page.[78]

In the *Spoon River Anthology* was included a narrative poem entitled "The Spooniad." As the time indicates it was to be for the Spoon River what the *Iliad* had been for Ilium or Troy. This mock epic opens with lines like those about the wrathful Achilles that begin Homer's epic. In fact, the Illinois poet invoked the same muse "that lit the Chian's face," and reminded us of the strife in the valley of another river—the Scamander.

Such a narrative poem in the Homeric manner and in blank verse was hardly original—and not likely to win the plaudits of a critic such as William Reedy, whose opinion Masters respected.[79] But it was Reedy who "pressed" upon Masters's "attention" a less familiar body of Greek verses, in June 1909. This was the *Greek Anthology*, a collection of Greek epigrams gathered from various sources, some as ancient as the seventh century B.C., but the most important being from the "Garland" (in Greek, "Anthologia" would be a flower gathering) compiled by Meleager in the first century B.C. Masters acknowledged to Reedy that it was "from contemplation" of the epitaphs of the *Greek Anthology* that "his hand unconsciously strayed to the sketches" that were to be printed in Reedy's *Mirror* beginning with the issue of May 29, 1914.[80]

Other factors, personal and literary, affected the free rhythms, spirit, and subject matter of the Spoon River epitaphs, but the important influence of Greek literature is clear, both the new experience of Masters with the *Greek Anthology* as well as his previous reading and studies over the years. Many allusions derived from that familiarity with Greek religion, history, mythology, poetry, and drama occur in the epitaphs,[81] and, though it might seem strange that so many of the men and women of a small Illinois town should make classical references, yet the allusions are appropriately made and without seeming affectation.

The gods are alluded to, though in a very familiar metaphor requiring no special learning, in the epitaph that carries the name of Masters's Greek teacher at Knox: "Professor Newcomer." His given name, Alphonso, also appears in the title of the epitaph, "Alfonso Churchill," that explicitly refers to Knox College. The second name in that title is that of the principal of the Knox Academy at the time Masters was a prep student there. But the actual subject of this epitaph is a third member of the Knox faculty, Professor Larkin. He was the self-taught village genius for whom the College, only the year before Masters enrolled, had built an observatory in order to mount the telescope that Larkin brought with him from the nearby town of New Windsor. Larkin's excitement about celestial studies and soaring imagination and dedication to the *"new"* sciences were quickly noted by the students, and there is reason to believe that in fact some of them laughed at his intensity.[82]

ALFONSO CHURCHILL

They laughed at me as "Prof. Moon,"
As a boy in Spoon River, born with the thirst
Of knowing about the stars.
They jeered when I spoke of the lunar mountains,
And the thrilling heat and cold,
And the ebon valleys by silver peaks,
And Spica quadrillions of miles away,
And the littleness of man.
But now that my grave is honored, friends,
Let it not be because I taught
The lore of the stars in Knox College,
But rather for this: that through the stars
I preached the greatness of man,
Who is none the less a part of the scheme of things
For the distance of Spica or the Spiral Nebulae;
Nor any the less a part of the question
Of what the drama means.

The epitaphs of Spoon River people appeared in the *Mirror* for many weeks, and then, in the issue of the *Mirror* for January 15, 1914, in Masters's own words, "I epitaphed myself under the pseudonym 'Webster Ford.' " This epitaph was an invocation to the Delphic Apollo, the god of poets.[83]

Fame never brought Masters back to the Knox College campus. Simonds did invite him "to be present" at the alumni dinner of 1917, but the letter inviting him failed to reach the poet at a summer place in Michigan until it was too late. At that time Masters remarked that he had not been in Galesburg "in eleven years, near as it is to Chicago."[84] A journalistic fraternity invited him to be their guest in the spring of 1919, and though he accepted "with delight" it is not certain that he came.[85] When Masters was about seventy years old, his greatest work became part of the reading in a course on the Midwest required of all freshman at Knox. President Carter Davidson about that time corresponded with the poet about establishing some kind of lectureship for him on the campus, but the compensation that could be offered was modest, Masters was not eager, and some of the trustees were dubious about the man whose later works had included an iconoclastic biography of Lincoln and a shockingly candid autobiography.[86] And at the age when a famous alumnus might expect to receive an honorary degree from his alma mater, Masters had a reputation for being difficult, even cantankerous. There was an insistent though secondhand report that he was offered such an honorary degree but refused to take it unless the same honor was also given to the friend of his youth, Edwin Reese, "then working as a night watchman."[87] There are serious factual flaws in such a story, but, as apochrypha often do, much of the story fits. Reese had been graduated from Knox in 1894 after a distinguished career as a student.[88] For a quarter century he edited or helped to manage newspapers in central Illinois and then in 1918 moved to the Chicago area in search of better medical care. He wrote feature articles for magazines and other periodicals. In 1929 he became associate editor of the *Federation News,* published by the Chicago Federation of Labor, and retained this connection until his death in 1940. In a memorial poem entitled "Farewell Edwin," Masters recalled:

> Edwin, that day you reached your sixtieth
> Birthday, we sat the whole long afternoon
> Talking in Housman's restaurant saloon,
> And canvassed life and death,
>
> Men and misfortune, fortune, politics,
> Women and love, and the long ended years,
> In which we two had watched the life careers,
> Of chums, of men defeated by the tricks
>
> Of fate, and of the republic, too, we talked
> How it was slipping, by idiocy long undermined
> With liberty discarded, long consigned
> To ignorance, or badly mocked. . . .[89]

During the Great Depression Reese advocated such reforms as a "tax on labor-saving devices proportionable to the number of men displaced," a thirty-hour work week, and a "referendum to the people before Congress can declare war."[90] One can well imagine Masters in an irascible mood testing the rather conservative Knox College board of trustees with the proposal that Edwin Reese, class of 1894, be given an honorary degree.

NOTES

1. Flannagan, Masters, 21.

2. *Poetry: A Magazine of Verse,* 5 (Feb. 1915), 247–48. "Ezra Pound perhaps blew the loudest blast of admiration in the London *Egoist,* 'At last!' he proclaimed, 'At last America has discovered a poet' " (Flannagan, *Masters,* 27).

3. *The Dial,* 59 (June 24, 1915), 28. If this seems like rather provocative rhetoric, it should be realized that *The Dial* was deeply committed to a defense of the genteel tradition, which was being so rudely violated by *Poetry,* the first issue of which appeared in Oct. 1912. The month that the epitaphs of the *Spoon River Anthology* first appeared in Reedy's *Mirror,* Harriet Monroe, editor of *Poetry,* issued an ultimatum to "our orthodox neighbor *The Dial*" (*Poetry,* 4 [May 1914], 63–64).

4. Putzel, *Man in the Mirror,* 214.

5. Masters, *Across Spoon River,* 399 (italics supplied). Masters did not use the name Edgar Lee until he joined a law firm in Chicago in 1893; at Knox he was known as Lee.

6. *Ibid.,* ch. 5.

7. In the academic year of 1889–90 there were 601 students, including those in all departments, from commerce to conservatory, and from junior preparatory to college senior. Statistics compiled from the catalogue for that year.

8. Masters, *Across Spoon River,* 109.

9. Masters to Jack Cecil, Mar. 16, 1947, Masters file. This letter was published in the *Knox Student,* Apr. 10, 1947, 4, 6.

10. Galesburg *Republican Register,* June 9, 1888, 1; Oct. 20, 1888, 2.

11. Simonds, "Knox College in 1888–1890."

12. James G. Needham, "Some Knox Academic History," *Fifty Year Club Bulletin,* 8 (June 1953), 4–8.

13. Masters, *Across Spoon River,* 109–10.

14. *Ibid.,* 110–11; Masters to correspondent in *Fifty Year Club Bulletin,* 6 (June 1951), 24–25.

15. *Coup D'Etat,* 9 (Dec. 1889), 53.

16. Masters, *Across Spoon River,* 115.

17. *Coup D'Etat,* Jan. 1890, 66. Authorship by Masters is confirmed by the letter from Masters in the *Fifty Year Club Bulletin,* 6 (June 1951), 24–25. Masters may also have been the "Humble Prep" who contributed a humorous verse on the "Janitor's Woodpile," in the *Coup D'Etat,* Nov. 1889, 41. Masters admitted (Masters to Cecil, Mar. 16, 1947) to playing a prank with the janitor's rooster. Capture of that fowl is mentioned in the poem.

18. That there was some personal identification intended by this matching of persons to quotations was cruelly apparent in the case of Frank J. Standard, a student from Masters's hometown and a classmate at Knox. He was matched to: "A gross, fat man, as fat as butter" (*Gale,* 1889–90, 136). In this same

yearbook (p. 21) there is a suggestion that he was very heavy; Masters later remembered him as a "huge fellow" (*Across Spoon River*, 198).

19. Calkins to Masters, Dec. 24, 1932, Calkins Papers.

20. A clipping in the Masters file of the Knox College Alumni Office.

21. *Gale*, 1889–90, 73; also the volume for 1890–91, 65. Charles Center, also a member of KEK that year, recalled that they paid "two dollars and twenty-five cents a week for twenty-one excellent meals."

22. From the poem "Farewell Edwin" published in the *Federation News* (Chicago Federation of Labor), of which Reese was associate editor at the time of his death in 1940.

23. Kimball Flaccus to E. E. Calkins, Oct. 18, 1955, Calkins Papers.

24. *Gale*, 1890–91, 87–88.

25. Masters to Cecil, Mar. 16, 1947.

26. *Coup D'Etat*, Sept. 1889, 9; Dec. 1889, 52; Feb. 1890, 79; June 1890, 144.

27. Masters to Cecil, Mar. 16, 1947.

28. Masters, *Across Spoon River*, 111–12.

29. *Gale*, 1890–91, 87–88.

30. *The Dial*, Oct. 1, 1913, 269; Oct. 16, 1913, 299; *Knox Student*, Nov. 4, 1913, 2.

31. Masters to Cecil, Mar. 16, 1947.

32. Masters to a correspondent in the *Fifty Year Club Bulletin*, 6 (June 1951), 24.

33. Masters to Cecil, Mar. 16, 1947.

34. *The Breeze* (Galesburg) 1, No. 13 (June 13, 1891).

35. *Coup D'Etat*, Sept. 1891, 11.

36. "Apollo Belvidere and one of Agamemnon," in Masters, *Across Spoon River*, 130.

37. *Coup D'Etat*, Sept. 1893, 12.

38. *Ibid.*, Feb. 1893, 1.

39. I owe this observation to Dr. Douglas Wilson, Knox College, for whose thorough reading and creative criticism of this monograph, while it was still a manuscript, I am greatly indebted.

40. *Coup D'Etat*, Sept. 1893, 1, 12; oct. 1893, 33; Nov. 1893, 37; Masters, *Across Spoon River*, 168–71.

41. *Knox Student*, Dec. 13, 1898, 161. It had appeared on p. 30 of Masters's *Book of Verses*.

42. *Coup D'Etat*, Dec. 1890, 63–65, reported Masters was at a meeting of the Knox Bateman Club of Chicago.

43. Flannagan, *Masters*, 17.

44. Masters, *Across Spoon River*, 251. There was no mention whatever of the book in the Chicago magazine of literary criticism, *The Dial*.

45. *Ibid.*, 60, 100, 105, 153–54.

46. *Knox Student*, Jan. 10, 1899, 171, 173.

47. Flannagan, *Masters*, 17.

48. Simonds, "The New Poetry and Free Verse in Illinois, Masters-Lind-

say-Sandburg"; Katherine Simonds Wensberg, "W.E.S. Recalls the Prairie Poets," *Fifty Year Club Bulletin*, 31 (June 1972), 12.

49. *The Dial*, May 1, 1903, 309.

50. Masters to Simonds, Simonds Papers. The letter is undated but probably was written in 1903. Flannagan, *Masters*, 17, notes that *Maxmillian* attracted little attention, although it was reviewed in the *Atlantic Monthly*. The reviewer was not favorably impressed, considering the basic story "worthy of being treated as opera bouffe."

51. *Knox Student*, Nov. 8, 1906, 139.

52. *The Dial*, Sept. 16, 1904, 139.

53. Masters to Simonds, undated letter published late in 1903, MS, Knox College Library; see *Knox Student*, Dec. 17, 1908.

54. Masters to Simonds, June 23, Dec. 30, 1904, MS, Knox College Library.

55. *Knox College Bulletin*, New Series, 1 (Dec. 1903). James Findlay's essay had been strongly anti-Hamiltonian. Was it unplanned irony or a soothing of ruffled feathers when President Thomas McClelland in reporting the Masters's essay contest to the Board of Trustees gave a great deal more attention to the fact that a Knox student had won second prize in the Oratory Contest sponsored by the Hamilton Club of Chicago? (*ibid.*, 1 [June 1903]).

56. Masters to Simonds, Jan. 18, 1906, MS, Knox College Library.

57. *Knox College Bulletin*, 2 (Dec. 1906), 2–3. The winning essay was published in full in this bulletin.

58. Edgar Lee Masters [Dexter Wallace], *The Blood of the Prophets*, prized by the *Dial* list at $1.00.

59. *The Dial* merely named it in a list of "New Books" under a catch-all head of "Poetry and Drama" (Dec. 1, 1905, 397). Search of this magazine for the next eighteen months found no further reference to it. There are three letters from Masters to Simonds that are largely concerned with the *Blood of the Prophets*. All are on letterhead stationery reading: Law Offices Darrow, Masters & Wilson 1202 Ashland Block Chicago. Only the third letter is dated: Jan. 18, 1906.

60. Letter not dated, probably written in 1903.

61. Masters to Simonds, Oct. 17, 1910, MS, Knox College Library.

62. William Morton Payne, "Recent Poetry," *The Dial*, Mar. 1, 1911, 162–67. Writing about this period of his life, Masters recalled: "So it was that the cords of the Lilliputians shot around my steps and entangled me. . . . I needed spiritual support in those days" (*Across Spoon River*, 315).

63. *The Dial*, June 24, 1915, 29.

64. Masters, *Across Spoon River*, 349.

65. Putzel, *Man in the Mirror*, 177–81.

66. Wensberg, "W.E.S. Recalls the Prairie Poets," 12–13; Simonds, "The New Poetry and Free Verse in Illinois."

67. Knox *Magazine*, 1 (Feb. 1915), 10, 11, 34.

68. William E. Simonds, "Ballads and Songs of the Shanty Boy, Book of

Verse by the late Franz Rickaby, '16," *Knox Alumnus,* June-July 1926, 194–96; see also *ibid.,* May 1925, 122.

69. Simonds in this passage is writing to a cousin, Wayland Chase, at the University of Chicago, Feb. 19, 1940, as quoted by Wensberg, "W.E.S. Recalls the Prairie Poets," 12–13.

70. Lindsay to Simonds, Apr. 13, 1913, Simonds Papers.

71. Simonds, "The New Poetry and Free Verse in Illinois."

72. Ruggles, *The West-Going Heart,* 236–37.

73. Masters, *Across Spoon River,* 325.

74. Masters to Cecil, Mar. 16, 1947.

75. Masters, *Across Spoon River,* 401–2. The notebook is among the papers of Masters at the Humanities Research Center, University of Texas, Austin (Robinson, *Edgar Lee Masters,* 28).

76. Masters, *Toward the Gulf,* 21. In this dedication to William Reedy, Masters writes of the way in which his continuing interest in Greek literature "had its influence both as to form and spirit."

77. Masters, *Across Spoon River,* 276.

78. Title page of the *Blood of the Prophets.*

79. Putzel, *Man in the Mirror,* 195.

80. Masters, *Toward the Gulf,* vii.

81. See the following epitaphs: "Dorcas Gustine," "Blind Jack," "Petit the Poet," "John Cabanis," "Editor Whedon," "Thomas Trevelyan," "Percival Sharp," "Oaks Tutt," "Henry C. Calhoun," "Archibald Bigbee," "Hamlet Micure," "William H. Herndon," "Scholfield Huxley," "Gustav Richter," and "Judson Stoddard."

82. See ch. 7 herein.

83. Masters, *Across Spoon River,* 353.

84. Masters to Simonds, Jan. 12, 1917, MS, Knox College Library.

85. *Knox Student,* Mar. 14, 1919, 1.

86. Personal knowledge of author.

87. Flaccus to Calkins, Oct. 1995, Calkins Papers.

88. He won prizes in essay writing and oratory and was editor-in-chief for both the college newspaper and the yearbook.

89. MS in the Reese folder of the alumni files.

90. *Federation News,* Sept. 3, 1938.

CHAPTER VII

NATURAL PHILOSOPHY AND
NATURAL SCIENCE

Among the things given in Prof. Hurd's last lecture was the com-
forting assurance that when the fields of coal are exhausted we
shall be able to utilize the sun's heat directly, an engine that thus
generates force having already been constructed (1876).[1]

The men at the universities in the seventeenth and eighteenth cen-
turies, who had been steeped in the classics and were knowledgeable of Plato and Aristotle, called the new experimental sciences
"natural philosophy," as differentiated from "moral philosophy"
or metaphysics. Even in the early nineteenth century opticians in
England still advertised themselves as "philosophical instrument
makers."[2] When the professor of natural philosophy at Knox in
1873 asked the "gentlemen of the Board of Trustees" to purchase
a compound microscope, a spectroscope, and a "full set of apparatus for meteoric observations," the request emanated from the
"Philosophical Department of the College."[3]

For the first half century and more at Knox College courses in
natural philosophy paralleled those in moral philosophy. The
founder himself, George Washington Gale, taught the course in
moral philosophy, and beginning in the catalogue for 1845–46 he
was listed as "Professor of Moral Philosophy and Belles Lettres."
Nehemiah Losey, who had been on the faculty with Gale at
the Oneida Manual Labor Institute in Whitesboro, New York,
was "Professor of Mathematics and Natural Sciences" in the

first Knox catalogue (1842), but his title was changed to "Professor of Mathematics and Natural Philosophy" in 1851. In 1869 Milton Comstock, who had been "Professor of Mathematics," became "Professor of Mathematics, Natural Philosophy, and Astronomy."[4]

Professor Losey taught the mathematics and science courses that were listed in the earliest catalogues: astronomy, chemistry, physiology, mineralogy, and geology. The College men were introduced to the sciences during the sophomore year by studying *Introduction to Natural Philosophy,* a two-volume work written by Denison Olmstead (1791–1859), who was on the Yale faculty. This widely used textbook, an edition of which was still used at Knox when it celebrated its semicentennial in 1887, opened with a classification of scientific knowledge that stated that the "material world consists of two parts—the *organized,* including the animal and vegetable kingdoms; and the *unorganized,* which comprehends the remainder."

> Organized matter is treated of in *Physiology,* and in those branches of science usually called *Natural History.* Unorganized matter forms the subject of *Natural Philosophy* and *Chemistry.* *Chemistry* considers the internal constitution of bodies, and the relations of their smallest parts to each other. *Natural Philosophy* deals principally with the external relations of bodies and their action upon one another. If, however, the bodies are so large as to constitute *worlds,* of which the earth itself is one, this science takes the name of *Astronomy.*
>
> The word *Physics* is much used to include both Natural Philosophy and Chemistry; but sometimes it is applied to the branches of Natural Philosophy.[5]

This division of science into the organized and the unorganized indicated the influence of taxonomy and Carl Linnaeus. Until the 1860s, well after Hurd and Comstock had started to teach at Knox, "chemistry had no chart of the elements, nor any standard principle of taxonomy beyond the very simple distributions between gases, liquids, and solids."[6]

Another course taught by Professor Losey may appropriately be regarded as applied science. This was the course named "Mensuration, Navigation and Surveying." Surveying was then a highly regarded profession, which as the West was being settled directly affected a great many people. George Washington had been a surveyor, and so had Abraham Lincoln. The mathematics required, though elementary, "put it beyond the reach of most and provided it with an element of mystery . . . and it was a career which fathers held up as an incentive when their sons fought their arithmetic."[7] Midwesterners of the twentieth century, not knowing the irregular, oblique, shifting, and curving contours of older landscapes, take for granted the square patterns that were put upon the land by surveyors, and that were to fix farm boundaries, direct the angle of furrows and crop rows, locate roads, lay out voting precincts, school districts, townships, and other local governing authorities, and impose a rectangular organization on living groups such as groves, prairies, and societies of animals and of people. From the township lines which had been surveyed in 1816, Professor Losey himself in 1836 laid out the village of Galesburg, locating and measuring its streets, lots, and public square. One of his students, George Churchill, before he joined the Knox faculty, helped to survey the right-of-way for the first railroads that entered the town and later, while principal of the Knox Academy, would serve the city as engineer, while more streets were extended out over the prairie and when the first water and sewer systems were projected.[8]

The early catalogues of Knox noted that there were subjects that could not be well taught only with textbooks and that "lectures in Natural Philosophy and also in Chemistry" were "given by Professors of the College, accompanied with experiments."[9] George Churchill recalled from his student years in Academy and College (1842–44, 1846–51) how these lectures attracted and fascinated the Hoosier visitors, the settlers from south of the Ohio River or by way of Indiana—whom Yankees regarded as less sophisticated than themselves:

> Prof. Losey, who taught the natural sciences, extemporized from nothing philosophical and chemical apparatus, with which he performed prodigies of wonders to us youngsters and to the curious natives who flocked in from the surrounding groves to see the Yankees light up their meeting-house with something that burnt without wick, grease or oil, or to see them play with the lightning and make it dance around the room at their pleasure. An evening lecture on Philosophy and Chemistry always brought out a house full of citizens, who were as eager as were the students, to see and hear and

learn, and if the worthy Professor announced to his Chemistry class, that on a certain day he would give an exhibition of the effects of laughing gas, everybody for miles around was on hand to see men get drunk on air, and many very comical scenes were beheld on the green in front of the academy on such occasions.[10]

During the summer of 1844 the College acknowledged the "acquisition of a valuable library and an excellent philosophical and chemical apparatus."[11] This educational equipment must have included gifts recently procured by President Hiram H. Kellogg while in Great Britain seeking contributions from evangelical and abolitionist philanthropists. At this time the College classes still met in the Academy near the center of the village, but by the summer of 1845 the College had constructed a building on the grounds set aside for the College at the southern edge of the village. Though not entirely finished, it had been used for part of the year past not only for lectures and recitations but also for the "Library" and for "Philosophical and Chemical apparatus."[12]

The word "laboratory" does not appear in a Knox catalogue until 1891.[13] Instead, beginning in 1853, reference was consistently made to the "Cabinets" and to the "collections" in them— geological, mineralogical, zoological, and botanical. The development of these "Cabinets" reflected the arrival of Albert Hurd, who joined the faculty in 1851, as "Tutor and Lecturer on the Natural Sciences." Three years later he was named "Professor of Natural Sciences." In 1870 his title became "Professor of Chemistry and Natural Science," at the same time that Comstock became "Professor of Mathematics, Natural Philosophy, and Astronomy." Professor Comstock taught what today would be called physics. Locally he was regarded as the authority on subjects such as "Sound" or "Gravitation,"[14] and he would be called upon to witness the fact that a baseball could be pitched with a curve.[15] From the time that Professor Losey retired from teaching in 1863 to 1888, for a quarter of a century, Hurd and Comstock were the science faculty of Knox College.

The earliest specific description of the "Cabinets" appeared in the catalogue for 1854–55, which stated that the "Mineralogical Cabinet" now contained 500 specimens and the "Geological Cabinet" contained 600. It also noted that the College had obtained during the year past "an excellent skeleton . . . for the illustration of anatomy." This was no doubt the same skeleton that the students discovered many years later had the body of a man "but the head, or skull of some woman."[16] Professor Hurd gave much of his attention to the procuring of new specimens for the "Cabinets" and to their classification, labeling, and exhibition. During his younger years as faculty member he made long summer journeys on foot to collect fossils, minerals, and plants that would belong to what by 1885 was called the "Museum." His travels took him as far away as Lake Superior. Judiciously he exchanged specimens that he had gathered for valuable items from other parts of the world.[17] In 1864 the College received a valuable collection of shells from the Smithsonian Institution,[18] for which Hurd's two daughters helped him to make small white boxes in which each shell could be kept along with its own carefully hand-written label.[19] The extra money that he earned by serving as the acting professor of Latin (in addition to his duties as a teacher of chemistry and the natural sciences) he accepted from the trustees on the condition that he might use it for "bettering the condition of the museum."[20] Fortunately, the most important addition made to the Museum by Hurd has been more carefully preserved than some of the other items, which have been rather carelessly handled by scientists with a different teaching style.[21] It was Hurd who negotiated the acquisition of the important Mead Herbarium, which contained "9,000 species, representing almost all the North American orders of Phanerogamia and Crytogamia besides hundreds of European and other foreign genera."[22]

With this addition, the Knox faculty "believed that no other institution in the West possessed an equally rich and extensive botanical collection."[23] It represented forty years of collecting and scholarly research by Dr. S. M. Mead, a Yale graduate who began the practice of medicine on the Illinois frontier in 1833 in Hancock County. Already in 1846 Dr. Mead had published in the *Prairie Farmer* a list of over 800 plants that grew "spontaneously in the state of Illinois," particularly near Augusta, in the west-central part. To over 180 plants on this list Dr. Mead ascribed some medical attribute, such as "emetic," "laxative," "narcotic," "caustic," "tonic," "antiseptic," "acrid," or just "poisonous." He distinguished between those plants that he thought were "native" and those "introduced," and he faithfully recorded where he found his plants: along rivers or creeks, on bottom land, in sand, on hills, in timber, in prairie, or in wet prairie or in the "barrens."[24] His work soon attracted the attention of botanists in New England and Europe with whom he made systematic exchanges. When his widow expressed a desire to sell the Herbarium, Professor Hurd went about Galesburg to raise the money for purchase of the collection and made himself responsible for organizing and preserving the materials.[25] Thus Knox acquired and preserved one of the special scholarly resources that, beginning in the second quarter of the twentieth century, made it possible to emphasize in its curriculum and by the research of its faculty the natural as well as the cultural features of the Midwest.[26]

Specimens from the "Cabinets" were used to illustrate Dr. Hurd's lectures. A student (class of 1891) who himself would become a distinguished scientist recalled Hurd's classroom presence and his teaching method:

> He demanded that students study. Some of the more timid members of his classes approached their turn in his recitations with fear and trembling. He had an uncanny discernment of a state of unpreparedness, and his questions were searching. He was a tall, spare man, smooth shaven, with black hair, and aquiline nose and a healthy ruddy complexion. There was fire in his eye and steadiness in his step. I can see him now as he entered the classroom, clad in a long black coat, white starched shirt and flowing tie. His black shoes were always neatly polished. He would take his seat at the side of a little table on the floor level, and adjust his spectacles to ride properly on the top of his nose. He would open the book on his knee, and glance assuringly at the faces of the students seated before him, with a pleased expression that seemed to say, "I am going to enjoy this hour with you. We will examine together a most interesting subject. Alert all!" But no such word was spoken; it was all conveyed in the serene assurance of his presence and in the glance of his eye.
>
> In his teaching there was no monotony of procedure; the element of surprise was never lacking. He taught all the sciences by the lecture method, as was the rule in the colleges of his day. But he was far from being content to have his pupils learn only by hearsay. He wished them to see things for themselves whenever possible. He had no laboratory. He had only a little cubicle of a room where he prepared his material for demonstration.[27]

For the botany class he would bring in fresh flowers and hand them to the students, who, following his directions, would examine them with the aid of pocket knives or pins, and, possibly, with a few simple tripod lenses known then as "linen testers."[28]

In 1881 Professor Hurd published a text book on chemistry, presenting the information he had used in his classes. It comprised 265 pages of exposition, definitions, and equations, with no problems or exercises such as would today be tried in a laboratory.[29] He himself performed the experiments as demonstrations for the class.[30] On one occasion in his class in what is now called Old Main considerable excitement occurred when his class "fired off a combination of oxygen and ethene, the report of which was like that of a young cannon. Those in the halls thought the building was going up. The girls screamed, and the boys were not much behind them in vocal demonstrations."[31] The building in 1888 of an Observatory gave a little more teaching space, and in 1889 Hurd "fitted up" on the first floor of the old West Bricks a chemical laboratory where he could oversee the students' work in "Chemical manipulations and analysis."[32] When this building was torn down in the summer of 1890 to make place for Alumni Hall, he was given better facilities in Old Main, and in 1891, for the first time, the catalogue used the word "Laboratory." It appeared in the same section of the booklet that now described the courses on "Chemistry and the Natural Sciences" as if they had become a "department."[33]

Hurd had earned his bachelor's degree at Middlebury College. For about six months in 1854–55, after he had been at Knox for three years, he studied at Harvard. Louis Agassiz impressed him greatly, as this master teacher did so many others, and Hurd remained a disciple of this great zoologist from Switzerland and France. Like Agassiz, Hurd accepted the proposition that the record of the fossils did not support a literal interpretation of the first two chapters of Genesis. Hurd's elder daughter, Harriet, who helped him make geological charts for his class, recalled that:

> Father used to present all there was to be said on his chosen subject from both points of view, always coming to the final conclusion that the glorious poetry of the first two chapters of Genesis could not possibly be regarded as the expression of literal, scientific fact, but was to be considered as an allegorical picture of the general course of progress of Creation, during the countless ages of time while it was unfolding in nature, and which has left its records in

the rocks of the earth's frame for man to read more and more understandingly.[34]

Not infrequently, Professor Hurd lectured on this topic in neighboring towns as well as in Galesburg.[35] A local newspaper in 1867 published this summary of his lectures on "Creation of the World" and on "Modern Science and the Bible:"

> It is fashionable with a certain class of superficially educated persons to charge that modern science disproves the statements of the Bible, and there are also a class of superficial theologians who having no knowledge of the true teachings of science take the ground that the Bible disproves the teachings of science, and therefore the deductions of science are false. Both are wrong, and as much mischief has been done by the theologians as by the so called scientific infidels. . . . Though the Bible is not intended to be a scientific book, it is in harmony with science.[36]

A student at Knox during the 1870s, who had preserved the notes she took from Professor Hurd's lecture on the creation, recalled how he differed with Professor Alexander F. Kemp, who taught the course in moral philosophy during the long interval from 1872 to 1875 when there was no president to teach that subject. Professor Kemp believed "that the deposits on the mountains corroborated the universal Flood which the scriptures said covered the face of the earth." Professor Hurd did not believe that the fossils indicated such a flood.[37]

Like Agassiz, however, Hurd did not accept the evolutionary hypotheses propounded by Charles Darwin in the *Origin of Species* during Hurd's seventh year on the Knox faculty. James Needham, who was a student of Hurd thirty years after that magnum opus was first published, recalled that Hurd's class lectures in zoology were "tinctured with the philosophy of Agassiz rather than of Darwin."[38] Agassiz believed that each species of animals and plants was a "thought of God."[39] Further, "homologies among the parts of different animals . . . and lines of differentiation among them . . . indicated a Creator's infinite resourcefulness, rather than blood relationship among animals."[40] Like Agassiz, Hurd fairly presented the facts on both sides, but he made it plain that he did not accept Darwinism. Unlike President Bateman, who wrote out his chapel speeches in full, Hurd used only brief notes for his weekly talks to the student body and no primary document has been preserved that exactly records what he said. However, newspaper reports of two lectures given in the academic year 1885–86 are available. In December 1885 Hurd spoke as follows to the faculty and students:

> "We all know there is much said on evolution in the present age. We are familiar with the names of the great expounders of this theory; with Huxley, Darwin, and Spencer. I am fearful sometimes that we place too much reliance on their dicta; that we are too easily led by them. I confess that when I read their works I often feel the discrepancies of their logic and can boldly meet them and give better, clearer, more accurate definitions. I shall read a few words this morning from an article by the bishop of Carlisle, a man but little known to the world compared with Herbert Spencer, and yet whose writings are immeasurably superior." Prof. Hurd then read a few paragraphs in which the writer showed the falsity of Spencer's definitions of life and then gave a definition which could withstand all objections.[41]

And the following month, after a detailed examination of certain zoological and geological data, he concluded that the "evolutionist rested his whole theory on an assumption wholly erroneous." He began this chapel talk by noting that Agassiz "was during his entire life an earnest, powerful opponent of the theory of evolution. He did not believe that plants and animals were created by any law of development."[42]

On the issue of evolution Hurd was probably more conservative than President Bateman or than Bateman's predecessor, President John Gulliver, both of these men being ex-officio the professors of moral philosophy for students in their senior year.[43] Bateman did not endorse or defend Darwinism,[44] yet sometimes he made an accommodation to Darwin's writings, at least rhetorically if not logically, as when he told the students: "Evolution is but the method by which the Builder wrought. It does not explain origins."[45]

When the Board of Trustees met at the conclusion of the academic year 1888–89, Hurd requested that he be relieved from duty as professor of natural sciences and be appointed professor of Latin. He had been teaching Latin as an extra duty for almost twenty years. The executive committee of the board accepted his request but later in the summer rescinded this action,[46] and Hurd continued as before to teach chemistry, Latin, geology, and the whole range of courses in what later would comprise biology. Possibly Hurd had ended the school year very tired, though he was very proud of his physical and mental vigor and once boasted to his colleague and former student, Professor Thomas Willard, "I have never known what it was to be tired. I don't know the sensation."[47] But he was now nearly sixty-six years old; he had worked himself hard; he had twice assumed some of the duties of president;[48] he had been active in the Congregational church, where he taught a popular Bible class on Sundays;[49] he served as the leader of a private library society before that became a public venture. He was allowed no time nor given the means by which to keep up with the rapid growth of scientific knowledge.

During the 1880s some students pressed for strengthening the requirements for the bachelor of science degree, which was regarded as a "short cut through college."[50] It differed from the arts degree only in that it did not require courses in Greek language and literature. In the spring of 1886 the College announced that the requirements for the bachelor of science degree would be stiffened and that as consequence it would take two years instead of one in the Preparatory Department to qualify as a freshman.[51] The increased requirements were not, however, made by adding science courses but by enlarging the number of stipulated courses in languages. Two years of German were now expected, not merely one; the amount of Latin was increased. During the sophomore year a year of French could be substituted for three terms of Latin; during the junior year French could substitute for one term of Latin and for the calculus in two terms.[52]

That students desired more learning in the sciences was shown in 1888 by the organization, on their initiative, of a Natural History Club.[53] A leader in this society was James G. Needham, who during his junior year was chosen "Superintendent of Scientific Investigation."[54] Members of his class (1891) "petitioned the faculty for the privilege of a little laboratory work in chemistry" and though this required "the reuse . . . of Professor Hurd's scanty materials and apparatus and . . . meant more work for him, he supported" the "petition and it was granted." Needham operated a taxidermy shop in one of the rooms of West or East Bricks, working his way through Knox "at odd hours mounting birds and mammals for exhibit purposes and for collections." In 1895 Needham would return to Knox to teach biology, the first man to give Hurd some help in teaching the natural sciences.[55] In 1898 he was awarded the degree of doctor of philosophy at Cornell University, where he had a very distinguished career as an entomologist, which was recognized by the honorary doctorate given him at Knox thirty years after he had received his baccalaureate. Another student of Hurd's, whose scientific achievements were similarly recognized by his alma mater, was George Latimer Bates (1885), who after theological training went to West Africa, prepared the first grammar of a native language, published a book on the ornithology of birds in that region, and became a famous collector of specimens for the British Museum of Natural History.[56]

The first addition in a quarter of a century to the teaching of sciences at Knox was not made, however, in natural sciences but in natural philosophy. Comstock was still in 1888 the professor of mathematics, natural philosophy, and astronomy. The mathematics needed to earn a degree either in science or in classics had during all that time remained unchanged. When the catalogue of 1889–90 for the first time listed what might be called "departments," it was noted that changes in the course of "Pure Mathematics" would "afford increased facilities" to those who wished "to make the studies of that department a specialty." Algebra would now be completed in the Preparatory Course and would be followed with two terms of geometry and two terms of trigonometry. Analytical geometry and calculus were, however, "optional." Even a student pursuing the science degree could substitute French for the calculus. Indeed, the formation of a calculus class in 1892 was still a newsworthy item for the college magazine.[57]

The textbooks used in the mathematics courses for more than two decades had all been written by Elias Loomis of Yale, who had succeeded Denison Olmstead at Yale as the professor of mathematics and natural philosophy. The culminating experience of the students at Knox with Loomis's text books was in the astronomy course, which, significantly, was listed in the mathematics column of the day-week class schedule. Astronomy had been required for the degree since the College began and had not changed its place in the curriculum and in the calendar since the catalogue for the year 1842–43 listed "Astronomy with Calculation of Eclipses." From the first it was taught to all juniors during the second term, both on the semester system (ante 1856–58) and thereafter, on the three-term system, during the winter. For years, the time for astronomy was the last period of the day, and this much, at least, remained the same when Edgar Lucien Larkin became in September 1888 "Adjunct Professor of Astronomy."[58]

Larkin came from New Windsor, a very small town to the northwest of Galesburg, just across the county line. Here he was the proprietor of the village drug store. On New Year's Day 1880 he had mounted his new telescope on a pier in the revolving tower that he himself had built, and thus he established the "New Windsor Observatory,"[59] which soon came to the attention of Knox faculty and students. The six-inch telescope was a very good one, purchased at the cost of $688 from Alvan Clark and Sons, the famous Boston lens-makers, whose craftsmanship was as honored in Europe as in the United States. It was a much better instrument than the portable one used by Professor Comstock at Knox, which had a three-and-one-half-inch glass and was estimated to be worth only about $100.[60]

The owner of the New Windsor Observatory was a self-taught amateur scientist, in 1880 still only thirty-three years old. Altogether he had only twenty-seven months of formal schooling, the last of it concluding below the high school level when he was still only sixteen. He could not have passed the entrance examinations of a college such as Knox, but he would become a professor at Knox College and later the director of the Lowe Observatory on Echo Mountain in California. He would write many scientific articles and four books. He had been born in a log cabin on a frontier farm in La Salle County, Illinois, in 1847 and at the age of eleven, after his father died, went with his mother to live at the home of her parents. Though his schooling was delayed and remained scanty, he found other learning in the library of a retired German physician who had settled on an adjacent farm in La Salle County.[61]

On a night in October 1858 he was greatly excited by the appearance of Donati's Comet. His grandmother used a gold coin she had hoarded to buy from his teacher a copy of Burrit's *Geography of the Heavens* and an atlas. A surveyor who lived nearby loaned him a four-inch lens, which he placed in a square tube with an eyepiece to make a telescope. And thus his self-instruction in astronomy began.[62]

By the winter of 1868–69 he was settled in New Windsor, which was a booming little village on the newly completed "American Central Railway."[63] As a merchant in this flourishing town Larkin made the money to buy science books and astronomical apparatus and, beginning in 1879, to travel to the meetings of the American Association for the Advancement of Science.[64] He concentrated especially on what was then called the "New Spectroscopic Astronomy."

Larkin contributed articles to leading scientific journals,[65] and his observatory came to have "free telegraphic communication" with an observatory in Cambridge, Massachusetts, and with the Smithsonian Institution in Washington, D.C.[66] In 1883, by ballot, the American Association for the Advancement of Science elected him a fellow, a title which he would wear as a badge besides the more ordinary academic degrees of his colleagues on the Knox faculty.[67]

As early as December 1883 Professor Comstock was in communication with Larkin regarding the longitude and latitude of different points in Knox County. This interest had been stimulated by the recent adoption of standard time, an event of particular relevance to a railway center such as Galesburg. Comstock used for his computations the longitude and latitude of the observatory in New Windsor.[68] The following summer several Knox students visited this observatory.[69] The leading newspaper in Galesburg published in 1887 several articles by Larkin, on topics such as "Celestial Photography," "Weather Prophets," "The Sun," and "Recent Discoveries in Physical Science."[70] The Larkins' son Ralph had enrolled in September 1886 in the Knox Preparatory Department, and the following June the father attended the celebration of the Knox semicentennial. Larkin would have had a special interest in the Knox alumnus who was chief orator for that occasion, for he was Stephen "Deacon" White, notorious Wall Street stock speculator, who owned "the largest and finest refracting telescope of any private observer in America," and had been elected president of the American Astronomical Association when it was founded in 1883.[71]

S. S. McClure at the time he graduated from Knox. Photograph from *Success Story: The Life and Times of S. S. McClure.*

Albert Brady and John Phillips, McClure's classmates at Knox and his associates on *McClure's Magazine.* Photographs from *Success Story: The Life and Times of S. S. McClure.*

Edgar Lee Masters, ca. 1894, about five years after he had left Knox to practice law in Chicago. Photograph from *Across Spoon River: An Autobiography.*

W. E. Simonds and A. G. Newcomer, two of Edgar
Lee Masters's most influential teachers.

The Observatory that was built for A. L. Larkin, Edgar Lee Masters's "Professor Moon."

Albert E. Hurd, professor of chemistry and natural science, 1860 (top; nine years after he had joined the faculty) and 1904 (bottom).

Knox condemns plot against George Wishart, as highly criticized and "falsely accused."

A great many observatories were built during the last quarter of the nineteenth century. They were an aspect of the academic style of that period when philanthropists of this Gilded Age underwrote several installations, the most notable occurring near the end of the century when Charles Yerkes, street railway titan, repaired a damaged personal reputation by paying for the observatory built in his name on Lake Geneva, where the University of Chicago installed a telescope with a forty-inch lens, the last "objective" made by the Clarks.[72] On a much more modest scale many small colleges also erected observatories, particularly during the 1880s. Only five miles away from Galesburg, St. Mary's School for Girls announced in March 1888 that a new observatory would be built to house a telescope eight feet long, mounted with brass clock works, whose six-inch object glass had been made by Clark and Sons, the whole including the building to cost about $8,000.[73]

To keep up, where would Knox get an observatory? Already in the summer of 1887 a Galesburg newspaper reported that Edgar Larkin was "seriously" contemplating a move from New Windsor to Galesburg.[74] In December the executive committee of the Knox board discussed a communication from Larkin "proposing that Knox College establish an observatory" and that he would "under certain conditions turn over his instruments and apparatus to the College" and offer his services as instructor in astronomy. The faculty voted to recommend to the trustees that Larkin's proposal be accepted,[75] and the students in January announced as an accomplished fact that steps had been "taken to secure an observatory . . . one of the best in the State," and, what was even better, would "have the benefit of an astronomer of more than local reputation."[76] Actually President Bateman first took the precaution of sending an emissary to New Windsor who would be competent to determine Larkin's qualifications and to assess the value of his scientific equipment. Accordingly, on April 3, 1889, Larkin received as a visitor the Reverend H. G. Sedgwick, the director of technology at Nebraska Wesleyan in Lincoln, who had been recommended to Bateman by Knox alumnus Charles Wesley Leffingwell, rector of St. Mary's in Knoxville, where Sedgwick was already under contract to build an observatory.[77]

On the same day Sedgwick wrote Bateman a strong and most enthusiastic recommendation of Larkin. His telescope, solar photographic attachment, spectroscopic attachment, stereoptician, solar-nebulae-steller views, and "choice library of astronomical works, from all over the world" constituted the "best selected, most carefully kept, observatory" that Sedgwick had "seen in the West, . . . a very rare outfit" that could not be duplicated for $2,500. His opinion of "*The Man,* in charge," was most favorable:

> I found him the best posted person in mathematical mechanical & downright *practical* astronomy it has been my pleasure to meet in many a day, and I meet professors every week—in different colleges with long titles. Yet I will venture the assertion, Mr. L. has forgotten more than many of them ever knew about astronomical science . . . and he is the first man I have met except the famous "Burnham" of Chicago whom I couldn't "stick" on the telescope. . . .
>
> Get some college to grant him a degree. *Set him to work.* If you have that instrument fixed up in proper shape for him, it won't be six months before your observatory will lead everything in the west for solid work.[78]

President Bateman followed his consultant's advice not to risk losing Larkin by delaying. Within three days Larkin's proposal had been accepted: he would become a professor at Knox; his astronomical equipment would come into possession of the College; an observatory would immediately be built on the Knox campus for which Larkin should draw up the plans and for which he should consult with Sedgwick, with whom before commencement 1888 a construction contract was made to build "the dome and its appurtenances at $1325 and the . . . observatory building $2275."[79]

By mid-September 1888 the telescope was mounted and "everything . . . was ready for the juniors to commence star gazing." Professor Larkin in great detail proudly described the new scientific installation for the Galesburg *Republican Register,* to which he would continue to provide articles with great frequency.[80] He welcomed all those who had "an odd hour between recitations" to visit the new building. It was the first entirely academic building constructed since Old Main in 1857; it was the first science building; it exceeded anything that had been done previously to provide laboratory experience for the students. Especially during the early years of the use of the building, it was newsworthy that students viewed a solar eclipse with the telescope, "gazed upon Venus in all her beauty," and saw "through the equatorial . . . some nebulae . . . and saw Saturn with his rings."[81] The student magazine published articles from Larkin, and by the spring of his first year he was given a regular assignment for speeches in chapel, where the scientific lectures he gave every other Friday were "highly appreciated."[82] He made celestial incidents such as the close conjunction of Jupiter and Venus important public events for the city of Galesburg. In May 1891 he reported in the *Republican Register* on "the transit of Mercury," which was for him obviously an important emotional and aesthetic happening as well as a significant astronomical observation. He explained that he had been asked by the Naval Observatory in Washington, D.C., to join with other "western observatories" in making and recording this transit of Mercury, which would not be visible in the eastern part of the United States. To his readers, Larkins explained: "These observations are required . . . to be used in computations to determine the quantity of matter making revolution around the sun, within the orbit of Mercury. . . . [The] fact that the perhelion of Mercury is moving at a rate of 38 sec. per century . . . can only be accounted for on the hypothesis that one quite large planet lies between Mercury and the Sun, or a multitude of small bodies."[83]

Larkin became much more than the College astronomer; already during his first term he taught the juniors "Optics" and took them to inspect the local electric light works after "a highly interesting lecture on the dynamo."[84] He taught subjects that today would occur in the introductory course in physics, a word that appeared in the catalogue for the first time in 1890, when college courses also for the first time were organized under departmental headings. Details about the nature of the physics he taught may be gleaned from articles he published in the *Republican Register* on "Mechanics," "Motion," "Mass," and "Pneumatics"—less conventional, certainly more transient, was "Etherodynamics," which Larkin described as "the Youngest Science. . . . Matter has a spirit, a refined essence more subtile [*sic*] than itself. It pervades all matter and cannot be separated from it. It is the ether, but it is matter also—a substance so rarified that hydrogen is a solid to it as iron is to hydrogen."[85]

It was appropriate that Larkin's title was changed in 1891–92 from "Professor of Astronomy and Director of the Observatory" to "Directory of the Observatory and Physical Laboratory." Occasionally now the articles he provided to the newspaper came over the date line of the "Knox Physical Laboratory" instead of the "Knox Observatory." He was not at all coy about the advantage Knox might gain from such publicity, once bluntly stating: "Oh! that the money of Galesburg . . . be given to the Knox scientific department."[86] In May 1893 he provided Dr. Bateman, who still was acting as president, with a special and detailed report on the "needs of the college in the department of physical science." He began the report with a vigorous plea for bringing Knox into line with the times: "The day has arrived when modern science should have a hearing in Knox College. I have reason to know that the case is urgent. . . . It is my judgment that immediate steps be taken by Knox if she would retain her renown and prestige. . . . She cannot hope to enter the area of science without modern equipment."[87] Larkin's plea made extended references to the fact that he intended to spend the summer at the Columbian Exposition in Chicago, which offered special opportunities to observe, test, and perhaps even acquire the latest and best scientific equipment.

Larkin had by this time developed a special interest and competency in "Electricity," the technology that particularly was symbolized by the Chicago World's Fair, the "White City." It was on this topic that he provided town as well as gown his most timely educational service. During the decade of the 1880s the urban areas of the more advanced countries of the western world began to develop public supplies of electric current—London in January and New York in September 1882. Even in Galesburg by May 1883 there was a "Galesburg Electric Illuminating and Power Company" that was selling stock and expecting to purchase a "forty light electrical machine." By the spring of 1887 an electric plant lighted certain downtown stores, and in June of that semi-centennial year, the large "wigwam" built by Knox south of Old Main to shelter the festivities was "illuminated by electric light"— the first Knox structure thus lighted.[88]

Larkin was an avid and enthusiastic expounder of the discoveries of Nikola Tesla, the Croatian immigrant who developed the induction motor, which used alternating current. This technology created less heat than direct current and simplified the methods by which electrical connections were made. In numerous lectures and newspaper articles Larkin reported on the new phenomena, interpreting but also exhorting.[89] He prophesized momentous consequences from the uses of electricty. Though his pronouncements were often quickly proved by actual events, still there were those who sneered at his ideas as "chimerical."[90] Scepticism in some auditors may have been provoked by the animated enthusiasm with which he lectured. One report spoke of his going into a "trance" and unveiling the future of Mississippi Valley when an electric railway between the cities of Chicago and St. Louis became the axis for "a continuous city" starting at Lake Michigan and terminating at the famous Eads Bridge. Even if much of Larkin's enthusiastic rhetoric on this and other topics proved to be prophetic, the truth was that he was sometimes simply unrestrained and flighty—his language simply boiled over.

Larkin's enthusiasm was one of the traits noted from the very first by the students. His hyperbolic style made him an easy target for student humor. Thus when he announced a total eclipse of the moon for the night of March 10, 1895, it was said that as evening approached he "was delirious with delight and still refuses food."[91] Did the students who laughed at him also call him "Professor Moon," as is suggested in the poem by Edgar Lee Masters about the man "who taught the lore of the stars at Knox College" and was jeered when he

> . . . spoke of the lunar mountains,
> And the thrilling heat and cold,
> And the ebon valleys by silver peaks,
> And Spica quadrillions of miles away,
> And the littleness of man.[92]

Repeated quips in the student magazine suggest that Larkin had difficulty maintaining order in his classes,[93] which is not surprising for a man who lacked even the experience of having been a high school student and was unfamiliar with the delicate classroom forces that affect the relations of a college teacher to his students. He tried, unsuccessfully, to hold them to higher standards of performance than they would tolerate. In 1891–92 he abjectly capitulated to the juniors taking astronomy, promising that he would teach them descriptive rather than mathematical astronomy and would give them an easier final examination.[94]

In his writings Larkin was defensive of his lack of conventional academic training, and it is reasonable to assume that his older colleagues may have been offended by public utterances about Larkin's being the harbinger of "new branches of science." To the trustees he described Knox as being behind the times and himself as ready to provide the needed "modern science." He referred to himself as introducing the "New" Astronomy or the "New" Physics, and even of supplementing Hurd's "regular chemistry" with a "New" Chemistry. Toward the end of Larkin's first year the student magazine wryly remarked: "It is not fair the way Prof. Hurd contradicts Prof. Larkin."[95]

Late in life Larkin admitted that for one period of six years in his life he had been interested in "occult" studies, inquiries in "Hindu, Iranian, Persian, Egyptian, and Greek philosophy and esoteric mysteries."[96] This involvement with occultism did not, as one might presume, occur after he migrated into the spiritual environment of California. It was apparent in newspaper articles he wrote even before he moved from New Windsor to Galesburg, articles that quoted the Vedas and the Upanishads. It was clear that he pursued the occult in the oldest sense of the world—as knowledge that was deliberately hidden, as the secret and undisclosed, not to be shown to the uninitiated; as knowledge concealed from view; the "mysterious," as that word is used to indicate a religious "mystery." This kind of occultism was described by Larkin in an article on "The Science of Antiquity," written for the *Republican Register* over the dateline: "Knox Observatory, Jan. 17, 1891."

> The most ancient civilized nations possessed a knowledge of the physical sciences. It has long been the habit to say that discoveries in natural law are recent, and that the ancients made little advancement in the study of nature. . . . But late researches in primeval history, translations of exhumed inscriptions, and the finding of philosophical instruments, have led archaeologists to admit that the ancient civilizations were more scientific by far than has been imagined. It is now known that the philosophers and hierophants of

Bactria, India, Media, Assyria, Chaldea, Egypt . . . Greece . . . Rome
. . . had much accurate knowledge of nature's laws. . . .

And all this knowledge was kept profoundly secret, the masses
never heard of these laws, and they were only communicated in the
rites of initiation. All philosophers of antiquity reasoned that the
multitude could not comprehend, and that it was best to keep
knowledge confined to the ruling classes. And when it was desired
to impress the common herd with an appearance of superhuman
wisdom the priests and kings performed philosophical experiments,
far beyond the understanding of those who beheld. . . .

All enlightened nations had mysteries, and these were but societies of learned men who conferred upon the candidates for initiation
in subterranean labyrinths the most profound truths of science,
under oath of death should they be revealed to the outsiders.[97]

Such ideas about a cult of ancient secrets corresponds very
closely with Rosicrucian belief in secret wisdom from ancient
times that is passed on only to those who have been initiated into
the secret brotherhood. This is not to say that Larkin was a Rosicrucian any more than it is to say that he was a Theosophist
because he believed that ancient esoteric wisdom, available only
to the few, had been handed down from ancient seers, mainly by
word of mouth. Larkin was a faithful Congregationalist, indeed,
an elder of that persuasion, but for him a scientific discovery could
also be a religious revelation, as he indicated in one of his very
first statements to Knox students, when he wrote in 1888 of a
modern scientific discovery as being "the mighty gate of a laby-
rinth, more inscrutable than the Egyptian."[98] Later he provided
an article for the *Coup D'Etat* about the Great Pyramid in which
he explained that it was a "sacred building" whose form and
proportions incorporated the astronomical and mathematical
knowledge of the builders, who "concealed the entrance with a
stone, seemingly intended to remain until wind and sand should
wear it away. . . . Their idea doubtless was that mankind would
be unable to comprehend the wisdom hidden in the interior, until
the elements would have time to batter the stone to dust. . . . They
sought to transmit the knowledge in unwritten stone to unborn
generations. . . . The Book of Revelations is a prophecy in Words,
the pyramid in stone. Both will be revealed in the fullness of time,

and all hear."[99] The books that Larkin would write after he left Knox and became director of the Lowe Observatory have titles that indicate that he continued to mingle esoteric subjects with more orthodox scientific themes; see, for example: *The Matchless Altar of the Soul, Symbolized as a Shining Cube of Diamond, One Cubit in Dimensions, and Set within the Holy of Holies in all Grand Esoteric Temples of Antiquity.*[100]

It is clear that his leaving Knox was a painful personal wrench, causing him to comment to Albert Perry, business manager of Knox College: "How exceedingly unfortunate for all concerned that I ever came to the institution."[101] In September 1894 Larkin had begun his seventh year at Knox. That month he and Mrs. Larkin moved into a house in the block just west of the campus.[102] There seemed to be no indications that this would be his last year with the College. But early in the summer of 1895 he was informed that the next year would be his last and that meanwhile his salary would be reduced to $500. Larkin "felt unable" to accept the reduction in salary, which not only was cut back to what it was when he started his Knox tenure but also suggested a diminishing importance on the campus. It was explained that the College needed to cut expenses by the teaching staff; Larkin's teaching load could more readily be distributed among the other faculty members for his classes were very small.[103] Perhaps Larkin's unconventional interest in the occult made some of his colleagues uneasy; it is likely that some were bothered by his extraordinary spells of enthusiasm—whatever it was that made a more junior colleague, Professor William Simonds, remember him as "turbulent." Larkin resigned and with little delay left the city to establish himself for a time, as a druggist in Antioch, Illinois.

The farewell notice in the student paper, however, placed a high value on his role at Knox: "His loss will be greatly felt by the spirit and thought of the College. An enthusiast in his line of work, he has kept before the college the wonders and the advances of electricity. He is thoroughly conversant with astronomy and electricity in every particular and we regret to lose him."[104]

The telescope that he had brought with him from New Windsor remained behind him, a circumstance that compounded his bitterness. In November 1897, more than two years after he left Knox, he commented: "As time goes on, my loss of the telescope grows more and more painful, and I now feel I shall never have the pleasure of looking through a telescope again."[105] Over a number of years the college paid interest on the "exact cost" of the telescope to Larkin, and then soon after he became director of the Mount Lowe Observatory he relinquished for a modest lump sum all claims to the instrument, explaining: "My only regret is that I was not able to give it entirely." The Observatory that had been erected for him in 1888 stood for seventy-five years, long after anyone on the campus knew anything about the man for whom it had been built.[106]

There is considerable justification for the view that the updating of science at Knox began during the last decade of the nineteenth century while Dr. John Finley was president. This was evident in the appearance of doctors of philosophy trained in Germany or in a similar type of American graduate school organized on the German model, such as John Hopkins, where President Finley himself did his graduate work. Two of the teachers who would see the George Davis Science Building completed in 1912 were appointed late in Finley's administration. But in the fields of astronomy and physics the renaissance of the sciences at Knox began earlier with Larkin, however amateur, home-grown, and self-cultivated his professional credentials were.

The career of Professor Larkin exemplified the profound changes occurring in American culture and in the relation of scientists to society at large. In the past the enrichment of scientific knowledge had to a large extent been accomplished by amateurs as a pastime or as an avocation. It now became the vocation of highly trained specialists for whom it was a livelihood and full-time profession. The term natural philosophy was becoming archaic as scientists were less and less perceived as scholars concerned with underlying causes or with principles of reality. More and more they were regarded as experts who provided the kind of knowledge that might be of practical use in an industrial economy that was ever ready for technological innovations. The interest shown by Galesburg audiences in Larkin's lectures on electricity exemplified this public expectation that science might be something useful.

NOTES

1. Professor Hurd continued: "As the smoker, with his sun glass lights his pipe in the harvest field; so will the engine in the mill generate the steam that turning ponderous wheels, grinds the corn" (Galesburg *Republican Register*, Nov. 18, 1876, 6). On the subject of smoking Hurd advised in a chapel talk: "if you must smoke get a meerschaum or a clay pipe with a long stem, or use your cigar or cigarette in a holder" (*ibid.*, Sept. 25, 1880, 5).

2. William Calvert Kneale, "Philosophy," *Encyclopedia Brittanica* (1967), 17:864–69.

3. MS dated June 24, 1873, and signed by M. L. Comstock, Knox College Library.

4. Dr. Lance Factor of the philosophy department of Knox College has provided this note: "The division of the English curriculum into 'Natural Philosophy' and 'Moral Philosophy' reflects Aristotle's distinction between 'theoretical' and 'practical' knowledge. For Aristotle ethics was practical wisdom. The distinction was re-enforced by Locke's division of knowledge into Ethics, Physics, and Logic (*Enquiry Concerning Human Understanding*). . . . After Newton, a friend of Locke, 'Natural Philosophy' became physics or the physical sciences. In fact it was any subject where the materialist assumptions were presumed to hold. The rest became 'moral philosophy' which included logic and metaphysics." After he retired from the presidency of Knox College, Newton Bateman continued as professor of moral philosophy until his death in 1897. The next year Professor Henry Thatcher Fowler was listed as professor of moral philosophy and elocution, but in 1899 the listing was simply professor of philosophy.

5. Olmsted, *Introduction to Natural Philosophy*, 1–3.

6. Note from Dr. Factor, philosophy department.

7. Buley, *Old Northwest Pioneer Period*, 1:122–23.

8. Biography of George Churchill in Perry, ed., *History of Knox County*, 2:310–14. For references to his career as city engineer, see the Knox catalogue for 1882–83, 58, and also Galesburg *Republican Register*, Sept. 27, 1873, 1.

9. Catalogue for 1846–47.

10. *Coup D'Etat*, Mar. 1884, 85.

11. Catalogue for 1843–44.

12. Catalogue for 1844–45.

13. Catalogue for 1890–91, 41.

14. See articles in Galesburg *Republican Register*, May 6, 1883, 2; June 23, 1883, 7; Mar. 21, 1882, 2; Apr. 7, 1883, 2.

15. See ch. 3 herein.

16. Galesburg *Republican Register*, Sept. 10, 1881, 6.

17. A sketch of Hurd's life was published in the *Knox Bulletin*, Ser. 2, 3 (Oct. 1906), 1–2.

18. Catalogue for 1863–64.

19. Notes by Mary Hurd, Albert Hurd Papers.

20. Executive Committee Minutes of the Board of Trustees, Jan. 7, 1884.

21. When the shell collections were moved to Davis Science Hall, they were, according to Mary Hurd, all dumped together.

22. Catalogue for 1889–90.

23. Catalogue for 1882–83, 29.

24. Issues of the *Prairie Farmer* for Jan., Feb., Mar., and Apr. 1846.

25. *Coup D'Etat*, Dec. 1881, 46–47; *Knox Student*, Dec. 1881, 35–36.

26. Edward Caldwell (1886) would contribute to the College an extraordinary collection of books and prints on the Old Northwest; Alvah Green (1890) would bequeath "Green Oaks" for biological studies. This is an open area with very old trees adjacent to a prairie carefully nurtured by Knox College.

27. James G. Needham, letter to the *Fifty Year Club Bulletin*, June 1953, 4–8. A student from the 1860s recalled: "Professor Hurd had small sympathy for a poor scholar. Someone said, 'you might as well kill a man as scare him to death.' I would not imply that Professor Hurd ever scared a girl to death, but he did many times scare the sense out of her, and if she really did know the answer to his question she would forget it when his sharp eye demanded an answer. He loved a bold brave answer even if it was wrong. It provoked discussion." *Knox Alumnus*, 6 (June-July 1923), 219, "Hurd Memorial Unveiled."

28. Needham, "How Biology Came to Knox," 365–72; Galesburg *Republican Register*, Feb. 19, 1881, 5.

. 29. The copy in the vault of the Memorabilia Department of Knox College has no title page. Reference to publication is made in Galesburg *Republican Register*, Aug. 20, 1881, 3.

30. Needham in *Knox Fifty Year Club Bulletin*, 7.

31. Galesburg *Republican Register*, Jan. 1, 1890, 1.

32. Albert Hurd to Mrs. Mary W. Anderson, Jan. 1, 1890, Hurd Papers.

33. Catalogue for 1890–91, 41. The character of the course in Chemistry was for the first time described in the catalogue as follows: "By the use of a text book and by experimental lectures, the instruction aims to secure a familiar acquaintance with the elementary facts and principles of Inorganic Chemistry. The student is taught to observe chemical phenomena and to explain them, write out fully by means of chemical equations each change as it occurs and solving various volumetric and stoichiometric problems until their underlying principles are well understood. He may then pass into the laboratory and by his own experiments gain a practical knowledge of the properties of the common elements and their compounds. The laboratory work embraces an elementary course of qualitative chemical analysis, sufficient to give some practice in manipulation and a fair acquaintance with the methods of investigation. The laboratory is open six hours a week for about ten weeks."

34. Harriet Hurd McClure to Mrs. Laura Wright Eddy, Apr. 19, 1929, in the *Knox Alumnus*, May 1929, 128. Hurd's beliefs regarding creation were reflected in a graduation essay by one of his students at the Female Seminary commencement in Jan. 1857. The young woman responded negatively to the

proposition: "Are the six days of Creation literal days?" See Charles Ferris Gettemy, "A Graduation Essay of 1857," *ibid.*, Jan. 1929, 18–22.

35. Hurd to Eddy, Apr. 19, 1929. In 1869 Hurd was engaged to deliver his "scientific course" of lectures in Joliet (Galesburg *Free Press,* Dec. 28, 1869, 3).

36. Galesburg *Weekly Register,* Jan. 17, 1867, 4.

37. A letter from Mrs. Laura Wright Eddy in the *Knox Alumnus,* Apr. 1929.

38. Needham, "How Biology Came to Knox," 367.

39. David Starr Jordan, "Louis Agassiz," in *Encyclopedia Brittanica* (1967), 1:319–21.

40. Needham, "How Biology Came to Knox," 367.

41. Galesburg *Republican Register,* Dec. 12, 1885, 2.

42. *Ibid.,* Jan. 30, 1886, 2.

43. Askew, "Liberal Arts College Encounters Intellectual Change," 67–68, 113–31. See the rather tolerant attitude toward Darwin expressed by Gulliver in 1882, when he had become Stone Professor of the Relation of Christianity and Science at Andover Seminary in "Address at Wells College, June 21, 1882," Gulliver Papers.

44. In his talks on science to Knox students he certainly did not feel compelled to warn them against Darwinism and obviously did not express a belief in the literal truth of the biblical creation story (Bateman Papers).

45. Needham, "How Biology Came to Knox," 370.

46. Executive Committee Minutes, Board of Trustees, July 3, 5, Aug. 1, 1889.

47. *Knox Alumnus,* June-July 1923, 219–22.

48. He had performed many of the functions of an acting-president for nearly three years, 1872–1875. While Bateman was absent on an extended tour in Europe in 1880, he also served as the de facto head of the institution (Galesburg *Republican Register,* Sept. 4, 1880, 1; Sept. 11, 1880, 1).

49. *Ibid.,* June 30, 1877, 1.

50. *Coup D'Etat,* Feb. 1885, 81–85.

51. Galesburg *Republican Register,* May 22, 1886, 1; *Coup D'Etat,* May 1886, 137; catalogue for 1885–86, 31.

52. *Coup D'Etat,* Sept. 1888, 10; Dec. 1888, 51; catalogue for 1887–88, 334.

53. *Coup D'Etat,* Dec. 1888, 51.

54. Catalogue for 1889–90, 54.

55. Needham, "How Biology Came to Knox," 366–71.

56. The best source for information of this kind about Knox alumni is the *Knox Directory, 1837–1863.*

57. *Coup D'Etat,* Dec. 1892, 51.

58. The information on Larkin that follows recapitulates a more fully annotated manuscript monograph by Muelder, "Edgar L. Larkin."

59. Basset, *Past and Present of Mercer County,* 1:58; *History of Mercer and Henderson Counties,* 759.

Natural Philosophy and Natural Science

60. Executive Committee Minutes, Knox College Board of Trustees, Oct. 5, Nov. 2, 1893.

61. Fred Shoop, "Mt. Lowe Observatory Director's Career Started in Illinois." This is a newspaper clipping; the article was written soon after Larkin's death in 1924. Shoop used extensively an autobiographical sketch available to him; hereafter this article will be noted as Shoop, "Larkin Autobiography."

62. *Ibid.;* Knox College *Gale,* 1888, 102. The comet carried the name of Giovanni Batista Donati (1826–73), who saw it first on June 2, 1858. He was a pioneer in celestial spectroscopy, which became a subject of special interest to Larkin.

63. Basset, *Past and Present of Mercer County,* 1:463–64; Galesburg *Free Press,* Nov. 10, 1869, 2.

64. Report by Larkin to Board of Trustees, dated May 29, 1893, Bateman Papers.

65. *Gale,* 1888, 102.

66. *History of Mercer and Henderson Counties,* 762–63.

67. See faculty lists in the catalogues, 1889–95.

68. Galesburg *Republican Register,* Dec. 15, 1883, 4.

69. *Coup D'Etat,* Sept. 1884, 10; Dec. 1884, 55.

70. Galesburg *Republican Register,* Apr. 23, 1887, 11; May 28, 1887, 1; June 11, 1887, 7; July 16, 1887, 4; Dec. 3, 1887, 7.

71. *Ibid.,* May 21, 1887, 3; June 11, 1887, 6; Warner, *Alvan Clark & Sons,* 107–9. White's telescope was given to Wellesley.

72. Warner, *Alvan Clark & Sons,* 112.

73. *Knox Republican* (Knoxville, Ill.), Mar. 3, 1888, 6.

74. Galesburg *Republican Register,* June 11, 1887, 1; July 9, 1887, 1.

75. Faculty Minutes, Dec. 9, 1887.

76. *Coup D'Etat,* Jan. 1888, 75.

77. Bateman to Larkin, Apr. 6, 1888, Bateman Papers. Larkin would refer later to Sedgwick as "that accomplished mechanic . . . [of] Davenport, Iowa" (*Pantheon,* 1888, 103). Since Sedgwick also constructed an observatory at Grinnell College this same year as well as the one at Knox (Warner, *Alvan Clark & Sons,* 64–65) and was under contract to build one for St. Mary's at Knoxville, Ill., he must have been located in this general area much of the year.

78. Sedgwick to Bateman, Apr. 3, 1888, Bateman Papers.

79. Bateman to Larkin, Apr. 6, 1888, Sedgwick to Bateman, Apr. 3, 1888, Bateman Papers; minutes of the Board of Trustees, June 12, 1888; *Coup D'Etat,* June 1888, 153.

80. Galesburg *Republican Register,* Aug. 4, 1888, 1; Aug. 12, 1888, 1; Sept. 15, 1888, 5; Sept. 22, 1888, 1.

81. *Coup D'Etat,* Jan. 1889, 74; Mar. 9, 1891, 105; Galesburg *Republican Register,* Jan. 5, 1889, 4; Feb. 2, 1889, 5; Mar. 9, 1889, 5.

82. *Coup D'Etat,* May 1889, 135. In 1894–95 he was still scheduled for Fridays, sharing the assignment with Professor Comstock and Lt. William Phillips. All these men had classes in mathematics or science. Lt. Phillips was

professor of military science, but he also taught mechanical engineering (*Student*, Sept. 26, 1894, 3).

83. Galesburg *Republican Register*, May 16, 1891, 2. This phenomenon, which Larkin and others were observing, was in fact "beyond the scope of Newtonian theory for an explanation. It required new concepts in space and time. Einstein's Relativity Theory would furnish both a logical and quantitatively precise explanation of Mercury's orbital precession." Note to the author by Professor Herbert Priestly, professor of physics, Knox College. The following February the observatory "was crowded" one evening "by the interested spectators who came to witness the close Conjunction" of Jupiter and Venus (Galesburg *Republican Register*, Feb. 13, 1892, 2).

84. *Coup D'Etat*, Dec. 1888, 58.

85. Galesburg *Republican Register*, Mar. 16, 1889, 2.

86. *Ibid.*, Jan. 30, 1892, 2; Feb. 20, 1892, 2.

87. "KNOX PHYSICAL LABORATORY, May 29th, 1893. To the President and Board of Trustees of Knox College. . . ," Bateman Papers.

88. Galesburg *Republican Register*, May 21, 1887, 1; May 28, 1887, 5; June 25, 1887, 1, 6; Webster, *Seventy-Five Significant Years*, 90.

89. Galesburg *Republican Register*, Feb. 14, 23, Mar. 7, 8, 15, 1893. For other references to his lectures see Muelder, "Edgar L. Larkin."

90. Galesburg *Republican Register*, Jan. 14, 1893, 1; Mar. 14, 1893, 1.

91. *Knox Student*, Feb. 20, 1895, 5; *Gale*, 1895, 73.

92. Masters, *Spoon River Anthology*, 252.

93. *Gale*, 1889, 36; 1890, 148; *Coup D'Etat*, Nov. 1889, 39.

94. "Larkin to the Junior Class," Bateman Papers.

95. *Coup D'Etat*, May 1889, 135.

96. Shoop, "Larkin Autobiography."

97. Galesburg *Republican Register*, Jan. 17, 1891, 10.

98. *Pantheon*, 1888, 102.

99. *Coup D'Etat*, Feb. 1892, 85–88.

100. Other books credited to him in *Who was Who in America* are: *Radiant Energy and Its Analysis; Its Relation to Modern Astrophysics; Within the Mind Maze; or Mentonomy, the Law of the Mind; Popular Studies in Recent Astronomy.*

101. Larkin to A. J. Perry, Nov. 15, 1897, MS, Knox College Library.

102. *Student*, Sept. 12, 1894.

103. *Ibid.*, Aug. 1895; Executive Committee Minutes, Sept. 21, 1893; Trustees Minutes, June 12, 1895, June 10, 1896.

104. *Student*, Aug. 1895.

105. Larkin to Perry, Nov. 15, 1897.

106. Larkin to Perry, Nov. 15, 1897, Larkin to Mary Scott, June 20, 1904, MS, Knox College Library.

CHAPTER VIII

"OLD SIWASH": FACT, FICTION, AND GEORGE FITCH

On a Monday morning in January 1899 Carl Sandburg[1] entered the chapel at Lombard College "in triumphal procession," for on the preceding Saturday night the newly organized Lombard basketball team had defeated Knox College 16 to 12, and Freshman Sandburg was credited particularly with "good goal throwing."[2] He had enrolled that autumn, immediately after he had been mustered out from service in the Spanish-American War; Lombard had admitted him and given him a year's free tuition,[3] even though his formal education had stopped after the eighth grade in the Galesburg public schools. Indirectly, at least, Knox College could claim some credit for the competency that he quickly showed in the use of the English language. Not only had a Knox alumna, who was his teacher in the sixth grade, made him aware of the popular poet, Eugene Field, a Knox alumnus,[4] but it had been under the tutelage of Knox students that Sandburg, a child of Swedish immigrants, first "sang for an audience, acted in a play and spoke a declamation for an audience," according to his own recollection.[5]

This public practice in the use of the English language occurred in the weekly classes and occasional entertainments staged at the City Mission, which was maintained on the "other side of the tracks," in the part of the city where Sandburg grew up. The City Mission had been established in 1858, originally as an interdenominational enterprise, and at first used a railway car of the C.B.&Q. for its meetings, thereafter a chapel located on railroad land,[6] and when Sandburg was ten years old it had been relocated at a site in the 500 block of South Seminary Street, less than four blocks from the Sandburg home on Berrien.[7] Carl attended the weekly mission classes on Sunday afternoons, after he had gone to the morning services conducted in Swedish at the Lutheran church. The City Mission had by 1888 become a Congregational enterprise, with most of the teaching done by Knox students, several of whom the poet and Lincoln biographer would later warmly remember.[8]

Such volunteer missionary work and similar religious services were still highly respected and quite popular among students as well as the faculty. The chief religious organizations for students were the YWCA, organized in 1883, and the YMCA, which in 1880 had succeeded to the older "Society for Religious Inquiry."[9] During the late 1880s and the 1890s the evangelical work of the Y was carried through the summer by a band of Knox men. With the attraction of musical performances, they conducted religious meetings in the towns of west-central Illinois, often with the help of Knox alumni in the localities, and, it was hoped, with the cooperation of the local clergy. In this way they brought "spiritual blessings" to the local citizenry, promoted the cause of the larger YMCA organization, and brought Knox College to the attention of potential patrons.[10] On the campus the Y cultivated Christian character for young men, stressed the importance of physical education and the manly sports, and thus contributed to the rising cult of athleticism during the closing decades of the nineteenth century. Indeed, it was during the academic year 1891–92 that James Naismith (who had dropped out of the ministry to study physical education) at the YMCA training school in Springfield, Massachusetts, invented basketball. The Y secretaries being trained there immediately taught the new game far and wide; by 1894 it was played on several college campuses;[11] by 1898 it was a sport that enlivened the long, gray winter months at both Lombard and Knox. "Gymnasium," which had meant a place for gymnastics or calisthenics, now came to mean more commonly the enclosure used for another kind of ball game played between football in the autumn and baseball in the spring.

For some students, however, the religiosity of the College was becoming tedious and burdensome.[12] Earnest Elmo Calkins, who was a student at Knox when Sandburg was a pupil at the City

Mission, regarded with some contempt a Y kind of student and long after he left Galesburg recalled with lingering distaste how the YMCA helped to make Sunday "as exacting as the 'hours' in a medieval convent" and then compounded the tedium by preempting Friday night for "devotional sessions."[13] A deeply contemptuous description of the college YMCA occurred in *Sons of the Puritans*, the autobiographical novel by Don Marquis,[14] who was a student in the Knox Academy during the autumn of 1898. Marquis particularly resented that "a pious little enclave" in the YMCA held prayer sessions concerning non-conforming and unregenerate students such as Marquis himself. In Calvin College (the name for Knox in this novel), the YMCA conducted a labor bureau to find jobs for needy students, but this agency discriminated against those who were not active in the Y and got the best jobs for "fellows who get up in the Y.M.C.A. meetings and pray longest and loudest."[15] Another student from the 1890s who was bothered by the pious posturing was George Fitch, who was graduated with the class of 1897. He had good friends in the YMCA,[16] but when he wrote his short stories about "Old Siwash" he frequently made the Y the butt of his humor.[17]

The YMCA was still a prestigious organization, however, as it had been in 1884, when a student explained to his parents that he had been arrested during a celebration of the oratorical victory of Charles Wyckoff along with the "flower of Knox College," which included the "President and ex-President of the Y.M.C.A." along with the president and vice-president of Adelphi, the editorial staff of *Coup D'Etat* and "our next years orator."[18]

Included in this listing of the "flower" of the College were the class officers. They, too, were still important while Fitch was a student. The class was the most significant group identification on the campus at the turn of the century, though its meaning was beginning to weaken with the recent appearance of sororities and the revival of fraternities. A senior class during the years of Calkins (1891) and Fitch (1897) had between forty and sixty members, still small enough for all members to know each other very well, still manageable for gatherings such as the class parties held in homes of class members who lived in the city.[19] Each class had its own motto, colors, and emblem. The meaning that might be attached to such symbols was suggested by this mocking comment of a junior in 1883: "The Juniors have white plug hats, the Seniors black ones and the Sophomores have canes. The slim light-weight seniors look top heavy under their stove-pipes. The Sophs swing their canes like ax helves or hoes, which goes to show that their ranks are recruited mainly from the country districts. But the tall and handsome Juniors support the dignity of the institution with their snowy tiles as if to the manor born."[20]

Such mockery might be taken quite seriously. In October 1880, when the seniors wore their "stove-pipe hats" to chapel, the preps taunted them by wearing "sham plugs" made of pasteboard in a variety of shapes, colors, and sizes. This precipitated a tussle in which the seniors shoved the preps down the great central stairway of the main College building.[21] There was obviously something about those senior hats that invited hostility.[22] In September 1887 when the seniors and juniors walked into chapel wearing "shiny new tiles," the sophomores had anticipated them and were on hand ready for a tussle. They had "taken possession of the Senior seats." However, "instead of showing fight, the Seniors stood in the aisles" near their seats, until President Newton Bateman noticed the situation and "commanded" the sophomores to take their proper places, at which point, it was reported in the local newspaper, they "crept sheepishly to their own quarters, while the remainder of the students gave them the laugh."[23]

The worst aspect of this class rivalry was associated with Washington's birthday, which during the Civil War became, by petition of the students,[24] a school holiday, the only release from scheduled classes, other than the recesses between terms, during the entire academic year. Formally the celebration of this patriotic holiday began after the usual daily chapel and consisted primarily of a program staged later in the day by students, with suitable musical and speaking exhibitions.[25] But informally by the 1880s it had become an occasion for testing faculty authority[26] and for student relaxation from the long days and full routine of the winter months. It became part of the contemplated rites for February 22 (and the night preceding) that there would be a "scrimmage" among the classes. Though each year varied in its confrontations, it became "the custom of contending classes to break into the college building at a late hour of night and to engage in a free-for-all scuffle, in which furniture was smashed, doors broken down, ceilings punched through, heads cracked, eyes blacked, noses tapped, and clothes torn, with an utter disregard of conse-quences."[27] Tactically, it was essential to get control of the great central stairway that before the restoration of Old Main in 1936 reached to the third floor from which it was possible to get to the cupola and the roof. Here a class would plant its colors and fight to hold off others who attempted to achieve this prestigious ter-ritory. On the afternoon of Washington's birthday in 1884 the program that had been scheduled in the chapel was held up for three-fourths of an hour by a melee on this stairway between freshmen and sophomores. The latter had arrived dressed in white robes and high paper cockades, which were in sad disarray before the scrimmage was over.[28] In 1886 the fight for the banner which sophomores had planted on top of the College ranged down across the mud in the city park and toward the Female Seminary.[29] In 1887 the women in the Seminary themselves had a "fierce strug-gle" before the main entrance over an effigy of a "Freshman Girl" rigged up ridiculously in a "red calico dress, very large shoes, and a tall Seminary hat." From the balcony the sophomore girls twitched a rope that caused "the big feet of the effigy to dance a comical jig."[30] In 1888, in a tussle before the Seminary, the senior men, who "had worn their customary insignia of dignity, plug hats and Prince Albert coats," were humbled "by the time they had rolled in that Tompkins Street mud."[31]

In 1890 the "free fight over class banners" at Knox College was reported by the New York *Mail and Express*. Knox students de-nied the exaggerated and inaccurate statement that "several stu-dents were forced from a roof . . . and suffered injury in falling to the ground." They also resented the unfavorable imputation that eastern colleges "glorified Father George" in a more decorous manner.[32] It is not surprising that at Knox there had been talk for some time of "abolishing the celebration."[33] In 1892 President Bateman forewarned the students "in a little talk" that "those scrimmages" had become a "scandal to the institution" which the trustees would not ignore. That year everything was "orderly and quiet" on Washington's birthday[34] and as the same holiday ap-proached in 1893 it was simply assumed that there would be no "repetition of the gory fights which used to mark the day."[35] By 1899, a reminiscent essay in the *Knox Student*, while not pleading for a revival of the scrimmages on February 22, regretted that there was no longer such strong evidence of school "spirit."[36]

As a festival, Washington's birthday remained on the calendar for many more years, but class skirmishes still occurred at other times. In 1905 a freshman may have been nearly killed during an "old fashioned class scrap."[37] In 1911, however, the fights were ritualized when the student council (established in 1909) adopted "Regulations for class Scraps," which set forth in detail rules controlling contests for class colors displayed on a greased pole.[38]

Rather more imagination had characterized the rivalry of the classes of 1896 and 1897, in which George Fitch participated. When he was a junior, his class (1897) presented a one-act play in an old hall on Main Street, "exposing the Senior class to the well earned contempt of the world and posterity." It was written by Fitch and was a "scather in every line." The juniors hired some local strong men to guard the stairs to the hall, but that did not keep the leading man from being roughed up by the seniors before he got there for the performance. Later that same academic year the seniors (1896) planned a farewell party in which elaborate attention was given to displaying their class colors, red and white, in the room decorations, in the girls' costumes, and in the candies, cakes, and ice cream. All went as designed until it was time for the desserts; then the candies, cake, and ice cream appeared not in red and white but in pink and green, the colors of the junior class, for Fitch and others of a committee of juniors had visited the restaurant owner, represented themselves as seniors, and ordered the colors changed.[39]

The local police who were, on occasion, at hand to restrain "class scraps"[40] understandably became impatient with disturbances staged by the students. While Fitch was a senior at Knox College, Chicago and local daily newspapers made a "monstrous riot," according to the Knox Student, out of a mere "racket" that Knox men made at a Democratic rally during the McKinley-Bryan presidential contest of 1896. One of the Galesburg policemen who quelled the disturbance complained in an open letter to the Galesburg Evening Mail about how college "boys" were allowed to get away with their disturbing pranks. "It is also a notorious fact that here in this city of colleges students have repeatedly flagrantly violated, not only the city ordinances, but the state laws as well, and have not been punished, until they seem to think that neither the statutory nor moral law applies to them, and in the interests of our beautiful city and the reputation of our colleges and college boys, such things should be frowned down upon."[41]

In this presidential contest of 1896 the Democratic candidate was the famous orator William Jennings Bryan, whose eloquence on "Justice" had impressed local critics in 1880 at a state oratorical contest for which Knox was the host.[42] In 1895 he was in Galesburg as one of a distinguished panel of judges for the interstate contest in oratory in which Otto Harbach of Knox carried off the championship.[43] The Republican candidate for president in 1896 was Ohio congressman William McKinley. Knox students the previous spring had made a different choice, for a group of students (mostly juniors and like Fitch from small towns in west-central Illinois) had successfully managed a campus campaign that organized a "Federal Party" in which Theodore Roosevelt won the presidency. At that time TR was not the household name he became by 1900 when elected vice-president. Fitch and his roommate were the leaders in the students' defection from their elders in 1896. In 1909 he proudly retold the story for the *Gale*, admitting that partly the students were merely seeking relief during the spring from the "deadly monotony of college life enlivened only by baseball, track meets, class fights, fraternity rows and campus plots." Identifying himself as a "life long Republican," he denied that the "Federal Party" at Knox in 1896 had been manipulated by Democrats; rather it was organized by Republicans. "It was the first protest against blind party fealty—an acorn of independence which never stopped growing until it triumphantly elected Roosevelt in 1904."[44]

The facts about the man whom the "Federal Party" at Knox chose for vice-president are quite as strange as the fiction Fitch would one day write about "Siwash." For Theodore Roosevelt's running mate the "Federals" chose Robert Wilson McClaughery, a graduate of Monmouth College, who had been a Knox trustee from 1886 to 1889. He had then been warden of the Illinois Penitentiary at Joliet since 1874. In June 1888, President Bateman having resigned, the Knox Board of Trustees elected this keeper of the state's chief penal institution to be the head of Knox College, Female Seminary, and Academy.[45] The selection had the odor of politics about it. Colonel Clark E. Carr was being promoted by some to be the new Knox president.[46] Major McClaughery did not immediately refuse the Knox post but asked that he be allowed to defer his decision until after the Republican Convention met on June 19 in Chicago. Clearly, he was hoping for some political plum, which eventually fell when he became the warden at Fort Leavenworth. In August he definitely declined the presidency of Knox;[47] a few days later Bateman withdrew his resignation[48] and thus, fortunately, retained the position to which four years later John Huston Finley would be elected. Even Fitch's imagination could hardly have contrived a stranger incident than the election of a jail keeper for the Knox presidency. Fitch explained that McClaughery had been chosen for vice-president of the United States by the Knox "Federals" in 1896 "for the same reason that all vice-presidential candidates are chosen—because no one in the world would think of electing him president."[49]

George Fitch became during the first two decades of the twentieth century a well-known contributor to widely circulated magazines such as *Ladies' Home Journal, American Magazine,* and *Collier's Weekly.* For many years after his death he was fondly remembered as the author of stories about "Old Siwash," the first of which appeared in the *Saturday Evening Post* of May 30, 1908. It was followed by a popular series of hilarious tales about college life at Siwash. These stories twice were collected for publication in book form. The term "humorist" seems too mild a classification for Fitch. His contemporaries at Knox obviously regarded him as a prankster who perpetuated in print new escapades such as they remembered from their own college years, 1894–97. He dealt with situations, however highly embellished, that were familiar to alumni from many other colleges: fraternity rows, competition among literary societies, athletic contests, college parties, campus events of many kinds. The stories were not fantasies but rather related to real college affairs and sometimes regarded as mildly satirical. Mostly, however, they simply were hyperbolic accounts of the kind of predicaments undergraduates created—undergraduates such as "Petey Simmons," "Allie Bangs," "Hogboom" (captain of the team), and "Ole Skjarsen," who reappeared in one rollicking Siwash story after another, to the delight of Fitch's fascinated readers.[50]

In 1909 Fitch concluded his memoir about the 1896 election with an admission that, though he wrote about actual events and real people, he could not "guarantee the absolute truth of all this information." This raises the broader question about the extent to which the books about Siwash College, which he began to publish at this time,[51] were about Knox College. He asserted that Siwash College was a montage of different colleges and universities,[52] but it is evident that when he wrote the Siwash stories he usually had Knox College and his experiences there in mind. Siwash was not an old eastern school like Harvard nor a new state university to the west like South Dakota, but rather a "middle age college"[53] founded, as was Knox, as a religious institution about 1840.[54] Its chief athletic rival, Kiowa College, was about ten years younger and was located about fifteen miles away, a description which rather closely fit Monmouth.[55] In Jonesville, where Siwash College was located, there was a Lincoln Park as there was in Galesburg[56] and also a stinking central sewer, which in Jonesville was Cedar Creek and in Galesburg Cedar Fork.[57] Like Knox, when Fitch was a student there, Siwash College still had its original Preparatory Department.[58] It was coeducational.[59] Both at Knox and at Siwash there were rival literary societies and their names were the same, Adelphi and Gnothautii; the campus roles of these organizations were the same at the real Knox and at the fictional Siwash.[60] A distinguished teacher at Siwash was Professor "Timmons"; at Knox he was Professor Simonds.[61] The name of the women's dormitory at the former was Browning; at Knox it was Whiting. Like Knox, Siwash was distinguished among the colleges of the "whole Northwest" for it oratorical champions;[62] indeed, the protagonist in *Old Siwash,* like Fitch, specifically when a freshman, helped to celebrate the victory of an interstate winner.[63] Siwash, like Knox, had a tradition of rather riotous celebrations and trouble between students and police on such occasions.[64]

At Old Siwash there was no aspect of college life that was left untouched by Fitch's wit, yet it would not appear that Fitch meant to provoke reform by exposing college customs to laughter. Nevertheless the Siwash—or Knox—about which he wrote was undergoing profound changes in student life. The older literary societies, no longer so venerable, were losing out to the secret societies. Forensic champions were being nudged on their pedestals by athletic heroes or by campus leaders wearing honors unashamedly won by social competition. The YMCA seemed somewhat old-fashioned in a more worldly community.

While Fitch was a student, it was repeatedly noted that the literary societies were declining. Professor George Churchill, reminiscing about Adelphi and Gnothautii, observed: "I am sorry to think that in the multiplicity of new things and fads, these societies are neither of them doing as much and as good literary work as they have done in years past."[65] The *Coup D'Etat* that same year (1895) reported that there was a "growing tendency to postpone meetings of our literary societies because of other engagements."[66] Each fall the two societies, with good resolutions, conscientiously renewed their former roles in the literary education, forensic preparation, and parliamentary training of students, but by spring the more prominent members, too deeply committed to other activities, neglected to attend, and in their absence the "mob" took over, so that at "some of these meetings the only sober proceedings" were "devotionals," whereafter came a kind of "intellectual rough house," impromptu, farcical, and disorderly.[67]

Though it was argued that the work of the literary societies was important and that they "should be reinstated in their old place of honor," the truth was that "today their glory is departed, and those who do not slight them altogether consider them a great bore."[68]

Though the literary societies persisted as respected organizations in the twentieth century and though Knox continued to excel in intercollegiate oratorical contests and other forensic activities,[69] the time had come when a dance for the benefit of the "football training fund" would be scheduled in conflict with what for years had been the weekday night reserved for the college literary societies.[70]

The divided loyalties of students who belonged both to a literary society and to a fraternity contributed to the diminishing status of the former.[71] At the time, during the early 1880s when fraternities were being restored on the Knox campus, local campus leaders had warned that they would injure the literary societies.[72] The revival of Phi Delta Theta was almost immediately reflected in the factionalism within Adelphi in 1881[73] that exacerbated the conflict over choice of the college orator,[74] alienated three Adelphians who left Knox the following autumn for Amherst,[75] and led to the campus split over control of the magazine and to the appearance of two rival publications in 1881–82.[76] Again in 1888, when the Beta Theta Pi chapter was reestablished at Knox, it was noted that its members were a group in Adelphi.[77]

"Eta Bita Pie" was the fraternity that appeared most often in the Siwash stories.[78] The name sound most like Beta Theta Pi, the fraternity to which Fitch belonged. Rather recently there had in fact been an "Eta Pie" fraternity at Knox, the Omicron Eta Pi, which had been organized on November 12, 1887,[79] as a local, which, when the Greeks published the first *Gale* at the end of 1887–88, had six members.[80] The members of this organization enlisted the interest of former Betas in reestablishing a chapter at Knox and were granted a charter by the annual Beta Theta Pi convention in July 1888. On September 5, 1888, Omicron Eta Pi was dissolved; the next day its members were initiated into Beta Theta Pi.[81] This chapter was designated as "Alpha Xi" until 1911, when the national convention changed the identification to "Xi" in order that the Knox chapter, so a member explained, "would have the standing of one of the earliest chapters in the fraternity, which rightfully belongs to us, and could claim the distinction of being the oldest chapter of any fraternity in the state."[82] Already in 1890 it was reported that the "Beta Theta Pi, a Knox College Secret Society, celebrates its Thirty-fifth anniversary," as if it had been in continuous existence since 1855.[83] That was a misleading impression, for though Beta Theta Pi had been secretly established at Knox College in 1855 and had become public in 1861,[84] it had ceased on the Knox campus in 1873.[85] Indeed, in November 1888, after Beta Theta Pi had been restored at Knox for two months, a reporter in the *Republican Register* made a point of stating, "The oldest Greek letter society in the College is Phi Delta Theta."[86]

The truth was that all the national fraternities existing at Knox by the end of 1888 had previously experienced an interruption in their existence at Knox. The other two fraternities were Phi Gamma Delta and Phi Delta Theta. The former had been established at Knox in 1867 but languished by the mid-1880s and lost its charter. Phi Delta Theta at Knox was given a charter in 1871, but it was transferred to Lombard in 1878. This failure of the

Greek secret societies reflected the declining College enrollment but also occurred when the literary societies were very active and when the opposition to secret societies was still strong.

As is evident in other midwestern colleges such as Oberlin, Grinnell, and Carleton, hostility to fraternities remained strong among many Congregationalists. The second president of Knox, Jonathan Blanchard, strongly opposed secret fraternities and was admired by many at Knox for thirty years after he was forced out of the presidency.[87] He carried his crusade into the decades after the Civil War and became the national leader of this cause, for which he published a fortnightly reform magazine entitled *Christian Cynosure*. This was the official organ of the National Christian Association, founded in 1867 with Blanchard's help and with the blessing of Charles Grandison Finney and the President of Oberlin.[88] President John Putnam Gulliver, the Congregationalist who succeeded the two Presbyterian Curtises as president of Knox, joined Blanchard in this cause and, along with a Knox alumnus, the Reverend Joseph E. Roy (later a trustee of Knox), promoted a resolution at the Pilgrim Memorial Convention in April 1870 that asked that the tablet be removed from the cornerstone of the national monument in Plymouth that the Masons had placed there. According to Blanchard, the fraternities at Knox were there against Gulliver's wishes. He loathed "college secret orders."[89] During the long interregnum after Gulliver's resignation it is significant that the faculty carefully avoided giving a "secret college society permission to meet in the college building."[90] In December 1881 a national convention of those opposed to secret societies, meeting in the Galesburg Opera House, nominated Blanchard for president of the United States.[91] Ten years later the National Christian Association held its convention in the First Congregational Church of Galesburg, which had been founded during the 1850s under the leadership of Dr. Edward Beecher on the northern edge of the Knox Seminary grounds. Like his predecessor, the pastor of this congregation in 1891, the Reverend H. A. Bushnell, was opposed to secret fraternities.[92] During the mid-1880s there were protests when the Masons laid the cornerstone for the new county courthouse that had been built on what was once the College Park. Those protesting this performance of a civic function, as if the Masons had some special status, included not only Blanchard but one of his former students, Edward P. Chambers, scion of one of the founding families that was ardently Congregationalist.[93]

Not all faculty of Knox disapproved of secret societies. During the 1860s the principal of the Academy, George Churchill, had become a member of Beta Theta Pi, as had Thomas Willard (1866), who became professor of Greek at his alma mater. Then, to the chagrin of Blanchard, as noted in the *Cynosure,* the trustees chose as the fifth president of Knox, Newton Bateman, who was a Mason, a circumstance of which some trustees may not have been aware when they voted for him.[94] There is no evidence that President Bateman promoted the development of secret societies on the campus; indeed, during the first years of his administration they continued to decline and then disappeared. In 1881, however, a freshman wrote to his parents that "Secret societies are festering" and stated that "one of them has been turned up in Adelphi."[95] This was a reference to the factional difficulties within the literary societies that culminated late that spring in the bitterly contested election by the College students of Nels Anderson as the Knox representative in the intercollegiate oratorical competition.[96] Anderson was a member of the chapter of Phi Delta Theta that had been reestablished at Knox the preceding December. His defeated opponent, Frederic Bancroft, member of a prominent local Congregational family, was not a fraternity member.[97]

Phi Delta Theta was the first of the faltering fraternities to be revived at Knox. A Knox chapter had been started when three Knox men, including Eugene Field, had been initiated at Monmouth College in 1871. By 1877 only three members remained, all seniors, and they were about to surrender their charter when it was instead transferred to Lombard University, just across town, with the expectation that Knox men might be initiated into this Delta chapter on the other campus. This expectation proved to be "impractical," and in 1880 a Lombard alumnus who had become "province president" of Phi Delta Theta arranged for the reestablishment of the Knox chapter, with the designation of "Zeta."[98]

Opposition to secret societies was still vocal at Knox as elsewhere. An editorial in the *Coup D'Etat* in April 1883 commented:

The secret society strife, the war between Frat. and Anti-Frat. still continues. This strife had been quite general and in some places has assumed extensive proportions and given rise to serious complications. . . . The advocates of Greek-letter Fraternities are very bitter in their denunciation of those who oppose them, alleging that charges are made without any knowledge of the workings of such fraternities. However this may be it seems to us that the direct results of the existence of secret societies in a college are too plainly apparent to the most superficial observer to admit of any doubt as to their pernicious influence. The journals published at colleges where such societies exist are frequently almost wholly devoted to quarrels and disturbances between rival fraternities. We are not making this attack blindly and ignorantly. We are not without experience in the matter, and we are pretty intimately acquainted with the workings of secret societies and the attendant results. It is our opinion that these societies are not only superfluous but also injurious. Particularly is this true where good literary societies exist.[99]

A year later another editorial expressed the hope that the secret society being revived at Knox "will find among us an uncongenial atmosphere."

Our college has had some experience with secret societies and we hoped that it had had its last. The very fact that the old organization, supported as it was by many of the best students in school, did not keep up its existence is evidence that there is no call for such a society. And further some of the strongest members of the old organization are among the most active opponents of the new thus proving that they feel that such a society is an injury to our college. At present there is a strong bond of good feeling among the students and between the literary societies. Never in the history of our college has there existed more universal harmony. Why introduce anything that shall tend to disturb the present existing good feeling? Wherever these societies have been they have tended to stir up strife and divide the students into cliques. Some of the older students remember how much strife the old organization caused. Nearly all the wirepulling and enmity in college was laid, justly or unjustly, to its charge.[100]

This editorial referred to the fact that Phi Delta Theta was being revived for the second time on the Knox campus. It had again been suspended in February 1882 but in March 1884,[101] having received reenforcement from Monmouth College, it was reestablished with the aid of the chapter at Lombard.[102] There were only four "original members" that had responded to this "call for re-organization";[103] but four seniors and a junior from Monmouth College were affiliated with these Knox men.[104] In January 1884 the Knox College faculty had decided that these students, who had been suspended from Monmouth, might be admitted to Knox if they brought papers showing that their only offense was "membership in a secret society."[105] Four of these students were then admitted "on trial" as seniors,[106] and were graduated from Knox the following June.[107] Another Monmouth student who joined the Knox Phi Delta Theta chapter, C. C. McClaughery, was admitted at this time as a junior; special arrangements were made for him to continue his studies at Knox,[108] and he was graduated in June 1885. When the Greeks published their first *Gale* in 1888, the paragraphs devoted to Phi Delta Theta emphasized the important role of these former Monmouth students in stimulating the development of fraternities at Knox: "They brought with them an energy and zeal in fraternity work which was quickly felt; the present fraternity awakening in Knox is the legitimate growth of the seed which they sowed."[109]

For ten years at Monmouth College fraternities and sororities had attempted to exist *sub rosa*, despite a ban against secret societies that had been imposed by that College in 1874 in response to requirements of the United Presbyterian Church. Under Presbyterian governance, a college could be held accountable in ways not possible in the loose, decentralized polity of Congregationalists. At Monmouth there was a special interest in the effect of this prohibition on two sororities, with whom it was maintained "the American sorority movement began." Both these sororities, Pi Beta Phi (founded in 1867) and Kappa Kappa Phi (founded in 1870), continued to exist underground, but in 1884 the national conventions of both societies found this kind of existence, despite faculty disapproval, unsatisfactory and withdrew the charters of both of these Alpha chapters.[110] It was in this year, during the same month that the suspended Monmouth fraternity men helped to revive Phi Delta Theta at Knox, that a chapter of Pi Beta Phi was established at Knox. It was the first time, at least to the knowledge of College authorities, that the women at Knox organized a secret society.

The generous manner in which the Knox faculty adopted the men suspended at Monmouth supported the report by a Knox student in 1888 that the Knox faculty had assumed a "tolerant policy" toward fraternities.[111] In December 1885 Phi Gamma Delta was reestablished, and in 1887 a local Greek letter society was organized that would effect the restoration of Beta Theta Pi.[112] By the opening of the year 1887–88 Knox had obviously adopted an open attitude to secret societies. A Galesburg newspaper noted: "Three new secret societies are about to be organized at Knox College. The Seminary students are talking up one of these. It is stated that all members of a certain secret society, now attending Monmouth College, talk seriously of coming to Knox on account of the hostility shown secret societies by the Monmouth College faculty."[113]

By 1888 Knox students were being differentiated as Greeks or barbarians,[114] and the desire of the Greeks to assert themselves on the campus was demonstrated in the confrontation over the publication of a yearbook, the first since a *Pantheon* had been published in 1873. To publish a *Pantheon* for 1887–88, a board was organized consisting of the presidents of the five literary societies and of the YMCA and YWCA.[115] Previous College enterprises certainly provided precedents for this mode of organizing an all-College activity. This board desired to have representation of "editors" from "all departments in the college including the fraternity chapters." But the fraternities, "claiming that they were publishing another annual," did not wish to appear to countenance the *Pantheon* and even consulted lawyers regarding the serving of an "injunction constraining the editors and publishers of the *Pantheon* from publishing the names of any fraternity men on the board of editors." The *Republican Register,* commenting on the "bad blood . . . brewing among the students," predicted: "We fear that this is only the beginning of a quarrel that promises to split into two factions the students of Knox College."[116]

Accordingly, in 1888 two yearbooks were published; one was a "college students annual" named the *Pantheon;* the other was a "fraternity annual," or "secret societies annual," as some would call it. The latter was named the *Gale.*[117] On the first page it proclaimed: FRIGIDA EST DIES CUM DESISTIMUS, which according to a teacher of classics at Knox may be read: "It'll be a cold day in Hell before we give up." The editorial differences reflected the desire of fraternities to emphasize membership in the Greek letter societies. Both yearbooks listed all the students according to their classes, from the College, the Seminary, and the Conservatory, but the *Gale,* in listing the students, identified those who belonged to a Greek letter society, making obvious those who did not belong to fraternities or sororities. To make possible this use of Greek letters, the *Gale* was published in Peoria, for the type of the Greek alphabet was not yet available in the Galesburg printing shops.[118]

The annuals for 1889, 1890, and 1891 were fraternity publications and continued to carry the name of *Gale.* In February 1889 the junior class met to consider publishing an annual,[119] but the fraternities (except for the Beta Theta Pi members) refused to participate on the editorial board. The juniors, after a "hot debate," challenged the *Gale* managers "to the appointment of an arbitrating committee," but the fraternity men declined.[120] "Hard feelings" prevailed while the second volume of the *Gale* was published. In 1889–90 the fraternities, including the Betas this time,[121] again organized to publish volume three.[122] The fourth volume, the *Gale* for 1891, was, "despite factional strifes," an attractive yearbook, but it was such a financial failure as to make promoters wary of such an undertaking in the future.[123]

Early in 1892–93 it was suggested in the *Coup D'Etat* that to assure the needed cooperation for the success of a college annual, "no fraternity or other society should try such a venture," and that instead the yearbook be published by the junior class.[124] This plan was not immediately adopted, however, and for the years of 1892, 1893, and 1894 there was no annual.[125]

During these years when the fraternities published the College yearbook, the total enrollment in the College and Seminary was approximately 200; about one-third of these students belonged to "secret societies."[126] The *Coup D'Etat* in February 1890 stated that there were "between two and three hundred Knox alumni . . . who during their college careers were connected with the Greek letter societies having chapters here."[127] These numbers were used to explain why this magazine began, for the first time, to have a news section specifically devoted to fraternities.[128] Comments in the columns of the *Coup D'Etat* became quite patronizing to those who had not been admitted to the privileges of fraternity or sorority membership, referring, for example, to those who did not know "just who belonged . . . and occasionally seem to have an idea that the members of the college secret societies are a sort of hobgoblin. They are very much like other people after all despite their supposed horrible incantations, profound mysteries, dreadful oaths and awful secrets."[129] When the students of the Preparatory Department chose to debate whether "secret organizations are detrimental to society," the *Coup D'Etat* editorialized, "There's nothing like opening an old sore."[130]

Regret over the neglected literary societies and concern over the declining amount and quality of their work was a recurring editorial theme in the *Knox Student,* when it was revived in 1894.[131] The editor-in-chief was James Harper Andrews, who was also president of the Adelphi.[132] Andrews was a leader of the "non-fraternity" and "anti-fraternity" students on the campus. During his junior year, under his editorship, his class published a College yearbook.[133] The practice of having the *Gale* be a junior class project became the College custom,[134] prevailing for more than half a century.

It was late in his junior year that Andrews led in forming the joint stock company that revived the *Knox Student* in competition with the monthly *Coup D'Etat,* which twelve years earlier had displaced a monthly *Student.* The new *Student* of 1894–95 was "definitely non-fraternity in its control," though it was not strenuous in its "anti-fraternity policies."[135] The *Coup D'Etat,* of which George Fitch was editor-in-chief in 1896–97, became a kind of monthly literary magazine but was published for the last time in 1897–98. At the end of that year the two College periodicals were amalgamated under the name of the *Student,* which now became more like a weekly magazine than a newspaper.[136]

Fraternities boasted that they "spiked" the best, the most prominent students for their membership.[137] They also identified themselves with what were the leading families in Galesburg[138] and came to recapitulate the social discriminations in the community. Thus, in the 1890s the older of the two sororities, Pi Beta Phi, presented as its "patronesses" four or five matrons from the city, including Mrs. Clark E. Carr and Mrs. George A. Lawrence,[139] both of whom lived in newly completed mansions on Quality Hill.[140] Mrs. Carr was the wife of the man most people, including himself,[141] regarded as the city's leading citizen. Mrs. Lawrence was heiress to thousands of acres of Illinois farm land, was the wife of a member of the city's leading law firm, and very active in the Daughters of the American Revolution. Both Colonel Carr and Lawrence were Knox alumni and members of the Knox Board of Trustees. A Knox alumnus who published one of the first scholarly studies of the social structure of an American city stated that Galesburg, where he had grown up, had rather less class differentiations than most communities, but then he proceeded to describe a complex and specific social structure based on education, livelihood, wealth, place of residence, ethnic origins, and family background. The families of the founders of Knox and Knox alumni ranked high in this social hierarchy.[142] His monograph was confirmed by the recollections of Earnest Elmo Calkins: "Even in a municipality so young and so small there was a definite social set, Presbyterians and Congregationalists, for society followed denominational lines. His mother was a Baptist, and Baptists and Methodists ranked lower, not only because they were poorer, but because they frowned on dancing and cards, the chief social diversions."[143]

Certainly the fraternities were beginning to offer facilities for coeducational social activities and entertainment that compared favorably with those available on the campus itself. The *Coup D'Etat* reported in great detail on the opening of a "new hall" on February 4, 1893, by Phi Delta Theta, in the newly completed Tunnicliff building at the corner of Simmons and Cherry streets, where the "entire third story" had been planned for fraternity use. It comprised "three main rooms, the chapter room, parlor and dancing hall. Also off the parlor . . . is a small room. Dressing rooms for the ladies and gentlemen connect with the dancing room. . . . The rooms can be thrown together, which makes the hall elegantly adapted to social purposes. . . . The hall and its equipment is certainly beautiful, and we doubt if many fraternities in the West are so well fixed as the Knox chapter of Phi Delta Theta."[144]

By the opening of the twentieth century the College no longer provided room or board for men. The West Bricks and the East Bricks had fallen into neglect and were demolished; the various efforts to manage dining rooms were abandoned; and men were left to fend for themselves, some boarding in the private homes where they slept (perhaps working for their keep), others joining eating clubs.[145] For some men it was therefore a very great comfort as well as symbolic advantage when the fraternities set up their own houses.[146] They also offered the rather conspicuous privilege of tennis courts for their members.[147] As the parties of the sororities and fraternities became accepted events in the College social calendar, the single most important occasion was the junior promenade, a formal party managed, not by the junior class, but by the Greeks.[148]

The anguished adolescent sense of rejection, of not belonging to the right set,[149] had of course existed at Knox long before sororities and fraternities dominated social affairs, but discrimination in social status was now repeatedly restated in the Greek letters and ritualized by the "rushing," by the "pledging," by the "initiations," and the recurring incidents that set "barbs" off from Greeks. The condescending attitude toward those not accepted into the formally privileged groups was expressed in paragraphs that appeared in the yearbook for 1905 and mocked the YMCA for its efforts to serve the College as a whole and characterized it as a society for "any student unable to get in elsewhere."

> The Knox Y.M.C.A. was born in the 80's and is a Twig from the big Tree. Its Mission is to redeem Souls under the Hammer. Very few Souls turn up for Redemption, but the Hammer keeps on Pounding. There is Anvil practice on Wednesdays when nothing else is doing. Now and then a Wise grad. from Africa or some other Monkeyfarm makes a long Hit and runs Home; then they all Yell. On big Days, they hire a Strong talker to Drum up Trade from the Knox pulpit.
>
> A committee Points out Central Church and the Public Library to the New student, and Fans him while Mary Scott writes the first Receipt. After that he can Stand alone. The Y.M.C.A. opens Knox social Life without a Cork-screw and Helps the Green ones to Mix and grow used to Harness. Church members only can get on the Inside, but any student Unable to get in elsewhere always finds the latch-string Out.[150]

That the YMCA was somewhat in tension with the fraternities is evident in an article which opened an issue of the *Student* in September 1911. The writer cited the "decentralizing force" of the "college fraternity system" and emphasized the importance of the "broad function of the Y.M.C.A." in the "crystallization of college spirit" and in fomenting "unity" by "representing all the men of the college."[151]

This disposition to put loyalty to the fraternity ahead of a devotion to the College was noted and deplored by John Corbin, who visited Knox and Beloit and published his mainly favorable impressions in the *Saturday Evening Post* in April 1908. He chose these two colleges because they had been "stamped . . . as standard in their respective districts," for small colleges, by Rockefeller's General Education Board. He was hopeful that the small college would deal better than the new state universities of the Midwest with the "personal equation" for the students seeking a liberal education, and was genuinely distressed when he spoke to a member of Beta Theta Pi about the "snobbish and unpatriotic spirit" that excluded deserving students from fraternities. He was "met with a helpless shrug."[152]

While deploring the failures of the fraternity system at Knox and Beloit to his *Post* readers, Corbin had described the problems of a brilliant football player at Beloit, whose insubordination had probably been brought on by resentment over the fact that none of the three fraternities on the campus had invited him to membership.[153] This was the very situation that George Fitch treated humorously in a short story that appeared in the *Saturday Evening Post* issue of May 30, 1908, about six weeks after the Corbin article had been published in the same periodical. Fitch's story tells about the lumberjack from the Wisconsin pineries, Ole Skjarsen, who performed marvelous feats as a fullback for Siwash College for three years of overwhelming victories, but then went on strike during his senior year because he had not been rushed nor pledged to any of the Siwash fraternities. It was difficult for the "frat" men to think of him as a member:

> "Doesn't he want to go to the Astor ball, too."
> Oh, this was rich! To think of Skjarsen, built like Texas steer and dressed like a cotton bale, rollin down to Saturday night cotillions. We laughed.[154]

When he first came to Siwash College, he did speak a little English, but as a senior this "white-eyebrowed leviathan in high-water trousers" still had embarrassing manners. "He drank his coffee from his saucer with a barytone gurgle, speared his bread with his fork, and treated his napkin with quiet indifference."[155] Yet his refusal to play football created such consternation that a member of Eta Bita Pie arranged for his own and other fraternities to give him, belatedly, the full attentions of rushing, and at the critical moment in the crucial game with Kiowa College he appeared to rejoin his teammates "in full football armour. . . . But that wasn't all. On one shoulder he wore, in a huge bow, the purple and white colours of Eta Bita Pie. On the other shoulder he wore the magenta and white of Alfalfa Delt. Around his waist he wore a red and black sash a foot wide. They were the colours of Chi Yi."[156]

This story, "The Big Strike at Siwash," was published in book form in 1909; it was the first of the Siwash tales. Others appeared during the next seven years, in the *Saturday Evening Post* and in two other books: *At Good Old Siwash*, 1911, and *Petey Simmons at Siwash*, which was published in 1916, the year after Fitch's untimely death.[157]

The sport of football fascinated Fitch; the noisy crowd performing its repertoire of well-drilled, rhythmic, alliterative, sound-repeating yells and the violence of assaults of backfield men upon the enemy lines. It was exciting; it was also amusing. He wrote about it in the pieces that he contributed frequently to the *Gale* for years after he had been graduated.[158] Hard-plunging backs were admired in the poem, "Football," that he published in the yearbook for 1903–4.

. . . .

The fullback crashes through the mass,
    Amid a wild and frantic shout
The injured writhe upon the grass,
    The umpire sorts the players out.
Beneath the pile, upon the ground,
    All pale and lifeless, face to face,
The opposing quarterbacks are found,
    Entangled in a fierce embrace.

. . . .

The halfback grabs the reeking ball,
    And pokes his head a player through;
A dozen men upon him fall,
    The fullback breaks an end in two

"Old Siwash"

The quarter stands a giant guard,
Upon his head there dives beneath,
The squirming mass and gains a yard,
At cost of half a dozen teeth.[159]

Two years before he presented Ole Skjarsen in the first of his Siwash stories, Fitch had already written for Knox students about an insuperable fullback, in the poem, "A Whitman on Football":

. . . .

Chief of the padded hulks is a behemoth in a rubber
    muzzle.
On him I gaze, awe rooted, in admiration.
He is big brother to the ox.
Towering, mastodonic, breathing steam clouds from
    his nostrils, cavernous, he paws from beneath him
    huge masses of earth.
Marvelling, I wonder who has taught him to stand on
    his hind legs.
Verily, he is a colossus of flesh.
At my right a delicate woman-thing is saying:
"Is he not sweet?"
. . . .

Look!
The shrieks of ten million planets, demon-infested
    have been loosed.
The mastodon has escaped his keeper.
On he rushes, implacable, froth wreathed, earth
    shaking.
He has hurled an opponent far into the west.
On others he has trampled, impetuous, roaring,
    relentless.
His steps are measured with writhing sons of mothers.
He is a mile high.
From the grandstand come whirlwinds of ecstacy,
    shouts, sobs, gurgles, splutters, whoops, bellows, yells
And unclassified insanity.
The game is over.
Bloodstained, the mountain of murderous meat stalks
    backward over the scene of his crime.
I linger to watch for the vigilance committee, ropes
    noosed and knotted.

247

It does not come.
Heavens! They have crowned the brute with flowers.
Ever at my side the slight girl, with pale cheeks,
   clear-glowing is murmuring in rapture
"Is he not sweet!"[160]

The more violent form of football that had derived from rugby (rather than from soccer) was adopted at Knox in 1891,[161] where previously a more open type of game had been preferred.[162] During the 1890s, also, the scheduling of athletic events and their management were separated from the association controlling oratorical contests, to which competitive sports had been subordinated.[163] The football played in the early years of the twentieth century, when Ole Skjarsen was at Siwash, was characterized by massed formations that today would be illegal and by crushing "momentum plays," such as a "flying wedge" that truly made football a dangerous, some would say, a brutal game.[164] Public outcry against the many serious injuries threatened the sport as an intercollegiate activity.[165] In December 1905 Knox participated at Milwaukee in a conference of eight colleges from Illinois and Wisconsin concerned about the "brutality, professionalism and kindred evils occurring in football." The conference adopted "strict rules" that prohibited "paid coaching" and "gifts" to players and that required ten "hours" of college work from each team member. Players guilty of brutality were to be barred from playing. All athletics was to be "under the complete supervision of the faculty."[166] That same month Galesburg High School and Lombard College abolished football for the next season, and when school opened at Knox in 1906 soccer was substituted for football, the substitution being made at the suggestion of President Thomas McClelland with the concurrence of the students in a meeting held in Adelphi Hall.[167] By this time the president of the United States had prompted formation of a national rules committee that reformed the game, forbidding certain kinds of mass formations and opening up the plays by legalizing the forward pass. There must have been those at Knox in 1915 that regretted the resumption of the rougher kind of football, for in mid-October a Knox player, Bryan Scott, was paralyzed from a back injury during a game at St. Louis University and died five days later. The team wanted to complete the season, but the faculty insisted that the games remaining on the schedule be cancelled.[168]

After 1907, when Knox resumed the rugby type of football, its competitors were consistently appropriate for a college of its type and size. Knox had been admitted in 1898 to the Western Intercollegiate Athletic Association, with only the University of Michigan dissenting, as it did to Notre Dame, which was refused admission because Northwestern and Lake Forest also objected.[169] During the ten years after Fitch's graduation (and while Ole Skjarsen was at Siwash) the games scheduled by Knox not only included schools in the immediate vicinity and some small colleges farther away but also the universities. Though it is true that the state schools had not yet become the academic municipalities of the period after World War I, they offered extremely tough competition for Knox, where the enrollment, exclusive of the Conservatory and Academy, ranged from 325 in 1897–98 to 224 in 1906–7. During that decade Knox played twenty-three games with the universities of Chicago, Illinois, Northwestern, Wisconsin, Iowa, Nebraska, Notre Dame, and Kansas. Twice Knox tied one of these opponents. It won against them only three times. Obviously it was competing out of its class, and after 1907 the Knox football schedules were more reasonable.[170]

Football had now crowded baseball out of the autumn months, but full baseball schedules prevailed in the spring, the number of contests reaching twenty-eight in 1902, though the sixteen in 1906 were more typical. Track and field contests also comprised a major sport. In these encounters during the early years of the century the universities were also Knox opponents.

There had come to be doubts as to whether sports always made for men of good moral character, as the YMCA literature alleged. At the time that football was suspended for a year at Knox there was open discussion of its moral evils as well as of physical injuries, of the "dishonesty" and "trickery" associated with intercollegiate competition.[171] In 1898 an editorial in the college yearbook had boasted, rather self-righteously, that Knox had "no 'hired men' " on any of its athletic teams.

The man who comes to Knox for an education will find no one standing in his way in athletics, bought and brought here for excellence in that department. Better no athletics at all than such as promote immorality, dishonesty or even excess and devotion to them at the expense of other legitimate work. It is to its legitimate students that the college plans to give all its advantages in athletics. Thus it not only lays good foundations for the future of the department, but also makes athletics contribute their large part to the development of that noble character, which is the ideal of Knox College.[172]

Yet the seniors who were graduated that June would well remember that Knox hired pitchers for its baseball team in 1894 in order to "play good ball to draw crowds and make money" to pay for the fence around the playing field.[173] The newly revived *Knox Student* editorialized a year later against the use of men who were not students on the baseball team.[174] It was noted by the local newspaper that in a football game with the University of Illinois in November 1891, both Knox and its opponent played their "trainers," as coaches were then called.[175]

There were ethical objections raised to such practices by some students, but not by all. In October 1887 some Preparatory students hanged a sophomore in effigy from an elm before Old Main because he had reported to the press how Knox recently had dishonorably won a triangular baseball match at Jacksonville.[176] One of the Knox players was paid $5 a day for his services and provided the expense for his tuition for a course in penmanship in the Academy so that he might be certified as a Knox student. At a secret meeting Knox men had raised the necessary money, justifying their action on the grounds that other colleges such as Monmouth also used hired players.[177]

In his Siwash tales Fitch made fun of the efforts of the faculty to regulate athletics.[178] Already in 1892 President Bateman had received from the president of Grinnell a letter about athletes who were recruited away from the Iowa school.[179] During the presidency of John Finley the faculty expressed its disapproval of the use of professional athletes and toward the end of his administration tried to bring intercollegiate sports under stricter control.[180] It was stipulated that any student who fell below a passing grade in any subject should be excluded from athletic competition.[181] It was also advocated that athletic expenses be entirely sustained by the College[182] rather than partially covered by an annual canvas among townspeople to pay the wages of the "trainers" for the College teams.[183]

In 1902 the faculty was embarrassed by abuse of its official standards for athletic eligibility, as now set forth in the College catalogue.[184] That autumn the football team had a particularly successful season; though defeated by the University of Chicago and the University of Nebraska by small scores (0–5 and 0–7), the team was victorious over the University of Kansas (5–0) and Northwestern University (15–0). On the first Saturday of December occurred the game with Notre Dame University, which had been advertised as deciding the "supremacy among the Western Colleges." It was played in Rock Island, but a special train carried Knox students to that city for only $1 for the round trip.[185] Knox won 12–5, and duly claimed to be the "Western College Champion," that is, "college" as distinguished from "university."[186]

The enthusiasm over this championship changed to anger, however, when local and Chicago newspapers alleged that the Knox victories were not honorable. They noted that two of the players in particular (the right and left guards, one of whom weighed 232 pounds) had entered College that autumn only after special examination by the faculty, that they had assured the faculty that they would stay in school, but that they dropped out of College as soon as the football season was over.[187] About 150 Knox students so resented this adverse publicity in the Galesburg *Republican Register* that they organized a parade that for more than a mile hauled a wagon carrying an effigy of the editor (Frederick Jelliff, class of 1878) to his home on North Broad Street, where they burned the effigy and daubed the cement walks and porch with tar and wrote the word "knocker" on every step.[188]

In truth only half of the celebrated Knox team of 1902 were enrolled in the College. Of the fourteen men listed on the team (as distinguished from the squad, which was a larger group), one was a student in the Academy, five were listed as "unclassified,"[189] and one was an alumnus who had been graduated at the preceding commencement. The last player was Charles Hopkins, a young man from Galesburg. It was noted that "at his old place at half" he could still "find a hole when every one else has been blocked," though he weighed only 148 pounds.[190] Altogether, beginning in 1897 he played football at Knox for six seasons, and also played baseball and competed in track at various times. When he was graduated in June 1902, he was the first black person, in all likelihood, to receive a degree at Knox since Barnabas Root in 1870.[191]

Obviously responding to the public disparagement of the legitimacy of some players on the championship team of 1902, a faculty committee in consultation with students prepared tighter rules that could be announced during the first week of February 1903.[192] The new regulations were more detailed and specific in defining who was a bona fide student, requiring that only Academy pupils who were in their final preparatory year and only special College students who had satisfactorily completed a full semester could join the regular College students on athletic teams.[193]

Certainly it was now quite evident that student athletics had become too important to be left entirely to the students. In 1903 it was hardly conceivable that only a decade earlier the members of the football team were chosen by a committee of the Athletic Association.[194] That was now the duty of a professional athlete. That athletics was a "department of college work" was recognized in 1901 when the trustees appointed a "Director of Athletics" who was "also a member of the college faculty."[195] This was John H. McLean, who presented credentials much more impressive than those of the "head coach" of the previous year, who had been physical director at a YMCA.[196] McLean was said to be an athlete of "international reputation" who had represented the University of Michigan "in the International Olympian games at Paris in 1900, where he made the best record in the broad jump and won second place in the high hurdles"[197]—a claim that was impressive, even though it could not later be substantiated.[198]

McLean left Knox after only two years and was succeeded by Nelson Willard who had an impressive record in sports both at Knox (class of 1896) and later at Columbia University.[199] He was the son of Knox's first dean, Thomas Willard (class of 1866). Dean Willard, a professor of Greek, more than any other faculty member was admired by the students for the encouragement that he gave to athletics and the improvement of sports facilities. During the euphoria over the football championship of 1902, the *Student* published letters he received from those he had solicited for contributions to the athletic program. Among these was a letter accompanying a check from the son of Abraham Lincoln, Robert Lincoln, who at the turn of the century was a Knox trustee.[200] Dean Willard's personal involvement in the development of athletics on what was then the south campus was recognized by giving the area his name, and Willard Field it would remain for more than sixty years, until the campus was enlarged and other sports areas were opened up.

The women at Knox had been provided professional directors of physical education much earlier than had the men, the first time being as early as 1866.[201] During the first decade of twentieth century, again with professional direction,[202] they were expected to participate in a program of diverse activities that ranged from indoor sports such as gymnastics (clubs and dumbbells), bowling, and basketball, to athletics such as golfing, tennis, and "cross country walks" in the appropriate seasons. Less conventional, in certain years, was "military drill," fencing, and the "Ladies Target Club," which practiced with rifles. All of these sports were intramural except for an occasional basketball game with Lombard College. For the public the most conspicuous athletic event for women was the "regatta," which was staged in the spring at Highland Park, east of the city, where there was an artificial lake.[203]

Indoor athletic activities for the women occurred in the large recreation room in the wing of the Female Seminary that had been built in 1885. The wooden gymnasium that had been erected with student labor in 1876 was so decrepit by the turn of the century that it had to be torn down—Fitch celebrating the decreptitude and the demolition in nostalgic verse published in the *Gale* in 1904:

> Then let us weep o'er its demise,
>   Each loyal college man;
> And honor it, although 'twas built
>   Upon a hay-barn plan.[204]

As a makeshift for a gymnasium the College men used the eastern part of the basement of Alumni Hall,[205] where ditches were dug into the dirt floor to make room "for flying rings and other stunts."[206] In 1902–3 an abandoned factory building at the corner of Simmons and Cedar streets was repaired and a cinder course constructed, upon which the track team could practice in the winter—total cost, $500.[207]

Though Knox played some intercollegiate basketball games at the turn of the century, competition with other schools was discontinued for seven years owing to the lack of a suitable place.[208] There was a team of Knox students, but they played in the local city YMCA league.[209] Basketball was permanently added to the list of intercollegiate sports in 1908 when a new gymnasium was completed. This new structure, costing with equipment about $30,000, was dedicated on Founders Day of 1908, the annual banquet for students, alumni, and friends being held in the new gym.[210]

These were the years of *Old Siwash*. When Fitch was a student at Knox, there was already a word that suggested a provincial college; it was the word "freshwater." During the mid-1890s Earnest Calkins was very defensive about the way easterners used that word as a "term of reproach." Against them he cited the famous Englishmen, "Dr. Arnold" and "Lord Bryce," and noted that "Octave Thanet" was giving the small colleges that "dot the upper valley of the Mississippi" a place in American literature. Calkins declared: "There is a native charm about this same freshness to which the glittering but often jaded life of a big eastern college is but a foil. . . . The fresh water college has a life at once simple and unconventional. It is the village of the college world. I was one of the rustic people. It was a freshwater college which set knowledge in a visible form before my eyes. . . . Incidentally, I learned many things not required by the curriculum, and for which degrees are not offered."[211] "Freshwater" in time would be largely displaced in the language by "Siwash." Where Fitch found that name is not known, nor exactly what he meant by the word. What the word meant then and what it came to mean in time is very clear, however. It was the French word for savage, that is *sauvage,* which voyageurs contributed to the intertribal or trade language of the Old Northwest, the Chinook jargon. It meant Indians of any tribe, often in a derogatory sense. Along the Pacific coast of the United States and Canada Siwash came to be used as an adjective meaning "no good" and might thus describe bad dogs or poor coffee.[212] The stories of George Fitch associated the word with colleges, and the word now designates "any small, provincial college."[213]

Despite the derogatory inference of provincialism, most alumni, students, and staff identified the name of Siwash with Knox College. Members of Knox athletic teams are now regularly called Siwashers. This preemption of this title began when Fitch's stories were being published. One may properly speculate how during the next fifty years this identification of Knox affected not only the view that outsiders had of the College but also how it shaped the image of their alma mater for Knox alumni.

The effect of the Siwash tales undoubtedly extended far beyond the Knox campus. During the quarter century before World War I practically all colleges endured the distractions caused by the development of football contests, and many also accepted the disunities effected by fraternities and sororities. Chicanery in these extracurricular affairs, having become the subject of laughter in Fitch's fiction, seemed more like tolerable peccadillos when they occurred in reality.

Certainly by the time that President Warren Harding announced a return to "normalcy," Knox was a secular institution or, to use less latinate language, a rather worldly place. It was less unified than it had been when teachers and most students agreed on common religious and moral principles. Loyalties were now divided. Though for most students the academic program was still intense and important, for some of the students the winning of a letter in football or the pin of the locally most prestigious sorority symbolized the most important achievement of their collegiate residency.

NOTES

1. He was baptized "Carl," assumed "Charles" as a youth, and resumed "Carl" after he left Lombard.
2. *Lombard Review,* 15 (Feb. 1899), 101, 103.
3. Sandburg, *Always the Young Strangers,* 423.
4. *Ibid.,* 117.
5. *Ibid.,* 70–76.
6. Galesburg *Republican Register,* July 3, 1875, 1.
7. *Colville's Galesburg City Directory for 1887–1888,* 136.
8. Sandburg, *Always the Young Strangers,* 70–76.
9. *Knox Student,* Nov. 1880, 9.
10. *Gale, 1899,* 81.

11. William G. Mokray, "Basketball," *Encyclopedia Britannica*, 3 (1967): 247–50.

12. Askew, "Liberal Arts College Encounters Intellectual Change," 141–44.

13. Calkins, *and Hearing Not*, 37–39, 52.

14. See Anthony, *Marquis*. Marquis's unfinished novel was published posthumously (474). Marquis had a difficult time at Knox during the two months he attended the Academy because the $20 he had borrowed fell far short of his needs. He was not even able to afford the services of a physician who could tend an injury he suffered playing football. Nevertheless, he would later testify to a life-long sentimental attachment to Knox (81, 84, 136, 409, 494–95).

15. Marquis, *Sons of the Puritans*, 243–60.

16. Allan Rearick, class of 1897, was regarded by some as the original of a character put into many of the Siwash stories. Rearick managed the football team, edited the *Gale*, and was "very active in the Y.M.C.A." According to Lyman Thompson (*Knox Alumnus*, Sept. 1921, 144–45) Fitch "was a great admirer of Allan Rearick."

17. For example, the reference to the "hymn singers at the Y.M.C.A." in Fitch, *At Good Old Siwash*, 56.

18. Fred Jones to his parents, May 11, 1884, MS, Knox College Library. For references to oratorical contests and the student celebrations over victories in these competitions see Fitch, *At Good Old Siwash*, chs. 3, 8.

19. A "Junior Jubilee Party" was held in the Calkins's home (Galesburg *Republican Register*, Oct. 27, 1888, 1).

20. *Ibid.*, Oct. 6, 1883, 1.

21. Fred Jones to his parents, Oct. 6, 1883, MS, Knox College Library.

22. In 1885, while the seniors were holding a party at the home of one of their members, students belonging to other classes put a ladder to an upstairs window, crept into a bedroom, and stole the "glossy plug hats and overcoats" of the senior men and "distributed" them "generally" all over the city, some on fence pickets, but some on the muddy roads, where they were "ruined" (Galesburg *Republican Register*, Nov. 28, 1885, 5).

23. *Ibid.*, Sept. 24, 1887, 6.

24. Faculty Minutes, Feb. 22, 1864; Feb. 21, 1865; Feb. 18, 1871.

25. Galesburg *Republican*, Feb. 24, 1872, 1.

26. See Faculty Minutes for the late winter and spring of 1870 relating to difficulties with a senior, Forrest Cooke, arising from an alleged impertinence by him on Feb. 22, 1870. The Galesburg *Republican Register*, Mar. 5, 1881, 6, reported the circulation in chapel on Feb. 22, 1881, of a document "disrespectful and insulting to some of the Faculty and to some of the students." Three days later the students assembled in chapel voted to condemn the "gross and outrageous insults toward members of the Faculty."

27. Galesburg *Republican Register*, Feb. 27, 1892, 5.

28. *Ibid.*, Mar. 8, 1884, 7.

29. *Coup D'Etat*, Mar. 1886, 106; Galesburg *Republican Register*, Feb. 27, 1886, 6.

30. Galesburg *Republican Register*, Feb. 26, 1887, 5.
31. *Student*, Feb. 1899, 243–45.
32. *Coup D'Etat*, Mar. 1890, 88–90. The *Gale* for 1890 had a cartoon related to this episode.
33. Galesburg *Republican Register*, Mar. 8, 1884, 7; Faculty Minutes, Feb. 24, 1888.
34. Galesburg *Republican Register*, Feb. 27, 1892, 2.
35. *Ibid.*, Feb. 21, 1893, 1.
36. *Student*, Feb. 1899, 243, 245.
37. A reminiscence of T. A. Roberts, 1909, in the *Knox Alumnus*, Jan.-Feb. 1937. Class fights were reported in detail in the Galesburg *Weekly Mail*, Nov. 3, 1898, 1; Galesburg *Republican Register* (weekly), Jan. 30, 1901, 16; *Student*, Oct. 19, 1911, 88.
38. *Student*, Nov. 23, 1911, 190–91.
39. Interviews on George Fitch for the Premiere *Siwasher* by John Barrow, Jr., May 1940, MS, Knox College Library. This interview was with the "leading man," J. J. Hammond.
40. Galesburg *Republican Register*, Feb. 27, 1886, 6; *Student*, Feb. 1899, 243, 245.
41. *Student*, Oct. 1896, 4.
42. *Ibid.*, Oct. 1880, 15; Galesburg *Republican Register*, Oct. 16, 1880, 1.
43. Prather and Groves, eds., *Winning Orations of the Inter-State Contests, 1890–1907*, 2: 109–10. While at Knox, Harbach was Hauerbach.
44. George Fitch, "The Campaign of '96," in *The Gale Nineteen Hundred and Ten. The Year Book of Knox College Published Annually by the JUNIOR CLASS* (1909), 131–35.
45. Galesburg *Republican Register*, June 16, 1888, 1; June 23, 1888, 3. *Coup D'Etat*, June 1888, 155, provided a biography of the man who students assumed would become president of Knox College.
46. "The Peoria *Journal* and Chicago *Daily News* are booming Col. Carr for President of Knox College" (Galesburg *Republican Register*, July 7, 1888, 1).
47. *Ibid.*, Aug. 4, 1888, 1, 5.
48. *Ibid.*, Aug. 18, 1888, 1.
49. Fitch, "The Campaign of '96," 133. It should be noted that in 1912 Fitch was elected to the Illinois General Assembly as a Progressive.
50. Simonds, *Fitch*.
51. The first of the Siwash tales was published in the *Saturday Evening Post*, May 30, 1908. This story was republished as a small book the next year: *The Big Strike at Siwash*.
52. George Fitch, "About Siwash College," in the 1912 *Gale* (published in 1911 for the year 1910–11), 147–48. See Simonds, "Siwash and Knox," in *Fitch*, 7–8.
53. Fitch, *At Good Old Siwash*, 87.
54. *Ibid.*, 51–61, 69.

55. Fitch, *Petey Simmons at Siwash,* 188–89.

56. *Ibid.,* 219.

57. Fitch, *At Good Old Siwash,* 142–43.

58. *Ibid.,* 61.

59. *Ibid.,* chs. 9, 10.

60. Fitch, *Petey Simmons,* 118, 123.

61. *Ibid.,* 94–95.

62. Fitch, *At Good Old Siwash,* 66.

63. *Ibid.,* ch. 7.

64. *Ibid.,* ch 3.

65. *Student,* Mar. 27, 1895, 2.

66. *Coup D'etat,* Apr. 1895, 134–35.

67. The *Gale* for 1905, 66–67, an essay on "Work and Play."

68. *Coup D'Etat,* Dec. 1895, 67.

69. *The Naught-Nine Gale* (published in 1908) listed Knox winners of first and second place in intercollegiate oratory contests and noted that Knox was "appointed as the only college among the leading institutions of the Middle West to participate in the annual contest in oratory held under the auspices of the Hamilton Club of Chicago" (91). In this contest Knox had done very well in competition with the great universities of the region.

70. *Student,* Oct. 24, 1895, 4.

71. *Coup D'Etat,* Apr. 1889, 114.

72. *Ibid.,* Apr. 1883, 97; Apr. 1884, 97–98.

73. Compare the roll call votes in the Business Meeting Minutes of Adelphi on Jan. 19, 1881, and Feb. 2, 1881, with the list of those to whom a Phi Delta Theta charter had been issued in 1880 and to the fraternity membership list in the *Gale* for 1889.

74. Fred Jones to his family, Apr. 29, 1881, MS, Knox College Library.

75. See ch. 3 herein.

76. See ch. 3 herein.

77. *Republican Register,* Nov. 10, 1888, 5.

78. Fitch, *The Big Strike at Siwash,* 31, 52–53; Fitch, *At Good Old Siwash,* 2. This rather obvious pun appeared as the name of a society in the *1903 Gale,* published by the junior class in 1902; see "Eta Pie."

79. *Pantheon,* 1888, 35.

80. *Gale,* 1888, 44.

81. "History of Beta Theta Pi at Knox College," MS in the Beta Theta Pi file of the Knox College Archives, apparently written during 1917–18.

82. *Annual Alumni Letter. Xi Chapter. Beta Theta Pi* (Knox College, 1911).

83. Galesburg *Republican Register,* May 31, 1890, 6.

84. See ch. 3 herein.

85. The editions of the *Gale* for 1889 and 1890 (volumes II and III) were published by the fraternities and give detailed information about the members initiated for each year and other fraternal history.

86. Galesburg *Republican Register,* Nov. 10, 1888, 5.

87. He lectured on Dec. 2, 1888, in the old colony church against "secret societies" (*Coup D'Etat,* Dec. 1888, 57).

88. Askew, "Liberal Arts College Encounters Intellectual Change," 56–57, ch. 5.

89. *Ibid.,* 71–72.

90. Faculty Minutes, Oct. 22, 1874, Apr. 15, 1875.

91. Galesburg *Republican Register,* Dec. 3, 1881, 6; June 17, 1882, 4. The national convention had been preceded by a state convention that met in the Swedish Lutheran church (*ibid.,* Dec. 3, 1881).

92. *Ibid.,* Nov. 7, 1891, 1; Nov. 21, 1891, 1, 10.

93. *Ibid.,* May 23, 1885, 4; July 18, 1885, 7, 8.

94. Askew, "Liberal Arts College Encounters Intellectual Change," 108–9, 136 In the Bateman Papers there is a long, undated address by Bateman expounding the goodness of the Order of Masonry and defending it. This address was made at a lodge in the presence of a Grand Master.

95. Fred Jones to his family, Feb. 27, 1881, MS, Knox College Library.

96. See ch. 3 herein.

97. Jones to his family, Apr. 29, 1881, MS, Knox College Library.

98. "History of [Phi Delta Theta] Delta Zeta 1871–1971," a manuscript in the Phi Delta Theta file of the Knox College Archives.

99. *Coup D'Etat,* Apr. 1883, 97.

100. *Ibid.,* Apr. 1884, 97–98.

101. Galesburg *Republican Register,* Mar. 15, 1884, 1.

102. "History of Delta Zeta [of Phi Delta Theta] 1871–1971."

103. Galesburg *Republican Register,* Mar. 15, 1884, 1.

104. *Gale,* 1888, 36–39.

105. Faculty Minutes, Jan. 3, 1884.

106. *Ibid.,* Jan. 11, 25, 1884.

107. *Ibid.,* June 20, 1884.

108. *Ibid.,* Jan. 11, 25, 1884. He was the son of Robert W. McClaughery, who became a Knox trustee in 1886 and was offered the presidency in 1888.

109. *Gale,* 1888, 37.

110. Davenport, *Monmouth College,* ch. 3.

111. Galesburg *Republican Register,* Nov. 10, 1888, 5.

112. For the dates claimed by Greek letter societies at the time of their founding, see the "Directory" in *Coup D'Etat,* Sept. 1889, 16.

113. Galesburg *Republican Register,* Oct. 1, 1887, 1.

114. *Ibid.,* Nov. 10, 1888, 5.

115. "Review of the Gales," *Gale,* 1903.

116. Galesburg *Republican Register,* May 5, 1888, 6.

117. *Ibid.,* Apr. 28, 1888, 1.

118. A. M. Harvey, "The Founding of the Gale," *Gale Nineteen Ten* (published in 1909), 105–6.

119. Galesburg *Republican Register,* Feb. 23, 1889, 1.

120. *Coup D'Etat*, Mar. 1889, 106.
121. Possibly the Betas objected to the seniority system for managing the *Gale*, which had been established by the fraternities in 1888 before the Betas had been restored to the Knox campus (*Gale Nineteen Ten*, 106).
122. *Coup D'Etat*, Jan. 1890, 66.
123. "Review of the Gales," *Gale*, 1903.
124. *Coup D'Etat*, Oct. 1892, 21.
125. "Review of the Gales," *Gale*, 1903.
126. See the students' list in the *Gale*, 1888–91.
127. *Coup D'Etat*, "Fraternity Notes," Feb. 1890, 81.
128. *Ibid.*
129. Galesburg *Republican Register*, May 3, 1890, 1.
130. *Coup D'Etat*, Jan. 1894, 86.
131. See *Student* references in this chapter; for another *Student* editorial on this theme, 1 (Mar. 6, 1895), 4.
132. *Ibid.*, Sept. 26, 1894, 7.
133. *Alumnus*, Mar.-Apr. 1932, 87.
134. "Review of the Gales," *Gale*, 1903.
135. *Alumnus*, Mar.-Apr. 1932, 87. See editorial comments: *Student*, Sept. 6, 1894, 4; Oct. 31, 1894, 4. The *Coup D'Etat*, Apr. 1895, editorialized that both itself and the *Student* should be kept out of politics by having the faculty choose the editorial boards (127–28).
136. *Gale*, 1900.
137. Galesburg *Republican Register*, Nov. 10, 1888, 87.
138. See the guest list for the reception opening the Phi Delta Theta Hall (*Coup D'Etat*, Feb. 1893, 76–77).
139. The *Gale*, 1898, 52; *Gale*, 1899, 63.
140. Quality Hill was located in an area adjoining East Losey between Cherry and Chambers streets. Resentment over the pretensions on Quality Hill were dramatized by political controversy during the early 1880s over the sewer that those on Quality Hill wanted to have dug down Kellogg Street to Cedar Fork, which was already "at certain states of the atmosphere" emitting "an amount of disgusting and nauseating smell perfectly sickening." The editor of the Galesburg *Republican Register* agreed with those who opposed building the sewer from Quality Hill. It would be "an imposition...on owners living between North and Losey streets.... It would...be a direct damage to the people living near the creek...by increasing the quantity of filth emptied into creek" (issue of Aug. 12, 1882, 1). After all, the ladies of the Seminary still had their privies; the men of the College did without a single water closet until Alumni Hall was completed in 1890 (Executive Committee Minutes, Apr. 3, 1882; June 24, 1891).
141. For a sharp satire of Colonel Carr's pretensions, see page 80 of the *Gale*, 1898.
142. Dunn, *Social Structure of a Western Town*. Dunn was graduated from Knox in 1893, and he served on the Knox faculty, 1895–96; he came from a Galesburg family. Tension between Knox students and "city boys" is sug-

gested by an incident on Halloween of 1881 (Galesburg *Republican Register,* Nov. 5, 1881, 1).

143. Calkins, *and Hearing Not,* 107.

144. *Coup D'Etat,* Feb. 1893, 76–77.

145. In 1856 the College removed a new dwelling house from the site selected for the Female Seminary to a lot southwest of the College and fitted it for a boardinghouse. The plan was that students would form "a Club and arrange a bill of fare which would be more satisfactory and more economical in point of expense, than board at the present rates in town" (*Reports Presented to the Board of Trustees of Knox Manual Labor College, at their Annual Meeting Held June 25th, 1856.* It was sold in 1863 (Executive Committee Minutes, Oct. 3, 1861). There was for a time a dining hall on the first floor of the West Bricks (1871), according to Fred R. Jelliff (1878) in "The Old Bricks," *Gale,* 1902. In 1874 a door was cut into the basement of the Female Seminary in order that men living in the Bricks might board with the ladies of the Seminary (Galesburg *Republican Register,* Jan. 17, 1874, 3). For fifteen men this was still the practice in 1887 (*ibid.,* Apr. 16, 1887, 5). The College also advertised for "families where boarders will be held subject to wholesome family regulations as to hours" (Galesburg *Republican,* Aug. 12, 1871, 4). An example of a boarding club is the KEK, described earlier, (*Gale,* 1890, 149; *Gale,* 1891, 65). Other eating clubs were reported in the Galesburg *Republican,* Apr. 6, 1872, 3; *Knox Alumnus,* Mar.-Apr. 1937, 100, by J. L. Pearce, class of 1872. Very satisfactory private boardinghouses were reported by Fred Jones (letter to his parents, Nov. 7, 1880) and Center, *Things Usually Left Unsaid,* 21. John H. Finley (1887) lived with the family of A. J. Perry and for his board cared for the horse and the cow and the furnace and the lawn (*Fifty Year Club Bulletin,* June 1951, 8).

146. Houses for the Betas, Phi Delts, and Phi Gams are pictured in the 1906 *Gale,* 92.

147. "The girls [of Whiting Hall] were allowed to use the Fraternity courts while the Whiting Hall court was remodelled." *Ibid.,* 77.

148. See the description of this event beginning with *Gale* for the year 1897.

149. About knowing your "place" and about who spoke to whom in the 1870s, see Prince, "Autobiography," 3–6.

150. The 1906 *Gale,* 117.

151. *Student,* Sept. 8, 1911, 23–24.

152. Corbin, "The Small College Versus the University," 7–8, 28–29.

153. *Ibid.,* 28.

154. Fitch, *The Big Strike at Siwash,* 22–23.

155. *Ibid.,* 39.

156. *Ibid.,* 52. Some alumni believed that the real life original of Ole Skjarsen was Arthur Harbaugh, a "demon football player and all around athlete" (1922 *Gale,* 106; *Knox Alumnus,* Nov.-Dec. 1926, 28). Harbaugh was at Knox from 1896 to 1901, being graduated with the class of 1900. He was twenty-four years old when he entered Knox in 1896. Another Knox alumnus,

James L. Crane, a fellow Beta with Fitch, believed that Skjarsen was a combination of two players. One was on the team of St. Albans school for boys in Knoxville. St. Albans in 1894 "fielded a team composed of two or three students, the balance of the team being made up of instructors, janitors and several well built men about town." On this team was a burly gentleman named Woolsey (a well digger) who "rendered" Crane "hors de combat" with a punch on Crane's jaw. A week later Knox, according to Crane, played the Athletic Club of Cambridge, Ill. "At the beginning of the second half" Knox was "surprised to see an entirely strange team come on the field which eventually proved to be a team from Augustana." On this new team was a "big Swede from Augustana." He became the other man in the "combination" that became Ole Skjarsen. This game broke up in a "free for all fight." James L. Crane to Carter Davidson, Apr. 22, 1940, Fitch Papers.

157. A bibliography of works by Fitch is provided in the memorial edited by William E. Simonds and Max Goodsill, *Supplement Knox College Bulletin*, 1918, new series, no. 3, 5.

158. The following pieces by Fitch have been identified: "Ye Book III of Ye Chronicles," a humorous account of the mock presidential election during Fitch's senior year, the 1897 *Gale*, 47–48; "Rough House," reminiscences regarding meetings of the Gnothautii literary society, the 1903 *Gale;* "Football," a poem, 1904 *Gale;* "A Smile," a poem, *ibid.;* "The Old Gym," a poem, illustrated with a picture of the ruins of the old wooden gymnasium, the 1905 *Gale*, 54; "A Whitman on Football," poem, 1907 *Gale*, 116; "The Way Dad Talked," a humorous poem about college yells, in the 1908 *Gale*, 141; "Seeing Knox Through a Megaphone," a humorous essay, the 1909 *Gale*, 9–12; "The Campaign of '96," the 1910 *Gale*, 131–35; "The Rooter," from his syndicated "Vest Pocket Essays," in the 1914 *Gale,*.

159. The 1904 *Gale*.

160. The 1907 *Gale*, 116–17.

161. Thomas Gold Frost, "Knox College and Athletics," *Coup D'Etat*, May 1891, 126–28; Frost, *Tales from the Siwash Campus*, ch. 2, deals with Knox athletics at the turn of the century; *Coup D'Etat*, Nov. 1891, 38; *Knox Student*, Oct. 21, 1897, 1.

162. See ch. 3 herein.

163. See ch. 3 herein. In Dec. 1891 Knox concluded the first season under the auspices of the Illinois Inter-collegiate Football league, which included the University of Illinois (*Coup D'Etat*, Dec. 1891, 52). In 1894 Knox, Normal University, Illinois College, and Eureka organized another "Football League" (*Knox Student*, Dec. 1894, 1).

164. "Football," *Encyclopedia Britannica* (1967), 9:570–71.

165. *Knox Student*, Dec. 7, 1905, 179; Jan. 25, 1906, 256.

166. *Galesburg Weeks Review*, Dec. 20, 1905, 10, 5.

167. *Ibid.*, Sept. 27, 1906, 21. Knox was able to find only one college soccer team in Illinois with which to compete; otherwise it played with professional or semiprofessional teams, such as the one at Farmington, where pos-

sibly British coal miners had introduced the game. Knox secured as soccer coach J. C. Purcell, an Oxford University player (1908 *Gale*, 143).

168. *Student,* first page for the issues of Oct. 19, Oct. 26, and Nov. 2, 1915.

169. Galesburg *Weekly Mail,* Apr. 21, 1898, 9.

170. Data compiled from the volumes of the *Gale* for this period.

171. *Student,* Dec. 7, 1905, 179; Jan. 25, 1906, 256.

172. *Gale,* 1899, 109.

173. *Coup D'Etat,* June 1894, 187, reported: "For the past two years there has been no pitcher in the college and so men were brought in to do this work. This has been very demoralizing to the team, but we had to play good ball to draw crowds and make money. Now that the fence is paid for, we need no longer follow this plan. Ball must be played for the sake of the students, not the people. Two men are rapidly developing as pitchers, and as they will play in the city league all summer, they will be in good trim for the fall. Two other men will develop into fairly good catchers, and by next spring we will have two good batteries that no college can kick on playing against because they are not bona fide students. All the other places will be filled by good men, so that there is no reason why Knox should not have a crack college team and no one but out-and-out students playing."

174. *Student,* May 22, 1895, 4; June 5, 1895, 4.

175. Galesburg *Republican Register,* Nov. 28, 1891, 7.

176. *Ibid.,* Oct. 15, 1887, 5.

177. *Coup D'Etat,* Oct. 1887, 19.

178. Fitch, *At Good Old Siwash,* ch. 8.

179. Letter from President Gates of Grinnell, Mar. 19, 1892, Bateman Papers.

180. Gettleman, "College President on the Prairie," 142–44.

181. *Gale,* 1899, 109; Faculty Minutes, Feb. 7, 1898.

182. Gettleman, "College President on the Prairie," 142–44.

183. *Gale,* 1899, 108.

184. See the statement in the catalogue for the year 1901–2, 76–77. See also Faculty Minutes for Feb. 2, 1900.

185. *Student,* Dec. 5, 1902, 90.

186. *Ibid.,* Dec. 11, 1902, 162.

187. *Ibid.,* 161.

188. *Ibid.,* 155.

189. The two men who dropped out of school immediately after the football season was over were among those on the list of "unclassified" students; they were George Martin and Richard R. France. The *Knox Student* occasionally spelled the name of the latter "Franz." He had attracted particular attention to himself at the Northwestern game, from which he was ejected for his "dirty" tactics (*Student,* Nov. 2, 1902, 96). The players on the team and on the squad are identified in pictures in the *Student* for Dec. 5, 1902, which issue is particularly devoted to the football season. Students are listed accord-

ing to their categories in the catalogue for 1902–3, 93–100. That Martin and France were indifferent students is suggested by the Faculty Minutes for Nov. 3, 1902.

190. *Student*, Sept. 18, 1902, 6.

191. See the activities listed for C. C. Hopkins in the senior class list of the *Gale* of 1903. See also the athletics section of the *Gale* for each of the previous four years. Hopkins resided at 931 West South Street. See the football section of the *Gale* of 1904, where he is pictured as a member of the team for the autumn of 1902. Elsewhere in this same *Gale,* he is listed as "alumni committeeman" of the Knox Republican Club. On the football squad of 1902 was another black man, William Corn, who was a student in the Academy for one year. He weighed 242 pounds. At least eight black students have been identified as attending between 1870 and 1897. None of these was graduated (see notes on the Civil War and Reconstruction by Muelder filed in the Knox College Archives). A black student, Lawrence H. Ferribee, was graduated from Knox in 1906, completing the course at Knox in three years. He was a member of Adelphi and active in forensics (*Gale,* 1907, senior class section).

192. *Student*, Feb. 5, 1903, 217; Faculty Minutes, Dec. 11, 1902; Dec. 17, 1902.

193. Catalogue for 1902–3, 87–88.

194. *Coup D'Etat*, Dec. 1893, 69.

195. *Gale*, 1903.

196. Walter Hempel; *Gale*, 1902.

197. *Gale*, 1903.

198. Standard reference works on sports list another man as the champion broad jumper in the Paris Olympics of 1900. The first claim for him in the *Student* (Sept. 19, 1901, 70) was merely that he was a member of the U.S. Olympic team of 1900. The *Student* of Nov. 28, 1901, 156; stated: "In 1900, with three others, McLean was sent to represent Michigan University in the International Athletic contest in Paris. There he won the broad jump and also won second place in the high hurdles." See Arlott, *Oxford Companion to Sports and Games*. McLean is not mentioned as a winner for any event in 1900.

199. The *Gale*, 1905, 128–29.

200. *Student*, Dec. 5, 1902, 131.

201. See ch. 2 herein. This was done when President William Curtis strengthened the Seminary faculty, preparatory to its entire separation from the College.

202. See "Athletes in the Hall," *Gale* of 1905, 151–52.

203. The *Gale* for these years consistently published a section on women's sports.

204. *Gale*, 1905, 54.

205. *Student*, Oct. 28, 1929, 7.

206. *Gale*, 1922, 106.

207. "Andrew Harrington Gymnasium," *Gale*, 1904.

208. *Gale*, 1909, 167.

209. *Gale*, 1908, 161.

210. Webster, *Seventy-Five Significant Years*, 105.

211. E. E. Calkins, "Remark Proofs," *Coup D'Etat*, Dec. 1894, 56–57. Calkins used essentially this same essay for an article: "Past and Present of Knox College. Being the History of Her Life, Her Achievements and Her Ideals," in *American University Magazine*.

212. Hodge, *Handbook of American Indians North of Mexico*, Part I: 214–15. See also Matthews, ed., *Dictionary of Americanisms on Historical Principles*, 2:1551; *A Dictionary of Canadianisms*, ed. Avis, 698–99.

213. *Random House Dictionary* (1969), 1333.

CHAPTER IX

THE INTELLECTUAL AND
FINANCIAL ASPECTS OF ACADEMIC
EXCELLENCE, 1892–1917

John Huston Finley spoke the valedictory for the class of 1887 in the large "wigwam," a temporary building erected to shelter the large crowd that came to celebrate the semicentennial of Knox College. Less than five years later the trustees chose him to be president. As if it were an apostolic succession, a picture was made of the venerable, white-bearded Newton Bateman placing on the shoulder of the younger, taller, and clean-shaven Finley the hand that was said to have been the last to shake that of Lincoln as his train pulled out of Springfield for Washington.[1] As one of Bateman's pupils, Finley had excelled in every way. He genuinely enjoyed the classics and was given advanced standing in Latin; for a time he taught Horace to the freshmen. He became president of Adelphi and wrote for the *Coup D'Etat*. That he did chores for his board and room was not unusual, but it was less typical that he learned to set type and to read proof at a local printery,[2] and that he himself set up and printed his *Catalogue of Books in the College, Adelphi, and Gnothautii Libraries* (Galesburg, 1887).[3] This catalogue included a section on magazines that was compiled by Edward Caldwell, and this was followed by a "Select List of the World's Best Books in the Department of General Literature," prepared by Professor Melville Anderson. This collaboration of Finley, Caldwell, and Anderson signified a common interest in books that years later would bring to Knox the extraordinary collection of works on the French pioneers in the Mississippi Valley, on which Finley became an authority and about which Caldwell, a learned bibliophile, collected and gave to his alma mater, the "Finley Collection."[4]

During the spring of his senior year Finley also won the first prize in the Inter-State Oratorical Contest with a speech on "John Brown" that linked his subject with other great rebels such as Emmet of Ireland, Wallace of Scotland, Garibaldi of Italy, and George Washington. Finley's glorification of Brown indicated that though Knox in many ways had become conservative, yet there persisted much of the old abolitionist tradition, enough to link the reforming evangelism of Charles Grandison Finney early in the nineteenth century with the muckraking of *McClure's Magazine* and the social gospel of the early twentieth century.[5] The special interest in social studies that would lead Finley to graduate studies at Johns Hopkins University was evident in his role as a founder of the Political Science Club in Galesburg in the autumn of 1886. Finley was the secretary-treasurer; the president was Jeremiah Whipple Jenks, who was just starting his first year at Knox as professor of political science and literature.[6]

When Finley became a graduate student at Johns Hopkins, it was only about ten years old, but the university was already becoming, after the model of German universities with their emphasis on the seminar method of teaching and on research, the prototype for the burgeoning graduate schools of the Midwest and being emulated in the Ivy League. Here Finley found not only great scholars but also concern with social reform, including pioneering attention to social work as a profession. In 1889, on the recommendation of the president of Johns Hopkins, Finley became secretary of the New York State Charities Aid Association, which supervised the public charities of the state. As the *Coup D'Etat* reported it, this was the agency "which has for its object the study and promotion of social questions and reforms, such as how to treat the insane, the pauper, the defective, and the criminal classes."[7] Soon after assuming his duties in New York he founded and edited the *State Charities Record* and then two years later started the *Charities Review: A Journal of Practical Sociology*. In 1891 Stanford University, which was just opening its doors, offered him an associate professorship of social science, and in Galesburg it was reported in November that he had accepted. It was, therefore, "news to Knoxites" when in February the Stanford

Sequoia announced that Finley had accepted the presidency of Knox College.[8] Actually such news was premature, for it was not until March 5, 1892, that Bateman reported that Finley would accept the position at Knox.[9]

Much was expected of Finley. It was anticipated that he would effect progressive changes and yet retain the piety with which, as an alumnus, he was familiar; he was known to revere the classics, yet the faculty had recently specifically requested better library and laboratory facilities and the addition of teachers of newer disciplines such as political economy and sociology. It was also hoped that Finley's experience with moneyed men who supported "charities" would help garner gifts for Knox.[10] Finley himself appreciated the need to raise money; indeed, he was immediately burdened with the necessity of raising $200,000 to match the offer of a $50,000 gift that was announced at the commencement of 1892. He requested and was given a year's leave of absence to do this while Bateman remained as the de facto president, administering routine matters and serving as chairman of the Executive Committee of the Board of Trustees until July 1893.[11] Finley never did become, as had his predecessors, the teacher of culminating courses for seniors on the "Evidences of Christianity" and "Moral Philosophy." Bateman remained for several years as the teacher of these subjects, and when he retired in 1877 he was succeeded by a new faculty member who became simply professor of philosophy.

Finley did not wait for changes in the curriculum and for new appointments to the regular faculty to enrich the intellectual life at the College. He immediately established special lecture courses that were taught by distinguished visiting scholars.[12] These were free to the students and available at low fees to the townspeople. Though they included lectures on scientific and literary topics, they were mostly in the area of history and the newer social studies. Among the nine lecturers for 1892–93 were Frederick Jackson Turner, who that same year would propound his important hypothesis on the "Significance of the Frontier," and the economist Richard T. Ely, who had instructed Finley on "Scientific Philanthropy" at Johns Hopkins and with whom Finley collaborated in the writing of a book. The next year Ely would return as one of nine visiting lecturers, along with Jeremiah Jenks.[13] For 1894–95 the ten special lecturers included men and women who were part of the social and intellectul vitalization of Chicago, foreshadowing the Chicago Renaissance of the early years of the twentieth century. One of the ten lecturers was Alice Freeman Palmer, formerly president at Wellesley and now a dean at the University of Chicago, which William Rainey Harper was transforming into one of the great universities of the world. Another was Graham Taylor, the first professor of social ethics in an American theological seminary, the Chicago Theological Seminary. Another was Jane Addams of Hull-House. And for a celebration of Knox Founders Day in February 1895 Harriet Monroe, later the founder of *Poetry,* recited "The Spirit of the Pioneers," a portion of the *Columbian Ode* that she had written and recited for the opening of the Columbian Exposition in Chicago in 1893.[14] Eugene Field, who received an honorary degree from Knox in 1893, had particularly encouraged and assisted her literary ambitions.[15] Edgar Bancroft, another Knox alumnus, she regarded as her lawyer-friend;[16] he spoke in the same lecture series of 1894–95 at Knox on "Political Ideals." Knox trustee John P. Wilson, class of 1865, served as general counsel for the Chicago World's Fair, which had an extraordinary effect on the scientific, cultural, and social enlightenment of the hundreds of thousands who attended it. President Finley's particular part in the numerous "congresses" convened for this exposition was to organize the International Congress of Charities, Correction and Philanthropy, to preside over it, and to edit a volume of the papers of this congress.[17]

When Finley was graduated in 1887, the curriculum was still limited in the choice of subject matter available to students; no departmentalization had occurred except for differences between the courses of study leading to the B.A. and the B.S. degrees, the latter requiring no Greek. Ten years later there were fifteen departments, not counting the Academy, the Conservatory, nor a short-lived School of Art. Some of these changes had occurred soon after Finley was graduated, such as the appointment of Edgar Larkin as director of the Observatory of 1888.[18] Also in 1891 the catalogue for the first time used the word laboratory. Space for such course work became available with the construction of an Observatory and by the shifting of the chapel and of the library rooms from Old Main to Alumni Hall, which had been completed in 1890. The expansion of the curriculum occurred with particular speed during the last four years of Finley's administration, which concluded in 1899 when Finley accepted an editorial post in the enterprises headed by S. S. McClure and associated Knox alumni. In 1895 James Needham (1891) was brought back to Knox to teach zoology and natural history, thus for the first time easing Professor Albert Hurd's duties in this area.[19] Needham would be succeeded by an instructor in biology in 1896, who had a laboratory assistant. In fact, the catalogue for 1897–98 would describe three departments (geology, biology, and chemistry) for the subject matter of natural science that Hurd had taught since before the Civil War. The modern languages of French, German, and Spanish also became departments, as did English literature. The area of Finley's special academic interest was apparent in the appointment in 1895 of an instructor in sociology, in the creation of a department of psychology and ethics, and in the formation of a department of history, economics, and political science.[20]

To teach this enriched and diversified curriculum the number of faculty members was increased from seventeen to twenty-five, not counting those that taught in the Conservatory and the Academy. Midwestern universities and Harvard, Yale, and Johns Hopkins were represented; three men were doctors of philosophy from Strasbourg, Bonn, and Leipzig. With the counsel of these new men the course structure was much revised, assuming a form that would still be quite familiar nearly nine decades later. Electives were increased, though there still remained general requirements in languages and in mathematics. The older emphasis on the classics was weakened so that it became possible to earn a B.A. with no course in Greek and only two courses in Latin at the College level. There was a more candid recognition that some students were preparing for vocations or would continue their studies elsewhere.[21]

What was becoming the characteristic American academic accounting system was adopted. Subject matter units from recognized secondary schools were substituted for the entrance examinations that formerly tested entering students on topics or books that had been stipulated in the catalogue. The courses of the College were now computed as part of the 120 credits needed to be graduated, each credit being equal to a certain accumulation of knowledge for one semester of class hours of fifty-five minutes.[22]

Still familiar at the middle of the next century would be the mechanics of the College operations. Professor Thomas Willard, having been appointed registrar in 1897, became dean in 1899. There was no longer a preceptress of the Female Seminary but instead, beginning in 1895, a dean of women.[23] Much of the routine business was no longer done by the faculty as a whole but by committees announced in the catalogue. The titles of some of these committees revealed what some of the recurring chores were: Excuses from Chapel, Excuses from Drill, Accrediting Schools. The burden of this last committee would be eased with the expansion of the North Central Association of Secondary Schools and Colleges, which was started in 1895. In 1896 the Knox faculty requested that the president seek listing of Knox in a prestigious roster of institutions of learning, *Minerva: Jahrbuch der gelehrten Welt,* published in Strasbourg, and in 1900 this cherished recognition was achieved.[24]

Such scholastic contrivances do not adequately reflect the glow of intellectuality that would be remembered from the seven years that Finley was the head of Knox. Much of the excitement came from the close relations of Knox and *McClure's Magazine,* which was started by Knox men of the class of '82 about the same time that Finley became president. As has been related earlier,[25] Knox's influence was often apparent in the issues of this popular periodical, and McClure was often in Galesburg expressing his enthusiastic interest in the College. His relations with Finley were most cordial. Writers for *McClure's,* such as the distinguished French journalist Madame Blanc and Ida Tarbell who wrote about the Lincoln-Douglas debates, visited the campus. Tarbell's article on this theme was coordinated in 1896 with the celebration in a most grand manner of the anniversary of the debate that had occurred on the Knox campus in October 1858. For this first ceremonial recollection of an historic political event, Robert Lincoln, son of the Civil War president, was a speaker, and a U.S. Senator and governor from Illinois and the head of its state university were on hand.[26] Thus Finley set the style by which Knox, its Old Main, and a Lincoln debate were repeatedly associated in the news for years to come, with visitors such as President William McKinley, John Hay and other members of the cabinet, Theodore Roosevelt, William Jennings Bryan, William Howard Taft, and Adlai Stevenson. After World War I the notables brought to the debate site at the east wall of Old Main were more likely well-known Lincoln biographers, not the least of whom would be Carl Sandburg, the Galesburg youth who had witnessed the first celebration staged by Finley.[27]

It was also Finley who started the practice in 1894 of having a Founders Day each February fifteenth, recalling the date when the Illinois legislature in 1837 had granted Knox a charter.[28] Until past the middle of the twentieth century this precedent of having the College involve the community and some of its churches in Founders Day was faithfully repeated.

Another example of what some regarded as Finley's showmanship was the centennial observance at Knox of the birth of the poet William Cullen Bryant, another instance of how the College could be associated with famous persons and noted events. Earnest Calkins, who had a part in the occasion, would later remark that, "without injustice to his other achievements," President Finley's "chief contribution was to make the college known."[29] In saying this Calkins did not intend to demean the quality of genuine intellectual enthusiasm that Finley stimulated. It was Finley who originated the Pundit Club to "stimulate literary and scientific activity" at Knox. The faculty members belonging to this club were privileged to name one member of the senior class to the society. In 1896–97 the twenty topics scheduled ranged all the way from "Henrik Ibsen," presented by Professor William Simonds, to "Brick Paving in Galesburg," discussed by Professor Willard.[30] Also there was for town and gown the club named Cadmus for the hero who brought the alphabet to Greece. Its interests included not only the reading but also the writing and the making of books. Among its dozen members were George A. Lawrence (1875), lawyer, landed squire, and bibliophile; Professor Simonds, who not only taught Shakespeare at the College but also reviewed the performance of the plays of Shakespeare in Chicago for *The Dial*, the literary magazine then published in Chicago; Calkins, whose interest in the arts of printing would influence the history of American advertising; and two professor-poets, Alphonso Newcomer (the idol of Edgar Lee Masters), and Philip Greene Wright from the Lombard faculty, on whose basement press the first volumes of poems by Sandburg would be published.[31] Calkins would later comment that the Cadmus Club gave Galesburg "a reputation for intellectuality it has since succeeded in living down."[32]

In the spring of 1898 students were distracted from usual campus routine by talk of war with Spain, and many of the men had to consider the prospect of an interruption of their college careers by military service. In so far as the *Knox Student* reflected the attitudes of students, it would appear that until war actually began they generally maintained a kind of detached patriotism. The editor, Albert Britt (later a president of his alma mater), noted early in March that it "was most gratifying" that Knox students had received the news of the sinking of the warship *Maine* in Havana harbor without the "mass meetings," "inflammatory speeches," and effigy burnings that occurred at other campuses. He asserted that the "quiet state of affairs at Knox" did not "betoken any lack of patriotism or bravery" but the "students should be the last class of men to desire hostilities."[33] A month later Britt commended President McKinley for holding out against "popular and Congressional clamor for war."[34] Even as hostilities were at hand, Dr. John P. Cushing, professor of history, while declaring for the liberation of Cuba whose "manifest destiny" it was to join the United States, decried "frenzied and hysterical war talk."[35]

The day after Congress voted the resolutions that led shortly to a formal declaration of war against Spain, it was reported in a local paper that Knox would answer President McKinley's call for volunteers with two companies of soldiers, to be led "by cadet alumni officers." In addition, there would be an "alumni volunteer company" of which President Finley would be captain, for he had been a captain of the Knox cadets while a student and was "qualified for leadership in every way. A man of magnificent physique, with great executive ability, thoroughly versed in military matters, of perfect temperment, and a natural leader of men, it is certain that Knox and Knox friends would be proud of her soldiers under his guidance."[36]

The head of the Knox military department, Captain J. G. Ballance, U.S. Army, was more cautious about the immediate enlistment of Knox men for military service. At a meeting of students, he warned them that the pay would be poor and that many of them would return from the tropics greatly impaired in health. He was quoted furthermore as saying: "The country don't need you. There are plenty of men who are unemployed, and who would be willing to go. It is their place to volunteer."[37]

With such advice from a West Point graduate, it is not surprising that only a few Knox students enlisted. Nothing came of the idea of forming several companies of Knox students and alumni; the Knox cadets, as such, did not go to war. Most of those that served in the army during this very short war did so in Company C of the Sixth Regiment of the Illinois National Guard.[38] There were ten Knox College or Academy students or alumni in Company C, which is now most often recalled because one of the privates was Carl Sandburg, to whom this military comradeship was a transitional experience that led to his going to college, but to Lombard and not to Knox.[39]

Like the soldiers in other military units that got into a combat area, the men of Company C suffered badly from military mismanagement, confused leadership, poor food, and, as the commander of the Knox cadets had warned, disease. The men of Company C came strongly to dislike their captain, one Thomas Leslie McGirr, of whom Private Sandburg years later would recall that he was a "second rate lawyer . . . who in the sight of his men . . . occasionally fed juicy sirloin steaks" to his Saint Bernard dog.[40] A member of the Knox class of 1898, George Martin, was the "special object of Captain McGirr's abhorrence" because he was the correspondent of the Galesburg *Evening Mail,* which "dared to voice the feelings of the boys toward him."[41] When they returned to Springfield, Illinois, late in September 1898, to await their mustering out, they circulated "a petition which was signed by all but four members of the company requesting that the people of Galesburg should not recognize Captain McGirr . . . at any public celebration given in their honor."[42]

A Knox alumnus, Congressman G. W. Prince, had "received the boys" when they landed in New York and provided them care that otherwise had been neglected. President Finley went to see them when they got back to Springfield, bringing "many desired neccessities and some luxuries which they had not had for months." And the new editor of the *Student*, Thomas Blodgett, who had been Editor Britt's business manager, pronounced: "We welcome our boys home and hope for the safe return of those still in the field and in the hospital."[43] Three weeks later he made this editorial judgment about what had happened:

> "REMEMBER THE MAINE" is a phrase unworthy of the American people. It is a sensational cry, taken up first by yellow newspapers and quickly copied on badges, buttons, etc., by people whose only desire was to make money. . . . When the *Maine* was destroyed yellow journalism rushed to the front, throwing the blame on the Spanish government. Anything more absurd could not have been imagined. Yellow journalism then forced the United States government into a war costing millions in money and thousands in men's lives and backed everything up with the false cry "Remember the *Maine*." Let us be done with this foolishness.[44]

When Blodgett made this pronouncement, he had already reported to the students that President Finley had received from the War Department a request "to report on the number of Knox men who had become members of the volunteer army." It was reasonable to determine whether the expense of maintaining a regular army officer at Knox for the cadet corps was justified by the number that responded when called upon for military service. Twenty-eight Knox men were known to have volunteered for the recent conflict, but records were incomplete about "students of earlier days."[45] Already in June the College had been informed that the business of the cadet corps at Knox was being "closed out."[46] Despite requests from the trustees,[47] it was not restored. A scholarly examination of the records of the War Department leads to the conclusion that the disbanding of the cadet unit at Knox was due to the "manifest lack of enthusiasm" for recent hostilities with Spain and the conquest—or "liberation"—of her colonial territories.[48]

President Finley resigned the Knox presidency in 1899 to assume an editorial role with McClure and soon thereafter went on to a professorship offered him at Princeton by Woodrow Wilson. It was during his brief stint as an editor for *McClure's Magazine* that he, with his brother-in-law Albert A. Boyden (who had studied at Knox Academy and College for five years but completed his degree at Harvard), brought Lincoln Steffens onto the staff, and it would be with Boyden family connections that Steffens would make the contacts in Chicago to start the memorable series of articles on municipal corruption that would be called "The Shame of the Cities."[49] Finley later returned to New York to be president of the City College of New York and then editor-in-chief of the New York *Times*. For Knox he became a member of the Board of Trustees in 1899 and served for forty years. As he had been present for the Knox semicentennial, so, as its most distinguished alumnus, he would participate in its centennial celebration in 1937.

Finley's strengthening of the faculty and expansion of the academic program were not accompanied with adequate improvement of the financial condition of the College. As he explained to the trustees, the times were not "propitious" for raising money. The depression connected with the Panic of 1893 endured during most of the time he was the head of Knox.[50] Even as he was about to give up the presidency in February 1899, he had only raised the matching money for one-fourth of the D. K. Pearsons fund of $50,000,[51] on which he had started to garner contributions immediately after being chosen president. Fortunately, the philanthropist was flexible in his expectations. Meanwhile every year the College finances fell behind, and by 1898 the accumulated deficit was very large, though Finley must have been surprised to read nearly three decades later in the eulogy of his successor, President McClelland, that the latter had "saved Knox College from disaster."[52]

To understand the special contributions made by Thomas McClelland as president from 1900 to 1917, it is helpful to know that he was suggested to the Board of Trustees by a top-level executive of the C.B.&.Q. Railroad, W. C. Brown, who later, while still on the Knox Board, became president of the New York Central. He and McClelland had become acquainted when McClelland, while a professor of philosophy at Tabor College in southern Iowa, had been the leader of a company that built a short branch line to the main line of the Burlington from the town of Tabor.[53] McClelland had been ordained as a Congregational minister but instead of making the ministry a career entered academic life, first on the faculty at Tabor and later as the president of Pacific University in Oregon, from which he moved to Knox. As a graduate of Oberlin and student at theologically liberal seminaries of the Northeast,[54] he had religious convictions broad enough to accept advanced views held by members of the Knox faculty who did not subscribe to literal biblical interpretations in areas such as biology. Significantly, it was during his presidency that Knox seriously contemplated a merger with the Universalists at Lombard,[55] the project failing mostly because of reluctance of the latter. It was an important mark of more liberal religious sentiments that in 1909 the centenary of the birth of Charles Darwin was celebrated in Beecher Chapel by members of the faculty from both colleges and by the pastor of Central Congregational Church.[56]

President McClelland's standing as a good Congregationalist was of use to him both at the local and the national levels, but his work for Knox relied on more secular connections. Professor Simonds, who was on the faculty when McClelland arrived and who would remain as the dean after McClelland retired, recalled that it was a particular trait that "he made friends and inspired confidence among men of affairs, notably those who had money to give or were responsible for the distribution of funds."[57]

Almost immediately after he assumed office, McClelland began a campaign that by the end of his second year as president had added $70,000 to the endowment. Such a fund must be measured in terms of purchasing power at the turn of the century, when the highest monthly salary of a professor at Knox was $162 and that of an instructor was $60.[58] On Founders Day of 1909 College and community enthusiastically celebrated in Central Congregational Church the successful gathering in gifts and promises of $260,000.[59] The money came from hundreds of friends of Knox and from alumni from coast to coast; citizens of Galesburg contributed about $88,000, but the largest sums came from the General Education Board, which administered the philanthropy of John D. Rockefeller, and from Andrew Carnegie, $50,000 each.[60] McClelland had carefully cultivated the friendship of the author of the *Gospel of Wealth* and had become a trustee of the Carnegie Foundation for the Advancement of Teaching when it was founded in 1905.[61] It should be noted that the corporate source of such funds did not go unnoticed in the trust-busting era. The *Knox Student* for Founders Day of 1906 noted that at Illinois College

William Jennings Bryan had resigned from the Board of Trustees because of its solicitation of funds from Carnegie. And on the same date a year later, Knox trustee, S. S. McClure, speaking at the Founders Day banquet for the seventieth anniversary of Knox, warned that gratitude to such benefactors as Rockefeller "would tend to blunt the sense . . . of approbrium toward the manner in which such wealth was acquired."[62] But the Knox trustees were hardly the same body of evangelists and zealots for reform in 1907 that they had been when the College was first incorporated. The last of the antebellum abolitionists on the Board, the Reverend Joseph Edwin Roy (class of 1848), died in 1906. Local Congregational and Presbyterian ministers were still chosen as trustees, but by the end of the McClelland administration the trustees were mostly influential lawyers, bankers, and powerful corporation executives. Even though they were not active participants in the business meetings of the board, trustees such as Robert Lincoln and Frank O. Lowden by their names alone would have impressed the financial community. The former was the son of Abraham Lincoln who served as legal counsel for the powerful (and in labor circles the notorious) Pullman Company; the latter was the son-in-law of George Pullman himself.[63]

Soon after the successful endowment effort of 1909, Knox College acquired what was the largest individual gift ever received up to that time. Dr. John Van Ness Standish and his wife gave real estate valued at $75,000.[64] He had been professor of mathematics at Lombard College and between 1892 and 1895 the president of this college whose faculty he had joined soon after it was founded. Misunderstandings and disputes over finances cooled his interest in Lombard.[65] In 1900 Knox accepted his offer to take over "beautifying the campus free of charge." The chestnut trees planted at that time as a border to the campus would still, eighty years later, testify to the special interest he took in the appearance of Knox.[66] Part of the gift made in 1909 was the Standish home on the site where the Knox library later would be built. For years its carefully tended yard and gardens had been the horticultural marvel of Galesburg. Standish gave them the same attention that he gave to the park across the street from Alumni Hall, the park that still carries his name and was once a remarkable arboretum.

The buildings at the northeastern part of the campus still indicate the improvements made under McClelland's management. A gymnasium was completed by 1908, costing, with its equipment, $30,000. A heating plant, since replaced on the same site, was constructed in 1911 at the cost of $40,000. During 1912, the year that Knox celebrated its seventy-fifth anniversary, Davis Hall, originally a science center, was dedicated. It cost $115,000, for which $25,000 had been donated by the son-in-law and daughter of George Davis, who had been treasurer of Knox from 1875 to 1890.[67]

A final endowment campaign in 1916 added another $500,000 to the College resources. In October 1914 President McClelland informed the board that he had received from the General Education Board a proposition stating that "in view of the present emergency caused by the European war and the general financial conditions," the General Education Board would contribute $100,000 from "the income of the late John D. Rockefeller Fund for Higher Education" to Knox for permanent endowment provided Knox would by May 1, 1916, raise $400,000.[68] Finley, who was present at this board meeting, remarked that "to undertake such an enterprise at that time showed a courage in President McClelland worthy of the Belgians." Finley helped substantially by securing $75,000 from the Russel Sage foundation.[69] And again the matching funds were collected, and a total of $500,000 was garnered for the College endowment.[70] This brought the total endowment of the college to approximately $980,000.[71] Even more of the wealth of Knox should, in the judgment of the man who became dean of the faculty in 1912, be credited to McClelland, for it was by him "that the two Seymour brothers, Lyman K. and Henry M., were confirmed in their purpose to add the men's dormitory and the new library building to the College equipment, although these benefactions were received during . . . two later administrations."[72]

While the president was away on his frequent trips raising money, running the College was to a large extent left to the faculty. The minutes of their meetings (at least two each month) show that the dean of the faculty very often presided. This new College office was created shortly before McClelland became president, and was first performed by Professor Willard. He served as acting president following the resignation of President Finley.

McClelland relied heavily on the judgment of the faculty in making new appointments of teachers, as he did in letting the faculty resolve academic problems. According to Dr. Simonds, who became the dean in 1912, some of the faculty criticized McClelland for his "lack of positive leadership." They also charged "that action taken, especially in cases of discipline, was too easily modified or reversed, when left in the president's hands."[73] He was not perceived as the intellectual leader that Finley had been.

At the very time that the indifference to scholarship apparent at "Old Siwash" was about to be associated with Knox, the faculty was refining the modern academic program as it had begun to take shape during the Finley presidency. In 1906 the faculty enhanced the recognition given to scholarly achievements by adopting a report of a committee chaired by Professor Herbert Neal, a Bates College graduate with a Ph.D. from Harvard in biology. This legislation established a new program of academic honors. Seniors were now to be graduated with the familiar latinate laudations: *Summa cum Laude, Magna cum Laude, cum Laude,* and *Rite.* In addition there were to be, as voted by the faculty, announced at commencement, and published in the catalogue, "General Honors" and "Special Honors" awarded by the departments with faculty concurrence. These were to be awarded to underclassmen as well as to seniors.[74]

Resources for scholarly work by both students and faculty were enriched by improvement of library services. In 1901 a public library building was constructed (partly with money from Carnegie) in the same block that the women's dormitory and Beecher Chapel were located. Its collection, which by 1912 counted 40,000 volumes, was thus readily accessible to Knox students.[75] Not for nearly thirty years would the College have as good a building for itself. However, beginning in Finley's time as president, much was done to provide Knox with a better library. During the year when Bateman still served as de facto president, Finley got promises from several of his scholarly friends, Professor Richard Ely, Dr. E. R. A. Seligman of Columbia, and Dr. Albert Bushnell Hart, that they would send copies of their own works and duplicates on their shelves to Knox. A discounting agreement was solicited from Columbia College, and the Newberry Library in Chicago sent fifty books. Finley secured twenty periodicals for one year at no cost from the publishers.[76] A new trustees' committee was appointed by Bateman, and Finley began to make arrangements to rent a large room from Gnothautii in the east wing of Alumni Hall so that the separate libraries of the college and the men's literary societies could be brought from three small rooms in Old Main and put together in one place. Even when this was done the collection was not very impressive. Many of the books had come off the shelves of deceased clergymen and "were as dead as their owners."[77] In 1898 an editorial in the *Student* (likely written by Britt) complained that

> the labors of Hercules were child's play compared with the task of searching through the college library for data on any particular subject. In the first place, the number of books is woefully incommensurate with the needs of the students. How seven thousand volumes will ever satisfy the various wants and necessities of four or five hundred students it is impossible to discover. . . . It is usually very difficult also to find the books that are in the library. . . .
>
> Some good system of cataloguing and the necessary rules to enforce the proper use should be adopted and rigidly adhered to.[78]

Twelve years later the College provided much improved library facilities in the large central section of Alumni Hall, where an auditorium had been built that had proved so poor in its acoustics that it was deserted for the Congregational Church north of Whiting Hall that was known as Beecher Chapel. The auditorium was adapted to library use by putting a level floor above the one that had sloped to the platform. As the 1,365 volumes were moved from the east wing, they were catalogued, being "numbered according to the decimal classification of Melvil Dewey," which an article in the *Student* explained "when once mastered will prove of great usefulness to the student in his search among the book stacks."[79] The library was adorned with pictures "that illustrated aspects of western culture." For nearly a score of years, the student coming from the outdoors into this more dimly lighted space was first attracted to the large white plaster cast of the *Winged Victory* that seemed to move toward the circulation desk. It had been given to the College by John Finley as a memorial to his brother Robert, also of the class of 1887.[80]

Some students certainly perceived that the College ought to be a place of independent scholarly inquiry beyond study assignments for undergraduates and preparations for classroom appearances by teachers. The yearbook issued for 1902–3 had a most unusual feature, a page listing "Publications of the Faculty."[81] Of the six professors who were represented, the listings for three were most impressive: Dr. William Simonds in English literature; Dr. Aladine Cummings Longden in physics; Dr. Herbert V. Neal in biology. Three of the articles attributed to Neal had appeared in a German scientific journal of anatomy, for, after completing his doctorate at Harvard in 1896, Neal studied at Munich a year before coming to Knox. He remained at Knox until 1913. Longden, who joined the Knox faculty in 1901, remained for a quarter of a century, until his retirement in 1926. During the last quarter of the nineteenth century there had been three professors at Knox whose exceptional careers as scholars earned them inclusion in the *Dictionary of American Biography*, but they were at Knox only a short time early in their careers.[82] For those who made Knox a life's vocation, a rigorous teaching schedule and recurring requests for community services[83] allowed little time for personal intellectual interest. Furthermore, there was a paucity of library and laboratory resources.

During the early years of the twentieth century the outstanding intellectual leader of the faculty was William Simonds. The *Gale* in 1903 took notice of the six books on English literature that he had edited or written. In addition, he was a frequent contributor to one of the important "little magazines" that encouraged and reviewed literature and reported literary events. This was *The Dial* of Chicago for which, beginning in 1894, with an account of the centenary of the birth of William Cullen Bryant as staged by Knox College,[84] he often reviewed Shakespearean and other dramatic presentations in Chicago[85] and wrote numerous other essays on literary topics such as the merits of Walt Whitman as an important poet.[86]

Two former members of the Knox faculty were also frequently contributors to *The Dial* during this same period,[87] even though they were in California where they had become members of the faculty of the new university established by the fortune of Leland Stanford. It was from richly endowed institutions such as Stanford and from those new schools perennially enriched and enlarged by state legislatures that most scholarly writing was now expected to come, for the teaching loads of these schools allowed for such labors by their scholars. Entirely new constellations of state-supported educational institutions changed the orbits of the private liberal arts colleges in the universe of higher education.

The role of Knox with reference to secondary education was much changed by the rapid growth of public secondary schools. Until the 1880s the Knox Academy enrolled more students than the College. In 1909 the trustees decided to close the Knox Academy.[88] Since 1887, when the Knox catalogue for the first time announced that "students from certain preparatory schools which have been approved by the Faculty" would "be admitted to suitable classes without examination,"[89] the enrollment in the Academy had been falling. Most of the fifty-four preps in the Academy in 1909 were in the final year of the curriculum designed to qualify them for admission to the College, having done most of their studies elsewhere, but needing "to make up deficiencies that could be covered in a single year of well ordered work." The thirty-five preps enrolled for 1909–10 were the last.[90] Dean Simonds in an essay about Knox published in 1912 approved of this abandonment of one of the original departments of the College as a means of concentrating on a good four-year liberal arts program. He also was pleased that, even earlier, Knox had discontinued "the so called commercial course" and a "department of art."[91]

The Knox Conservatory of Music, however, was thriving and perhaps was at its prime. Though still an autonomous enterprise, financed from its own fees, it was located on the Knox campus (in Whiting Hall) and closely associated with the College. As Knox approached the celebration in 1911–12 of its seventy-fifth anniversary, there were 346 students in the College and 256 in the Conservatory, forty-three of them being enrolled in both institutions. That year there were forty-nine seniors in the College and seventeen seniors in the three-year Conservatory program. College students not taking courses or lessons in the Conservatory might still enjoy the advantages of the glee clubs, oratorio societies, and choirs directed by teachers in the Conservatory.[92] Both College and Conservatory had close ties with the nearby Central Congregational Church, where one of the features of the seventy-fifth anniversary celebration was the dedication of the organ to the "great triumvirate,"[93] Albert Hurd, Milton Comstock, and

George Churchill, whom alumni so warmly remembered. In Central Church the head of the Conservatory, William Bentley, directed the choir, while the organist was his close and long-time partner in Conservatory affairs, John Winter Thompson. Both of these men were the leaders of the Galesburg Musical Union, which did much to bring College and Conservatory and community together. For example, during its twelfth season in 1910, the Musical Union for the second time staged a May Festival. It was described in the *Knox Student* as the "greatest musical event of the year," being attended by a "large proportion" of Knox students, and the "greater part of cultured Galesburg, while special trains brought hundreds of music lovers from nearby cities to swell the throng." The chorus of the Musical Union in the afternoon sang Gounod's *Faust* in Central Church "in the style of the oratorio." That evening the Minneapolis Symphony presented a concert. The reporter for the *Student* could hardly contain his enthusiasm for the way the Galesburg Musical Union had for years been financing such "cultural uplift of this city."[94]

By 1912 students had initiated the dramatic activities that would lead to the appointment for the first time of a theatre director after World War I. That there should be a theatre at all betrayed a considerable shift in campus mores since some of the older alumni on the Board of Trustees had themselves been students. For as Royall Tyler, one of the earliest American playwrights had complained, the theatre was widely believed to be a place where the follies of the world are hung up on the "tenterhooks of temptation." As late as 1875 the Adelphi debated whether "modern theatrical entertainments are pernicious in their effects upon society."[95] It is true that sometimes the literary societies had staged pieces that tended to a dramatic form—so-called conferences or colloquies, in which there was dialogue on some patently moral theme. During the 1860s Gnothautii and Adelphi occasionally staged short dramatic pieces written by themselves for "exhibitions" in their own halls.[96] It was an important departure from campus customs, however, when LMI (Ladies' Moral Improvement Society), which was raising money for a better hall, was given special permission by the trustees to present a play called *School,* with a cast of both men and women, at the Opera House just off the town square.[97] The players had been trained by

Melvina Bennett, who had been since 1880 instructor in elocution, and who was much admired for her coaching of the Knox men who had won many championships in oratory. The staging of *School* in March 1882 was so well received that one hundred "citizens of Galesburg" asked that it be repeated. This LMI agreed to do with the "addition" of the court room scene from the *Merchant of Venice*.[98] Miss Bennett played Shylock; the other players were students of the Female Seminary.[99] In the late 1880s "theatricals" were not uncommon but their staging off the campus was inhibited because in December 1886 the Opera House burned and a new auditorium was not "dedicated" until 1890.[100] By the turn of the century class plays were a regular feature of the yearly calendar and an important means of rivalry between seniors and juniors and between sophomores and freshman.

A College Players Club was organized in November 1911.[101] This organization raised money and did much of the work to remodel the space that became available to the public speaking department on the third floor of Old Main as the chemistry laboratories were relocated in the new science building. This new auditorium was named Grace Chamberlain Hall to honor the woman who had been instructor in elocution from 1891 to 1896. The stage, which had a front opening of nine by eighteen feet, looked out upon an auditorium where 200 opera chairs had been installed. An electrical system in fire-proof conduits provided current for "footlights, strip lights, and border lights."[102]

In January 1912 this theater was opened with the performances of dramatic sketches, one written by Kenneth Andrews, president of the dramatic club, and the other by Jesse Crafton.[103] Crafton, later in the year, won first place in the state oratorical contest, staged at Lombard by the Intercollegiate Peace Association of Illinois, and then won the second place in the Interstate Contest of the same association.[104] He repeated this oration for the ceremonies of the seventy-fifth anniversary of the chartering of Knox College.[105]

After graduation from Knox, Andrews, Crafton, and several other members of the Players Club became active in the movement called the Little Theatre, the name for the amateur theatrical groups that to some extent followed after the numerous professional road companies and local stock companies that once had flourished but had declined with the advent of moving pictures. One of these alumni was Franz Rickaby, who came from Springfield, where his interest in literature and other arts had been directly influenced by Vachel Lindsay.[106] Crafton after his graduation from Knox in 1912 studied at Harvard in the famous "47 Workshop Theatre" of Professor George Pierce Baker.

In the fall of 1915 Crafton returned to Galesburg and with two companions, from Smith College and from Dartmouth,[107] converted the old White House saloon on the east side of the town square into a "little theatre," which opened in November 1915 as the Prairie Play House.[108] This venture was soon hailed as "the first little theatre in a small city in America." The New York *Times* and the *Christian Science Monitor* publicized it, as did three national magazines. Alumni, students, and faculty participated in its activities.[109] Already in its first season, in the spring of 1916, a faculty meeting discussed "the demands of the Prairie Playhouse upon the time of the students taking part in the play."[110]

Unfortunately, this venture was cut off in its third season by the entry of the United States into World War I, during which Crafton served with the Air Force in France. Nonetheless, when Crafton returned to the Knox campus twenty years after his graduation to receive an honorary degree, he stated that Knox could "claim to contribute a larger share toward" the development of the little theatre in the United States "than any other college in the middle west."[111]

For the commencement of 1912 the faculty voted that they would wear academic costume. The colors of the hoods they wore in the procession represented distinguished colleges and graduate schools. There were twenty-two members of the faculty, exclusive of the Conservatory, and nine of them were doctors of philosophy, one each from Chicago, Northwestern, Wisconsin, Columbia, Yale, and Harvard, and three from German universities. The occasion celebrated seventy-five years of Knox history and the completion of a new science building. The teaching of the sciences had probably improved the most during the last decade; in chemistry under the guidance of Professor Herbert E. Griffith; in biology by Professor Herbert Neal; in physics with Professor Aladine Longden. An emerging leader of the faculty at this time, in the department of history and political science, was Dr. John L. Conger, who had come to Knox from graduate studies with Frederick Jackson Turner. He would continue to serve the College for nearly four decades following his arrival in 1907, being distinguished among his colleagues for political activism, being elected mayor of Galesburg in 1915, even though he was a Democrat in a strongly Republican community. This feat was made possible by the recently enfranchised women, who unlike the male voters gave Professor Conger strong majorities in both the primary and the general elections.[112] He was a stimulating teacher, especially for those truly interested in the study of history and government, and he sent on to graduate work a steady series of Knox seniors. His pride in their accomplishments was illustrated by a gallery of their photographs. By the time he was retired, this display nearly covered the back wall of his favorite classroom in Old Main. It is worthy of note that among these protégés of Dr. Conger were several brilliant women. Three of them, Chloe Owings, class of 1910, and Alice Felt Tyler, class of 1913, and Alice Jeannette Paddock Nichols, class of 1913, would later be recognized by Knox with honorary doctorates for their scholarly achievements.

In the latter years of his presidency McClelland was failing in health and often hardly able to carry the burden of his office.[113] His son, Kellogg, was in 1912 appointed "assistant to the president,"[114] but in 1917 the president decided to retire, weary from his labors, full of years, and yet surely proud of what had been achieved at Knox during the last seventeen years. The high standing of Knox had been officially recognized by the U.S. Bureau of Education in 1910 "as one of the five colleges west of the Alleghenies to be placed" by its rating system in "Class I."[115] This meant that it was one of the twenty-one colleges and thirty-nine universities in the United States "whose graduates would ordinarily be able to take the master's degree at any of the large graduate schools in one year after receiving the bachelor's degree."[116] Knox was also the first educational institution in Illinois to be granted by the Carnegie Foundation for the Advancement of Teaching the considerable benefit of retirement allowances for its professors.[117]

In 1911 the Harvard Exchange was established. This was an agreement among Harvard and five midwestern colleges—Knox, Beloit, Grinnell, Carleton, and Colorado. Harvard would send a professor for half a year to these colleges who would divide his time equally among them and give such regular instruction in their courses as they required. The five colleges in return were to send Harvard each year a teacher for half a year who served as an assistant for one-third of his time and used the rest of his time doing graduate work or research in Harvard University. The first Harvard professor to visit Knox, in 1911–12, by this arrangement was the distinguished historian Albert Bushnell Hart. The Exchange lasted into the academic year 1935–36. It was modified in 1920 by adding Pomona as a sixth college, with two Harvard professors visiting three colleges each for five weeks, now offering their own courses for regular college credit.[118]

In March 1916 the senate of Phi Beta Kappa authorized the issuing of a charter to a chapter of this honorary fraternity at Knox College. This would be the first chapter established at a college in Illinois, following those issued to the three leading universities in Illinois. In the view of many scholars dedicated to the teaching of the liberal arts, this was the most widely esteemed sign that Knox had become an excellent academic institution.

NOTES

1. A photograph, probably made in 1892, by "Osgood Galesburg, Illinois," Knox Archives.

2. Gettleman, "John Finley's Illinois Education," 147–69.

3. During his freshman year he also dusted law books in the office of Edgar Bancroft, a young Knox alumnus about to launch a distinguished career as attorney and civic leader in Chicago (*ibid.*).

4. Finley, "Pioneers of France in the New World." To compensate John Finley for this catalogue, the trustees forgave the tuition of his brother Robert for the past term and voted that John should not be charged for his diploma (Executive Committee Minutes, Apr. 11, 1887).

5. See chs. 3 and 5 herein.

6. *Coup D'Etat*, Nov. 1886, 44.

7. *Ibid.*, Feb. 1889, 94.

8. *Ibid.*, Nov. 1891, 40; Feb. 1892, 94.

9. Executive Committee Minutes, Mar. 5, 1892.

10. Gettleman, "College President on the Prairie."

11. Executive Committee Minutes, Feb. 13, 1892, July 6, 1893; *Coup D'Etat*, June 1893, 135.

12. William E. Simonds, "Knox College—1892–1934: The Four Presidents." (On this typed manuscript is written in Dean Simonds's handwriting:

"For personal use of E. E. Calkins in compiling his book 'They Broke the Prairie,' 1937. W.E.S.")

13. These lecture courses are described in the catalogues for 1892–93, 1893–94, 1894–95.

14. *Coup D'Etat*, Nov. 1894, 46, Feb. 1895, 100–102. *Knox Student*, Feb. 20, 1895, 2, 7. Miss Monroe wrote about this Founders Day celebration in the *Critic* (*Knox Student*, Feb. 27, 1895, 5) and said of Knox: "The Pilgrim Fathers themselves were scarcely more heroic than this little band of scholars, who left comfortable eastern homes to sow the seeds of the higher culture in the wilderness." Calkins, "Past and Present of Knox College," 226–33.

15. Monroe, *A Poet's Life*, 78–84, and *passim*.

16. *Ibid.*, 234, 244. Bancroft was one of the original five-year underwriters of *Poetry*. He was present at the famous *Poetry* banquet for Yeats in 1914.

17. Gettleman, "College President on the Prairie," 144.

18. See ch. 7 herein.

19. Needham, "How Biology Came to Knox College," 365–72.

20. Students' awareness of the academic improvements was evident: *Coup D'Etat*, Sept. 1896, 5; *Student*, Feb. 1904, 288.

21. Gettleman, "College President on the Prairie," 137–39.

22. *Ibid.*, 150.

23. Executive Committee Minutes, Jan. 29, 1895. A distinctive course for women was abandoned in 1891. From 1891 to 1901 the College offered a Bachelor of Literature Degree. An art department had been established in 1883 and a decade later was "comfortably settled in the new quarters in the Adelphi wing of Alumni Hall" (Galesburg *Republican Register*, Feb. 25, 1893, 1). Art had originally been taught in the Female Seminary.

24. Gettleman, "College President on the Prairie," 140.

25. See ch. 5 herein.

26. Webster, *Seventy-Five Significant Years*, 100.

27. Sandburg, *Always the Young Strangers,* p. 302.

28. Webster, *Seventy-Five Significant Years*, 98–100.

29. Calkins, *They Broke the Prairie*, 405–7. Calkins was the publisher in Galesburg of the Bryant Centennial booklet (*Coup D'Etat*, Nov. 1894, 53).

30. *Gale*, 1896–97, 74; for 1897–98, 79; for 1905–6, 88–89.

31. *Gale*, 1896–97, 78, listed eighteen members, four of whom were non-resident and five of whom were honorary.

32. Quoted from Calkins, *and Hearing Not*, 193–40, in which Calkins described the origins and membership of the Cadmus Club. See also Calkins, "Prairie Book Club," *Knox Alumnus*, June 1943.

33. *Student*, Mar. 10, 1898, 4.

34. *Ibid.*, Apr. 7, 1898, 4.

35. *Ibid.*, Apr. 28, 1898, 4; May 26, 1898, 1.

36. "The Sons of Knox Will Go to War," Galesburg *Weekly Mail*, Apr. 21, 1898, 3.

37. *Ibid.* As late as May 12, 1898, there was an expectation that the "Knox College Cadet Volunteer Company" would join a regiment being raised in

Peoria (*ibid.*, 1). The *Knox Student* of Apr. 28, 1898, 2, summarized the discouraging counsel of Captain Ballance as follows: "Monday noon, after the last recitation, the office of Captain John Green Ballance was crowded with cadets who had assembled for the purpose of considering the possibility and advisability of forming a volunteer company of Knox cadets for the war with Spain. The boys were given a thoughtful address by the commandant of cadets, who considered that it was better for the cadets not to enroll just at present, there being men without particular purposes ahead who would gladly go to the front, whereas with the students at college such a step would imply a considerable sacrifice. He hoped the boys would wait, or at least carefully consider the importance of the matter of going out to war. The possibility of losing health and strength was mentioned."

38. Upon the return of the Sixth Regiment to Springfield in Sept. 1898, President Finley went there to visit with the Knox men. He brought back to Galesburg a list of the Knox men who were serving with the Sixth Regiment, and it was published in the Galesburg *Weekly Mail*, Sept. 22, 1898. Company C from Galesburg included these men from the College: George Martin, 1898; Walter Coolidge, 1899; Thomas Thomson, 1900; Howard Pettitt, 1901; Roy Pendarvis, 1901; Fred Harms, 1901; Ralph Matteson, 1899; and Warren Williamson, 1897. It included these men from the Academy: Oscar Wilson, 1890–98, and Charles Winders, 1897–98. Company B from Geneseo included these men from the College: Ira Cardiff, 1897, and Otho Gray, 1898. In Company D from Abingdon was Lester Hittle, 1897–98. President Finley also noted the following Knox men in "different commands": Julius Reed, Fiftieth Iowa; Bert Smith, Third U.S. Volunteers, Jefferson Barracks; Ralph Boyd, Third Illinois; George Vincent, Second Illinois; and Clark Shipp, Fifth Illinois.

39. Sandburg, *Always the Young Strangers,* 423.

40. *Ibid.,* 409.

41. Galesburg *Weekly Mail,* Dec. 1, 1898, 2.

42. *Ibid.,* Sept. 22, 1898, 1, 10. Two Knox students, being unable to go with this Galesburg company, went to California and joined the Fifth Regiment of volunteer infantry of that state. One of these men, Pvt. Charles Stuart, was wounded while serving with Merritt's forces in the Philippines (*ibid.,* Aug. 11, 1898, 1). The other, Lt. Jesse Lowenberg, earned some distinction for the ardor with which he helped to run down the Filipino patriot, Emilio Aguinaldo (*Gale* for 1899–1900).

43. *Student,* Sept. 27, 1898, 21.

44. *Ibid.,* Oct. 18, 1898, 60–61.

45. *Ibid.,* Oct. 4, 1898, 32–33.

46. Executive Committee Minutes, June 2, 1898.

47. Minutes of the Board of Trustees, June 26, 1901.

48. Gettleman, "College President on the Prairie," 144.

49. See ch. 5 herein.

50. Gettleman, "College President on the Prairie," 133–35.

51. *Student,* Feb. 1899, 242; May 2, 1912, 530–31.

52. *Knox Alumnus,* Feb., 1926, 86.

53. *Ibid.,* Feb. 26, 1926, 85.

54. He was a student at Union Theological Seminary and was graduated from Andover Seminary in 1880 ("Thomas McClelland," in Perry, ed., *History of Knox County,* 1:1127–28).

55. Minutes of the Board of Trustees, Dec. 9, 1911.

56. "The Darwin Centenary," *Student,* Feb. 25, 1909, 395–96.

57. Simonds, "Knox College—1892–1934," 4–7.

58. Knox College, *Fifty Year Club Bulletin,* June 1965, 27.

59. Webster, *Seventy-Five Significant Years,* 106–7.

60. Simonds, "Knox College," in Perry, ed., *History of Knox County,* 1:562–577.

61. Askew, "Liberal Arts College Encounters Intellectual Change," 256–57.

62. *Student,* Feb. 15, 1906, 308; Feb. 21, 1907, 333.

63. Lincoln was a trustee from 1897 to 1902; Lowden, from 1904 to 1923.

64. Simonds, "Knox College," in Perry, ed., *History of Knox County,* 1:575.

65. Swanson, "A History of Lombard College."

66. Minutes of the Board of Trustees, June 13, 1900; "Campus Improvements," *Gale,* 1901.

67. Simonds, "Knox College," in Perry, ed., *History of Knox County,* 1:575–76.

68. Minutes of the Board of Trustees, Oct. 16, 1914.

69. "Remarks of J. Finley. Board of Trustees, Knox College, June 3, 1916," Alumni File, MS, Knox College Library.

70. Minutes of the Board of Trustees, June 3, 1916.

71. Obituary of President McClelland, Galesburg *Republican Register,* Feb. 29, 1926.

72. Simonds, "Knox College—1892–1934," 6.

73. *Ibid.*

74. Minutes of the Faculty, Apr. 9, 1906. For example, in June 1914, five students were graduated *Magna cum Laude;* twenty students were graduated *cum Laude.* "General Honors" were voted to nine seniors, five juniors, six sophomores, and nine freshmen. "Special Honors" were voted to two students in biology, one in economics, five in English, one in German, eight in history, five in Latin, four in philosophy, and six in physics (Minutes of the Faculty, June 8, 1914).

75. Perry, ed., *History of Knox County,* 1:408.

76. Finley to Bateman, Dec. 1, 1892, Bateman Papers.

77. Professor Simonds as quoted in the *Student,* Feb. 17, 1910, 330.

78. *Student,* Feb. 10, 1898, 4.

79. *Ibid.,* Mar. 3, 1910, 370–71.

80. *Ibid.,* Feb. 10, 1910, 331.

81. *Gale,* 1904.

82. These were John W. Burgess, at Knox, 1869–71; Melville Anderson, 1881–86; Jeremiah Jenks, 1886–89.

83. An extreme example would be George Churchill, who may be regarded as the father of the public school system of Galesburg. He was a member of the city school board for thirteen years, and he was also city engineer for twenty-two years, on the library board for twenty-three years, on the park board for eight years, and was an alderman for two terms. He was president of the Mechanics Homestead and Loan Association from its organization in 1882 to his death in 1899.

84. W. E. Simonds, "Bryant's Day at Knox College," *The Dial*, Nov. 16, 1894, 301–2. In this same issue (p. 300) there is mention of J. H. Finley "of Knox College" as author of a special report on "The Public Treatment of Pauperism."

85. *Ibid.*, June 16, 1896, 348–49. An article by Simonds in the issue of July 1, 1899, 11–12, opens: "Continuing our annual midsummer survey of the drama of Chicago" and refers to the dates: June 16, 1896, July 16, 1897, July 1, 1898. See also the issue of Oct. 16, 1905, 230–31.

86. *Ibid.*, Nov. 16, 1906, where he reviewed a book on Whitman by Bliss Perry, with whom he had been a student companion at Strasbourg. See also the issue of June 16, 1909, 404–5. Perry provided the *Gale* an appreciative essay about "Professor Simonds" (*Gale Nineteen-Ten*, 7).

87. Melville Anderson and Alphonso Newcomer.

88. *Student*, Mar. 3, 1910, 370–71, featured a brief history of the Academy. The catalogue of 1889–90 (71–71) reaffirmed that the "paramount educational need of the West is a supply of well-organized and well-equipped Secondary Schools, or Academies." There was still talk of providing the Knox Academy a new building in 1893 (Galesburg *Republican Register*, Feb. 14, 1893).

89. Catalogue, for 1886–87, 26–27. The four schools approved at this time were the high schools in Peoria, Galesburg, and Princeton and Geneseo Collegiate Institute.

90. Simonds, "Knox College," in Perry, ed., *History of Knox County*, 1:575.

91. *Ibid.*, 576.

92. *Student*, May 5, 1910, 556.

93. Bronze tablet in the foyer of Central Congregational Church.

94. *Student*, May 5, 1910, 556–58.

95. The "Program Minutes" of both Adelphi and Gnothautii show that the theater was a recurring subject of debate.

96. At their business meetings on Dec. 5, 1860, and Jan. 9, 1862, the Adelphi voted to spend money for a "curtain" and for printed programs for their forthcoming "exhibition."

97. Warren, "Development of Theatre at Knox College."

98. Galesburg *Republican Register*, Mar. 18, 1882, 1, 5.

99. Warren, "Development of Theatre at Knox College."

100. See reference in the catalogue to the financial loss of Adelphi lecture

series because the Opera House had burned (catalogue, 1887–88, 38). Articles about the building or rebuilding of "Public Halls in Galesburg": Galesburg *Republican Register,* Christmas ed., 1885, 6; Jan. 1, 1887, 1; Sept. 22, 1888, 1; Nov. 29, 1890, 1. A Galesburg Literary and Dramatic Association was organized in 1874 (*ibid.,* Aug. 1, 1874, 1; Oct. 31, 1874, 6).

101. *Student,* Nov. 2, 1911, 132.

102. *Ibid.,* Jan. 18, 1912, 267–68; Jan. 27, 1912, 288–89; May 16, 1912, 5.

103. *Ibid.,* Jan. 27, 1912, 286–89.

104. *Ibid.,* Mar. 7, 1912, 391; Apr. 18, 1912, 477; May 2, 1912, 529–30.

105. Webster, *Seventy-Five Significant Years,* 177.

106. Katherine Simonds Wensberg, "W.E.S. Recalls the Prairie Poets," *Fifty Year Club Bulletin,* 31 (June 1972), 12–13.

107. Abby Merchant of Smith College and Mark W. Reed of Dartmouth and the MIT School of Architecture.

108. Opening article of the *Knox Student,* Nov. 1915.

109. *Student,* Jan. 11, 1916, 4; Jan. 18, 1916, 4; Mar. 7, 1916, 1; Mar. 14, 1916, 1; Apr. 14, 1916, 2.

110. Administrative Committee, Faculty Minutes, Mar. 14, 1916.

111. An address delivered by Jesse Crafton, then head of the dramatics department of the University of Kansas, during the Knox commencement of 1932, MS, Knox College Library.

112. *Student,* Mar. 2, 1915, 1; Apr. 13, 1915, 1.

113. Simonds, "Knox College—1892–1934."

114. Minutes of the Board of Trustees, June 13, 1912.

115. Simonds, "Knox College," in Perry, ed., *History of Knox County,* 1:576.

116. Webster, *Seventy-Five Significant Years,* 114.

117. Simonds, "Knox College," in Perry, ed., *History of Knox County,* 1:576.

118. *Ibid.;* catalogue for 1935–36, section on "Lectures."

CHAPTER X

... FOR DEMOCRACY, AT KNOX, 1914–24

In 1914 Dean William Simonds could share memories of student
years at Strasbourg with two colleagues at Knox, recollections of
the old dormered houses of that ancient city, of the horological
marvels measuring time in the cathedral, and of the great sculp-
tured arch of the main portal where Eve was carved in stone
carrying a stone apple and with toads and snakes crawling on her
back. That city is now at the border of Germany and France. In
August 1914 it was spelled Strassburg. The high Gothic nave of
the cathedral was the work of Germans building in a French tradition. "La Marseillaise" was composed and written in this city in
1792 by a captain of engineers. In 1870 the city became part of
the new German Empire. At its university Dean Simonds had done
his doctoral dissertation about an English poet of the sixteenth
century, Sir Thomas Wyatt, noted among other humanistic accomplishments for his translations of Italian sonnets.

One of Simonds's scholarly companions at this university was
Bliss Perry, who became a widely known member of the faculty at
Harvard. In 1909 he provided the *Gale* with an essay of appreciation of Professor Simonds. Perry noted that the stress put upon
philological studies had diminished during the past twenty years
and that the "emphasis upon the necessity of preparation in Germany had 'suffered some alteration.' " He continued, "Very likely,
if Simonds and other good men of his day had studied in Paris
rather than in Germany, American literary criticism would have
been enriched, and our knowledge of linguistic sources not essentially impoverished." Perry also recalled the nightingales "singing

in the Alsatian gardens" and how Simonds "had an eye for picking good restaurants in an unpromising street."[1]

There were at the commencement of 1914 nine teachers of the College and the Conservatory who had studied at Strassburg, or Heidelberg, or Halle-Wittenberg, or Marburg, or Leipzig, or Berlin.[2] On August 3, 1914, Germany declared war on France; a world war later numbered "I" had begun, and in ways most profound the lives of Knox students and teachers would never again be the same. Even memories and the understanding of history would be transformed.

Like the American economy in general, Knox College prospered while Europe learned how to wage what would be called total warfare. The College enrollment, which was at the number of 300 in 1910, had increased to 350 in September 1914 and then for the year 1916–17 grew to over 500. Though the war and the threats of American involvement were ever in the news, life at Knox went on rather much as usual: classes were met, studies done, contests held, theatricals presented, and parties enjoyed rather routinely, until the early spring of 1917. Events in February and March of that year, including German resumption of unrestricted submarine warfare, the breaking off of diplomatic relations with Germany by the United States, and America's arming of merchant ships, made it seem more likely that the United States would go to war. Some of the men at Knox became "anxious" for some kind of military training, and this the captain of the local national guard unit, Alfred E. Miller, agreed to give them. The first drill was held in the gymnasium on the night of March 20, 1917.[3] On that day President Woodrow Wilson's cabinet unanimously advised him that we should go to war. The next day he called Congress back into special session; by April 6, responding to his address urging a war to save democracy, both houses had passed resolutions declaring war.

About 150 Knox men were by now organized into two companies and a military band, drilling an hour and a half three afternoons a week. When Captain Miller and a national guard unit from Galesburg were ordered to camp in Texas, a local insurance man, Ron Wohlford, who had been a sergeant in the regular army took over the drilling at Knox. On May 8 he and many of the Knox men entered the officers' training camp at Fort Sheridan, near Chicago. They would become commissioned officers commanding the men who waited—to be drafted. As other men enlisted and went to other training camps, the two companies that had been drilling at Knox were combined into one, under the instruction of W. A. Barton, an officer who had formerly been military instructor in Abingdon at Hedding College.[4] When classes resumed in September 1917, the *Knox Student* reported that the College enrollment was down 28 percent from the previous year.[5]

In June 1917, on the recommendation of the faculty, the trustees established a department of military training. Two credits in "gymnasium work or military drill were to be required for graduation of all students," a policy that would persist for many years after the war. Military drill was expected of "all able bodied Freshmen and Sophomore men." It was hoped that an army officer, if necessary one who had retired, could be found to put in charge of this new department.[6] No one with such qualifications could be found in the fall, but two companies of Knox men practiced the fundamentals of close order drill and the manual of arms under student commanders, who, whenever possible, were assisted by local recruiting officers. In December, "due to a lack of an inside place to drill," this activity ceased until March, when Captain Miller again took over, having been retired from active service for physical disability.[7]

Meanwhile, week by week, some men were leaving for military service who otherwise might have been graduated with the classes of 1918, 1919, or 1920. By December the *Student* reported that at least seventy men had left.[8] By that time three faculty members also had enlisted. One was a football coach, Curtis Redden, who would become a lieutenant colonel in the famous Rainbow Division and die in January 1918 while serving in France.[9] Another, Ira Neifert, would return after the war to resume teaching chemistry and become a very influential member of the faculty during the next four decades.[10]

During this school year the curriculum also made adaptations to war needs. Some existing courses were modified to emphasize an interest in the war. Several new courses were introduced that might have some practical use in the war effort, civilian as well as military. These were: Food and the War, Conversational French, International Law, European Geography, and Analytic Mechanics.[11] However, the student publications for this year indicate that normal athletic, forensic, and social activities, while curtailed to some extent, were not interrupted.

How drastically war might at another time alter college life became apparent in the fall of 1918. All the men were now expected to live in the gymnasium, which became the barracks, and to eat in a common mess hall, built by the College. Further, to equip the campus for the realities of war, a bayonet run was erected, and trenches and shell holes were dug in the Knox "battlefield."[12] These actions were part of the program of the Student Army Training Corps (SATC), which had been established at Knox, one of about 500 such units on college and university campuses throughout our country. In the morning the men attended regular college classes and then went to chapel as usual, but the afternoon was committed to military training.[13] In connection with the SATC a course on War Aims was taught by various members of the faculty under the direction of Dr. Frederick Middlebush,[14] who had done graduate study at Paris, London, and the Hague. Even the women of the freshmen and sophomore physical education classes did military drill under the command of Dr. Lucius Elder, the English instructor who during the summer of 1918 had completed a "military course" at Fort Sheridan.[15]

Fortunately, the war ended about a year and a half after the United States had become directly involved. The armistice of November 11th immediately removed the necessity for and relaxed the rigor of the military training program. Four days before Christmas, after existing less than four months, the SATC was mustered out.[16] Moreover, it should be noted that the demands of war had not become so total that there were no men available to field a football team, a schedule of six games having been played that fall when the war ended.[17]

To commemorate the patriotic service of Knox alumni during this war, a flagpole with a large granite cube for its base was erected on the front campus in 1919. Each Memorial Day for many years classes were briefly suspended for a service at this site, remembering the 660 Knox men who had done their military duty in this war and recalling the sixteen men who had died and whose names were recorded in bronze.[18] Taps and other military rituals were performed by the men in the uniform of the Reserve Officers Training Corps (ROTC).

Immediately after the war units of the ROTC had been established at the universities and at some of the colleges in the United States, including Knox. Many of the freshmen and sophomores elected to enroll in military training instead of in physical education, as the faculty and the board had provided in 1917. Some of these men, as juniors and seniors, if accepted by the department of military science, would continue their military education under the direction of commissioned and noncommissioned officers detailed to Knox by the U.S. Army and would be commissioned as second lieutenants at commencement. For such students a considerable part of their college education had occurred in the military department. Its presence was much apparent; once a week all cadets wore uniforms to their classes all day, the juniors and seniors in the better-tailored suits becoming student officers; once a year a military ball was an important social event; in the spring there was an inspection with a grand review and the awarding of military prizes bestowed at the hands of coeds garbed in the purple and gold colors of Knox—they were called "sponsors." Often in good weather one could hear the band sounding while the cadets marched on the back campus athletic field. On the faculty there were a few who were disturbed by all this panoply of war, fearing that at worst it sanctioned a kind of deference to authority instead of independent scholarship, or that at least it was a vocational training not suited to the liberal arts. Undoubtedly the availability of this officers' training attracted some students to Knox, especially during the late 1930s, when, after less than a score of years, rumors of war and then war in Europe increased the likelihood that students would be called up for military service in a war even more total than the last one.[19]

The prevailing mood of the nation after World War I was spoken in the phrase "return to normalcy," which was pledged by Warren Gameliel Harding when he campaigned for the presidency of the United States in the fall of 1920; he was elected overwhelmingly. This very ordinary man, who was expected not to fret the country with novelties such as a League of Nations, had been nominated by the Republicans when the convention deadlocked between General Leonard Wood and the governor of Illinois, Frank O. Lowden, a Knox trustee whom the College had honored with a doctorate of laws in 1919. A comparable resolve to maintain what had been traditional before the war on the Knox campus

was apparent in 1921 in the publication of a *Campus Handbook*
by the YMCA and the YWCA. Each freshman received a copy at
the reception, which opened the academic year of 1921–22.[20]

These Christian associations had been providing such a sociable
at the beginning of each year for at least thirty-six years, for the
purpose of enabling the new students to become acquainted with
one another as well as with the old students.[21] It had by 1921
acquired the name "Pumphandle,"[22] because each student as he
came to the reception shook hands with those ahead of him and
then joined them in forming a spiraling line.

The *Campus Handbook* issued in the last week of September
1921 described the traditions that the "old students" held "dear."
An editorial in the *Student* that same week stated that it was "a
matter of the deepest concern to the student body, to the alumni,
to the faculty, and to all concerned that the customs and traditions
of Old Siwash be upheld and supported." Six of these traditions
were selected in this editorial for special attention as a test of a
student's loyalty to his alma mater. These were:

1. Every Freshman "man" should wear a green cap; every
   Freshman "girl" should wear a green ribbon "following the
   order by the upperclassmen."
2. "Rough Neck Week" should be observed in the spring. This
   tradition, like number one, it was noted, would be "enforced
   by violence in case of disobedience."
3. Knox students should touch their hats when they met members of the faculty on the street or campus.
4. When passing out of chapel, underclassmen should wait
   "until the class just preceding them has passed out."
5. Only "men" should root at athletic games. "Girls" might
   join in the songs but should not yell. Indeed "dates" were
   not favored at games because they might interfere with the
   rooting.
6. Students should honor a tradition of which the students were
   "most proud," that smoking was "voluntarily tabooed on
   the campus."[23]

That these traditions were thus emphasized in 1921 and that all
of them would be forgotten or ignored twenty-five years later
suggest some of the changes in cultural values and social mores

occurring in the nation as well as on the campus during that quarter century, a period that included the Great Depression and then a second total war.

The president of Knox in 1921 was, by Knox precedents, not traditional. Except for President John Finley, the men presiding over Knox affairs had done post-baccalaureate studies in theology. The graduate studies of President James Lukens McConaughy were in education. He was thoroughly an Ivy League product; he had been educated at a prestigious private academy, earned a B.A. at Yale, taught briefly at Bowdoin, acquired his doctorate in education at Columbia, and was professor of education at Dartmouth when the Knox trustees, after consultation with two Ivy League presidents, chose him in 1918 to preside at Knox. At the age of thirty-one, he was the youngest college president in the nation. Knox proved to be only one stage in the career of a young man intent on mounting ever higher rungs as a chief executive. He would leave Knox after six years to preside at Wesleyan in Connecticut and, then, in due time, he became the governor of that state.[24] Before he left Knox, McConaughy had become "governor" for Rotary of all downstate Illinois.

McConaughy, in his inaugural address, asserted that a "college that is not Christian is not a college at all. The administration of the college should be Christian, believing in the Christian doctrines of responsibility and the second chance. The faculty must be Christian in spirit and in their daily lives; the university may have a place for the professor who is an agnostic; the college certainly has not."[25] However, McConaughy's rhetoric about Christian training was vague as to how it would affect character development. He provided no theological definitions and affirmed no particular principles of piety. There certainly was no expression of the evangelical zeal with which the College had been founded, nor any expectation that patrons of the College would again tally the number of converts in the student body who could report redeeming individual religious experiences. It had been more than a decade since a local religious revival had received the special cooperation and prayers of the faculty and the public approbation of the president.[26] This had been in 1907 when first "Gypsy" Smith and then "Billy" Sunday had brought their rather considerable entertaining and evangelizing talents to Galesburg. Of "Billy"

Sunday (professional ballplayer become YMCA worker), it was reported that he converted a large "quantity" of students, even among a particularly "fast," or wicked, wine-tippling fraternity. "Among the young women his harvest was vast," so that the "unregenerate" despaired that they would find partners with whom to dance on the newly finished gymnasium floor, for "Billy" Sunday had forbidden dancing.[27]

To restore such old-time religion was not McConaughy's intention. He spoke proudly of how Knox was nonsectarian. He wanted members "of different denominations" to "learn" that we all worship the same God.[28] When he appointed a Jew for the first time to the Knox Faculty there was "only slight apprehension."[29] Dr. George Hunter, who was appointed chairman of the biology department in 1920, proved in 1925 to be the author of a textbook used by the John T. Scopes who was prosecuted in Tennessee for teaching evolution. The mood on the campus was pride, not apology.

About the time that McConaughy came under consideration for the Knox presidency, he had published an article in a widely known educational journal that raised the question "Have we an Educational Debt to Germany?" He noted: "In this day, when America is looking with searching eyes upon German influence in this country, it may be pertinent to inquire the sources of educational influence here, the exact types of schools and educational practices which we borrowed from Germany." He greatly deplored the ways in which our public schools had imitated those of Germany:

> the eight-year elementary school, and the institution for training teachers—the normal school. It seems fair today to indict Germany for many of the educational ills from which we are now suffering. . . . This eight-year elementary school . . . has brought about the problem of children leaving school at the completion of the grades, or the age of fourteen, a situation to Germany's liking, but incompatible with our ideas of a free, democratic education.

Similarly he strongly regretted:

> the aping of Germany as seen in our higher institutions of learning . . . the pernicious type of Ph.D. scholarship, too often resulting in useless research and soulless teaching; the insertion of a four year

college course between high schools and professional training; the lecture method of instruction, so wasteful of energy of both students and teachers.[30]

Though the war was over when he was inaugurated at Knox, McConaughy charged that Germany "hideously exemplified a nation of highly trained minds and of undeveloped, selfish characters." He cited the example of Germany in his defense of the integrity of a full, four-year liberal arts college curriculum against those who wanted to hurry students into vocational training by reducing colleges to junior colleges or by accepting college students into professional schools at the end of their sophomore year:

> Germany led the world in practical, vocational education; her pupils began in their early teens the specialized training for their professions. France, on the other hand, insisted on a general training first, and a postponement of specialization as long as possible; no student is admitted to her universities to begin his professional work until he has secured his bachelor's degree in a college. Which country should America copy?[31]

The patriotic answer, in 1919, was still pretty obvious: "Postponement of specialization as long as possible."

This apparently did not mean that courses preparing students for a vocation were to be eliminated from the curriculum. In fact the scope of such training greatly broadened under McConaughy's leadership, so that by 1925 the number of vocational courses had increased considerably. Whereas ten years earlier there had been only two courses in pedagogy, taught by the professor of philosophy, there was now an entire department of education with classes taught by President McConaughy, the professor of psychology, the city superintendent of schools, and the principal of the high school. Most striking was the number of courses offered in economics; where there had been one year courses on the "Phases of Business" before the war, there were during the last year of McConaughy's tenure courses in banking, insurance, marketing, sales and retailing, labor problems, corporation finance, principles of business administration, transportation, accounting, and advanced accounting. Apologists for this part of the curriculum emphasized that these courses were only electives and that the College still insisted on "standard courses in Latin, Greek, and

Mathematics," and other good "old fashioned ideas of scholarship."[32]

The one course in journalism offered in 1915 was augmented to six courses in 1925, all taught by the Knox alumnus who was also in charge of publicity and alumni relations. This vocation had indeed been one in which Knox men and women had long excelled. This history of the College has already examined the very special relation of Knox to *McClure's Magazine* and to the *American Magazine*. Knox alumnus, Eugene Field, it should be recalled, wrote the column "Sharps and Flats," for the Chicago *Daily News* which was favored reading for Knox student Edgar Lee Masters and Lombard student Carl Sandburg. George Fitch, who created Old Siwash, was a syndicated columnist who edited the Peoria *Transcript*. Other distinguished Knox alumni were involved in editing or publishing well-known magazines such as the *Nation, Review of Reviews, Public Opinion,* and *World's Work*. After McConaughy the next president of Knox would be Albert Britt, who edited *Outing*. Former Knox President, John H. Finley, would in 1926 become an editor for the New York *Times*. In the nineteenth century Knox men edited or published religious serials such as the *Sunday School Times* and denominational periodicals such as *Pilgrim Quarterly* and *Advance* (Congregational) and *Living Church* (Episcopalian). With their training in language at Knox and very likely with experience on the College magazines, they later directed vocational organs such as *Stockman, Packer, Electrical World, Commercial, Charities Record, Moving Picture Digest,* a *Normal Monthly* for Iowa, and a *Journal of Education* for the Pacific Northwest. Edgar Lee Masters's special friend, Edwin Reese, became editor of the magazine published by the Chicago Federation of Labor.[33]

At a time when journalism was still regarded as a male profession, three graduates from the Knox Female Seminary had earned distinction in this calling: Mary Allen West (class of 1855); Ellen Browning Scripps (class of 1859); Mary Frances ("Fanny") Bagby (class of 1872). When West became the first woman to be elected to public office in Knox County as superintendent of schools, she started the practice of providing a weekly section in a local newspaper to keep the public informed of what was being done in their schools. Later she became very active in the Woman's Christian

Temperance Union and editor of their magazine, the *Union Signal*. The Women's Press Association of Illinois elected her president in 1892.[34] Scripps was literary editor of the Detroit *Evening News*, served as its foreign correspondent, and with her brothers founded a very influential newspaper network.[35] Bagby became literary editor of the St. Louis *Chronicle*.[36] This role did not put her above less noble assignments, such as reporting on a murder case or on a fight between heavyweight boxers. The Galesburg *Republican Register* in December 1883 reprinted from the Chicago *Daily News* an account of her presence at the fight between Sullivan ("The Great John L.") and the Maori, Herbert Slade:

> The only lady present at the Sullivan slugging benefit in St. Louis was Miss Fannie M. Bagby, managing editor of the *Evening Chronicle* of that city. She occupied a seat in a box with several other newspaper folks and seemed to be deeply interested in the proceedings on the stage. Many people in the audience supposed she was Sullivan's wife.

After the fight she interviewed the defeated Slade:

> The charming young editress felt of his muscle and knuckles, and fired more questions at him in ten minutes than he could have answered in six months.

This story, coming from the Chicago *Daily News*, may be one of Eugene Field's practical jokes played on a friend, an entirely imaginary anecdote, but the Galesburg newspaper accepted it as straightforward reporting.[37]

Except in the Old South, Knox alumni edited, published, managed, and wrote for scores of newspapers whose names provide a veritable glossary of titles. Some revealed political leaning, as in *Whig, Free Democrat, Republican,* and *Independent.* The titles of some had classical allusions, as in *Mercury* and *Tribune.* Others used Latinate words such as *Transcript* or *Pantagraph.* Some simply called themselves *Record, News, Register, Journal,* or *Times.* Others more grandly entitled themselves *Herald, Graphic, Chronicle, Gazette, Gazetteer,* and *Nonpareil,* or used metaphors such as *Spectator, Hawkeye, Beacon,* or *Plain Dealer.* In these many ways the language and learning of Knox—distributed by other alumni from pulpit, platform, and podium—enlightened many thousands of newspaper columns.

Students were well aware and proud of the Knox tradition in journalism. In 1917 a professional journalistic fraternity, Sigma Delta Chi, was established at Knox; three years later an honorary journalistic fraternity for women, Theta Sigma Phi, received a charter.[38] It was not, however, until 1918 that a woman edited a major student publication at Knox. When school opened that year, the men were enlisted in the Student Army Training Corps for an unfinished war. The editor of the *Student* and of the *Gale* was a junior, Florence Merdian. Furthermore, the business managers were also women: Katherine Harrington, a senior for the *Student*, Dorothy Gordon, a junior, for the *Gale*.

A curiosity from the catalogue of 1924–25 was that from the entire course of studies pursued in the Knox Conservatory only eight credits would be accepted toward a degree in the College, and these had to be in the "theory" of music, not in "applied" music. Yet a student could also apply toward the Bachelor of Arts degree eight course credits in the "Coaching of Athletics." President McConaughy was a warm supporter of athletics. Athletic teams traveled greater distances than ever before, including trips to the East.[39] The director of athletics during most of his administration was Justin McCarthy Barry, who six decades later was one of the first men to be enrolled in the Naismith Basketball Hall of Fame.[40] Under his tutelage Knox teams in all sports were so consistently and so overwhelmingly victorious that many alumni from those years were never thereafter satisfied with Knox athletic performances.[41] Some influential New York alumni, however, such as Finley, Edward Caldwell, and Albert Britt, let McConaughy know that they were fearful that the president would allow certain zealots to "commercialize athletics" at Knox, and they objected to the fact that the head coach succeeding Barry received a higher salary than full professors. They criticized a scholarship plan that offered special financial inducements to athletes.[42] More important than any transient effect this president may have had on any athletic contests during his tenure at Knox was his leadership in organizing a Midwest Conference of the best colleges in Illinois, Iowa, Wisconsin, and Minnesota.[43] Not only did this mean that most of the athletic contests by Knox teams hereafter would be with colleges of its own calibre; it also established effective faculty oversight on athletic policies. Under the constitution of this Midwest Conference it was not the coaches but a commission of faculty representatives that made rules about schedules, eligibility, and recruitment. Basic changes in policy, furthermore, required the assent of the several faculties.

A faculty member in 1920 established what became the most highly prized athletic honor at Knox, the Hunter Trophy.[44] It is a prize carrying the name of the distinguished professor of biology, Dr. George Hunter, who donated the cup on which the winner's name has each year been inscribed. It is awarded to an athlete of "high academic standing" who excelled in two sports during his junior year. The first winner was Adolph "Ziggy" Hamblin; he was a young black man from Galesburg who discovered that in the classroom and on the athletic field, at least, he was an acceptable associate, if not elsewhere. And, on one occasion, when the operator of a movie house insisted that he take a seat in the gallery called "nigger heaven," his teammates walked out with him.[45]

The changes effected by McConaughy in the curriculum and in managing the internal affairs of the College occasioned considerable friction. He had come to Knox "with ideas of his own, confident of their value and insistent on their adoption." His "arbitrary" style of administration contrasted with the "quiet and rather unassertive" manner of his predecessor, who was often ready to defer to the "counsel of others." Faculty whose departments were affected by the curriculum changes desired by McConaughy resented "the disappearance of the good old democratic principle of unlimited discussion and rule of the majority." These characterizations of the president were made by Dean William Simonds, to whom fell the duty "of serving as a 'buffer' between disagreeing and unduly excited parties." After two or three years this tension moderated. For the faculty the president brought "the painfully inadequate salaries . . . up to a fair and comfortable level."[46]

A campaign for endowment brought $750,000 to the capital funds of Knox, at least "nominally," according to Simonds.[47] He meant, perhaps, that the campaign was declared a "success" even though certain funds not gathered during the stipulated times were counted in the total, a not uncommon practice then as later. Bequests from Edna Smith Brown (class of 1887) and John Burrows Brown (class of 1866, trustee since 1899) in 1920 brought the

College large tracts of land in the Illinois River Valley near Beardstown.[48] Knox thus, it was boasted, became the proprietor of a "vast and scattered estate, larger in extent than the landholdings of many great feudal proprietors" and "one of the greatest farmers in the United States," producing in a single season "60,000 bushels of corn and thousands of bushels of other staple products."[49] The business manager for these assets of the College was Kellogg McClelland, son of President Thomas McClelland, who had first served as business manager under his father (1912–14) and who became treasurer of the College in 1922, a role he retained until 1961. For many years one of his main concerns was oversight of large areas of the flood-threatened bottom land near Beardstown, which had been transformed into a drainage district.

Among the characteristics of the College that McConaughy had called for in his inaugural was that "social organizations" should be "democratic in ideals." He specifically stated that "young men and women may learn to take their share of responsibility for the welfare of the College" through participation in a "student council."[50] Such a council had existed at Knox since 1909, when each of the four classes elected a representative to meet with the social committe of the faculty to plan social activities. These representatives came to form a "self-constituted student council," which reached for broader control over student affairs.[51] At the time it was noted that in fact "student self-government" had already appeared in many phases of student life: "The Oratorical Association regulates, exclusive of faculty control, the oratorical contests of the College. The students alone manage the Literary societies and through the Student Stock Company the official publication of the College. The Athletic Association through its officers and managers, under faculty guidance, regulates athletics. The girls of Whiting Hall annually elect officers who manage many affairs which relate to the girls only, particularly those of a social nature."[52] The exact mode of student representation in the council would undergo many changes in the years to come. As organized in 1909–10 it comprised a president and secretary (both seniors), two other seniors, three juniors, two sophomores, and one freshman.[53] It would gradually replace the YMCA and the YWCA in its unifying concern with student affairs.

McConaughy used the student council to bring the traditional class fights under control;[54] they now became primarily a tug-of-war between sophomores and freshmen.[55]

"By and within itself"[56] in the spring of 1922 the council decided (after it had been "ordained by the Powers that Be"[57]) that the custom of "Roughneck Day" had "outlived its usefulness." This tradition had started in 1917 as the climax to "Rough Neck Week," during which men did not shave and wore old clothes and the women did not use face powder and wore short, or long, saggy and ragged skirts. The week culminated in the wearing of "outlandish costumes" on Friday to chapel services, at which the girls violated customary procedure by taking the seats always occupied by the men, thus forcing them to sit on the "north side of the great divide" that ran down the middle of Beecher Chapel. Students who refused to conform were threatened with being "chucked under the pump." These events were declared a "huge success" by the *Student*, which expressed the hope that this would become an annual affair.[58] With the student council in charge this "Rough Neck Week" was celebrated the next few years,[59] reaching a tumultuous climax in the second week of May 1921, when on Friday men came to class in pajamas, and most classes were broken up by irregular ringing of the Old Main bell. A piano was rolled out of the gym and played on the campus. At chapel there was only mockery, after which students paraded downtown to a movie theater. Two students who refused to be "uncouth" were in fact dunked in the horse trough on the public square.[60]

It was the following spring that the student council substituted for Rough Neck Day a more decorous "Flunk Day." To the surprise of all the faculty and students, except for the very few who were in on the secret plans, posters appeared on May 11, 1922, that called off classes. A jazz concert in chapel, a movie downtown, and a picnic in a park in Knoxville filled out the day.[61] Flunk Day did indeed become a tradition. The manner of celebrating would vary, but the essential element of springing a surprise holiday persisted, along with the nuisance to the faculty of students not preparing lessons in the premature anticipation of Flunk Day.

According to one of his warm admirers, President McConaughy had "at once" started a reorganization so as to effect a greater "democracy."[62] The opportunity to do this was much improved by the gift of $100,000 in 1919 from Carrie Kay Robbins Seymour, who had been matron in the Female Seminary in 1893–94.[63] This money was to be used to build a men's dormitory in memory of her husband, Lyman Kay Seymour,[64] who had attended Knox from 1882 to 1885 and had become a prosperous farmer and banker near Quincy. Since the 1870s, when Knox for a time admitted men as boarders in the Female Seminary, the College had made no special provision for the feeding of male students. The situation was described in 1912 by an unhappy student as follows:

> One of the most trying things with which the non-resident man at Knox has to deal is the board situation. By the time a man has finished his college course he has experienced everything from a short order lunch counter or a Phila Quita Gapa hash house, where the rule is to grab a bite and run, to a hotel or more expensive boarding place, where he meets business and professional men instead of college students. . . . If he had any table etiquette upon coming to college he immediately begins to forget it.
>
> A rough count shows there to be about 140 men in the institution exclusive of the conservatory. Approximately 35 of these live in Galesburg. Twenty more work for their board by waiting on tables, etc. Of the eighty-five that are left, thirty-five live in the fraternity houses, leaving approximately fifty who are boarding in town. This last group are paying from three-fifty to five dollars a week for their board. . . . The fraternity houses in Galesburg furnish board for about $4.00 a week to a table of ten or a dozen.[65]

In arguing for a college commons equipped and run by the College this student not only stated that the students would get good board at no greater cost, but he also emphasized that the men would get "that fellowship with the men of the College which is one of the greatest assets of college life and which is best attained around the festive board." A "Commons" run by the College "would fill a great need for uniting the men of the College. The Y.M.C.A. this year has done much in that respect, but if supplemented by something that would tend to bring the men together still more its efforts would be vastly more effective."[66]

Not until after World War I was any concerted effort made to deal with the very real power of the fraternities in campus affairs so as to create better unity with the College in general.

McConaughy found that the fraternity houses were widely scattered, two of them nearly a mile from the campus. The trustees in 1907 had voted that "no portion of the campus be devoted to chapter houses."[67]

One of the early actions of the board after McConaughy began to preside was to adopt a proposal that on "the matter of the men's dormitory" that was being planned, no student should in the future "be allowed to board in fraternity houses and that no freshman be allowed to room in fraternity houses." The trustees also approved the policy that "fraternity houses should be located as near the college as practicable."[68] This policy was implemented when Lyman K. Seymour Hall was completed in 1920. As the "Greek" men joined the "barbarians" in the "Commons," "the table sittings were arranged in such a way that all men of the College were enabled to become acquainted." The alumni-secretary, a member of the class of 1919 and of Beta Theta Pi, commented: "It was virtually the first time that a college had put all the men on a plane of equality by a single reform."[69]

For the fraternities the College acquired land near the campus and helped them financially to occupy sites in the immediate vicinity. Two of them were assisted in building new, attractive chapter houses. The administration agreed that each fraternity would be allowed to serve two meals each week in its house, but since the brothers would eat their "regular meals" at the College Commons, the newly built houses had only limited dining and kitchen facilities.[70]

At the same time McConaughy strove "for better democratic principles for the life of the girls." They had never had chapter houses and mostly lived in Whiting Hall. Rushing was scheduled earlier in the year with the expectation that this would "put less emphasis on sorority life." Sorority membership became less exclusive with the organization of two new local organizations. For both sororities and fraternities the president used his influence to control expenses.[71]

It is quite probable that the ultimate effect of these changes, after McConaughy returned to the East in 1925, was to strengthen the hold of fraternities and sororities on student affairs. His successor, Albert Britt, early in his administration, tried to establish the policy that no freshmen would be pledged during their first year in the College, but by June 1932 he admitted to the trustees that this policy met with much "criticism and opposition from the student body, ... creating more friction than" could "be justified by any good results," and the restriction was removed.[72] Meanwhile, in October 1928, the trustees voted that those fraternities that so desired should be permitted "to establish dining rooms in their houses for their members."[73] When the College celebrated its centennial in 1937, there were thirteen fraternities and sororities on the campus. Their rushing, pledging, and hell week for initiates and their chapter parties, coordinated by an Inter-Fraternity Council and a Pan-Hellenic Association, were conceded high priority in College schedules. An organization of non-fraternity men, called "Union," comprised a feeble minority. As members of their brotherhoods, the "Greeks" fostered acts of snobbery and racism and exhibited anti-intellectual attitudes that many as individuals would have condemned. Though often embarrassed and irritated by fraternity activities, members of the faculty did not overtly express discontent. Even those who were deeply offended assumed that fraternities and sororities had become so deeply entrenched in the College traditions, in the loyalties of alumni, and in influence on the Board of Trustees that they had to be tolerated.[74] Seymour Hall, which once had been a symbol of democratic reform, did become the primary social center for both students and faculty, for student parties and for festivities on Founders Day, homecoming, and commencement.[75] It can hardly be said, however, that it eradicated the "breeding" of separate "group" spirits at the "various fraternity houses," which was the hope of the student who described the formal opening of Seymour Hall in January 1921, when Mrs. Seymour lighted the first fire in the great fireplace of the large parlor where students might get together.[76]

During the flush times of the mid-1920s optimistic schemes about a greater Knox seemed sensible. The College enrollment, which had exceeded 500 for the first time just before the entry of the United States into World War I, reached 600 in 1921 and 656 during 1925–26. President McConaughy and the trustees, working toward a Campus Plan, purchased property adjacent to the College grounds.[77] Henry M. Seymour, class of 1884, in 1920 (only about four months after Knox received the gift for the men's dormitory built in honor of his brother, Lyman) promised a library building.[78]

In the fall of 1924 Wesleyan University of Connecticut made a flattering offer of its presidency to McConaughy. He offered to remain at Knox until the end of the school year, but his resignation "was accepted to take effect immediately—at mid year." His relations with the board, particularly over financial policies, had not been "altogether harmonious." According to Dean Simonds, the executive committee, in which local trustees figured strongly, resented his "attitude," and in the minds of some he "left an unpleasant feeling towards him." Though the "critical attitude of the Faculty" had "moderated somewhat,"[79] after he had gone he was hardly ever spoken of when his former colleagues reminisced about the past.[80]

Dr. Charles E. McKinley, a trustee since 1918, was chosen to serve as acting-president. He was the pastor of Central Congregational Church, which had built the imposing Romanesque edifice on the public square, direct successor on that site to the first church built by the Galesburg-Knox colony.[81]

NOTES

1. Bliss Perry, "Professor Simonds," *Gale Nineteen Ten,* 7–8.
2. Catalogue for academic year 1913–14, *passim.*
3. The 1919 *Gale,* 27.
4. *Ibid.*
5. *Student,* Sept. 27, 1917, 1.
6. Trustees' Minutes, June 11, 1917.
7. The 1919 *Gale,* 27; *Student,* Oct. 4, 1917, 1; Nov. 16, 1917, 1.
8. *Ibid.,* Dec. 21, 1917, 1, 6.
9. *Ibid.;* the 1920 *Gale,* 21.
10. The third was Robert E. Williams, who taught public speaking in 1916–17 and returned for one year in 1919–20.
11. Catalogue for 1917–18, 50.
12. See pictures in the 1920 *Gale,* 27, 35.
13. *Student,* Oct. 4, 1918, 1; Oct. 11, 1918, 1.
14. Catalogue for 1918–19, 33.
15. *Student,* Sept. 27, 1918, 1.
16. The 1920 *Gale,* 26.
17. *Ibid.,* section on "Athletics."
18. Their military careers are described in *ibid.,* 19–24.

19. Recollections of the author.

20. *Student*, Oct. 3, 1921, 2.

21. Catalogue for 1885–86, 37.

22. *Student*, Oct. 3, 1921, 2.

23. *Ibid.*, Oct. 3, 1921, 4. An editorial in the *Student* (Feb. 14, 1919, 2) protested against the rule that women should not yell at games. He could find no other school where this "antiquated" custom prevailed.

24. Askew, "Liberal Arts College Encounters Intellectual Change," 279–81.

25. *The Inauguration of James Lukens McConaughy Ninth President of Knox College* in *Knox College Bulletin*, New Series, 13, no. 10, n.p.

26. Faculty Minutes, Jan. 21, 1907; Askew, "Liberal Arts College Encounters Intellectual Change," 273–74.

27. Corbin, "Small College Versus the University," 7–8, 28–29.

28. *Inauguration of James Lukens McConaughy*, address by President McConaughy.

29. Askew, "Liberal Arts College Encounters Intellectual Change," 285.

30. McConaughy, "Have we an educational debt to Germany?," 361–76 *passim*.

31. *Inauguration of James Lukens McConaughy*, address by President McConaughy, n.p.

32. John M. Baker, class of 1919, director of publicity, a press release, Oct. 18, 1925, on the occasion of the announcement that McConaughy would become president of Wesleyan in Connecticut (MS, Knox College Library).

33. These names occur in a list of Knox journalists that has been compiled by the author and that is on deposit in the College Archives.

34. Galesburg *Republican Register*, Jan. 23, 1892, 3.

35. Ellen Browning Scripps is the subject of an essay in the *DAB*. Knox references to her career: *Student*, Nov. 1878, 17; catalogue, 1883, 77; *Pantheon*, 1888, 125–26.

36. *Coup D'Etat*, Feb. 1882, 83.

37. Galesburg *Republican Register*, Dec. 8, 1883, 6.

38. "Knox in Journalism," *Knox Alumnus*, Jan.-Feb. 1922, 192–93.

39. Baker, press release.

40. Dean, "Justin 'Sam' McCarthy Barry Named to Hall of Fame," 33–34.

41. During his four year tenure at Knox "the four major sports teams won a total of 102 games, while losing 49 and tying 2." For his recruiting and promotional tactics, see *ibid*.

42. Edward Caldwell to McConaughy, Apr. 23, 1923, McConaughy to Caldwell, Apr. 26, 1923, Albert Britt to A. C. Rearick, May 1, 1923, Rearick to Caldwell, May 2, 1923, Caldwell to McConaughy, May 29, 1923, McConaughy to Caldwell, May 31, 1923, McConaughy file.

43. Baker, press release; Dean, "James Lukens McConaughy, Ninth President of Knox College," 45–46.

44. *Student*, Jan. 14, 1921, 1.

45. Related to the author.

46. Simonds, "Knox College—1892–1934," 7–10.

47. *Ibid.*, 10.

48. *Knox Fifty Year Club Bulletin,* 7 (June 1952), 18.

49. Baker, press release.

50. *Inauguration of James Lukens McConaughy,* n.p.

51. *Student,* Jan. 21, 1909, 290.

52. *Ibid.,* Feb. 4, 1909, 290.

53. The 1911 *Gale,* 25. The constitution of the student council as revised in 1919 gave the council fifteen members. One was elected from the Conservatory. The others were elected by classes in the College with considerable advantage to upper classmen and some preference to men. *Student,* Feb. 21, 1919, 3; Mar. 3, 1919, 5.

54. Baker, press release.

55. The 1922 *Gale,* 37; the 1923 *Gale,* 174.

56. *Student,* May 16, 1922, 2.

57. The 1924 *Gale,* 165.

58. *Student,* Nov. 2, 1917, 2, 4.

59. *Ibid.,* Mar. 28, 1919, 1; May 7, 1921, 5; May 21, 1920, 5.

60. *Ibid.,* May 13, 1921, 1, 8.

61. *Ibid.,* May 6, 1922, 1, 3.

62. Baker, press release, 1.

63. Catalogue for 1893–94, 7.

64. The gift from Mrs. Seymour was to be added to the $20,000 left by Lyman K. Seymour's will for a men's dormitory (*Student,* Oct. 24, 1919, 1).

65. *Student,* May 9, 1912, 530–31.

66. *Ibid.*

67. Trustees Minutes, June 12, 1907.

68. *Ibid.,* Dec. 14, 1918. This was a specially called meeting (*Student,* Dec. 20, 1918, 1).

69. Baker, press release. The leading article of the *Student,* Oct. 25, 1924, reported that McConaughy was to leave Knox. The reporter stated that "in student eyes the most important" of "many forward steps" occurring during his administration was the "centering of fraternity houses near the campus where the men may all eat at Seymour Hall."

70. Baker, press release; *Student,* Dec. 12, 1919, 1.

71. Baker, press release.

72. Trustees Minutes, June 6, 1932.

73. *Ibid.,* Oct. 19, 1928.

74. Recollections of the author. President Albert Britt, 1925–36, in a postmortem read to a session of the North Central Associaiton, made these comments on fraternities: "Another one of the sideshows over which administrators and faculties labor, about which the trustees worry and for or against which alumni fulminate, is something that is euphemistically called the social program. ... It is not necessary to live through many rushing seasons or hell weeks on a college campus to begin to entertain serious doubts about the extent to which our social organizations train young men and young women

in brotherly or sisterly love and concord. In many cases the college has helped the fraternity to finance a new chapter house in the naively blissful idea that a fraternity house was a suitable investment for college funds. Now the fraternity and the college are attempting to live together effectively, the college providing a social chairman or a dean of men or some other individual whose purpose it is to coordinate to a common end activities that to the unprejudiced observer seem directed to opposite points of the compass." Referring to the scholarship contests among fraternities and sororities on some campuses, Dr. Britt commented: "There is something irresistibly amusing in the very idea of a scholarship competition which becomes ironically tragic on discovering, as we usually do, that the competition is not between A's and B's but between D's and F's. In other words, the scholarship competition, of which the fraternity magazines make so much, is in reality not a test of excellence but of safe mediocrity. If this be scholarship, God save the American college, because nobody else can." Albert Britt, "Eleven Years a College President."

75. Dean, "James Lukens McConaughy, Ninth President of Knox College," 45–46.

76. *Student,* Jan. 7, 1921, 1.

77. Dean, "James Lukens McConaughy, Ninth President of Knox College," 45–46.

78. *Student,* Feb. 13, 1920, 1.

79. Simonds "Knox College—1892–1934"; Trustees Minutes, Oct. 25, 1924.

80. Recollections of the author.

81. Trustees Minutes, Feb. 17, 1925.

CHAPTER XI

THROUGH ADVERSITY TO CELEBRATION
1924–37

At the first session of the board with a new president, on November 20, 1925, a woman was for the first time chosen to be a trustee. She was Janet Greig Post of Chicago, class of 1894, member of the faculty from 1896 to 1902, and recipient of an honorary degree in 1919. Previous to 1919 only eight women had received such recognition from Knox, while 142 such degrees had been awarded to men.[1] The honorary master of arts bestowed on Post may be regarded as one of the signs of a broadening appreciation of the roles of women in American life. In 1920, for example, Knox for the first time granted an honorary degree to a woman who had no special connection to Knox (such as being a former student or faculty member). This was Louise deKoven Bowen, a Chicago social worker associated with Hull-House. Post, who was a leader among the women of Chicago in philanthropic and civic affairs, was familiar with Bowen's work. Indeed, Post had been appointed to the committee of the national YWCA to help select women during World War I for canteen duty overseas.[2] During James McConaughy's tenure as president ten women received honorary degrees, more than doubling the total of those given. These were all, however, at the level of the master's degree. In 1929 what was only the third doctorate given to a woman by Knox was awarded to Mary Margaret Bartelme, lawyer and judge in the juvenile court and circuit court in Chicago.[3] During the presidency of McConaughy's successor seven honorary doctorates were given to women in eleven years. The commencement of 1932 was particularly notable, when three of the four doctoral degrees went to women. One of these was Ella McBride Rainey, class of 1880. Her husband, Henry T. Rainey, who attended Knox from 1878 to 1881, would be reelected the next fall to the House of Representatives and then serve as Speaker, helping Franklin D. Roosevelt to implement the New Deal.

To succeed McConaughy, the trustees chose Albert Britt,[4] one of the group of distinguished Knox alumni in New York City who followed Knox affairs rather closely. Some of the trustees had reservations about his being able at the age of fifty-one to master an entirely new vocation. Certainly as compared to his predecessor, a professional educator, Britt would begin as an amateur. Unlike McConaughy, however, he was one of Knox's own. Though sometimes perceived as an easterner he had in fact come to Knox from a small town, Utah, only about a dozen miles northwest of the campus. He spent seven years in the Knox Academy and College, being graduated in 1898. He was one of the numerous alumni that S. S. McClure beckoned to New York by the prospect of a journalistic career, and in that vocation Britt's links to Knox held fast. After serving for a time as editor of *Public Opinion,* he became associated with Thomas Blodgett (class of '99) in the publication of *Outing, Yachting,* and *All Outdoors.* Their close friendship had already been apparent during Britt's senior year at Knox, when he was editor of the *Student* and Blodgett was the business manager.[5]

When Britt came back to the campus as president, there were many reminders of his own days as a student. Post, newly elected to the board, had been a College student when Britt was in the Academy and a faculty member when he was a senior in the College. The venerable professor of German, Thomas Willard, lived in retirement in Galesburg; his daughter Florence Willard was an assistant professor of French. During Britt's first five years as president, the dean was William E. Simonds, who had been his teacher of literature thirty years earlier. William Bentley and John Winter Thompson were still teaching in the Conservatory.

Much of what Britt found to be familiar at his alma mater was, however, failing—fading remnants of the "gay" 1890s that did not fit into the "roaring" 1920s. The Gnothautii, of which Britt had been president, did not bother to organize in 1926; the Adelphi came to an end the next year after eighty-four years. Oratory, which had been their prime concern and pride, ceased as a student activity. The last prize contest in this art occurred in 1928, and at the commencement of that year, for the first time, no student appeared on the program as a speaker for the graduates. Debaters still contested with teams from other colleges, as they did when Britt had been on a Knox team, but they now rarely attracted audiences of any size, partly because the debaters were trained to make technical points that impressed the judges, rather than to make a persuasive impression upon an audience, as was once the case when one's peers in the weekly meetings of Adelphi and Gnothautii voted on who had proved his proposition. In the public speaking department it was now dramatics that was most popular and prestigious.

The YMCA became inactive in 1927. Britt remarked to a colleague on the faculty that this club, in which he had been active as a student, had outlived its usefulness.[6] Some friends of the College in Galesburg felt that during Britt's presidency the "standing of Knox as a Christian college ... suffered." It was noted after his arrival that in *Who's Who* he was labeled as a Unitarian, and though he resumed a connection with a Congregational church to which he belonged as a student, there lingered a fear that at Knox there was a "lack of religious leadership on the part of the administration."[7] Chapel still met in Beecher Chapel three times a week; the women still were separated from the men by a waist-high partition down the central section of pews. The organ was played; the doxology sung; the Lord's Prayer repeated; but the brief program that followed was in content rarely sacred and sometimes quite worldly.[8] The historical association of Knox with founders who were Congregationalists and Presbyterians was acknowledged by staging commencement in Central Church at the public square, where the original colony church had stood, and by conducting a baccalaureate service in the Presbyterian Church on the preceding Sunday. Britt regularly was the speaker at this service, but what he spoke was more appropriately called an "address" than a "sermon." Though his speech to the seniors in June 1927 began with a familiar quotation from the Apostle Paul about completing the "course,"[9] his speech of June 1936 was a charming elaboration of a well-known aphorism, "Knowledge is Power," which Britt remembered from his boyhood copybook by Platt R. Spencer.[10]

John Huston Finley. Knox B.A., 1887; Johns Hopkins University Ph.D.; president of Knox College, 1892-99; eventually editor-in-chief of the New York *Times*.

President William McKinley spoke at the anniversary of the Lincoln-Douglas debate in Galesburg, 1899.

William Howard Taft spoke at this anniversary of the Lincoln-Douglas debate, 1908.

Janet Greig Post, at the west portal of Old Main; the renovation of this building for the Centenary in 1937 was in large part due to her efforts.

Carl Sandburg recited his "Ode" to Old Main at the rededication of the
building during the Centenary of 1937.

The way to Knox College.

Knox had departed far from the kind of evangelical orthodoxy which after sixty-eight years still prevailed in Illinois at Wheaton College, from the time President Jonathan Blanchard had gone there after he was forced out of the presidency of Knox in 1857, and where his son, Charles, had perpetuated his father's religious convictions. A comparison between the two colleges was made in a doctoral dissertation partly based on interviews with persons who were at Knox during Britt's time as president. If judged by the conservative standards of Wheaton, the appointment of Britt as president represented a "milestone in the religious history of Knox." He and the faculty "were committed to the great human-istic values of the Judeo-Christian tradition, but as a major force in setting educational goals, the evangelical Christianity of the school's founders and early professors lived on only in the memory of the elderly alumni."[11] This transformation was not effected by Britt but rather exemplified by him; it was the consequence of "successive periods of gradual change" in which Knox had moved "from the orthodox cosmopolitanism of Gulliver, to the loosely-defined evangelicism of Bateman, to the acceptance of new ideas under Finley, to the candid liberalism of McClelland, to open-minded freedom under McConaughy and Britt."[12]

A kind of apostolic succession, quite reverently, was suggested by a photograph taken of Britt with the right hand of John H. Finley upon his shoulder, just as Newton Bateman had placed upon the shoulder of Finley, then the very young college president, the hand that was said to be the last that Abraham Lincoln had clasped while he stood on the rear platform of the train that started his trip from Springfield to Washington, never to return. Soon after Britt assumed leadership of Knox, plans were begun to celebrate the seventieth anniversary of the Lincoln-Douglas debate in Galesburg in 1928. Previous commemorations had relied prin-cipally on the presence of prominent politicians. The renewal of the Galesburg debate in 1928 was more literary in quality. On the evenings of October 5 and 6, the play *Abraham Lincoln* by John Drinkwater was presented in the Knox theater by students sup-porting Frank McGlynn in the title role. McGlynn had become famous in theatrical circles for his performances in this play, which had an extensive run from 1919 to 1923; he had carefully studied the character of Lincoln, to whom he had an amazing physical resemblance.[13] For the pageant on October 7, the actual anniversary date, McGlynn again acted the part of Lincoln, as a parade moved from the site of the home where Lincoln had slept overnight on October 6, 1858, to the east door of Old Main. Among the many hundreds who had gathered there were numerous collectors of Lincolniana, scholars, and biographers of Lincoln.[14]

Some of these distinguished students of Lincoln's life participated in the commemorative program. One of the speakers, Emanuel Hertz, would make a gift of 3,500 Lincoln items to the Knox Library. Of them all, the biographer that would be best remembered when the 100th anniversary was celebrated was the native son of Galesburg, Carl Sandburg. His two volume *Prairie Years,* published in 1926, was the beginning of his six-volume *magnum opus* about Lincoln, which would be completed in 1939 and win a Pulitzer Prize. In his hometown of Galesburg, in 1928, he was, however, for many a prophet without honor—folk singer, rebel poet, political radical. In making Sandburg a doctor of literature on this occasion, Knox conferred the highest honor on an alumnus of Lombard College who dropped out just short of completing his baccalaureate. President Britt, introducing Sandburg, placed the poet squarely back in the neighborhood where he had been born and reared, by reading from the *Prairie Years* these lines: "Twenty thousand people sat and stood listening. They had come from the bank of the Cedar Fork Creek, the Spoon River, the Illinois, the Rock and Mississippi rivers, with hands toughened on the plow handles, legs with hard-bunched muscles from tramping the clods behind a plow team, with ruddy and wind-bitten faces. They were of the earth; they could stand the raw winds of the earth as long as any two lawyers wished to speak to them. What if one cow-milking was missed or the hogs had to root for themselves for a day?"[15] Sandburg spoke in words that anticipated the poetic affirmation of democracy that he would make in *The People, Yes* in 1936:

> Three great actors or human forces took part in the Lincoln-Douglas debates. The orators, Lincoln and Douglas, were two of the actors in the drama. The third was the People. They came in the cold and almost frozen rain of a raw October day to stand and listen three hours to the speakers of the day. That crowd of 20,000 was an instrument, a factor in history, that the minds and tongues

of the orators tried to control. In seven years both of the great orators were dead. But the people go on and on. Perhaps a thousand years from now there will be a millenial celebration of the event of seventy years ago on this spot. The very words of all great orators testify and cry that while the orators turn to dust the People go on and on.[16]

The folding chairs were stacked away and the platform again dismantled and hauled off. But already there were plans for an even grander celebration, to occur when Knox completed its 100th year. On February 15, 1927, the Board of Trustees adopted proposals for a Centenary Fund of $5 million to be raised by Founders Day of 1937. This fund was intended first to bring Knox "up to our present needs in a degree not true as yet of any college west of the Alleghenies" and then "to keep pace with the natural growth of student population and the diversifying of our desires and activities."[17] With some of this money appropriate attention could be given to the three College buildings that by 1937 would be eighty years old: Beecher Chapel, Whiting Hall, and Old Main. The last of these was to be restored, but there was considerable uncertainty about the future of the other two. At the least Beecher Chapel would require temporary refurbishing. Possibly Whiting Hall might become part of a quadrangle erected in that block beyond the county courthouse. There certainly would be a new theater and, it was hoped, a college union, and more dormitories for men, perhaps a faculty club. Of course, there would be extended fields for the sports. More territory would be needed for the campus. After all these physical improvements, there still ought to be left for endowment $3,250,000.[18] It should then be possible to overcome the salary disadvantage that caused Knox to lose some of its best teachers, such as Dr. George Hunter.[19] Such heady optimism also characterized the national mood two and a half years before the Crash.

The construction of a new library, which Henry M. Seymour had promised in 1920, was underway during the fall of 1926. It would be a gift from Seymour in the most literal sense, for he selected the architect, received the bids for construction, and hired the contractor. The walls were built of limestone quarried in a gorge on Fall Creek, which passed through Seymour's land near Payson, Illinois. When it was finished, he turned the building over to the College, and the handsome Tudor Gothic structure was dedicated on Founders Day of 1928.[20] The library collection, which had grown in ten years from slightly more than 5,000 volumes to about 16,000,[21] was carried from the utterly inadequate quarters in the central section of Alumni Hall to the new building, and Dr. Lucius Elder reported a tripling of the student attendance at this new educational facility, noting triumphantly as a teacher of philosophy and literature: "Two hundred of our students are known as constant readers."[22]

The quality of the library collection owed much to the prudential management of its growth by Dr. Elder. From time to time it was enhanced by the special interests of alumni such as Edward Caldwell (creator of the Finley Collection on the history and romance of the Old Northwest) or Lysander Cassidy (class of 1889) and Elizabeth Cassidy (class of 1891), who endowed a collection on international relations and world peace.[23] By the time Knox was at its centennial the books in its library numbered nearly 45,000.[24] Earnest Calkins, aficionado of good printing and fine bookmaking, upon his return to Galesburg to research a history of his hometown and his alma mater, found the Henry M. Seymour Library the most pleasant place in the city.[25]

The space in Alumni Hall vacated by the library became a new theater that was opened on March 31, 1928. This area had originally been built as an auditorium but abandoned because of intolerably bad acoustics. To remedy this problem the width of the area was now narrowed and reshaped with echo-absorbing wall board, outward from the stage like a fan. In the rounded wall at the back of the stage was a cyclorama to use for exterior sets; it was given by Otto Harbach, class of 1895, playwright and lyricist for musical plays. It was a sign of the effect of competition from movies that in the storage space for this new theater, which would seat 650 persons, were kept the two sets bought in 1927 when a theatrical company presenting *What Price Glory* at the theater downtown had to abandon its tour.[26] Thus the presentation at Knox of legitimate drama acquired a special significance.

Further enrichment of the experience of the Knox students came from the philanthropy of William L. Honnold, who had attended the Knox Academy briefly in 1886–87 and received the degree of L.L.D. from the College forty years later. After training as a mining engineer in Michigan, prospecting for gold in California, and working as an engineer in Mexico, he became associated with an English syndicate and subsequently made a fortune from gold and diamonds in South Africa. In March 1928 it was announced that he had established the "William L. Honnold Lectureship Foundation" for the purpose of bringing to Knox "distinguished visitors" who were to be in residence for a period of six weeks. They would not only lecture in a formal way but also be available for conversations with students and faculty members in "personal conferences or discussions in small groups." It was intended that the lecturers were to be "chosen as far as possible from active professions and pursuits of a non-academic character."[27]

The first Honnold Lecturer, as intended, was indeed a "person of note" who had had "a large part in the activities of the outside world." She was Ida M. Tarbell, who came to Knox early in November 1928 and until the Christmas recess lived in Whiting Hall; she was "an active and interested participant in the college."[28] She was hardly a stranger to many Knox alumni, for she had been a writer on the staff of *McClure's Magazine* and in 1909 had been the first woman to receive an honorary doctorate from Knox College.[29] A similar connection with *McClure's Magazine* was apparent in the career of Will Irwin, the third Honnold Lecturer.[30] Following the stipulation originally made in this lectureship, the visitors did make their home on the Knox campus for an extended period of time, though the critic and poet, Louis Untermeyer, in 1937 was able to do so only for three weeks.[31]

Though the Honnold program discriminated against use of professional scholars, there was a significant humanistic bias in the fellowship that Honnold established at Knox in 1929. This award to a graduate "for advanced work either in America or abroad" made this important distinction, that "preference will be given to candidates preparing for scholarly work, although candidates headed for the learned professions such as law, medicine, and engineering, if sufficiently outstanding in qualifications and attitudes and in need of assistance, may be placed on equal footing with those preparing for scholarly careers."[32]

The amount of the stipend was to be "governed largely by the plans and needs of the student." With so generous an arrangement, the first two recipients of the fellowship both went abroad to the University of Oxford where each of them earned the degree of B. Litt.[33] Earnest Emmanuel Sandeen, who was the first fellow, was the son of the custodian of the College gymnasium; his first language was Swedish.[34] He would one day receive an Alumni Achievement Award from Knox for his accomplishments in literature, as a poet and teacher at Notre Dame University. The second fellow, Mary McEldowney, would also receive an Alumni Achievement Award and later become an influential member of the Board of Trustees.

At homecoming 1929 the boom times that were reflected by the philanthropy of William Honnold, by the building of the library, and by the providing of a new theater, all since Britt had become president, were about to end abruptly. In his annual report to the trustees for the year 1928–29 President Britt alluded to the fact that in the agricultural regions of the South and West the hard times of the 1920s had "reached a climax and many families" had "found their reserves exhausted and themselves under the lowest possible level."[35] He referred to the competition of the new junior colleges. He noted that there was a slackening in general of college attendance and that at Knox, in particular, the size of the freshman class had been falling off, possibly because of more selective admissions requirements (though Knox at that time had no standard of reference such as the College Entrance Examination for comparing the scholastic qualities of entering classes). President Britt reported that during the past year the College had "worked more intensely than ever before to find through … alumni teachers the names of promising students, particularly in cities and states remote from Galesburg" and had sought to interest such students in Knox. He hoped thus to give Knox "a wider base."[36]

It was true that Knox was still overwhelmingly an Illinois school. The data compiled by James A. Campbell, registrar, for the years 1926 to 1930 (while the enrollment was declining from 646 to 525) showed that, consistently, all but 10 percent of the students came from Illinois and that 25 percent of them (or more) came from Galesburg.[37] One-third of them, during Britt's first year as president, came from small towns within seventy-five miles of the Knox campus,[38] already an easy round trip in one day on the newly built "hard roads," or easily accessible on the considerable number of passenger trains that came through Galesburg. In these little county seats, farm marketing towns, and tiny flag-stops, the accumulated debt by mortgages on land and the gap between prices for grain and the prices of securities by speculation on the stock market had indeed become overwhelming.

Even as President Britt was preparing, presenting, and filing his annual report, the Crash came. Bad breaks in the stock market occurred on October 24 and 27. By the time of the Thanksgiving recess the losses in the market value of listed stocks had continued until about $30 billion had been "wiped out."[39] That this panic would lengthen and deepen into the Great Depression was yet part of the future, as meanwhile thousands of enterprises went bankrupt.

What hard times might do to a college was exemplified within six months of the Crash by the failure of Lombard. There was hardly anywhere this college could seek help. The very small number of Universalists of the Midwest (with whom it had been identified until 1928 by its divinity school) did not give enough help. Other denominations would not likely come to the rescue; the fundamentalists still were horrified by the liberal theology of Universalism; members of the more respectable denominations, to whom dogmas no longer mattered much, would have no particular reason for selecting Lombard for patronage because there were now many institutions with latitudinarian admissions policies. In the eighty-ninth year after Liberal Institute had been founded in Galesburg, its successor, Lombard College, could no longer find the financial credit with which to operate.

On April 1, 1930, a Tuesday, President Britt was asked by spokesmen from Lombard whether Knox would favor a merger with Lombard. The next day the presidents of the two schools, and Dean Charles M. Poor of Lombard and Kellogg McClelland, Knox treasurer and business manager, met and agreed that the executive committees of the trustees of both colleges should convene on Saturday. On that date the executive committee for the Knox board resolved that there should be "an appropriate union with Lombard College" and authorized President Britt to appoint a committee to formulate a plan for such a union.

Thus swiftly Lombard lost its living identity. Carl Sandburg, who endorsed the action in a letter, thought it would be a merger: "I believe it would be good news to many people, both of Knox and Lombard alumni and former students, as well as a considerable public which is interested, to hear that the two institutions have been merged. The time and occasion arrives when unity and solidarity bring more blessings all around, more direct and tangible benefits, than by rivalry and diffusion of effort."[40] In the early discussions it was indeed hoped that by a merger the united schools might enjoy the considerable financial advantage of the clause in the Lombard charter that had conferred upon it an unlimited tax exemption. This, the lawyers determined, was not feasible. The best that could be done was for Knox to accept Lombard students immediately, for Lombard to close its doors, and for a local bank to take over its buildings and campus to cover the accumulated debt.

Accordingly Lombard seniors completed their studies at Knox and were duly graduated. The juniors were told that they could get their degrees if they completed a year of study at Knox. All Lombard students were assured that for the next year the tuition would be the same that it had been at Lombard, namely $200, and that they would be considered for scholarships on the same basis that Knox students were.[41] As of July 1, 1930, Knox assumed the considerable responsibility of custodian of Lombard scholastic records, agreeing to issue transcripts for all those who ever attended Lombard. During the next three years about fifty former Lombard students did continue their education at Knox, eighteen being graduated in 1931, nine in 1932, and eight in 1933. Three members of the Lombard faculty became teachers at Knox. One of these, Carl Hanson, professor of education, would remain at Knox for a quarter of a century. The other two remained only three years.[42]

Lombard alumni were accorded the opportunity of celebrating their class reunions at Knox, and with time were absorbed into the Knox alumni activities. To the memory of Lombard a bell tower was erected in 1936 at the heart of the Knox campus.[43] With the passing years it became most meaningful to those who came to Knox because the bell hanging there was the one which Carl Sandburg, to help work his way through college, had rung on schedule to summon his schoolmates to their classes.

Of the four presidents with whom Dr. William Simonds had served as professor and dean, he believed that Britt had a "harder situation" to deal with than any of the three men who preceded him.[44] There was a temporary increase in the enrollment from 1930 to 1932, partly from the transfer of students from Lombard, but in September 1932 the number had sharply declined and by the beginning of the next academic year was down to 504, the lowest since 1920.[45] Because of the accumulating deficit, in February 1933 the board "released" nine members of the faculty, effective as of the end of that school year. This "drastic and painful course," along with a 20 percent reduction in faculty salaries, seemed to the trustees "an absolute necessity as a means of adjusting the budget to the financial situation." Even two senior faculty members were "released." They were eligible to receive the retirement benefits of the Carnegie Foundation. In the case of one of them, whose wife had inherited a large estate, this was no hardship. In the case of the other senior professor, it meant that because he was retiring early only the minimum pension was forthcoming, substantially less than if he taught two or three years longer.[46] Obviously Knox teachers did not escape the skimping, the insecurity, and some of the bitter frustration that others endured during the depression. But when President Britt resigned early in 1936 it was noted that few colleges in the Midwest could "boast," as could Knox, "that punctually on the first of each month during the entire period salary checks lay in faculty mail boxes."[47] By that time there was actually one benefit coming to teachers from a program of the New Deal—the National Youth Administration. The NYA came into being by executive order in June 1935 as part of the Works Projects Administration (WPA). It extended funds for the part-time employment of young people, including needy college students.[48] Faculty members, even those of junior status, found themselves provided with clerical assistants, which usually had been available only to administrators.

Some supporters of Knox were critical of Britt because he did not pursue a more aggressive policy for recruiting students. They probably did not know that this was an activity about which Britt had learned something as a student. In June 1896 the executive committee of the board had authorized Albert Britt and four other members of the "Y.M.C.A. band" to go out "to do evangelistic work and at the same time secure students for the College." For six weeks work at this task they should each receive $30 to apply on their tuitions.[49] Forty years later such church connections no longer were of much help to Knox, though there were two or three members of the faculty who in the event of an emergency would "fill the pulpit" in a church that was easily reached for a Sunday service. Of course, the good will of Knox students was important in persuading their peers back home to come to Knox. Alumni, especially those who were teachers, were urged to bring Knox to the attention of students, and in some instances there was a continuity of students who came to Knox from the influence of such an alumnus. Brochures were placed where high school students might see them. Opportunities were sought to bring high school students and teachers to the campus, such as a high school press association or a convention of classics teachers. One of these events that occurred annually in the spring was the Military Tract Meet,[50] which brought teams from medium-sized towns in west-central Illinois to Knox for interscholastic contests in declamation and music as well as for competition in field and track.

All of these contacts fell short of direct recruiting of students by members of the College staff. The nearest approximation of such a policy was the sending of faculty members to high schools to speak about Knox. This practice, resumed under Britt's leadership, had occurred during the presidency of McConaughy, but the point was then plainly made that these faculty members were not "proselyting"[51]—a word suggesting something like getting someone to change his religion or offering special inducements for one to change his loyalty. On this Britt remained loyal to the principles of the amateur. The merits of a college were not for merchandising; it was there for those to come who loved mankind and cherished learning. It is true that during the last years of his presidency a plan was developed by Harold Way, assistant professor of physics, for a "special representative of the College to make personal contacts with students" from whom the College had received "reply cards" as a result of the visits made by faculty members, especially in the Chicago area.[52] There was no director of admissions until the next president took over; the office of admissions was until then the part-time duty of a teacher.

President Britt was an amateur in the finest sense: a lover of good reading, good writing, good speaking, good conversation, good scholarship, good sports. His own publications as well as his chapel talks were models of thrifty exposition and intellectual forthrightness and were modestly and lucidly presented. The devotee of literature and the arts, the concerned citizen, the seeker after truth, the person who wanted to try out a new idea found him a congenial companion. By the standards of academic performance that were established after World War II, it must be noted that some of the students of the 1930s could hardly be graded very high and were graduated with very mediocre records. Yet Knox was also a place where many very able students received an excellent education, having an exciting, stimulating intellectual experience. In some respects intellectual pursuits were, during the 1930s, more enjoyed for their own sakes than they would be later in the decade of the 1960s with its clamor for relevance or in the decade of the 1970s with its anxieties over vocational goals.

It is meaningful that when Britt became president the number of professional courses in journalism was drastically reduced. Whereas there were six courses in this area of Britt's previous vocation in 1925, there was by 1926–27 only one course in this area. It was listed in the English department and taught by Britt himself:

> Advanced Writing. Two hours.
> Practical work in different forms of professional writing, news stories, feature articles, editorials, and reviews. Limited to fifteen students of approved standing.[53]

As it did when he was a student, the curriculum when Britt became president still favored the classics. Even if a freshman had studied Greek or Latin in preparatory school, he still needed to study "Latin Prose Composition" for a year at Knox if he wished to become a bachelor of arts; otherwise he had to settle for a bachelor of science degree by taking foreign language courses and an additional year of science. After September 1913 this was changed; thereafter anyone could pursue the arts degree by taking either the ancient or the modern foreign languages, and the B.S. was no longer granted.

This modification of the graduation requirements was related to the adoption in 1930 of a "group system of courses" in which about four-fifths of a student's work was "directed" toward a broadening intellectual experience, and the remainder "left open to free election on his part."[54] For this purpose all courses were designated as belonging to one of four groups. Group I comprised literature, art, music, and speech; Group II included the languages; Group III offered history, philosophy, psychology, and the social studies; Group IV comprised mathematics and natural and physical sciences. In the language group the studies required of the student depended on the number of units certified by his high school transcript. In Group I he was expected to take freshman English and six more hours; in Group III, twelve hours; in Group IV, two years.[55] President Britt assured the trustees that this new curriculum pattern "was intended to provide more flexibility and the possibility of distribution of work without a mere spotting of the students' selections among presumably easy courses. . . . The intention was also to keep group requirements definitely in the first two years in order that more and more genuinely advanced work might be required in the junior and senior years."[56]

Another curriculum revision related more particularly to the teaching of music. This subject had first been taught in the Female Seminary and then, beginning in 1883, in the Knox Conservatory of Music. This institution was autonomous, beholden to the same trustees as the College, to which it was parallel but interconnected in faculty and student activities. At first it published its own catalogue; later this information was provided in a special section of the College catalogue. For example, in 1926 the College catalogue had a section on the "Music Department" detailing courses in music (limited to twenty-four hours) that might be accepted toward a College degree. However, there was also a more detailed section for the Conservatory. By then the director of the Conservatory for forty years had been William Bentley, and there was discussion of the need to redefine the relation of College and Conservatory. This was not effected, however, until after Professor Bentley's death, from injuries suffered in an automobile accident while returning with the Knox choir from a small town in a neighboring county where the Knox students had provided the Palm Sunday music.[57] The Conservatory now lost its separate identity and a much more detailed description of the offerings of a "Music Department" appeared in the catalogue for 1936–37. By action of the faculty in May 1936 and with the concurrence of the trustees, the Conservatory was incorporated in the College, which now offered a B.A. degree with a major in music.[58]

The College year during the 1920s and 1930s concluded with three academic processions: one to a concluding chapel for the seniors; one for the baccalaureate service; the last one for commencement. College life had a recurrence of formalities about it, a degree of ritualization, that would have amazed and probably irritated the blue-jean clad students of the 1970s. In this respect campus affairs were much as they had been during Britt's years, when his contemporary George Fitch wrote about Siwash: "This formal party business was a vice at Siwash. It affected all classes and did not spare the young, the old, the good, the beautiful, or old pluggers who were gumming up their middle-aged intellects with Greek and Latin."[59] During the 1930s the hard times did not deter some faculty from staging dinner and bridge parties for guests who were expected to come formal—the men in black, single-breasted jackets with notched silk lapels that revealed white shirts with stiffly starched fronts. This attire would also be worn to the all-college winter prom and in the spring to the Military Ball. On most Fridays and Saturdays, once rushing was over and school got underway, one or more of the fraternities had a "formal," which some of the faculty were obliged to attend as chaperones.

The secret societies, as many would still have called them in Britt's student years, now dominated campus affairs. Nothing for the College was ever scheduled on a Monday night, when the six fraternities and seven sororities held weekly chapter meetings. Defenders of these social organizations pointed to their rivalry for scholarship honors, "the proof of which" was "an ornate silver cup resting now on the mantel of this fraternity house and now on that, except when it" had "been borrowed surreptitiously by a third fraternity which probably ranked the lowest of all the previous semester."[60] Unfortunately, as President Britt noted, this competition was not between "A's and B's but between D's and F's ... in reality not a test of excellence but of safe mediocrity."[61]

The politics of the rivalry of the Greeks permeated extracurricular activities and thus compounded the exclusion of the "barbarians" or "independents" that was implicit in the nature of fraternities. Britt noted the lunacy of the situation when the faculty was obliged to take under its supervision "the election of college editors in order to prevent the honor from becoming a football of campus politics."[62] Under the influence of Professor John Conger, who taught politics as well as history, elections to the all-College student government were conducted by the Hare method of voting, so as to assure proportional representation of minorities in the student body.[63] Those who helped him to tally the ballots were always interested in looking for signs that "combines" on the campus had tried to manipulate this system.[64]

There were at least fifty extracurricular organizations (exclusive of athletic teams) at Knox in 1935–36.[65] The men's literary societies (Adelphi and Gnothautii) were mentioned in the catalogue (probably for the benefit of older alumni) with the acknowledgment that they had not been active in recent years. The women's literary society, LMI, still offered its membership to the women of College and Conservatory.[66] These three societies, which had dominated campus affairs in the nineteenth century, had now been replaced by an amazing diversity of clubs and societies[67] that made great demands on the time and talent of students and required much attention from faculty and administrative officers. Even the eight so-called honorary groups, such as Phi Beta Kappa, Curtain Call (theater), or Scabbard and Blade (military), created work for students and teachers. The students in the Chapel Choir, the ROTC band, and the debaters of the Open Forum might even earn course credits for faithful performance in an activity that had close faculty supervision. In 1936 the faculty allowed up to eight hours of credit for such activities,[68] the equivalent of a half semester of study in the more ordinary part of the curriculum.

Even the teachers whose departments sponsored such extracurricular organizations became concerned with how they interfered with the quality of students' scholarly achievements. Several means were used to place limits on excessive noncurricular involvement. The eligibility requirements that had for years been applied to athletes were now extended to participation in dramatics, publications, debates, "and all other activities involving the appearance of students before the public as representatives of the college."[69] Unless a student had an exceptional scholastic record, he had to reduce his academic load if he became editor or manager of a publication. Similarly, he was not to participate in more than two major activities, such as athletics and the theater.[70] Such elaborate legislation to restrain extracurricular affairs was what President Britt referred to in a speech to a session of the North Central Association of Colleges and Secondary Schools in Chicago on April 23, 1936, as "the side show problems over which administrators and faculties labor," problems which imposed "too many responsibilities on the faculty" and which were "at least apart from their main objectives and frequently opposed to them."[71]

In years to come what many alumni of Knox would hear when they identified their alma mater was the remark that during the 1930s its football team had achieved an intercollegiate record for successive losses, tied by the end of the 1935 season to twenty-seven games. This "disaster," as many patrons of Knox regarded the events, involved President Britt in a defense of principles of amateurism that he had stated when Knox had been winning. For these principles he was a well-qualified spokesman, who could not be accused of pedantic prejudices against manly sports. He had managed the football team as an undergraduate. Forty years later in the *Saturday Evening Post* he said of himself: "I suppose I am really a professional athlete. At one time, as editor of an outdoor magazine, I wrote football articles."[72] Similarly, recalling the years when he had been editor of the *Outing* magazine, he explained in the *Knox Alumnus* that it had "been my good fortune to see more football, good and bad, than most people, and a good deal of it from a rather close point of view, from association with coaches, players and football writers. I have known most of the great football coaches in the country, so that I speak rather by the card in what I have to say about football."[73]

That he was a realist about the game was evident in his opinion that during the active season teachers might "ease up a little in class room requirements"—only, however, if the player was required "to make up his average after the athletic training and strain" of representing the College no longer made it difficult to maintain his "standing" in the class with students who were not involved in the game. He expressed this opinion in 1923 to one of the New York alumni who like himself became concerned over the financial tactics favoring athletes that were tolerated by President McConaughy.[74] That there was also concern on this matter among the faculty at Knox between the time that McConaughy departed and that Britt took over is suggested by a minute in the record of the administrative committee of the faculty "regarding inducements offered to athletes" and "extended discussion" about funds that were used for this purpose.[75]

To his fellow New York alumni Britt had expressed as his ideal regarding collegiate sports a strong deemphasis on varsity competition which may not have been known to some of the trustees back in Illinois when he was elected to the Knox presidency. To Allan C. Rearick, class of 1897, New York lawyer and trustee for Knox from 1921 to 1936, he had written about two years before he became president: "I was hoping that 'Knox' would do what Andover did a few years ago; that is, come frankly out and say our purpose is to give athletic training of the right kind to every man and woman in the college—if the varsity suffers, so much the worse for the varsity. It would mean hard going for a few years, but I am convinced that it would be the biggest thing ultimately that any western college has ever done. Evidently, there is a lot of missionary work needed before the western alumni will even think about such a stand."[76]

During the autumn of 1929, Britt's fourth on the campus as president, the football team completed what was characterized as the "greatest football season of the decade," claiming the best record in the Little Nineteen (the Illinois conference). In the Midwest Conference one game was lost and three were won, among them the game with Monmouth on Thanksgiving Day.[77] The homecoming celebration this fall (which would mostly later be remembered for the Crash) was unanimously pronounced by the executive committee of the Alumni Association as the "best ever known," consisting as it did, during two days, of a chapel memorializing General Henry Knox, of the dedication to his name of the large elm tree behind Seymour Hall, of the performance by Players in the Knox theater, of a pep rally, bonfire, and parade with seventeen floats lavishly decorated so as to symbolize events of the Revolutionary War, and then the football game, followed by the homecoming dinner, concluding with the homecoming dance at which a cup was awarded to the fraternity with the best decorated house![78]

It was in the time of this kind of winning, not in an apology for losing, that President Britt provided the alumni two essays about the subject of football, coinciding with a report of the Carnegie Foundation of a study regarding the relation of colleges to athletics. One of these essays, "The Place of Athletics," appeared in the *Alumnus* for April 1929; the second that same year in December raised the question: "Football: A Business or a Game."

What most baffled sports fanatics about Britt was his attitude toward "winning." He did not "deride the desire to win"; in fact, he could at a particular event be quite excited over victory. But he repudiated the idea that the "proper policy" for athletics was to produce "winning teams." Inherently such a policy was contradictory, for at any time one of the contestants was bound to lose. He commented that "the situation reminds me of that existing during the World War in which every nation called upon God to bring success to their arms and confidently assured the world that they had every reason to believe that God was on their side. What must have been the doubt and uncertainty in heaven at that time."[79] It was "winning" as a "policy," he noted, that caused some colleges to connive at hiring athletes, to discriminate in favor of athletes on their campuses, to lower scholastic standards, and to set athletic success "above ordinary, every day academic honesty."[80]

President Britt posed the question: "What is the place of athletics in the college scheme?" He answered: "Because we want to play. I do not know of any better reason, or sounder, or more final."[81] He proposed these tests for college sports: Were they "fun for the participants?" Did they assist students in "forming habits of helpful play which they can carry on through their lives?"[82] He scoffed at the idea that football made any special contribution as compared with other sports and expressed doubts about the "athletic sanity of a nation which so seriously permits the idolatry of a game."[83]

President Britt restated standards of amateurism that he knew were being evaded at other colleges. At Knox, he announced: "We treat an athlete as a man who wants to go to school for an education. That he is proficient in some branch of sport does not affect our feelings nor treatment of him either before he enters or afterwards."[84] Coaches should not come into contact with prospective students; athletes should expect no special treatment in college employment. As for recruiting: "The function of a coach is to give the best coaching possible to the men in college who come out for the teams. It stops right there. The instant he becomes a field agent for the college, a recruiting officer for the football squad, he may be paving the way to victory, but he is laying up trouble for the college."[85]

As Knox football teams during the early 1930s began to lose more games than they won and finally to lose them all, many alumni wondered why Knox men were "nothing to brag about physically," why Knox had no better "varsity material," why changing coaches three times effected no improvement. They resented the "left-handed advertising" that was given to their alma mater in the newspapers and demanded that something be done about the "honor" of Knox. The discontent of such fans became angry resentment when Knox tied the all-time record for consecutive losing games—twenty-seven.[86]

President Britt, in the face of this national publicity, reaffirmed his fidelity to amateur ideals in an article in the issue of March 23, 1935, of the *Saturday Evening Post* entitled "Taking it on the Chin." It was in this same magazine, more than a quarter of a century earlier that George Fitch had written about the extraordinary backfield feats of Ole Skjarsen of "Old Siwash." Britt acknowledged that Knox really was Siwash, "the original and only Siwash," and that the "gifted creator" had been Britt's "housemate in the Golden '90s." He admitted that he, too, was "anxious to see my college win her share of whatever she wants to win," but he showed no contrition for the humiliation of those alumni who suffered because of losses at football. Again he stated that he liked the players and liked the game, but that he did not like much of what was associated with football.

Among the events that clouded Britt's pleasure with football was its exploitation by sports writers and newspapers. To increase circulation and sales they invented "championships" for leagues that had none: they contrived "averages and ratings and awards"; they promoted intersectional and after the season contests. He noted: "In general, it is fair to say that newspapers have taken football out of the hands of the colleges, and any attempt to reclaim it is greeted with the suggestion that the profs mind their own business."[87]

Britt appreciated that coaches were the victims of publicity, too, but he thrust his sharpest jibes at this vocation. He acknowledged that there were many coaches not guilty of the evils performed by some who achieved considerable success and much attention; but his scarcasm was rather embracing:

> His name gradually becomes more important than the name of the college. Stories are told of his psychological acuteness, of his skill in "handling men," of his great influence on the character of the young. He is in demand as an after-dinner speaker, he broadcasts his views on many things, even football, and the president of the college looks with envy at his contract with the newspaper syndicate for the articles which someone else will write. ... Coaches are heroes, no doubt of it. This is proved by the scores of letters I have received in the past month from men all over the country, willing to stake their lives, their fortunes and their sacred honor on their ability to end our slump. One or two have even offered to take over the job for a share in the increased gate. ...
> No, dear sporting writer, football coaches do not produce character, except the kind they need to win games. Unfortunately, young men possess in abundance the simple virtues of courage, hardihood, intelligence, obedience, endurance. The game demands these, and usually it strengthens them. If character grows on the field, the game and the boys deserve the major credit.[88]

In phrases that endeared him to those who shared his amateur values he concluded by expressing his pride in how Knox had endured its defeats:

> What's the matter with football? I might have written the answer in one word—victories! Everyone wants to win and every healthy man sets out with that intention. Even a college president likes the taste of victory. But only a fool turns a defeat in sport into a badge of mourning and despair. The only defeats to regret are those we bring upon ourselves by folly or half-heartedness. ...
> Victory in football proves one thing and one thing only: That at that particular time and place one team is better than another. It's too bad to shatter cherished illusions, but that's all there is to it. ...
> The game has its own values, if we will only look at them. For the past three years I have watched at close range a group of boys lose every game and keep on fighting. In the last game I saw them play they were hopelessly outplayed and outscored, but they were

in the opponent's territory when the game ended. If you're looking for character in football, dear critics, there's some for you.[89]

The convictions of President Britt uttered in the *Saturday Evening Post* certainly did "not meet with universal approval" among alumni. The issue of the *Alumnus* immediately following, edited by a member of the class of 1899 who owned a local laundry, stated that there was widespread dissatisfaction, which might in a different kind of corporation be regarded as dissent against the board chairman by the house organ. The editor referred to "many letters" and quoted from the sports page of the local newspaper the argument that if football was "just a game" and if "defeat was as acceptable as victory," then there was no need for "coaching."[90] In fact, during the winter a committee of three faculty members and two Galesburg alumni screened 275 applications for the position of football coach, and by mid-January a member of that committee, a local mortician, could announce that they were ready to submit ten names to the president.[91] And in the fall the losing streak was broken when Knox in its opening game defeated Principia, a Christian Science college,[92] was next victorious over a nearby teachers' college, and went on to complete the schedule with a total of five victories, two ties, and two defeats.[93]

The enormous amount of attention given to Knox during its troubles with football was not entirely negative. Comments about its athletic weakness were mingled with appreciative recognition of its scholarly strength. In a magazine published for alumni of Ohio State University appeared an article "Old Siwash Comes Through," which centered on the football fortunes of Knox but also noted:

> It's the kind of place you and I imagined a college was, before we went. Winding walks, tall ancient trees, weathered old brick buildings, chapel set in a quiet atmosphere, where everyone knows everyone else, and is darn glad of it. . . .
>
> We were shown the names of men of national, even international fame who today carry on the spirit which Old Siwash gave them. Few colleges of its size have made a greater contribution to the intellectual, spiritual, literary, and political progress of the country than Knox. It is an enviable spirit which the Old Siwash followers possess.[94]

And in Tulsa, Oklahoma, the tough-minded editor of the *Tribune,* Richard Lloyd Jones, expressed his admiration for the way Knox took it on the chin, noted its special identification with Lincoln, and would later become a trustee and underwrite a special lecture course at Knox on American civilization.[95]

The affairs of Knox were improving by 1936, but Britt, who had accumulated many critics, resigned on January 25, 1936, effective at the end of June.[96] At that time there were the usual encomiums detailing his accomplishments, but there was a chief legacy that at the time could not be perceived. It was the secure understanding by a group of young faculty members of what with the right kind of leadership a liberal arts college could stand for. They had come to understand that the purpose of a college, as Britt had so often affirmed, was really intellectual and that to that end they as teachers should be freed from institutional snarls. When he said at the beginning of his administration that they were limited in their freedom only by their obligation to their students,[97] he had meant it. It was they and not the alumni nor even the trustees who should know what needed to be taught and should be free to do it.[98] Two-thirds of the faculty with him during the final year of 1935–36 had been appointed during his tenure. They included a young history instructor who, as a Knox undergraduate, had embarrassed Britt by broadcasting a protest against the ROTC; the sociology teacher who made the first effort in Galesburg to organize a chaper of the National Association for the Advancement of Colored People; the biology professor who earned a national reputation for his efforts to effect innovations in science teaching; the mathematician whose first degree had been in music and who would be a tower of strength for the faculty under five presidents, two of whom he would have much voice in choosing; and the director of athletics whose integrity was unimpeachable and who always insisted that the students' classroom obligations come prior to those of the playing fields. The eagerness for curriculum adaptation, the resistance to commercial values, and the readiness for a higher degree of faculty self-governance, all apparent in the succeeding administrations, owed much to a group of young teachers who acquired their self-assurance with Albert Britt as a companion.[99]

The appointment of Britt's successor, Carter Davidson, was announced on commencement day of 1936. His doctorate in English literature had been of less significance to those who appointed him than his thorough apprenticeship under Dr. Donald J. Cowling, the highly regarded president of Carleton College. Davidson had had experience with admissions, student aid, a college budget, and other details of academic management at Carleton.[100]

During his first year it fell to Davidson to preside over the Knox Centenary. The plans for this year-long celebration had, however, been thoroughly formulated under the direction of Janet Post. The first plans for a Centenary had been presented on March 11, 1928, in the old Bryan Lathrop house at 120 Bellevue Place, Chicago, to which it had "amused" Post as a member of the Fortnightly Club, a women's society, "to invite a man's committee to meet." The others present were Britt, Edward Caldwell, Kellogg McClelland, and an architect, for at that time there were discussions of grand plans to reconstruct the College with a Centenary Fund.[101]

The Crash and the Great Depression drastically reduced these optimistic expectations and at the board meeting of October 31, 1930, the trustees concurred when Britt stated that "it did not seem advisable to proceed with active solicitation for subscriptions to the Centenary Fund until general conditions, the country over, were more favorable."[102] However, on November 30, 1932, there occurred an informal meeting of twelve trustees at the apartment of Dr. and Mrs. John Finley in New York City. At the request of President Britt, Post proposed to the men, mostly from New York, that despite the financial difficulties of the College, Old Main should be restored, and she indicated that she was "anxious on her own behalf" to undertake this project and that Dr. Finley had assured her that he would help.[103] Accordingly a campaign asking for contributions was launched on the following anniversary of Lincoln's birthday with such success that in August 1933 the exterior of Old Main began to be restored. At the trustees' meeting of June 12, 1934, Post's responsibilities were extended; she became chairman of a national committee to prepare for the Centenary celebration, for which she had already done considerable planning.[104]

Post refused to have her many board and club connections listed with her name in the Knox catalogue and those not familiar with her were only vaguely aware of how she became a woman of consequence in Chicago and in the suburb of Winnetka. But even without benefit of a dossier revealing her achievements, those who met her were soon impressed by this remarkable person, intelligent, widely read and traveled, gracious, genuinely interested and knowledgeable about her companions, and possessed of a courtly presence that assured, without demanding, attention and respect. Her very extensive correspondence, by long hand, carried the same kind of presence.

Janet Greig had come to Knox from a farm near the small town of Oneida, near Galesburg, and was graduated in 1894 with the degree of Bachelor of Literature. Then she did what was often done by men, but then exceptional for a woman: she went abroad for further studies. For a year she lived with a French family and studied at the Sorbonne. This had been preceded by a year with a German family whose son studied at Bonn University. Years later she recalled that he "brought home students and I went skating on the Rhine and I learned a lot from those Bonn students."[105]

When Greig returned to the United States in 1896, President Finley appointed her as instructor in German; a year later she became dean of women. Her protégés in Whiting Hall would recall how careful she was about their dress (e.g., proper hat, gloves) when they went out, whether for class, church, or athletic events. They also recalled that she started the practice of having the girls dance after dinner in the evening, except on Sundays—which became a long-lasting custom, interrupted only when evangelists such as Billy Sunday or Gypsy Smith were in town.[106]

In 1902 Greig married a member of the class of 1887, Philip Sydney Post, son of a Civil War general, who was consul to Vienna (where Philip was born), and who was congressman from the district that included Galesburg. Philip Post had already been a county judge since 1898 and a trustee of Knox since 1901, serving on the board until his death in 1920. He became legal counsel for the International Harvester Corporation in Chicago and one of its vice-presidents. Janet Post became familiar with the powerful McCormick family and deeply involved in its philanthropic affairs, helping to establish the Elizabeth McCormick Memorial Fund for the Betterment of Child Life. She also helped to plan the Harriet McCormick YWCA on North Dearborn Street, for which she was still chairman of the committee of management in 1935, when she was also serving as chairman of the Knox Centenary committee.[107] Other enterprises for which she served as a board member or officer were the Chicago Women's Club, the Chicago Association of University Women, the Congregational Training School for Girls, and the Illinois Training School for Nurses.[108] She was a friend of Jane Addams, who as death came near, wanted Janet Post to have the hood for the honorary degree that Knox awarded in 1934 to the founder of Hull-House.[109]

One would not have perceived Janet Post as a feminist, but she did bring women who should be recognized to the attention of President Britt,[110] and he also knew that she believed that women did not always get their just rewards. In a letter to his successor about the first woman to head a department at Knox, Professor Mabel Heren, Janet Post said: "I am in no way, ever inclined to 'favor women'—because they are women—in positions such as Miss Heren's—but—if her name were 'Mark' instead of Mabel—and attached to a man—she would have been receiving the salary merited—both by her superior ability and by reason of long tenure of position."[111] The department was mathematics.

The *Record of the Centenary of Knox College,* a volume of 356 pages, reveals Janet Post's extraordinary talent for enlisting men and women for the commemorative events that began with a radio program (the first of four) broadcast in Chicago on November 10, 1936, and concluded about eleven months later with a celebration of the Lincoln-Douglas debate anniversary of 1937. In Galesburg the first major program was that for Founders Sunday on February 14, 1937, sponsored by the Congregational and Presbyterian churches whose founders had also founded the City and the College. The next day 1,200 persons, many of them in costumes recalling the attire of the 1830s, were served at a banquet in the National Guard Armory and regaled with music, toasts, and dramatic interludes appropriate to the hundredth birthday of both town and gown. The scale and thoroughness of the entire centennial observation is suggested by the logistics of this event for which there were ten committees, four different singing groups, and five groups of actors.[112]

During the Centennial commencement week special events involving the entire community began with a parade to the Burlington Depot, where there were speeches by the president of the railroad, by the president of the College, and by the mayor of the City, while the relatively new and shiny Denver Zephyr made a stop that extended beyond its published schedule. Thrice during that week the College presented "A Masque of Prairie Pioneers," written by Earnest Elmo Calkins and arranged for production by the director of the Knox Theater, Paul Foley. This pageant, staged in a city park by the shore of Lake Storey, was viewed by about 7,000 persons. Its cast of 200 actors and singers was supported by a crew of "workmen, guards, hostlers, ushers, trouble shooters," numbering another hundred. A brace of oxen and about sixty horses and ponies were also used; a "genuine broncobuster" was employed to handle them. The pageant was a tremendous community effort.[113]

At the baccalaureate service the sermon was delivered by the dean of the chapel of the University of Chicago and the benediction spoken by Albert Blanchard Kellogg, a superintendent of schools from Claremont, New Hampshire; Kellogg concluded with sentences from the farwell sermon of Jonathan Blanchard of January 1, 1860, which included these lines: "Sown like a wheatfield in these prairies before fences were erected, exposed not only to every wind of doctrine which has blown over them, but to whomsoever might wish to devour your liberties in Jesus Christ, you have maintained, so far as I can judge, a calm, quiet and consistent testimony for Christ. You have been orthodox without bigotry. You have been reformers without fanaticism."[114]

And finally there was the graduation of seniors of 1937, whose role was rather diminished by the granting of twelve honorary degrees and by the inauguration of Carter Davidson, to whom the "Charge" was given by the editor of the New York *Times,* John H. Finley, who fifty years earlier had delivered the valedictory for the class of 1887.

Certainly the massive efforts made to stage an impressive and successful Centenary had brought Knox to the attention of thousands of people, had brought scores of important persons to the campus, had instructed many Knox patrons as to its history, and renewed the pride of alumni in their alma mater. How lasting such accomplishments were it is difficult to determine. There were some things, however, that are still readily apparent to those that want to notice them. One of these accomplishments was the collection and improved organization of historical materials about Knox. Since the summer of 1936 there has been continuously a staff member of the library particularly concerned with gathering, preserving, and arranging for research the college memorabilia and archives. During the Centenary there were several historical publications, by far the best and most important being the account of the founding of town and college and of its history in the nineteenth century by Earnest Elmo Calkins, *They Broke the Prairie: Being some account of the settlement of the Upper Mississippi Valley by religious and educational pioneers, told in terms of one city, Galesburg, and of one college, Knox.*[115] Also, citizens of Galesburg still can observe many of the twenty bronze markers set up in June 1937 to instruct them regarding the original boundaries of the pioneer village, to explain the names of the oldest streets, and to fix the site of important events early in the annals of town and college.[116]

The most conspicuous and best remembered achievement of the Centenary, however, was the restoration of the exterior of Old Main and the rebuilding of its interior. The extraordinary efforts of Janet Post had effected the refurbishing of the exterior, free of debt, by August 1934; she had procured from the secretary of the interior on June 4, 1936, the designation of Old Main as a national historic site;[117] she saw the interior ready for classes by September 1937. On June 15, 1937, she presented the building for its rededication. Other speakers were John H. Finley, Henry Horner, Democratic governor of Illinois, and John Gilbert Winant, three times Republican governor of New Hampshire and now at the head of the newly established Social Security board. Of those who spoke on this occasion the most likely name to be familiar at the Knox bicentenary would be Carl Sandburg. In his "Ode" to Old Main he recited these words:

> Old Main as a living instrument today might be saying:
> "One thing I know deep out of my time: youth when lighted and alive and given a sporting chance is strong for struggle and not afraid of any toils or punishments or dangers or deaths.
> "What shall be the course of society and civilization across the next hundred years?

"For the answers read if you can the strange and baffling eyes of youth."[118]

NOTES

1. List of honorary degree recipients, with a brief comment on each, *Knox College Directory*, 1963, 387–93.
2. Ida M. Tarbell received the degree of L.H.D. in 1909, the first doctorate given by Knox to a woman. Though not an alumna, she was closely associated in her career with S. S. McClure, John S. Phillips, and John Finley. At the Galesburg home of the latter she had lived while writing the article on the Lincoln-Douglas debates in which Knox was prominently featured. A discussion of the career of Janet Post occurs later in this chapter.
3. The second honorary doctorate Knox gave to a woman was awarded to Ellen Browning Scripps in 1912.
4. Elected Aug. 15, 1925, Trustees Minutes, Aug. 1925.
5. *Alumnus*, Jan.-Feb. 1922, 192–93.
6. Askew, "Liberal Arts College Encounters Intellectual Change,"286; based on an interview with Professor Howell Atwood.
7. Simonds, "Knox College—1892–1934."
8. Recollections of the author.
9. *Alumnus*, June-July 1927, 220.
10. *Ibid.*, July-Aug. 1936, 116.
11. Askew, "Liberal Arts College Encounters Intellectual Change."
12. *Ibid.*, 293.
13. *Alumnus*, Nov. 1928, 259–60.
14. *Ibid.*, 251–54.
15. "President Britt introducing Sandburg," Britt Papers.
16. *Alumnus*, Nov. 1928, 256.
17. Trustees Minutes, Feb. 15, 1927.
18. *Alumnus*, Feb. 1927, 90–92.
19. Trustees Minutes, Jan. 26, 1928, June 10, 1929.
20. *Alumnus*, Nov.-Dec. 1926, 20; Mar. 1928, 67–68.
21. *Ibid.*, Sept. 1927, 264–65.
22. *Ibid.*, Sept.-Oct. 1929, 203.
23. *Ibid.*, June 1935, 79.
24. *Ibid.*, Jan.-Feb. 1936, 43.
25. *Ibid.*
26. *Ibid.*, Apr. 1928, 111. The funds for reconstructing this theater came from Senator William B. McKinley (Trustees Minutes, Feb. 14, 1928).
27. *Alumnus*, May 1927, 224–25; Jan. 1929, 3–4; see also Trustees Minutes, June 11, 1928.
28. *Alumnus*, Jan. 1929, 4–5.

29. See ch. 5 herein.

30. The *Knox Alumni Directory* for 1963 provides a list of lecturers, pp. 382ff.

31. *Alumnus,* Jan.-Feb. 1937, 60.

32. Catalogue for 1935–36, 101–2; Trustees Minutes, Jan. 26, 1929.

33. Catalogue for 1935–36, 102.

34. *Knox Now,* Fall 1978, 1.

35. *Alumnus,* Sept.-Oct. 1929, 203–4.

36. *Ibid.,* 204–5.

37. The registrar's reports, with detailed statistical analysis, appeared during these years in the September issues of the *Alumnus.*

38. Compiled by the author from the student lists in the catalogues.

39. Morris, ed. *Encyclopedia of American History,* 337–38, 539.

40. *Alumnus,* May 1930, 116.

41. Trustees Minutes, June 9, 1930; *Alumnus,* June 1930, 151.

42. Elbert Smith, who taught Romance languages, and Charles Poor, who succeeded Simonds as dean. Already in January 1930, Simonds had indicated that he wished to resign (Trustees Minutes, Jan. 24, 1930).

43. *Alumnus,* Nov.-Dec. 1936, 26.

44. Simonds, "Knox College—1892–1934."

45. *Alumni Directory,* 1963, 370.

46. Simonds, "Knox College—1892–1934." For the younger faculty members the trustees in 1929 adopted the pension program administered by the Teachers' Insurance Annuity Association. This became obligatory in 1931 (Trustees Minutes, June 10, Oct. 25, 1929, June 8, 1931). The 20 percent salary reduction remained in effect until 1937 (Trustees Minutes, Oct. 27, 1937).

47. *Alumnus,* Jan.-Feb. 1936, 40.

48. Morris, ed., *Encyclopedia of American History,* 351.

49. Minutes of the Executive Committee of the Board of Trustees, June 4, 1896.

50. The Military Tract was the area between the Mississippi and Illinois rivers set aside for war veterans' land bounties in 1815. It extended north approximately to Rock Island.

51. *Alumnus,* Mar. 21, 1919, 5; Mar. 28, 1919, 5.

52. Trustees Minutes, Feb. 15, 1934.

53. *Ibid.;* catalogue for 1926–27, 39. It was still so listed in catalogue for 1935–36.

54. Catalogue, 1935–36, 43.

55. Both the "Old Plan" and the "New Plan" are described in the catalogue for 1930–31, 18–22.

56. Trustees Minutes, June 5, 1930.

57. *Alumnus,* May-June 1936, 93.

58. Faculty Minutes, May 21, Oct. 28, Nov. 18, 1936; Trustees Minutes, June 8, 1936.

59. Fitch, *Petey Simmons at Siwash,* 61.

60. Britt, "Eleven Years a College President," Britt Papers.

61. *Ibid.*

62. *Ibid.*

63. Apparently the first student organization to adopt the Hare proportional representational method was the Knox Woman's Government Association, after "explanation" by Dr. Conger (*Student,* Nov. 15, 1918, 1). Conger promoted this form of voting abroad as well as at home (*ibid.,* May 28, 1919, 1; Feb. 6, 1920, 5). Thomas Hare, an Englishman, set forth a system of voting in a volume published in 1859. In this system "the distinctive feature of the system is the transferable vote. In casting his ballot under the Hare system, the voter indicates first, second, third, fourth choices, and so on, depending on the number of names on the ballot. When all the ballots are in, the total number of valid ballots is determined and a 'quota' is ascertained. The formula for obtaining the quota is to divide the total number of ballots by one more than the number of places to be filled and add one to the resulting quotient. The formula sounds incomprehensible, but it is all quite simple." Or so we are assured by V. O. Key in his *Politics, Parties and Pressure Groups,* 395–97.

64. Recollections of the author.

65. Catalogue, 1935–36, 104–5, 126–27.

66. *Ibid.,* 104–5.

67. Many of these, like the social organizations, had Greek titles.

68. Faculty Minutes, Nov. 18, 1936.

69. *Ibid.,* Nov. 26, 1935, Mar. 26, 1936.

70. *Ibid.,* Mar. 30, June 9, 1937.

71. Britt, "Eleven Years a College President."

72. Britt, "Taking it on the Chin," 27.

73. Britt, "Football: A Business or a Game," 271–72.

74. Britt to A. C. Rearick, May 1, 1923, MS, Knox College Library.

75. Faculty Administrative Committee Minutes, Feb. 19, 1925. McConaughy left Galesburg during the last week of January, 1925 (*Student,* Jan. 22, 1925, 1).

76. Britt to Rearick, May 1, 1923.

77. *Alumnus,* Dec. 1929, 264–66.

78. *Ibid.,* Nov. 1929, 231–35.

79. Britt, "The Place of Athletics," 77–78.

80. *Ibid.*

81. *Ibid.*

82. Britt, "Football, Bane or Blessing," 184–85.

83. Britt, "Football: A Business or a Game," 271–72.

84. *Alumnus,* Dec. 1929, 269.

85. *Ibid.,* Apr. 1929, 77–78.

86. *Ibid.,* Dec. 1934, 20; Jan.-Feb. 1935, 35–36. The recollections of some Knox alumni present an interesting problem to the historian. They insist that Knox did break, not merely tie, the record for successive defeats in football. Contemporary publications make it clear that by defeating Principia in the

first game of the 1935 season, Knox was saved that distinciton. See *ibid.*, Dec. 1934, 21; *Knox Student*, Sept. 26, 1935, 4; *Centennial Gale*, 46 (1937). Thomas Gold Frost class of 1886, in his *Tales from the Siwash Campus*, included a section on "The Decline of Football at Knox" that stated: "never in the history of Knox College, have the loyal alumni of that institution been more humiliated or filled with resentment than at the results of this three year period of 'deflated' football effort." He quoted a "prominent" but unnamed Knox Alumnus as saying: "If reports are true, orders from the President and a Faculty conference" to the coaches "deflated athletics and greatly discouraged its prominence in the College" (111). Frost, who had during the 1880s helped to start intercollegiate football competition at Knox, blamed the faculty at Knox during the 1930s for indifference to football, saying they were "jealous of anything that threatened to weaken the allegiance of the student body to classroom drill and work" (112).

87. Britt, "Taking it on the Chin," 51.

88. *Ibid.*, 52–53.

89. *Ibid.*, 54.

90. *Alumnus*, Mar.-Apr. 1935, 51–52.

91. *Ibid.*, Jan.-Feb. 1935, 35–36.

92. *Ibid.*, Sept.-Oct. 1935, 5–6.

93. *Ibid.*, Nov.-Dec. 1935, 25.

94. *Ibid.*, 28.

95. Recollections of the author. Richard Lloyd Jones reminded his audience at the anniversary of the Lincoln-Douglas debate in 1937: "Already Knox has attracted national attention as the college that does better head work than foot work." (Sherwin, ed., *Record of the Centenary of Knox College*, 321).

96. Trustees Minutes, Jan. 25, 1936.

97. *Alumnus*, Jan.-Feb. 1936, 39–40.

98. Britt, "Eleven Years a College President."

99. Recollections of the author. These professors were: Dean Trevor (athletics), Rothwell Stephens (mathematics), Lee Furrow (biology), Howell Atwood (sociology), and Hermann Muelder (history).

100. *Alumnus*, July-Aug. 1936, 108.

101. Janet Greig Post, "The Genesis of the Knox College Centenary," in Sherwin, ed., *Record of the Centenary of Knox College*, 9–11.

102. K. D. McClelland, "The Centenary Plan," *ibid.*, 17–18.

103. Trustees Minutes, Nov. 30, 1932.

104. McClelland, "The Centenary Plan," in Sherwin, ed., *Record of the Centenary of Knox College*, 17–19.

105. Janet Greig Post to Hermann R. Muelder, Aug. 11, 1961, Post Papers.

106. Memorandum, Sharvy Umbeck to Max Goodsill, Feb. 4, 1964, MS, Knox College Library.

107. The papers of Janet Greig Post, *passim*.

108. *Ibid.*

109. Janet Post to Albert Britt, Apr. 28, 1934, *ibid.*

110. Post to Britt, Memorial Day, 1934, *ibid.*

111. Janet Post to Carter Davidson, July 20, 1942, *ibid.*
112. Sherwin, ed., *Record of the Centenary of Knox College*, 95–152.
113. John Wilson Pennington, "Supplying the Centenary," in *ibid.*, 324–26.
114. *Ibid.*, 216–17.
115. It was published in New York in 1937. See *ibid.*, 356.
116. *Ibid.*, 201–7.
117. *Ibid.*, 19.
118. *Ibid.*, 258.

BIBLIOGRAPHY

MANUSCRIPTS

Adelphi Society. Business Meeting Minutes, 1846–1927.*
———. Program Meeting Minutes, 1853–1907.
American Home Missionary Society. Papers. Hammond Library, Chicago Theological Seminary.
American Missionary Association. Papers. Amistad Research Center, Dillard University, New Orleans.
ATWOOD, J. HOWELL. Papers, 1930–60.
BANCROFT, FREDERIC. Papers.
BASCOM, FLAVEL. "Autobiography." Hammond Library, Chicago Theological Seminary.
BATEMAN, NEWTON. Papers.
BEAUCHAMP, WILLIAM THEODORE, SR. Papers, 1926–47.
BENDER, VICTOR E. Papers, 1882–1919.
"Biographical Scrapbook." Galesburg Public Library.
BRINK, SAMUEL HEZEKIAH. Papers, 1855–63.
BRITT, ALBERT. "Eleven Years a College President." North Central Association, Apr. 25, 1936.
———. "President Britt Introducing Sandburg."
CRAFTON, JESSE. An address delivered during the Knox commencement, 1932.
CALDWELL, EDWARD. Collection, 1833–1949.
CALKINS, EARNEST ELMO. Papers and correspondence, 1868–1964.
CHAMBERS, E. P. "Reminiscences of Early Days," one of the papers of the now defunct Knox County Historical Society.
CHURCHILL, GEORGE. Papers, 1854–1913.
COWLES, HENRY. Papers. Oberlin College Library, Ohio.
DUNN, E. M. "List of Donors to Knox College, 1836–1895."
FINLEY, JOHN H. "Pioneers of France in the New World."
———. "Tribute to the Memory of Robert J. Finley by His Brother, John H. Finley."

---

*Unless otherwise noted, manuscripts listed here are located in the Knox College Archives, Galesburg Ill.

FINNEY, CHARLES GRANDISON. Papers. Oberlin College Library, Ohio.
FITCH, GEORGE. Papers.
GALE, GEORGE WASHINGTON. Account Books.
———. "Autobiography."
———. Gale Family Papers, 1820–62.
GALE, WILLIAM SELDEN. "Autobiography."
GETTEMY, CHARLES FERRIS. "A Memoir of Silvanus Ferris, 1773–1861."
Gnothautii Society. Business Meeting Minutes, 1849–1926.
———. Program Meeting Minutes, 1849–1940.
GULLIVER, JOHN. Papers.
HITCHCOCK, HENRY EATON. Hitchcock Family Papers, 1840–98.
HITCHCOCK, MARGARET GALE. Papers, 1835–1943.
HURD, ALBERT. Papers.
HURD, ETHEL EDGERTON. Correspondence, 1861–63.
JONES, FRED D. Letters, 1879–84.
Knox College. Old Business Records, such as tuition accounts and "Blotter A," "Blotter B," and "Blotter C."
———. Executive Committee of the Board of Trustees Minutes.
———. Faculty Administrative Committee Minutes.
———. Faculty Minutes.
———. Trustees' Minutes.
LMI (Ladies Moral Improvement Society). Minutes, 1863–66.
McCONAUGHY, JAMES L. Papers, in file for Knox presidents.
MASTERS, EDGAR LEE. File.
MORSE, LUCY SMITH (MRS. EDWARD CALDWELL). Letters, 1881–92.
MUELDER, HERMANN R. "Edgar L. Larkin."
———. "Gulliver among the Lilliputians."
———. "Knox College and the Muckrakers."
POST, JANES GREIG. Papers in Faculty file.
PRINCE, GEORGE W. "Autobiography."
Presbytery of Knox. Records, 1839–44.
REVELS, HIRAM. "Autobiography." Library of Congress, Washington, D.C.
Scrap Book Number Two. Galesburg Public Library (examined by author before the library was destroyed by fire in 1958).
SHOOP, FRED. "Mt. Lowe Observatory Director's Career Started in Illinois."
SIMONDS, WILLIAM EDWARD. "Knox College—1892–1934. The Four Presidents."
———. "The New Poetry and Free Verse in Illinois. Masters—Lindsay—Sandburg."
———. Papers, 1877–1958.

Bibliography

SWANSON, JAMES A. "A History of Lombard College."
WARREN, LORNA. "The Development of Theatre at Knox College."
WEST, MARY ALLEN. "How Galesburg Grew," dated May 23, 1873. Galesburg Public Library, Galesburg, Ill.
WILLARD, THOMAS RIGNEY. Papers, 1800–1896.
WRIGHT, SAMUEL G. Journal, 1839–60.

NEWSPAPERS AND PERIODICALS

American Missionary Association. *American Missionary,* 1846–76. New York.
American University Magazine, 1894–97. New York.
The Breeze, June 1891. Galesburg Ill.
Chicago *Democrat,* 1842.
Chicago *Tribune,* 1866.
Educational Review, 1891–1928. New York.
The Dial, 1880–1929. Chicago.
Galesburg *Evening Mail,* 1891–1927.
Galesburg *Daily Mail,* 1895.
Galesburg *Free Democrat,* 1854–60. Concurrent with this weekly, the *Semi-Weekly Free Democrat* was also published in 1859–60.
Galesburg *Free Press,* 1865–76.
Galesburg *News Letter,* 1850–53.
Galesburg *Register,* 1866–73.
Galesburg *Republican,* 1870–73.
Galesburg *Republican Register,* 1873–1919.
Galesburg *Weekly Mail,* 1898.
Galesburg *Week's Review. An Illustrated Weekly Review of Past Events.* 1905.
Genius of Liberty, 1841–42. Lowell, Ill.
Genius of Universal Emancipation, 1839. Lowell, Ill.
Harper's New Monthy Magazine, 1850–. New York.
Illinois State Historical Society. *Journal,* 1899–. Springfield.
———. *Papers and Transactions,* 1900–1942. Springfield.
Knoxville [Ill.] *Journal,* 1849–55
Knoxville [Ill.] *Republican,* 1850–61.
Lombard [College] *Review,* 1884–1930. Galesburg, Ill.
McClure's Magazine, 1893–1929. New York.
Monmouth College. *College Courier,* 1 (Apr. 1868). Monmouth, Ill.
Northwestern Gazetteer, 1849. Galesburg, Ill.
Oquakwa [Ill.] *Spectator,* May 16, 1861.
Peoria [Ill.] *Register and Northwestern Gazetteer,* 1837–43.

Poetry: A Magazine of Verse, 1912–42. Chicago.
Prairie Farmer, 1841–. Chicago.
Reedy's Mirror, 1891–1925. St. Louis, Mo.
Saturday Evening Post, 1821–. Philadelphia.
Scientific Monthly, 1915–. Washington, D.C.
Western Citizen, 1842–53. Chicago.

PRINTED MATERIAL: BOOKS, ARTICLES, THESES,
DISSERTATIONS

ANDER, OSCAR FRITIOF. *T. N. Hasselquist: The Career and Influence of a Swedish Clergyman, Journalist, and Educator.* Rock Island, 1931.
ANDERSON, L. F. "The Manual Labor School Movement." *Educational Review,* 46 (Nov. 1913), 369–86.
ANTHONY, EDWARD. *O Rare Don Marquis, a Biography.* New York, 1962.
ARLOTT, JOHN. *Oxford Companion to Sports and Games.* London, 1975.
ASKEW, THOMAS. "The Liberal Arts College Encounters Intellectual Change: A Comparative Study of Education at Knox and Wheaton Colleges, 1837–1925." Ph.D. Dissertation, Northwestern University, 1969.
AVIS, WALTER S., ed. *A Dictionary of Canadianisms.* Toronto, 1967.
BAILEY, J. W. *Knox College, by Whom Founded and Endowed.* Chicago, 1860.
Baker's Biographical Dictionary of Musicians. 5th ed. New York, 1958.
BAKER, RAY STANNARD. *American Chronicle. The Autobiography of Ray Stannard Baker.* New York, 1945.
BALDWIN, THERON. "Historical Sketch of the Society." *Proceedings at the Quarter Century Anniversary of the Society for the Promotion of Collegiate and Theological Education at the West, Marietta, Ohio, Nov. 7–10, 1868.* New York, 1868.
BANCROFT, EDGAR A. *The Chicago Strike of 1894.* Chicago, 1895.
BARTON, WILLIAM E. *Joseph Edwin Roy: A Faithful Servant of God and His Generation.* Oak Park, Ill., 1908.
BASSET, ISAAC NEWTON. *Past and Present of Mercer County.* Chicago, 1914.
BEARD, AUGUSTUS FIELD. *A Crusade of Brotherhood: A History of the American Missionary Association.* Boston, 1909.
Beasley's Galesburg City Directory for 1877–78. Galesburg, 1877.
BEECHER, EDWARD. *The Papal Conspiracy and Protestantism Defended in the Light of Reason, History, and Scripture.* Boston, 1855.

Bibliography

BENDER, VICTOR E. "The Bricks." *Pantheon*, 1888, 97–98.

BENTLEY, W. H. *History of the 77th Illinois Volunteer Infantry, Sept. 2, 1862–July 10, 1865*. Peoria, 1883.

BENTLEY, WILLIAM F. "The Knox Conservatory of Music." *Knox Alumnus* (Feb. 1918), 68–69.

BIRNEY, JAMES GILLESPIE. *Letters of James Gillespie Birney, 1831–1957*, ed. Dwight L. Dumond. 2 vols. New York, 1938.

BLANC, MADAME (TH. BENTZON). "A Prairie College. An Eminent Frenchwoman's Study of Co-Education in America." *McClure's Magazine* (May 1895), 541–48.

BLANCHARD, JONATHAN. *Baccalaureate Address before the Senior Class of Knox College, June 22, 1856*. Galesburg, Ill., 1856.

———. *Memoir of Rev. Levi Spencer: Successively Pastor of the Congregational Church at Canton, Bloomington, and Peoria, Illinois*. Cincinnati, 1856.

———. *Public Men and Public Institutions. Published with George Washington Gale, A Brief History of Knox College*. Cincinnati, 1845.

———. *Secret Societies: An Argument before the State Congregational Association Delivered in Two Discourses in the First Presbyterian Church in Galesburg, June, 22, 1850*. Chicago. 1851.

———. *Sermon on Slaveholding: Preached by Appointment before the Synod of Cincinnati at Their Late Stated Meeting at Mount Pleasant, Ohio, October 20, 1841*. Cincinnati, 1842.

———. *Sermons and Addresses*. Chicago, 1892.

———, and NATHAN LEWIS RICE. *A Debate on Slavery: Held in the City of Cincinnati on the First, Second, Third, and Sixth Days of October, 1845, upon the question: Is Slavery in Itself Sinful, and the Relation between Master and Slave, a Sinful Relation*. Cincinnati, 1846.

BOWERS, CLAUDE G. *Beveridge and the Progressive Era*. New York, 1932.

British and Foreign Anti-Slavery Society. *Minutes of the General Anti-Slavery Convention ... 1840 ...* London, 1840.

———. *Proceedings of the General Anti-Slavery Convention ... 1843*. London, 1843.

———. *Second Annual Report of the British and Foreign Anti-Slavery Society ... 1841*. London, 1841.

———. *Third Annual Report of the British and Foreign Anti-Slavery Society ... 1842*. London, 1842.

BRITT, ALBERT. "Football: A Business or a Game." *Knox Alumnus* (Dec. 1929), 271–72.

——. "Football, Bane or Blessing." *Knox Alumnus* (Apr. 1931), 184–85.

——. "The Place of Athletics." *Knox Alumnus* (Apr. 1929), 77–78.

——. "Taking It on the Chin." *Saturday Evening Post* (Mar. 23, 1935), 25.

——. *Turn of the Century*. Barre, Mass., 1966.

BROWNING, ORVILLE H. *Diary of Orville H. Browning, 1850–1865*. Illinois Historical Collections, vol. 20. Springfield, 1925.

BULEY, ROSCOE C. *The Old Northwest: Pioneer Period, 1815–1840*. 2 vols. Indianapolis, 1950.

BURGESS, JOHN W. *Reminiscences of an American Scholar*. New York, 1934.

CALKINS, EARNEST ELMO. ... *and Hearing Not*. New York, 1946.

——. "I Remember..." *Knox Alumnus* (Oct. 1947).

——. "Past and Present of Knox College, Being the History of Her Life, Her Achievements and Her Ideals." *American University Magazine*, 1895.

——. "A Prairie Book Club." *Knox Alumnus* (June 1953).

——. *They Broke the Prairie: Being Some Account of the Settlement of the Upper Mississippi Valley by Religious and Educational Pioneers, Told in Terms of One City, Galesburg, and One College, Knox*. New York, 1937.

——, ed. *Log City Days: Two Narratives on the Settlement of Galesburg, Illinois*. Galesburg, 1937.

CARR, CLARK E. *My Day and Generation*. Chicago, 1908.

——. *The Illini: A Story of the Prairies*. Chicago, 1904.

CARRIEL, MARY TURNER. *The Life of Jonathan Baldwin Turner*. Jacksonville, Ill., 1911.

CENTER, CHARLES D. *Things Usually Left Unsaid*. Quincy, Ill., 1927.

CHAPMAN, CHARLES C., AND CO. *History of Fulton County, Illinois*. Peoria, Ill., 1879.

——. *History of Knox County, Illinois*. Chicago, 1878.

——. *History of Tazewell County, Illinois*. Chicago, 1879.

——. *Portrait and Biographical Album of Henry County, Illinois*. Chicago, 1885.

——. *Portrait and Biographical Album of Knox County, Illinois*. Chicago, 1886.

COLE, ARTHUR. *The Era of the Civil War, 1848–1870*. Centennial History of Illinois, vol. 3. Springfield, 1919.

Coleville's Directory of the City of Galesburg, vols. 1 (1883–84) to 5 (1892–93). Galesburg.

Bibliography

Congregational General Association of Illinois. *Minutes of the General Association of May 1862.* Quincy, Ill., 1862.

CONROW, ROBERT. *Field Days, the Life, Times, Reputation of Eugene Field.* New York, 1974.

COOKE, JACOB E. *Frederic Bancroft, Historian....* Norman, Okla., 1957.

CORBIN, JOHN. "The Small College Versus the University—The Personal Equation in Education in the Middle West." *Saturday Evening Post* (Apr. 18, 1908), 7–8, 28–29.

CROSS, WHITNEY R. *The Burned-over District: The Social and Intellectual History of Enthusiastic Religion in Western New York, 1800–1850.* Ithaca, N.Y., 1950.

CURTIS, HARVEY. *Inaugural Address: The College—Its Mission, June 24, 1858.* Chicago, 1858.

DAVENPORT, F. GARVIN. *Monmouth College. The First Hundred Years, 1853–1953.* Cedar Rapids, Iowa, 1935.

DEAN, WILLARD. "James Lukens McConaughy, Ninth President of Knox College." *Knox Alumnus* (Feb.-Mar. 1929), 45–46.

———. "Justin 'Sam' McCarthy Barry Named to Hall of Fame." *Knox Now and Knox Alumnus* (Spring 1979), 33–34.

Dewey's County Directory: Galesburg City Directory. Galesburg, 1868.

DUNN, ARTHUR. *An Analysis of the Social Structure of a Western Town. A Specimen Study according to Small and Vincent's Method.* 1896.

DUNNING, ALBERT E. *Congregationalists in America: A Popular History of Origin, Belief, Polity, Growth and Work.* New York, 1894.

ELLIOTT, ISAAC H. *History of the Thirty-third Veteran Volunteer Infantry in the Civil War 22nd August, 1861, to 7th December, 1865 by General Isaac H. Elliott with Company and Personal Sketches by Other Comrades also Complete Historical Posters Compiled by Virgil G. Way Secretary and Treasurer of the Regimental Association, by whom this Work Has Been Prepared for Publication.* Gibson City, Ill. 1902.

FEE, JOHN GREGG. *Autobiography of John G. Fee.* Berea, Ky., 1891.

———. *Non-Fellowship with Slaveholders the Duty of Christians.* New York, 1855.

FAULKNER, HAROLD UNDERWOOD. *The Quest for Social Justice.* History of American Life Series. New York, 1931.

FINLEY, JOHN HUSTON. *Catalogue of Books in the College, Adelphi, and Gnothautii Libraries.* Galesburg, Ill. 1887.

FINNEY, CHARLES GRANDISON. *Memoirs of Charles G. Finney.* New York, 1876.

First Church of Christ of Galesburg. *Semi-Centennial Celebration of the Organization of the First Church of Galesburg.* Galesburg, Ill., 1887.

FISCHER, JULIA. *Blessed Memories, Life of Mrs. Mary Blanchard.* N.p., n.d.

FITCH, GEORGE. *At Good Old Siwash.* Boston, 1911.

⸻. "The Big Strike at Siwash." *Saturday Evening Post* (May 30, 1908).

⸻. *The Big Strike at Siwash.* New York, 1909.

⸻. "The Campaign of '96." *Gale Nineteen Hundred and Ten: The Year Book of Knox College,* 20 (1909), 131–35.

⸻. *Petey Simmons at Siwash.* New York, 1916.

FLANAGAN, JOHN T. *Edgar Lee Masters: The Spoon River Poet and His Critics.* Metuchen, N.J., 1974.

FLETCHER, ROBERT S. *A History of Oberlin College from Its Foundation through the Civil War.* Oberlin, Ohio, 1943.

FROST, THOMAS G. "Knox College and Athletics." *Coup D'Etat* (May 1891), 126–28.

⸻. *Tales from the Siwash Campus.* New York, 1938.

GALE, GEORGE WASHINGTON. *Articles of Faith and Convenant of the Presbyterian Church of Galesburg.* Galesburg, Ill. 1849.

GARNER, JAMES WILFORD. *Reconstruction in Mississippi.* New York, 1901.

General Association of the Congregational Churches and Ministers. *Report on Knox College, Presented to the General Association of Illinois, May 24, 1861.* Quincy, Ill., 1861.

General Congregational Association of Illinois. *In Commemoration of the Fiftieth Anniversary of the Organization of the General Congregational Association of Illinois.* Ottawa, Ill., 1894.

GETTLEMEN, MARVIN E. "College President on the Prairie: John H. Finley and Knox College in the 1890s." *History of Education Quarterly* (Summer 1969), 133–44.

⸻. "John Finley's Illinois Education." *Journal of the Illinois State Historical Society,* 62 (Summer 1969), 147–69.

GETTMEG, CHARLES FERRIS. "A Graduation Essay of 1857." *Knox Alumnus* (Jan. 1929), 18–22.

HARVEY, A. M. "The Founding of the Gale." *Gale Nineteen Hundred and Ten: The Year Book of Knox College,* 20 (1909).

HENDRICKS, BURTON J. "The Story of Life Insurance." *McClure's Magazine* (May-Oct. 1906).

History of Mercer and Henderson Counties, Together with Biographical Matter, Statistics, etc. Chicago, 1882.

Bibliography

HODGE, FREDERICK W., ed. *Handbook of American Indians North of Mexico.* Part I. U.S. Bureau of American Ethnology, Bulletin 30. Washington, 1907.

HOFFMAN, FRANK S. *Tales of Hoffman.* Schenectady, N.Y., 1926.

Holland's Galesburg City Directory. Chicago, 1891.

HOLMES, JESSIE. *Knox Missionaries.* Galesburg, Ill., 1901.

HURD, ALBERT. "Reminiscences." *Knox Student,* 11 (Feb. 18, 1904), 305–8.

Illinois Society of Church History, Congregational. *Historical Statement and Papers.* Chicago, 1895.

JORDAN, DAVID STARR. *The Days of a Man: Being Memories of a Naturalist, Teacher and Minor Prophet of Democracy.* New York, 1922.

KELLOGG, HIRAM H. *Education for the People, an Inaugural Address Delivered at Galesburg, February 2, 1842.* Peoria, Ill., 1842.

KEY, V. O. *Politics, Parties and Pressure Groups.* New York, 1948.

LA FOLLETTE, BELLE CASE. *Robert M. La Follette, June 14, 1855–June 18, 1925.* New York, 1953.

LAWYER, KENNETH. "John Putnam Gulliver, D.D., Fifth President of Knox College." *Knox Alumnus,* 10 (May 1927), 239–40.

LITTLE, ARTHUR W. "College Days." *Gale,* 1894.

Lombard College. Catalogues, 1852–53 to 1929–30.

LYON, PETER. *Success Story—The Life and Times of S. S. McClure.* New York, 1963.

McCLURE, S. S. *My Autobiography.* New York, 1914.

———, ed. *History of College Journalism.* Chicago, 1882.

McCONAUGHY, JAMES LUKENS. "Have we an educational debt to Germany?" *Educational Review* (May 1918), 361–76.

MARQUIS, DON. *Sons of the Puritans.* New York, 1939.

MARS, HIRAM. "Recollection of Half a Century." Galesburg *Republican Register,* June 19, 1909.

MASTERS, EDGAR LEE. *A Book of Verses.* Chicago, 1898.

———. *Across Spoon River, an Autobiography.* New York, 1936.

———. *Songs and Satires.* New York, 1916.

———. *Starved Rock.* New York, 1919.

———. *Toward the Gulf.* New York, 1918.

——— [DEXTER WALLACE]. *The Blood the Prophets.* Chicago, 1905.

MASTERS, HARDIN. *Edgar Lee Masters, a Centenary—Memoir.* 1972.

MATHER, ROBERT. "Knox in Politics." *Gale* (1894), 62–63.

MATHEWS, MITFORD M. *A Dictionary of Americanisms on Historical Principles.* Chicago, 1951.

MEREDITH, ROBERT. *The Politics of the Universe: Edward Beecher and Orthodoxy.* Nashville, Ky., 1968.

MONROE, HARRIET. *A Poet's Life: Seventy Years in a Changing World.* New York, 1938.

MOORE, ALBERT BURTON. *History of Alabama.* Tuscaloosa, Ala., 1951.

MORRIS, RICHARD, ed. *Encyclopedia of American History.* New York, 1961.

MUELDER, HERMANN R. *Church History in a Puritan Colony of the Middle West.* Galesburg, Ill., 1937.

———. "Congregationalists and Presbyterians in the Early History of the Galesburg Churches." *Papers in Illinois History and Transactions for the Year 1937.* Springfield, 1938.

———. *Fighters for Freedom: A History of Anti-Slavery Activities of Men and Women Associated with Knox College.* New York, 1959.

———. "Printer's Error in Call for Antislavery Convention." *Journal of the Illinois State Historical Society,* 47 (1954), 321–22.

NEEDHAM, JAMES G. "How Biology Came to Knox College." *Scientific Monthly,* 60 (May 1945), 365–72.

———. "Some Knox Academic History." *Knox College Fifty Year Club Bulletin,* 8 (June 1953), 4–8.

NEWCOMBE, ALFRED. "Olson J. Streeter." *Journal of the Illinois State Historical Society,* 38 (Dec. 1945) and 39 (Mar. 1946).

OLMSTED, DENISON. *An Introduction to Natural Philosophy; Designed as a College Text-Book.* 2nd ed. rev., E. S. Snell. New York, 1870.

PAULIN, CHARLES O. "Henry Thomas Rainey," *DAB,* first supplementary vol.

PERKINS, FREDERIC T. *A Statistical Paper.* Galesburg, Ill., 1866.

PERRY, ALBERT J., ed. *History of Knox County.* 2 vols. Chicago, 1912.

PERRY, BLISS. "Professor Simonds." *Gale Nineteen Hundred and Ten: The Year Book of Knox College,* 20 (1909), 708.

PHILLIPS, JOHN S. *Albert A. Boyden, April 10, 1875–May 2, 1925. Reminiscences and Tributes by His Friends.* New York, 1926.

POWELL, BURT E. *The Movement for Industrial Education and the Establishment of the University 1840–70 ... with an Introduction by Edmund J. James, Fourth President of the University of Illinois.* Urbana, 1918.

PRATHER, EDGAR PRATHER, ed. *Winning Orations of the Inter-State Oratorical Contests and Biographies of the Contestants.* Topeka, Kans., 1891.

PRATHER, EDGAR, and J. E. GROVES. *Winning Orations of the Inter-State Oratorical Contests, with Biographies of Contestants, 1890–1907.* Topeka, Kans., 1914.

PRINGLE, HENRY F. *Theodore Roosevelt. A Biography.* New York, 1931.

Bibliography

PUTZEL, MAX. *Man in the Mirror*. Cambridge, Mass., 1963.

RAMMELKAMP, CHARLES HENRY. *Illinois College: A Centennial History*. New Haven, Conn., 1928.

Report of the Adjutant General of the State of Illinois. Vol. 4 and Vol. 7. Springfield, 1901.

ROBINSON, FRANK. *Edgar Lee Masters. An Exhibition in Commemoration of the Centenary of his Birth, Catalogue and Checklist of Books*. Austin, Tex., 1968.

RUGGLES, ELEANOR. *The West-going Heart. A Life of Vachel Lindsay*. New York, 1959.

ROOT, OMI E. *Root's Galesburg City Directory for the Year 1861*. Galesburg, Ill., 1861.

SANDBURG, CARL. *Always the Young Strangers*. New York, 1953.

SELBY, PAUL, NEWTON BATEMAN, W. SELDEN GALE, and GEORGE CANDEE GALE, eds. *Illinois and Knox County*. Chicago, 1899.

SEYMOUR, MARY IVES. *Life and Letters of Louis Moreau Gottschalk* [by] *Octavia Hensel* [pseud.] *His Friend and Pupil*. Boston, 1870.

SHERWIN, PROCTER, ed. *Record of the Centenary of Knox College and Galesburg*. Galesburg, Ill., 1938.

SIMONDS, WILLIAM E. *George Fitch. A Memorial*. Galesburg, 1918.

———. "Newton Bateman, L.L.D., Superintendent of Public Instruction, State of Illinois, 1859–62, President of Knox College, Galesburg, Illinois, 1875–1892." *Transactions of the Illinois State Historical Society for the Year 1935*. Springfield, 1937.

———. "Siwash and Knox." *George Fitch, a Memorial. Knox College Bulletin*, New Series, 12, no. 3 (1918).

SMITH, EMMET. "Field at Knox." *Knox Alumnus*, 14 (Apr. 1931), 195.

SOLBERG, WINTON U. *The University of Illinois, 1867–1894: An Intellectual and Cultural History*. Urbana, 1968.

STANTON, ELIZABETH CADY, and JOSLIN GAGE, eds. *History of Woman Suffrage*. Orig. publ., 1886; reprint ed. New York, 1970.

STEELE, W. L. *Galesburg Public Schools: Their History and Work, 1861–1911*. Galesburg, Ill., 1911.

STEFFENS, JOSEPH LINCOLN. *Autobiography of Lincoln Steffens*. New York, 1931.

———. *The Letters of Lincoln Steffens . . .*, edited with introductory notes by Ella Winters and Granville Hicks. New York, 1938.

SULLIVAN, MARK. *Our Times. The United States, 1900–1925: America Finding Itself*. New York, 1927.

TARBELL, IDA M. *All in the Day's Work*. New York, 1939.

————. "The Lincoln-Douglas Debate and Old Main." *Knox Alumnus* (Jan.-Feb. 1934).

THOMAS, BENJAMIN P. *Theodore Weld, Crusader for Freedom.* New Brunswick, N.J., 1950.

TAPPAN, LEWIS. *History of the American Missionary Association.* New York, 1855.

WARNER, DEBORAH JEAN. *Alvan Clark & Sons, Artists in Optics.* Washington, D.C., 1968.

WEBSTER, MARTHA FARNHAM. *Seventy-Five Significant Years: The Story of Knox College, 1837–1911.* Galesburg, Ill., 1912.

WELD, THEODORE DWIGHT. *Letters of Theodore Dwight Weld, Angelina Grimke Weld, and Sarah Grimke, 1822–1944,* ed. Gilbert H. Barnes and Dwight L. Dumond. 2 vols. New York, 1934.

WENSBERG, KATHERINE SIMONDS. "W.E.S. Recalls the Prairie Poets." *Knox College Fifty Year Club Bulletin* (June 1972), 12–13.

WHEATLY, R. "The New York Stock Exchange." *Harper's New Monthly Magazine,* 31 (Nov. 1895), 829–53.

WHITE, WILLIAM ALLEN. *Autobiography of William Allen White.* New York, 1946.

WILLARD, SAMUEL. "Memorial of Newton Bateman." *Coup D'Etat* (Feb. 1898), 150.

WILSON, HAROLD S. *McClure's Magazine and the Muckrakers.* Princeton, N.J., 1970.

WILSON, HOWARD A. "William Dean Howells's Unpublished Letters about the Haymarket Affair." *Journal of the Illinois State Historical Society,* 56 (Spring 1963), 5–19.

KNOX COLLEGE PUBLICATIONS

Knox College. *Addresses delivered at the Inauguration of Rev. John P. Gulliver as President of Knox College, Galesburg, Illinois, June 25th, A.D., 1869.* Galesburg, 1869.

Knox College. *The Adelphi Quarterly,* Oct. 1860–July 1861. Published jointly by Adelphi and Gnothautii literary societies. Galesburg, Ill.

Knox College. *Alumnus,* Vol. 1 (Oct., 1917) to vol. 53 (Nov., 1973). After 1973 this periodical may have other titles. Galesburg, Ill.

Knox College. *Annual Letter. XI Chapter. Beta Theta Pi.* Galesburg, Ill., 1911.

Knox College; Arnold, Wade. *College Hero Old Style.* Galesburg, Ill., 1948.

Knox College. *Bulletins.* Periodicals such as the *Alumnus* were part of a series of *Bulletins.* Where possible, titles rather than *Bulletin* numbers have been used. Special bulletins without titles are listed with serial numbers.

Knox College. *Knox College Bulletin,* New Series, 1, no. 4, Dec. 1905. New Series 2, no. 4, Dec. 1906. New Series, no. 3, 1918.

Knox College. Catalog, 1842–. Title varies, e.g., 1857–63, 1873–74, Annual Catalogue; 1862–72, 1875–88, Catalogue of the officers and students in Knox College, etc.

Knox College. *Catalog, Illinois Female Collegiate Department.* Galesburg, Ill., 1866.

Knox College. *Knox Collegiate Magazine.* Published jointly by Adelphi and Gnothautii literary societies. Galesburg, Ill., 1857–58.

Knox College. *Coup D'Etat* (spelling varies to *Coup d'Etat*), a monthly magazine, published by students. Oct. 1881–June 1899. 17 vols. Galesburg, Ill.

Knox College. *Knox Directory, 1837–1863,* edited by Marshall Max Goodsill and Arthur Walton. Galesburg, Ill., 1963.

Knox College. *Fifty Year Club Bulletin,* 1944 to the present. Galesburg, Ill.

Knox College. *Gale.* Yearbook, published by students. Volume 1 (1888) was published by the fraternities in Peoria. Later volumes were published, in Galesburg, by the juniors of each academic year. They entitled the *Gale* with the date of the year that the juniors would be graduated. To avoid chronological confusion, these annuals are dated in the notes as of the academic year in which they were published. None were published for 1892–93 nor 1896–97.

Knox College. *The Inauguration of James Lukens McConaughy Ninth President of Knox College . . . Galesburg, Illinois, Wednesday and Thursday, April Twenty-Nine and Thirty. Knox College Bulletin,* New Series 13, no. 10.

Knox College. *The Inauguration of Newton Bateman, President of Knox College, Galesburg, Illinois, June 23d. A.D.* Galesburg, Ill.

Knox College. *Knoxiana,* 1850–57, published by the Adelphi literary society. Galesburg, Ill.

Knox College. *Leisure Hour,* published by students during summer months. In 1890 by James Needham and George Perry. In 1894 by E. E. Calkins. Galesburg, Ill.

Knox College. *Mischmasch,* yearbook for 1870–71 published by students. Galesburg, Ill., 1871.

Knox College. *Oak Leaf,* published in 1856–57 by Gnothautii, a literary society. Galesburg, Ill.

Knox College. *Pantheon,* yearbook published by students for 1869–70, 1872–73, 1887–88. Galesburg, Ill.

Knox College. *Reports Presented to the Board of Trustees of Knox Manual Labor College, at their Annual Meeting, Held June 25th 1856.*

Knox College. *The Student.* A magazine published by students, vols. 1–4 (1878–82). New Series, vol. 1 (Sept. 6, 1849–).

Knox College. *Vacationist.* Published during the summer of 1889 by students. Galesburg, Ill.

INDEX

Index

Index

Index

Index

Index

Princeton, Ill.: student source for Knox, 8
Principia: football opponent, 338
Public Opinion, 158
Pumphandle, 299
Pundit Club: originated by J. Finley, 272

Racial discrimination: absence of in young ladies Domestic Seminary, 1–3; Kellogg speaks on at World Anti-Slavery convention, 10; Root on "Prejudice," 49
Rainey, Ella McBride: honorary degree, 317
Rainey, Henry T.: campus politics, 142–43; speaker of U.S. House of Representatives, 317
Read, Henry: alumnus joins faculty, 67; origin of Interstate Oratorical Contest, 81; and Masters, 176
Rearick, Allan C.: on athletic policy, 334
Redden, Curtis, 296
Reedy, William: recognition of Masters, 172; *Greek Anthology* pressed on Masters, 191
Reese, Edwin Parsons: lifelong friend of Masters, 174, 176, 183; journalistic career, 192–93; memorial by Masters, 193
Reconstruction: role of Knox men and women, 24–27; Revels, 25; American Missionary Association and education for blacks, 25–27
Record of the Centenary, 342
Religion: emphasis on, 67–68; diminishing significance under Britt, 318–19
Republican party: supported by Knox College, 1864, 24
Reserve Officers Training Corps (ROTC): established at Knox, 297–98
Revels, Hiram Rhodes, 25
Review of Reviews (R. Finley), 157

Rickaby, Franz: and Lindsay, 188–89; *Songs of Knox*, 188–89; *Set of Sonnets*, 189; Little Theatre, 286
Roosevelt, Theodore: denounces muckrakers, 133; Lincoln-Douglas debate celebration, 161; candidate of Federal party at Knox, 231
Root, Barnabas: at Knox, 47–48
Roseboro, Viola: at *McClure's Magazine* and influence of J. Finley, 163
Rough Neck Week: described, 308
Roy, Joseph E.: western agent for AMA and field superintendent in South, 26; and election to Knox board, 27; opposed to secret societies, 236

St. Mary's School for Girls: shares Laux with Knox, 121
Sandburg, Carl: hears about Field while in grade school, 73; memories of oratory celebrations, 88; Lincoln-Douglas debate celebration, 162; tribute to Masters, 172; meets Masters, 173; basketball at Lombard, City Mission, and Knox students, 225; Spanish-American War experience, 274–75; honorary degree on occasion of Lincoln-Douglas debate celebration, 1928, 320–21; approves union of Lombard and Knox, 325–26; "Ode to Old Main," 344–45
Sandeen, Earnest: Honnold Fellowship, 323–24
Scabbard and Blade: military honorary group, 332
Science building: George Davis Science Hall, 279
Science courses: teaching materials for philosophical department, 198; experiments, 200; philosophical and chemical apparatus, procured by Kellogg, 201; cabinets, 201; laboratory, 201; Mead Her-

379

Index

Streeter, Alson J.: perennial presidential candidate for agrarian-labor third parties, 151–52

Student: publishes Field poetry while McClure editor, 73; on College needs, 116; and Knox campus politicians, 141–43; article on Masters, 183–84; revived, 1894; on foolishness of Spanish-American War, 275; first woman editor, 1918, 305

Student Army Training Corps (SATC), 291

Student Council, 307 ·

Sunday, Billy: religious revival in Galesburg, 300

Taft, Alphonse: as oratory contest judge, 85

Taft, William Howard: and Lincoln-Douglas debate celebration, 161, 272

Talledega, Ala.: education for blacks by Knox missionaries, 25

Tarbell, Ida Minerva: *McClure's Magazine* staff, 157; Lincoln-Douglas debate at Knox, 271; first Honnold lecturer, 323

Taylor, Graham: lecturer, 1894–95, 269

Telescopes at Knox, 208

Theta Sigma Phi: journalistic fraternity for women, 305

Thirty-third Regiment of Illinois Infantry Volunteers, 21–22

Thompson, John Winter: organist and on music faculty, 128

Turner, Frederick Jackson: lecturer, 1892–93, 268

Turner, Jonathan Baldwin: protagonist for agricultural schools, 39

Tyler, Alice Felt: graduate studies in history, 287

Universalists: found Lombard College, 34

University of Illinois (Illinois Industrial University): founded, 39–41; participated in first interstate oratory contest, 82

Untermeyer, Louis: Honnold lecturer, 323

Vacationist, 158

Wabash College: recipient of funds from Western College Society, 12–13

Wallace, Dexter. *See* Masters, Edgar Lee

Ward, Susan Hayes: Female Seminary principal appointed by Gulliver, 57; author of *Salvinna Hacket* and *Christus ad Portam,* 57

Woman's Christian Temperance Union: chapter of Knox, 150–51

Webster Ford. *See* Masters, Edgar Lee

Weld, Theodore, 3

West Bricks: erected 1844, 8; hall for Adelphi, 76; succeeded by Alumni Hall, 89; first floor fitted up for chemical laboratory, 204

West College. *See* West Bricks

West, Mary Allen: schools for blacks in Galesburg, 36; career reviewed, 303–4

Western Citizen, 10

Western College Press Association: founded by McClure, 144–46

Western College Society: Blanchard seeks aid from, 11–13

Western Reserve College: recipient of funds from Western College Society, 12–13

Wheaton College. *See* Blanchard, Jonathan

A NOTE ON THE AUTHOR

Hermann R. Muelder is College Historian and professor
emeritus of history at Knox College, Galesburg, Illinois.
He graduated from Knox College with a bachelor of
science degree in 1927 and, except for one year, has
been at Knox College since the completion of his Ph.D.
(at the University of Minnesota) in 1933. For a dozen
years he served his classmates as dean of the College.
From 1973 to 1974 he was acting president of Knox.
His previous publications include *Fighters for Freedom:
A History of Anti-Slavery Activities of Men and Women
Associated with Knox College* (Columbia University
Press, 1959) and *Years of This Land: A Geographical
History of the United States* (co-author; Appleton-
Century Co., 1943).